CIMA
DICTIONARY OF
FINANCE AND
ACCOUNTING

CIMA DICTIONARY OF FINANCE AND ACCOUNTING

BLOOMSBURY

A BLOOMSBURY REFERENCE BOOK
Created from the Bloomsbury Business Database
www.ultimatebusinessresource.com

Copyright © CIMA 1982, 1991, 1996, 2000, 2003
Copyright © Bloomsbury Publishing Plc 2003
Management terms © Chartered Management Institute 2003

First published in 2003 by
Bloomsbury Publishing Plc
38 Soho Square
London W1D 3HB

British Library Cataloguing in Publication Data
A CIP record for this book is available from the British Library.

ISBN 0-7475-6689-5

Design by Fiona Pike, Pike Design, Winchester
Typeset by RefineCatch Limited, Bungay, Suffolk
Printed in Great Britain by Clays Ltd, St Ives plc

All papers used by Bloomsbury Publishing are natural, recyclable
products made from wood grown in sustainable, well-managed forests.
The manufacturing processes conform to the environmental regulations
of the country of origin.

Contents

User's Guide

The *CIMA Dictionary of Finance and Accounting* provides clear, concise definitions to more than 5,000 key financial terms and ratios. Combining approved terms from CIMA's *Official Terminology* and also drawing on the wealth of updated and expanded material in the *BUSINESS: The Ultimate Resource™* database, the dictionary is based on the real experiences of management accountants and is an essential guide for both practitioners and students.

ORDER OF TERMS

All terms are listed in strict alphabetical order, apart from when a term is part of a phrase. In these cases, the definition is shown at the most valid element of the phrase.

STANDARD AND EXTENDED DEFINITIONS

Each term in the dictionary is succinctly defined in the context of its application in today's business environment. For example:

cash flow the movement through an organisation of money that is generated by its own operations, as opposed to borrowing. It is the money that a business actually receives from sales (the cash inflow) and the money that it pays out (the cash outflow).

Mini-essays are used to illustrate more complex terms and concepts in greater depth:

National Market System in the United States, an inter-exchange network system designed to foster greater competition between domestic stock exchanges. Legislated for in 1975, it was implemented in 1978 with the Intermarket Trading System that electronically links eight markets: American, Boston, Cincinnati, Chicago, New York, Pacific, Philadelphia, and the NASD over-the-counter market. It allows traders at any exchange to seek the best available price on all other exchanges that a particular security is eligible to trade on. *Abbr* **NMS**

WORKED EXAMPLES

Financial ratios are illustrated with worked examples to demonstrate how each ratio functions. These examples are indicated by the ⬚EXAMPLE⬚ icon:

conversion ratio an expression of the quantity of one security that can be obtained for another, for example, shares for a *convertible bond*.

The conversion ratio may be established when the convertible is issued. If that is the case, the ratio will appear in the indenture, the binding agreement that details the convertible's terms.

⬚EXAMPLE⬚ If the conversion ratio is not set, it can be calculated quickly: divide the par value of the convertible security (typically £1,000) by its conversion price.

£1,000 / £40 per share = 25

In this example, the conversion ratio is 25:1, which means that every bond held with a £1,000 par value can be exchanged for 25 ordinary shares.

CROSS-REFERENCES

Cross-references are used throughout the Dictionary to link terms that are closely related, or which expand on information given in another entry. For example, at this entry

abnormal shrinkage the unexpectedly high level of *shrinkage* that has contributed to an *abnormal loss*

the concept of 'abnormal loss' is referred to, and highlighted in bold italics to show that it has an entry in its own right:

abnormal loss any losses which exceed the normal loss allowance. Abnormal losses are generally costed as though they were completed products.

Terms that are defined at another headword (as part of an associated concept), or which are less preferred versions of a standard term, are cross-referred to the term whose definition contains the primary information. For example:

mercantile paper *see commercial paper*

ABBREVIATIONS

The Dictionary features over 100 abbreviations and acronyms. Where the abbreviation is the most commonly used version of a term or phrase, the abbreviation's definition is given at that entry:

ISA *abbr* Individual Savings Account: a portfolio created according to rules that exempt its proceeds, including dividends and capital gains, from taxes. It was launched in 1999 with the intention that it would be available for at least ten years. Individuals may invest up to £7,000 each year, £3,000 of which may be invested in a savings account and £1,000 in life assurance. Either the remaining £3,000, or the entire £7,000, may be invested in the stock market.

In cases where the full form of an abbreviation is the most commonly known form of the concept, there is a cross-reference from the abbreviation to the full form, where the definition is shown:

CA *abbr* chartered accountant *or* certified accountant

chartered accountant in the United Kingdom, a qualified professional accountant who is a member of the Institute of Chartered Accountants. Chartered accountants are qualified to audit company accounts and some hold management positions in companies. *Abbr* **CA**

Variant names of a word or phrase are also presented:

good title the legally unquestionable title to property. *Also known as* **clear title**

FACTS AND FIGURES

Expanding on the wealth of knowledge in the Dictionary, this section contains a variety of helpful information, including contact information for accounting organisations in the United Kingdom, the United States, Australia, and New Zealand, and fascinating data on the world economy.

For more information about *BUSINESS: The Ultimate Resource*™ and other related titles, please visit: **www.ultimatebusinessresource.com**

To register for free electronic monthly upgrades, please go to: **www.ultimatebusinessresource.com/register**, type in your e-mail address, and key in your password: **Vroom**

CREDITS

The following terms and their definitions are reproduced with the kind permission of the Accounting Standards Board (ASB):

accounting bases; concepts; consolidation accounting; dominant influence; fair value; financial liability; fundamental accounting; prudence concept; write-down

CIMA
DICTIONARY OF
FINANCE AND
ACCOUNTING

A

AAA *abbr* American Accounting Association

AAD a unit of account used between member states of the Arab Monetary Fund

AAIA *abbr* Associate of the Association of International Accountants

AARF *abbr* Australian Accounting Research Foundation

AAS *abbr* Australian Accounting Standard

AASB *abbr* Australian Accounting Standards Board

AAT *abbr* Association of Accounting Technicians

abacus a counting device used for making basic arithmetical calculations, that consists of parallel rods strung with beads. Still widely used in education worldwide and for business and accounting in China and Japan, its origins can be traced back to early civilisations. Australia's oldest accounting journal bears the same name.

abandonment option the option of terminating an investment before the time that it is scheduled to end

abandonment value the value that an investment has if it is terminated at a particular time before it is scheduled to end

abatement a reduction in a payment, for example, if a company's or individual's total assets are insufficient to cover their debts or legacies. Such a reduction may lead to the eventual cancellation of the payments.

ABA transit number a number allocated to a US financial institution, such as a bank (it appears on US cheques in the top right-hand corner, above the 'check routing' symbol)

ABB *abbr* activity-based budgeting

abbreviated accounts a shortened version of a company's annual accounts that a company classified as small or medium sized under the Companies Act (1989) can file with the *Registrar of Companies*, instead of having to supply a full version

ABC *abbr* activity-based costing

ABI *abbr* Association of British Insurers

ability-to-pay **1.** taxation that takes into account the taxpayer's ability to pay. Thus, the greater the income or wealth to be taxed, the higher the level of taxation. In the United Kingdom, both income tax and inheritance tax operate according to this system. **2.** the ability of a borrower to meet interest repayments on long-term obligations, such as loans

ability-to-pay principle a theory which holds that taxes should be paid only by those who can best afford them

ABM *abbr* activity-based management

ABN *abbr* Australian Business Number: a numeric code that identifies an Australian business for the purpose of dealing with the Australian Tax Office and other government departments. ABNs are part of the new tax system that came into operation in Australia in 1998.

abnormal gain any reduction in the volume of process loss below that set by the normal loss allowance. Abnormal gains are generally costed as though they were completed products.

abnormal loss any losses which exceed the normal loss allowance. Abnormal losses are generally costed as though they were completed products.

abnormal shrinkage the unexpectedly high level of *shrinkage* that has contributed to an *abnormal loss*

abnormal spoilage the unexpectedly high level of shrinkage that has contributed to an *abnormal loss*

abnormal waste the unexpectedly high level of *waste* that has contributed to an *abnormal loss*

above par used to describe a security that trades above its *par value* or its *nominal value*

above-the-line 1. used to describe entries in a company's profit and loss accounts that appear above the line separating those entries that show the origin of the funds that have contributed to the profit or loss from those that relate to its distribution. Exceptional and extraordinary items appear above the line. *See also **below-the-line** (sense 1)* 2. in macroeconomics, used to describe a country's revenue transactions. *See also **below-the-line** (sense 2)*

abridged accounts financial statements produced by a company that fall outside the requirements stipulated in the *Companies Act*. Abridged accounts are often made public through the media.

ABS *abbr* Australian Bureau of Statistics

absolute title land registered with the Land Registry, where the owner has a guaranteed title to the land. It also applies to leasehold land, giving the proprietor a guaranteed valid lease.

absorb to assign an overhead to a particular cost centre in a company's production accounts so that its identity becomes lost. *See also **absorption costing***
   to absorb a loss by a subsidiary to write a subsidiary company's loss into the main accounts
   to absorb a surplus to take back surplus stock so that it does not affect a business
   to absorb overheads to include a proportion of overhead costs in a production cost (this is done at a certain rate, called 'absorption rate')

absorbed account an account that has lost its separate identity by being combined with related accounts in the preparation of a financial statement

absorbed business a company that has been merged into another company

absorbed costs the indirect costs associated with manufacturing, for example, insurance or property taxes

absorbed overhead an overhead attached to products or services by means of **absorption rates**

absorption costing an accounting practice in which fixed and variable costs of production are absorbed by different cost centres. Providing all the products or services can be sold at a price that covers the allocated costs, this method ensures that both fixed and variable costs are recovered in full. However, should sales be lost because the resultant price is too high, the organisation may lose revenue that would have contributed to its overheads. *See also **marginal costing***

absorption rate *see **overhead absorption rate***

abusive tax shelter a tax shelter that somebody claims illegally to avoid or minimise tax

ACA *abbr* 1. Australian Communications Authority 2. Associate of the Institute of Chartered Accountants in England and Wales

Academy of Accounting Historians a US body founded in 1973 that promotes 'research, publication, teaching and personal interchanges in all phases of Accounting History and its interrelation with business and economic history'

ACAS *abbr* Advisory, Conciliation and Arbitration Service

ACAUS *abbr* Association of Chartered Accountants in the United States

ACCA *abbr* **1.** Association of Chartered Certified Accountants **2.** Associate of the Association of Chartered Certified Accountants

ACCC *abbr* Australian Competition and Consumer Commission: an independent statutory body responsible for monitoring trade practices in Australia. It was set up in November 1995 as a result of the merger of the Trade Practices Commission and the Prices Surveillance Authority.

accelerated cost recovery system a system used in the United States for computing the depreciation of some assets acquired before 1986 in a way that reduces taxes. *Abbr* **ACRS**

accelerated depreciation a system used for computing the depreciation of some assets in a way that assumes that they depreciate faster in the early years of their acquisition. *Also known as declining balance method*

acceleration the speeding up of debt repayment

acceleration clause a section of a contract which details how a loan may be required to be repaid early if the borrower defaults on other clauses of the contract

accept
  to accept a bill to sign a bill of exchange to indicate that the drawee promises to pay it
  to accept a bill of exchange to sign a bill of exchange to indicate that you promise to pay it

acceptance the signature on a bill of exchange, indicating that the drawee (the person to whom it is addressed) will pay the face amount of the bill on the due date

acceptance bonus (*US*) a *bonus* paid to a new employee on acceptance of the job. An acceptance bonus can be a feature of a *golden hello* and is designed both to attract and to retain staff.

acceptance credit a line of credit granted by a bank to an importer against which an exporter can draw a bill of exchange. After acceptance by the bank, the bill can either be sold in the market or held until maturity.

acceptance house an institution that accepts financial instruments and agrees to honour them should the borrower default

accepting bank the bank that accepts a bill of exchange drawn under a *documentary credit*

Accepting Houses Committee the main London merchant banks, which organise the lending of money with the Bank of England. These banks receive slightly better discount rates from the Bank.

acceptor the person to whom a signed bill of exchange is addressed

access the right to sell goods or services into a particular market without contravening related legislation

access bond (*S Africa*) a type of mortgage that permits borrowers to take out loans against extra capital paid into the account, home-loan interest rates being lower than interest rates on other forms of credit

ACCI *abbr* Australian Chamber of Commerce and Industry

accommodation address an address used for receiving messages, which is not the real address of the company

accommodation bill a bill of exchange where the drawee who signs it is helping another company (the drawer) to raise a loan. The bill is given on the basis of trade debts owed to the borrower.

account 1. a business arrangement involving the exchange of money or credit in which payment is deferred, or a record maintained by a financial institution itemising its dealings with a particular customer **2.** a structured record of transactions in monetary terms, kept as part of an accounting system. This may take the form of a simple list or that of entries on a credit and debit basis, maintained either manually or as a computer record.

to account for to explain and record a money deal

to open an account to ask a shop to supply goods which you will pay for at a later date

to pay money on account to pay an amount of money to settle part of a bill

to settle an account to pay all the money owed on an account

to stop an account to stop supplying a customer until he or she has paid what is owed

trading for the account the buying of shares and the selling of the same shares during an account, which means that the dealer has only to pay the difference between the price of the shares bought and the price obtained for them when they are sold

accountability concept management accounting presents information measuring the achievement of the objectives of an organisation and appraising the conduct of its internal affairs in that process. In order that further action can be taken, based on this information, it is necessary at all times to identify the responsibilities and key results of individuals within the organisation.

accountancy the practice of accounting

accountancy bodies professional institutions and associations for accountants

accountancy profession collectively, the professional bodies of accountants that establish and regulate training

entry standards, professional examinations, as well as ethical and technical rules and guidelines. These bodies are organised on national and international levels.

accountant a professional person who maintains and checks the business records of a person or organisation and prepares forms and reports for financial purposes

Accountants' International Study Group a body of professional accounting bodies from the United States, Canada, and the United Kingdom that was established in 1966 to research accounting practices in the three member countries. After publishing 20 reports, it was disbanded in 1977 with the foundation of the International Federation of Accountants.

accountant's letter a written statement by an independent accountant that precedes a financial report, describing the scope of the report and giving an opinion on its validity

accountant's opinion a report of the audit of a company's books, carried out by a certified public accountant

accountants' report in the United Kingdom, a report written by accountants that is required by the London Stock Exchange to be included in the prospectus of a company seeking a listing on the Exchange

account code a number assigned to a particular account in a numerical accounting system, for example, a *chart of accounts*

account day the day on which an executed order is settled by the delivery of securities, payment to the seller, and payment by the buyer. This is the final day of the *accounting period*.

account debtor a person or organisation responsible for paying for a product or service

account form a balance sheet laid out in horizontal form (it is the opposite of 'report' or 'vertical' form)

accounting a generic term for all the activities carried out by accountants, for example, bookkeeping and financial accounting. Accounting involves the classification and recording of monetary transactions; the presentation and interpretation of the results of those transactions in order to assess performance over a period and the financial position at a given date; and the monetary projection of future activities arising from alternative planned courses of action. Accounting in larger businesses is typically carried out by financial accountants who focus on formal, corporate issues such as taxation, and management accountants who provide management reports and guidance.

Accounting and Finance Association of Australia and New Zealand an organisation for accounting and finance academics, researchers, and professionals. The Association has a variety of aims, including the promotion of information on accounting to the public, and the provision of programmes in continual professional development to both members and non-members. The Association's name was changed in 2002 to incorporate the Accounting Association of Australia and New Zealand (AAANZ) and the Australian Association of University Teachers in Accounting (AAUTA). *Abbr* **AFAANZ**

accounting bases the methods used for: applying fundamental accounting concepts to financial transactions and items; for the purpose of preparing financial accounts and in particular; for determining the accounting periods in which revenue and costs should be recognised in the profit and loss account; and for determining the amounts at which material items should be stated in the balance sheet

accounting concept any of the general assumptions on which accounts are prepared. The main concepts are: that the business is a going concern; that revenue and costs are noted when they are incurred and not when cash is received or paid; that the present accounts are drawn up following the same principles as the previous accounts; and that the revenue or costs are only recorded if it is certain that they will be incurred.

accounting concepts *see accounting conventions*

accounting conventions the fundamental assumptions that govern the practice of accounting, for example, *consistency* and **prudence**. *Also called accounting concepts. See also conceptual framework*

accounting cost the cost of maintaining and checking the business records of a person or organisation and the preparation of forms and reports for financial purposes

accounting cycle the regular process of formally updating a firm's financial position by recording, analysing, and reporting its transactions during the accounting period

accounting date the date on which an accounting period ends. It is usually 31st December for annual accounts, but it can in fact be any date.

accounting entity the unit for which financial statements and accounting records are prepared, for example, a limited company or a partnership. *See also reporting entity*

accounting equation 1. a formula in which a firm's assets must be equal to the sum of its liabilities and the owners' equity. *Also known as balance sheet equation* **2.** the basic formula that underpins *double-entry bookkeeping*. It can be expressed most simply as 'assets + expenses = liabilities + capital + revenue' where the debit amounts to the left of the equals sign must be equivalent to the credit amounts to the right. *Also called **balance sheet equation***

accounting event a transaction recorded in a business's **books of account**

accounting exposure the risk that foreign currency held by a company may lose value because of exchange rate changes when it conducts overseas business

accounting fees fees paid to an accountant for preparing accounts (such fees are deductible against tax)

Accounting Hall of Fame a means of recognising the achievements of eminent accountants. The system was established by the Ohio State University in the United States in 1950.

accounting insolvency the condition that a company is in when its liabilities to its creditors exceed its assets

accounting manual a collection of accounting instructions governing the responsibilities of persons, and the procedures, forms, and records relating to the preparation and use of accounting data. There can be separate manuals for the constituent parts of the accounting system, for example, budget manuals or cost accounting manuals.

accounting period an amount of time in which businesses may prepare internal accounts so as to monitor progress on a weekly, monthly, or quarterly basis. Accounts are generally prepared for external purposes on an annual basis.

accounting policies the specific *accounting bases* selected and consistently followed by an entity as being, in the opinion of the management, appropriate to its circumstances and best suited to present fairly its results and financial position. For example, from the various possible methods of *depreciation*, the accounting policy

may be to use ***straight-line depreciation***.

accounting principles the rules that apply to accounting practices and provide guidelines for dealing appropriately with complex transactions

Accounting Principles Board *(US)* the professional body which issued Opinions that formed much of US *Generally Accepted Accounting Principles* up to 1973, when the Financial Accounting Standards Board (FASB) took over that role. *Abbr* **APB**

accounting procedure an accounting method developed by an individual or organisation to deal with routine accounting tasks

accounting profit the difference between total revenue and explicit costs

accounting rate of return the ratio of profit before interest and taxation to the percentage of capital employed at the end of a period. Variations include using profit after interest and taxation, equity capital employed, and average capital for the period.

accounting ratio an expression of accounting results as a ratio or percentage, for example, the ratio of *current assets* to *current liabilities*

accounting records *(US)* all documentation and books used during the preparation of financial statements

accounting reference date the last day of a company's *accounting reference period*

accounting reference period the period for which a company makes up its accounts. This period is normally, although not necessarily, 12 months. Also used for taxation where it represents the period for which corporation tax is calculated.

accounting software computer programs used to help maintain **books of account** electronically. Such software can be used for a variety of tasks, including preparing statements and recording transactions.

accounting standard an authoritative statement of how particular types of transaction and other events should be reflected in financial statements. Compliance with accounting standards will normally be necessary for financial statements to give a true and fair view.

Accounting Standards Board a UK standard-setting organisation established on 1 August 1990 to develop, issue, and withdraw accounting standards. Its aims are 'to establish and improve standards of financial accounting and reporting, for the benefit of users, preparers, and auditors of financial information'. *Abbr* **ASB**

Accounting Standards Committee the UK accounting standards issuing body whose functions were taken over by the *Accounting Standards Board* in 1990

accounting system the means, including staff and equipment, by which an organisation produces its accounting information

accounting year the annual *accounting period*

account payee the words printed on most UK cheques indicating that the cheque can only be paid into the account of the person or business to whom the cheque is written, or be cashed for a fee at an agency offering a cheque cashing service

account reconciliation 1. a procedure for ensuring the reliability of accounting records by comparing balances of transactions **2.** a procedure for comparing the register of a chequebook with an associated bank statement

account sales a statement rendered to a consignor of merchandise by the consignee, giving particulars of sales, the quantity remaining unsold, gross proceeds, expenses incurred, consignee's commission, and net amount due to the consignor

accounts department the department in a company which deals with money paid, received, borrowed, or owed

accounts payable the amount that a company owes for goods or services obtained on credit

accounts receivable the money that is owed to a company by those who have bought its goods or services and have not yet paid for them. *Abbr* **AR**

accounts receivable ageing a periodic report that classifies outstanding receivable balances according to customer and month of the original billing date

accounts receivable factoring *(US)* the buying of accounts receivable at a discount with the aim of making a profit from collecting them

accounts receivable financing a form of borrowing in which a company uses money that it is owed as collateral for a loan it needs for business operations

accounts receivable turnover a ratio that shows how long the customers of a business wait before paying what they owe. This can cause cash-flow problems for small businesses.
EXAMPLE The formula for accounts receivable turnover is straightforward. Simply divide the average amount of receivables into annual credit sales:

Sales / Receivables = Receivables turnover

If, for example, a company's sales are £4.5 million and its average receivables are £375,000, its receivables turnover is:

4,500,000 / 375,000 = 12

A high turnover figure is desirable, because it indicates that a company collects revenues effectively, and that its customers pay bills promptly. A high figure also suggests that a firm's credit and collection policies are sound.

In addition, the measurement is a reasonably good indicator of cash flow, and of overall operating efficiency.

accredited investor an investor whose wealth or income is above a particular amount. It is illegal for an accredited investor to be a member of a private limited partnership.

accreted value the value of a bond if interest rates do not change

accretion the growth of a company through additions or purchases of plant or value-adding services

accretive relating to company policies or strategies that involve accretion

accrual a charge that has not been paid by the end of an accounting period but must be included in the accounting results for the period. If no invoice has been received for the charge, an estimate must be included in the accounting results.

accrual basis *see accrual method*

accrual bond *see zero coupon bond*

accrual concept the idea that income and expense items must be included in financial statements as they are earned or incurred. *See also* **cash accounting**

accrual method an accounting method that includes income and expense items as they are earned or incurred irrespective of when money is received or paid out. *Also known as accrual basis*

accrual of discount the annual gain in value of a bond owing to its having been bought originally for less than its par value

accrual of interest the automatic addition of interest to capital

accruals basis a concept that accounts are prepared with financial transactions *accrued*. Revenue and costs are both reported during the period to which they refer and not during the period when payments are received or made.

accruals concept *see accruals basis*

accrue **1.** to include an income or expense item in transaction records at the time it is earned or incurred **2.** to increase and be due for payment at a later date, for example, interest

accrued expense an expense that has been incurred within a given accounting period but not yet paid

accrued income income that has been earned but not yet received

accrued interest the amount of interest earned by a bond or similar investment since the previous interest payment

accrued liabilities liabilities which are recorded, although payment has not yet been made. This can include liabilities such as rent and utility payments.

accruing added as a periodic gain, for example, as interest on an amount of money

accumulated depreciation the cumulative annual depreciation of an *asset* that has been claimed as an expense since the asset was acquired. *Also known as aggregate depreciation*

accumulated dividend the amount of money in dividends earned by a stock or similar investment since the previous dividend payment

accumulated earnings tax *or* **accumulated profits tax** the tax that a company must pay because it chose not to pay dividends that would subject its owners to higher taxes

accumulated profit profit which is not paid as dividend but is taken over into the accounts of the following year

accumulated profits tax see *accumulated earnings tax*

accumulated reserves reserves which a company has put aside over a period of years

accumulating shares ordinary shares issued by a company equivalent to and in place of the net dividend payable to ordinary shareholders

accumulation unit a unit of a unit trust that retains dividend income instead of distributing it to individual investors

accumulation units units in a unit trust for which dividends accumulate and form more units, as opposed to income units, where the investor receives the dividends as *income*

acid test an accounting ratio used to measure an organisation's liquidity. It is calculated by taking the business's current assets, minus its stocks, divided by its current liabilities. The higher the ratio, the better: a low ratio is usually a sign that a company is overstretched.

acid-test ratio an accounting ratio used to measure an organisation's liquidity. The most common expression of the ratio is:

(Current assets – Inventory) / Current liabilities = Acid-test ratio

EXAMPLE If, for example, current assets total £7,700, inventory amounts to £1,200 and current liabilities total £4,500, then:

(7,700 – 1,200) / 4,500 = 1.44

A variation of this formula ignores inventories altogether, distinguishes assets as cash, receivables, and short-term investments, then divides the sum of the three by the total current liabilities, or:

Cash + Accounts receivable + Short-term investments / Current liabilities = Acid-test ratio

If, for example, cash totals £2,000, receivables total £3,000, short-term investments total £1,000, and liabilities total £4,800, then:

(2,000 + 3,000 + 1,000) / 4,800 = 1.25

In general, the ratio should be 1:1 or better. It means a company has a unit's worth of easily convertible assets for each unit of its current liabilities.

acquirer or **acquiring bank 1.** a financial institution, commonly a bank, that processes a merchant's credit card authorisations and payments, forwarding the data to a credit card association, which in turn communicates with the issuer. *Also known as clearing house* **2.** an organisation or individual that buys a business or *asset*

acquisition see *merger*

acquisition accounting the standard accounting procedures that must be followed when one company merges with another

ACRS *abbr* accelerated cost recovery system

ACT *abbr* Advance Corporation Tax

active asset an *asset* that is used in the daily operations of a business

active fund management the managing of a unit trust by making judgments about market movements instead of relying on automatic adjustments such as indexation. *See also passive investment management*

active portfolio strategy the managing of an investment portfolio by making judgments about market movements instead of relying on automatic adjustments

activist fiscal policy the policy of a government or national bank that tries to affect the value of its country's money by such measures as changing interest rates for loans to banks and buying or selling foreign currencies

activity-based budgeting the allocation of resources to individual activities.

Activity-based budgeting involves determining which activities incur costs within an organisation, establishing the relationships between them, and then deciding how much of the total **budget** should be allocated to each activity. *Abbr* **ABB**

activity-based costing a method of calculating the cost of a business by focusing on the actual cost of activities, thereby producing an estimate of the cost of individual products or services.

An ABC cost-accounting system requires three preliminary steps: converting to an *accrual method* of accounting; defining cost centres and cost allocation; and determining process and procedure costs.

Businesses have traditionally relied on the cash basis of accounting, which recognises income when received and expenses when paid. ABC's foundation is the accrual-basis income statement. The numbers this statement presents are assigned to the various procedures performed during a given period. Cost centres are a company's identifiable products and services, but also include specific and detailed tasks within these broader activities. Defining cost centres will, of course, vary by business and method of operation. What is critical to ABC is the inclusion of all activities and all resources.

Once cost centres are identified, management teams can begin studying the activities each one engages in and allocating the expenses each one incurs, including the cost of employee services.

The most appropriate method is developed from time studies and direct expense allocation. Management teams who choose this method will need to devote several months to data collection in order to generate sufficient information to establish the personnel components of each activity's total cost.

Time studies establish the average amount of time required to complete each task, plus best- and worst-case performances. Only those resources actually used are factored into the cost computation; unused resources are reported separately. These studies can also advise management teams how best to monitor and allocate expenses that might otherwise be expressed as part of general overheads, or go undetected altogether. *Abbr* **ABC**

activity-based management a system of management that uses activity-based cost information for a variety of purposes including cost reduction, cost modelling, and customer profitability analysis. *Abbr* **ABM**

activity cost pool a grouping of all cost elements associated with an activity

activity driver *see* *cost driver*

activity driver analysis the identification and evaluation of the activity drivers used to trace the cost of activities to cost objects. It may also involve selecting activity drivers with potential to contribute to the cost management function with particular reference to cost reduction.

activity indicator a calculation used to measure labour productivity or manufacturing output in an economy

act of God an unexpected and unavoidable event or occurrence, such as a storm or a flood, that is not covered by an insurance policy

actual cash value the amount of money, less *depreciation*, that it would cost to replace something damaged beyond repair with a comparable item

actuals earnings and expenses that have occurred rather than being only projected, or commodities that can be bought and used, as contrasted with commodities traded on a futures contract

actual to date the cumulative value realised by something between an earlier date and the present

actual turnover the number of times during a particular period that somebody spends the average amount of money that he or she has available to spend during that period

actuarial age the statistically derived life expectancy for any given person's age, used, for example, to calculate the periodic payments from an annuity

actuarial analysis a life expectancy or risk calculation carried out by an actuary

actuarial science the branch of statistics used in calculating risk and life expectancy for the administration of pension funds and life assurance policies

actuarial tables lists showing how long people of certain ages are likely to live, used to calculate life assurance premiums

actuary a statistician who calculates probable lifespans so that the insurance premiums to be charged for various risks can be accurately determined

ACU *abbr* Asian Currency Unit

ADDACS *abbr* Automated Direct Debit Amendments and Cancellation Service

addend the initial number added to an *augend* in order to complete an *addition*

addition an arithmetical operation consisting of adding together two or more numbers to make a sum

additional voluntary contributions extra money paid by an individual into a company pension scheme to improve the benefits he or she will receive on retirement. *Abbr* **AVCs**

ADF *abbr* Approved Deposit Fund

adjustable peg a method of pegging one currency to another, but with the possibility of adjusting the exchange rate from time to time

adjustable rate mortgage a mortgage where the interest rate changes according to the current market rates

adjustable rate preferred stock preference shares on which dividends are paid in line with the interest rate on Treasury bills

adjusted book value the value of a company in terms of the current market values of its assets and liabilities. *Also known as* **modified book value**

adjusted futures price the current value of a futures contract to buy a commodity at a fixed future date

adjusted gross income the amount of annual income that a person or company has after various adjustments for income or corporation tax purposes. *Abbr* **AGI**

adjusted present value where the capital structure of a company is complex, or expected to vary over time, discounted cash flows may be separated into (i) those which relate to operational items, and (ii) those associated with financing. This treatment enables assessment to be made of the separate features of each area. *Abbr* **APV**

adjusting entry in accounts, an entry which is made to correct a mistake

adjustment credit a short-term loan from the US Federal Reserve to a commercial bank

adjustment trigger a factor (such as a certain level of inflation) which triggers an adjustment in exchange rates

administered price the price of a good or service that is fixed by a manufacturer and which cannot be varied by a retailer

administration costs costs of management, not including production, marketing, or distribution costs

administrative expenses the cost of management, secretarial, accounting, and other services which cannot be related to the separate production, marketing, or research and development functions

administrative receiver a receiver appointed by a *debenture* holder to liquidate the assets of a company on his or her behalf

ADR *abbr* American depository receipt: a document that indicates a US investor's ownership of stock in a foreign corporation

ad valorem a tax or commission, for example, Value Added Tax, that is calculated on the value of the goods or services provided, rather than on their number or size

ad valorem duty a duty based on the value of a product or service

ad valorem tax *see ad valorem duty*

Advance Corporation Tax formerly, in the United Kingdom, a tax paid by a company equal to a percentage of its dividends or other distributions of profit to its shareholders. It was abolished in 1999. *abbr* **ACT**

advance payment an amount paid before it is earned or incurred, for example, a prepayment by an importer to an exporter before goods are shipped, or a cash advance for travel expenses

advance payment guarantee *or* **advance payment bond** a guarantee that enables a buyer to recover an advance payment made under a contract or order if the supplier fails to fulfil its contractual obligations

adverse action the action of refusing someone credit

adverse balance the deficit on an account, especially a nation's balance of payments account

adverse balance of trade a situation where a country imports more than it exports

adverse opinion a statement in the auditor's report of a company's annual accounts indicating a fundamental disagreement with the company to such an extent that the auditor considers the accounts misleading

advice note *see delivery note*

advice of fate immediate notification from a drawer's bank as to whether a cheque is to be honoured or not. This special presentation of a cheque bypasses the normal clearing system and so saves time.

Advisory, Conciliation and Arbitration Service a public body, funded by taxpayers, that aims to prevent and resolve problems between employers and their workforces. The government established the first voluntary conciliation service in 1896, but the modern ACAS was founded in 1974 when the organisation moved away from government control and became independent. It hosted talks between opposing sides in many of the high-profile labour disputes in the 1970s and 1980s, including the miners' strike in 1984. *Abbr* **ACAS**

advisory funds funds placed with a financial institution to invest on behalf of a client, the institution investing them at its own discretion

advisory management an advisory service offered by some stockbrokers in which clients are able to discuss a variety of investment options with their broker and receive appropriate advice. No resulting action may be taken, however, without a client's express approval.

AFAANZ *abbr* Accounting and Finance Association of Australia and New Zealand

affiliate a company that is controlled by another or is a member of a group, or either of two companies that owns a minority of the voting shares of the other

affiliated enterprise a company which is partly owned by another (though less than 50%), and in which the share-owning company exerts some management control or has a close trading relationship with the associate. *Also known as* **associate company**

affinity card a credit card issued to members of a particular group, for example, past students of a college, owners of a particular make of car, or supporters of a particular charity. The organisation may benefit from a donation upon issue or first use, and a small percentage of the card's subsequent turnover. Other cards give benefits such as air miles.

affluent society a community in which material wealth is widely distributed

AFTA *abbr* ASEAN Free Trade Area

after-acquired collateral collateral for a loan that a borrower obtains after making the contract for the loan

after date *see bill of exchange*

after-hours buying buying, selling, or dealing in shares after the Stock Exchange has officially closed for the day, such deals being subject to normal Stock Exchange rules. In this way, dealers can take advantage of the fact that because of time differences, the various stock exchanges round the world are open almost all twenty-four hours of the day.

after-tax relating to earnings or income from which tax has already been deducted

AG *abbr* Aktiengesellschaft: the German, Austrian, or Swiss equivalent of PLC

against actuals relating to a trade between owners of futures contracts

that allows both to reduce their positions to cash instead of commodities

age analysis of debtors the amount owed by debtors, classified by age of debt

aged debt a debt that is overdue by one or more given periods, usually increments of 30 days

aged debtor a person or organisation responsible for an overdue debt

agency bill a bill of exchange drawn on the local branch of a foreign bank

agency broker a dealer who acts for a client, buying and selling shares for a commission

agency theory a hypothesis that attempts to explain elements of organisational behaviour through an understanding of the relationships between principals (such as shareholders) and agents (such as company managers and accountants). A conflict may exist between the actions undertaken by agents in furtherance of their own self-interest, and those required to promote the interests of the principals. Within the hierarchy of firms, the same goal incongruence may arise when divisional managers promote their own self-interest over the interests of other divisions and of the company generally.

agent bank (*ANZ*) a bank that acts on behalf of a foreign bank, or a bank that participates in another bank's credit card programme, acting as a depository for merchants

age pension (*ANZ*) a sum of money paid regularly by the government to people who have reached the age of retirement, currently 65 for men and 60 for women

aggregate demand the sum of all expenditures in an economy that makes up its *GDP*, for example, consumers' expenditure on goods and services, investment in *capital stocks*, and government spending

aggregate depreciation *see accumulated depreciation*

aggregate income the total of all incomes in an economy without adjustments for inflation, taxation, or types of double counting

aggregate output the total value of all the goods and services produced in an economy

aggregate supply the total of all goods and services produced in an economy

aggressive relating to an investment strategy marked by willingness to accept high risk while trying to realise higher than average gains. Such a strategy involves investing in rapidly growing companies that promise capital appreciation but produce little or no income from dividends and de-emphasises income-producing instruments such as bonds.

aggressive growth fund a unit trust that takes considerable risks in the hope of making large profits

AGI *abbr* adjusted gross income

AGM *abbr* annual general meeting, a yearly meeting at which a company's management reports the year's results and shareholders have the opportunity to vote on company business, for example, the appointment of directors and auditors. Other business, for example, voting on dividend payments and board- and shareholder-sponsored resolutions, may also be transacted. *US term **annual meeting***

agreement among underwriters a document which forms a syndicate of underwriters, linking them to the issuer of a new *share issue*

agreement to sell a contract between two parties in which one agrees to sell something to the other at a date in the future

agricultural produce *see biological assets*

AICPA *abbr* American Institute of Certified Public Accountants

AIFA *abbr* Association of Financial Advisers

AIM *abbr* Alternative Investment Market: the London market trading in shares of emerging or small companies not eligible for listing on the London Stock Exchange. It replaced the Unlisted Securities Market (USM) in 1995.

air bill a US term for the documentation accompanying a package sent using an express mail service

air waybill a UK term for a receipt issued by an airline for goods to be freighted

AITC *abbr* Association of Investment Trust Companies

Aktb *abbr* Aktiebolaget, the Swedish equivalent of PLC

alien corporation a company which is based in one country, but registered in another

all equity rate the interest rate that a lender charges because of the apparent risks of a project that are independent of the normal market risks of financing it

alligator spread (*US*) a *spread* which remains unprofitable even with good market conditions, usually as the result of high *commissions* paid to *brokers* or agents (*slang*)

All Industrials Index a subindex of the Australian All Ordinaries Index which includes all the companies from that index that are not involved in resources or mining

All Mining Index a subindex of the Australian All Ordinaries Index which includes all the companies from that index that are involved in the mining industry

allocate to assign a whole item of *cost*, or of *revenue*, to a single cost unit, centre, account, or time period

All Ordinaries Accumulation Index a measure of the change in *share* prices on the Australian Stock Exchange, based on the All Ordinaries Index, but assuming that all dividends are reinvested

All Ordinaries Index the major index of Australian share prices, comprising more than 300 of the most active Australian companies listed on the Australian Stock Exchange. *Abbr* **All Ords**

All Ords *abbr* All Ordinaries Index

all-or-none underwriting (*ANZ*) the option of cancelling a public offering of shares if the underwriting is not fully subscribed

allowable deductions deductions from income which are allowed by the Inland Revenue, and which reduce the tax payable

allowable losses losses (as on the sale of assets) which are allowed to be set off against gains

All Resources Index a subindex of the Australian All Ordinaries Index which includes all the companies from that index that are involved in the resources industry

alpha rating the return a security or a portfolio would be expected to earn if the market's rate of return were zero. Alpha expresses the difference between the return expected from a stock or unit trust, given its *beta rating*, and the return actually produced. A stock or trust that returns more than its beta would predict has a positive alpha, while one that returns less than the amount predicted by beta has a negative alpha. A large positive alpha indicates a strong performance, while a

large negative alpha indicates a dismal performance.

To begin with, the market itself is assigned a beta of 1.0. If a stock or trust has a beta of 1.2, this means its price is likely to rise or fall by 12% when the overall market rises or falls by 10%; a beta of 7.0 means the stock or trust price is likely to move up or down at 70% of the level of the market change.

In practice, an alpha of 0.4 means the stock or trust in question outperformed the market-based return estimate by 0.4%. An alpha of –0.6 means the return was 0.6% less than would have been predicted from the change in the market alone.

Both alpha and beta should be readily available upon request from investment firms, because the figures appear in standard performance reports. It is always best to ask for them, because calculating a stock's alpha rating requires first knowing a stock's beta rating, and beta calculations can involve mathematical complexities. *See also beta rating*

alpha value a sum of money paid to an employee when he or she leaves a company that can be transferred to a concessionally taxed investment account such as an *Approved Deposit Fund*

alternate director a person who is allowed to act for an absent named director of a company at a board meeting

alternative investment an investment other than in bonds or shares of a large company or one listed on a stock exchange

Alternative Investment Market *see AIM*

alternative mortgage instrument any form of mortgage other than a fixed-term amortising loan

AM *abbr* asset management

amalgamation the process of two or more organisations joining together for mutual benefit, either through a *merger* or *consolidation*

ambit claim (*ANZ*) a claim made to an arbitration authority for higher pay or improved conditions that is deliberately exaggerated because the claimants know that they will subsequently have to compromise

American Accounting Association a voluntary organisation for those with an interest in accounting research and best practice. Its mission is 'to foster worldwide excellence in the creation, dissemination, and application of accounting knowledge and skills'. The AAA was founded in 1916. *Abbr* **AAA**

American depository receipt *see ADR*

American depository share *see ADR*

American Institute of Certified Public Accountants founded in New York in 1887, AICPA is the national association for certified public accountants in the United States. *Abbr* **AICPA**

American option an option contract that can be exercised at any time up to and including the expiry date. Most exchange-traded options are of this style. *See also* **European option**. *Also known as* **American-style option**

American Stock Exchange *see AMEX*

American-style option *see American option*

AMEX *abbr* American Stock Exchange: a New York stock exchange listing smaller and less mature companies than those listed on the larger New York Stock Exchange (NYSE)

amortisation 1. a method of recovering (deducting or writing off) the capital costs of intangible assets over a fixed period of time.

For tax purposes, the distinction is not always made between amortisation and depreciation, yet amortisation remains a viable financial accounting concept in its own right.

EXAMPLE It is computed using the straight-line method of depreciation: divide the initial cost of the intangible asset by the estimated useful life of that asset:

Initial cost / useful life = amortisation per year

For example, if it costs £10,000 to acquire a patent and it has an estimated useful life of 10 years, the amortised amount per year is £1,000. The amount of amortisation accumulated since the asset was acquired appears on the organisation's balance sheet as a deduction under the amortised asset.

While that formula is straightforward, amortisation can also incorporate a variety of non-cash charges to net earnings and/or asset values, such as depletion, write-offs, prepaid expenses, and deferred charges. Accordingly, there are many rules to regulate how these charges appear on financial statements. The rules are different in each country, and are occasionally changed, so it is necessary to stay abreast of them and rely on expert advice.

For financial reporting purposes, an intangible asset is amortised over a period of years. The amortisable life–'useful life'–of an intangible asset is the period over which it gives economic benefit.

Intangibles that can be amortised can include:

Copyrights, based on the amount paid either to purchase them or to develop them internally, plus the costs incurred in producing the work (wages or materials, for example). At present, a copyright is granted to a corporation for 75 years, and to an individual for the life of the author plus 50 years. However, the estimated useful life of a copyright is usually far less than its legal life, and it is generally amortised over a fairly short period.

Cost of a franchise, including any fees paid to the franchiser, as well as legal costs or expenses incurred in the acquisition. A franchise granted for a limited period should be amortised over its life. If the franchise has an indefinite life, it should be amortised over a reasonable period not to exceed 40 years.

Covenants not to compete: an agreement by the seller of a business not to engage in a competing business in a certain area for a specific period of time. The cost of the not-to-compete covenant should be amortised over the period covered by the covenant unless its estimated economic life is expected to be less.

Easement costs that grant a right of way may be amortised if there is a limited and specified life.

Organisation costs incurred when forming a corporation or a partnership, including legal fees, accounting services, incorporation fees, and other related services. Organisation costs are usually amortised over 60 months.

Patents, both those developed internally and those purchased. If developed internally, a patent's 'amortisable basis' includes legal fees incurred during the application process. A patent should be amortised over its legal life or its economic life, whichever is the shorter.

Trademarks, brands, and trade names, which should be written off over a period not to exceed 40 years.

Other types of property that may be amortised include certain intangible drilling costs, circulation costs, mine development costs, pollution control facilities, and reforestation expenditures.

Certain intangibles cannot be amortised, but may be depreciated using a straight-line approach if they have 'determinable' useful life. Because the rules are different in each country and are subject to change, it is essential to rely on specialist advice.

2. the repayment of the principal and interest on a loan in equal amounts over a period of time

amortise to reduce the value of an *asset* gradually by systematically writing off its cost over a period of time, or to repay a *debt* in a series of regular instalments or transfers

amortised value the value at a particular time of a financial instrument that is being amortised

AMPS *abbr* auction market preferred stock

analytical review the examination of ratios, trends, and changes in balances from one period to the next, to obtain a broad understanding of the financial position and results of operations and to identify any items requiring further investigation

angel investor an individual or group of individuals willing to invest in an unproven but well-researched e-business idea. Angel investors are typically the first port of call for Internet start-ups looking for financial backing, because they are more inclined to provide early funding than *venture capital* firms are. After investing in a company, angel investors take an advisory role without making demands.

angel network a network of backers, organised through a central office which keeps a database of suitable investors and puts them in touch with entrepreneurs who need financial backing

announcement a statement that a company makes to provide information on its trading prospects which will be of interest to its existing and potential investors

announcement date *see declaration date*

annual accounts *see annual report*

annual charge a management fee paid yearly to a stockbroker or collective fund manager by a client to cover a range of administrative costs and *commission*

annual depreciation provision the allocation of the cost of an *asset* to a single year of the asset's expected year

annual general meeting *see AGM*

annualised percentage rate yearly percentage rate, calculated by multiplying the monthly rate by twelve. It is not as accurate as the *APR*, which includes fees and other charges.

annual meeting *(US)* = *AGM*

annual percentage rate *or* **annualised percentage rate** *see APR*

annual percentage yield the effective or true annual rate of return on an investment, taking into account the effect of *compounding*. For example, an annual percentage rate of 6% compounded monthly translates into an annual percentage yield of 6.17%. *Abbr APY*

annual report a document prepared each year to give a true and fair view of a company's state of affairs.

Annual reports are issued to shareholders and filed at Companies House in accordance with the provisions of company legislation. Contents include a profit and loss account and *balance sheet*, a *cash-flow statement*, directors' report, *auditor's report*, and, where a company has subsidiaries, the company's group accounts.

The *financial statements* are the main purpose of the annual report, and usually include notes to the annual accounts. These amplify numerous points contained in the figures and are critical for anyone wishing to study the accounts in detail.

annual report and accounts a report from the directors on a company's financial situation at the end of a financial year, together with the balance sheet, profit and loss account, statement of source and application of funds, and the auditor's report, all prepared for the shareholders of the company each year

annual rest system a system in which extra payments or overpayments made to reduce the amount borrowed on a mortgage are credited to the account only once a year

annuity a contract in which a person pays a lump-sum premium to an insurance company and in return receives periodic payments, usually yearly, often beginning on retirement.

There are several types of annuity. They vary both in the ways they accumulate funds and in the ways they disperse earnings. A **fixed annuity** guarantees fixed payments to the individual receiving it for the term of the contract, usually until death; a **variable annuity** offers no guarantee but has potential for a greater return, usually based on the performance of a stock or unit trust; a deferred annuity delays payments until the individual chooses to receive them; a **hybrid annuity**, also called a **combination annuity**, combines features of both the fixed and variable annuity.

annuity contract a contract under which a person is paid a fixed sum regularly for life

annuity in arrears an *annuity* whose first payment is due at least one payment period after the start date of the annuity's contract

anticipation note a bond that a borrower intends to pay off with money from taxes due or money to be borrowed in a later and larger transaction

anticipatory hedging hedging carried out before the transaction occurs to which the hedge applies. *See hedge*

anti-dumping intended to prevent the sale of goods on a foreign market at a price below their *marginal cost*

anti-trust laws US legislative initiatives aimed at protecting trade and commerce from monopolistic business practices that restrict or eliminate competition. Antitrust laws also attempt to curb trusts and cartels and to keep them from employing monopolistic practices to make unfair profits.

ANZCERTA *abbr* Australia and New Zealand Closer Economic Relations Trade Agreement

APB *abbr* **1.** Auditing Practices Board **2.** (*US*) Accounting Principles Board

APEC Asia-Pacific Economic Co-operation Forum, an organisation designed to promote trade and economic co-operation among countries bordering the Pacific Ocean. It was set up in 1989. Its 21 members include Australia, Indonesia, Thailand, the Philippines, Singapore, Brunei, Russia, the United States, and Japan.

applied economics the practical application of theoretical economic principles, especially in formulating national and international economic policies

apportion to spread revenues or costs over two or more cost units, centres, accounts, or time periods

appreciation 1. the value that certain assets, particularly land and buildings, accrue over time. Directors of companies are obliged to reflect this in their accounts. **2.** the increase in value of one currency relative to another

appropriation a sum of money that has been allocated for a particular purpose

appropriation account in trading and non-profit entities, a record of how the profit/loss or surplus/deficit has been allocated to distributions, reserves, or funds

approved accounts accounts that have been formally accepted by a company's board of directors

Approved Deposit Fund (*ANZ*) a concessionally taxed fund managed by a financial institution into which *Eligible Termination Payments* can be transferred from a superannuation fund. *Abbr* **ADF**

APR *abbr* Annual or Annualised Percentage Rate of interest: the interest rate that would exist if it were calculated as simple rather than compound interest.

EXAMPLE Different investments typically offer different compounding periods, usually quarterly or monthly. The APR allows them to be compared over a common period of time: one year. This enables an investor or borrower to compare like with like, providing an excellent basis for comparing mortgage or other loan rates. In the United Kingdom, lenders are required to disclose it.

APR is calculated by applying the formula:

$$APR = [1 + i/m]m - 1.0$$

In the formula, **i** is the interest rate quoted, expressed as a decimal, and **m** is the number of compounding periods per year.

The APR is usually slightly higher than the quoted rate, and should be expressed as a decimal, that is, 6% becomes 0.06. When expressed as the cost of credit, other costs should be included in addition to interest, such as loan closing costs and financial fees. *See also **effective annual rate**. Also known as **nominal annual rate***

APRA *abbr* Australian Prudential Regulation Authority

APV *abbr* adjusted present value

APY *abbr* annual percentage yield

AR *abbr* accounts receivable

arbitrage the buying and selling of foreign currencies, products, or financial securities between two or more markets in order to make an immediate profit by exploiting differences in market prices quoted

arbitrage fund a fund which tries to take advantage of price discrepancies for the same *asset* in different *markets*

arbitrage pricing theory a model of financial instrument and portfolio behaviour that provides a benchmark of return and risk for capital budgeting and securities analysis. It can be used to create portfolios that track a market index, estimate the risk of an asset allocation strategy, or estimate the response of a portfolio to economic developments.

arbitrage syndicate a group of people formed to raise the capital to invest in arbitrage deals

arbitrageur a firm or individual who purchases shares or financial securities to make a windfall profit

arithmetic mean a simple average calculated by dividing the sum of two or more items by the number of items

armchair economics economic forecasting or theorising based on insufficient data or knowledge of a subject (*slang*)

arm's-length price a price at which an unrelated seller and buyer agree to deal on an *asset* or a product

articles of association an official document governing the running of a company, that is placed with the *Registrar of Companies*. The articles of association constitute a contract between the company and its members, set out the voting rights of shareholders and the conduct of shareholders' and directors' meetings, and detail the powers of management of the company. A *memorandum of association* is a related document. US term *bylaws*

articles of incorporation in the United States, a legal document that creates a privately held company whose powers are governed by the general corporation laws of the state in which it was founded

articles of partnership see *partnership agreement*

ASB *abbr* Accounting Standards Board

ASC *abbr* Accounting Standards Committee

ASEAN Free Trade Area a conceptual regional free trade agreement supported by Singapore to foster trade within the region. *Abbr* **AFTA**

A share 1. a non-voting share in a company issued to raise additional capital without diluting control of the company **2.** in the United States, a type of mutual fund share that has a sales charge associated with it

A shares (*US*) = *non-voting shares*

Asian Currency Unit a book-keeping unit used for recording transactions made by approved financial institutions operating in the Asian Dollar market. *Abbr* **ACU**

ASIC *abbr* Australian Securities and Investments Commission

ask 1. the *bid price* at which a dealer in stocks and shares, commodities, or financial securities is prepared to buy **2.** (*US*) the price at which a security is offered for sale, or the net asset value of a mutual fund plus any sales charges. *Also known as* **asked price**, **offering price**

asked price see *ask* (*sense 2*)

asking price the price that a seller puts on something before any negotiation

assessed loss the excess of tax-deductible expenses over taxable income as confirmed by the South African Revenue Service. It may be carried forward and deducted in determining the taxpayer's taxable income in subsequent years of assessment.

assessed value a value for something that is calculated by a person such as an investment advisor

asset any tangible or intangible item to which a value can be assigned. Assets can be physical, such as machinery and consumer durables, or financial, such as cash and accounts receivable.

Assets are typically broken down into five different categories. *Current assets* include cash, cash equivalents, marketable securities, inventories, and prepaid expenses that are expected to be used within one year or a normal operating cycle. All cash items and inventories are reported at historical value. Securities are reported at market value. Non-current assets, or long-term investments, are resources that are expected to be held for more than one year. They are reported at the lower of cost and current market value, which means that their values will vary. *Fixed assets* include property, plant and facilities, and equipment used to conduct business. These items are reported at their original value, even though current values might well be much higher. *Intangible assets* include legal claims, patents, franchise rights, and accounts receivable. These values can be more difficult to determine. FR10, published by the Accounting Standards Board of the Institute of Chartered Accountants for England and Wales is essential reading for dealing with this issue. Deferred charges include prepaid costs and other expenditures that will produce future revenue or benefits.

asset allocation (*ANZ*) an investment strategy that distributes investments in a portfolio so as to achieve the highest investment return while minimising risk. Such a strategy usually apportions investments among cash equivalents, shares in domestic and foreign companies, fixed-income investments, and property.

asset-backed security a security for which the collateral is neither land nor a land-based financial instrument

asset backing support for a share price provided by the value of the company's assets

asset-based lending the lending of money with the expectation that the proceeds from an asset or assets will allow the borrower to repay the loan

asset conversion loan a loan that the borrower will repay with money raised by selling an asset

asset coverage the ratio measuring a company's solvency and consisting of its net assets divided by its debt

asset demand the amount of assets held as money, which will be low when interest rates are high and high when interest rates are low

asset financing the borrowing of money by a company using its assets as collateral

asset for asset swap an exchange of one bankrupt debtor's debt for that of another

asset management an investment service offered by some financial institutions that combines banking and brokerage services. *Abbr* **AM**

asset play the purchase of a company's stock in the belief that it has assets that are not properly documented and therefore unknown to others

asset pricing model a pricing model used to determine the profit that an asset will yield

asset protection trust a trust, often set up in a foreign country, used to make the trust's principal inaccessible to creditors

asset restructuring the purchase or sale of assets worth more than 50% of a listed company's total or net assets

asset side the side of a balance sheet that shows the economic resources a firm owns, for example, cash in hand or in bank deposits, products, or buildings and fixtures

assets requirements the assets needed for a business to continue trading

asset-stripper a company that acquires another company and sells its assets to make a profit without regard for the acquired company's future business success

asset-stripping the purchase of a company whose market value is below its asset value, usually so that the buyer can sell the assets for immediate gain. The buyer usually has little or no concern for the purchased company's employees or other *stakeholders*, so the practice is generally frowned upon.

asset substitution the purchase of assets that involve more risk than those a lender expected the borrower to buy

asset swap an exchange of assets between companies so that they may divest parts no longer required and enter another product area

asset turnover the ratio of a firm's sales revenue to its total assets, used as a measure of the firm's business efficiency

asset valuation the aggregated value of the assets of a firm, usually the capital assets, as entered on its balance sheet

assign to transfer ownership of an *asset* to another person or organisation

assigned risk a poor insurance risk that a company is required by law to insure against

associate (*ANZ*) a member of a stock exchange who does not have a seat on it

associate company company which is partly owned by another (though less than 50%), and where the share-owning company exerts some management control or has a close trading relationship with the associate

Associate of the Association of International Accountants *abbr* **AAIA**

Association of British Insurers an association that represents over 400 UK insurance companies to the government, the regulators, and other agencies as well as providing a wide range of services to its members. *Abbr* **ABI**

Association of Chartered Accountants in the United States a non-profit professional and educational organisation that represents over 5,000 chartered accountants based in the United States. The Association was founded in 1985. *Abbr* **ACAUS**

Association of Chartered Certified Accountants an international accountancy organisation with over 300,000 members in more than 160 countries. It was formed in 1904 as the London Association of Accountants. *Abbr* **ACCA**

Association of Financial Advisers a trade association that represents the interests of independent financial advisers

Association of Unit Trusts and Investment Funds *abbr* **AUTIF**

assumable mortgage a mortgage that the buyer of a property can take over from the seller

assumed bond a bond for which a company other than the issuer takes over responsibility

assurance a standard form used in Australia to report **PAYG** instalment payments on investment income

assured shorthold tenancy a tenancy for a fixed period of at least six months during which the tenant cannot be evicted other than by court order. Any new tenancy without a written agreement is an assured shorthold tenancy.

assured tenancy a tenancy for an indefinite period during which the tenant cannot be evicted other than by court order

ASX *abbr* Australian Stock Exchange

ASX 100 a measure of the change in share prices on the *Australian Stock Exchange* based on changes in the stocks of the top 100 companies. Similar indexes include the ASX 20, ASX 50, ASX 200, and ASX 300.

asymmetric taxation a difference in tax status between parties to a transaction, typically making the transaction attractive to both parties because of taxes that one or both can avoid

at best an instruction to a stockbroker to buy or sell securities immediately at the best possible current price in the market, regardless of adverse price movements. It is also applicable to the commodity or currency markets. *See also at limit*

at call used to describe a short-term loan that is repayable immediately upon demand

at limit an instruction to a stockbroker to buy or sell a security within certain limits, usually not to sell below or not to buy above a set price. A time limit is stipulated by the investor and if there has been no transaction within that period, the instruction lapses. It is also applicable to the commodity or currency markets. *See also at best*

ATM an electronic machine from which bank customers can withdraw paper money using an encoded plastic card. *Abbr of automated teller machine*

ATO *abbr* Australian Taxation Office

at sight *see bill of exchange*

attachment a process that enables a judgment creditor to secure dues from a debtor. A debtor's earnings and/or funds held at his or her bankers may be attached.

attendance bonus (*US*) a financial or non-financial incentive offered to employees by an employer to arrive for work on time

attestation clause a clause showing that the signature of the person signing a legal document has been witnessed

at-the-money used to describe an option with a strike price roughly equivalent to the price of the underlying shares

auction market preferred stock stock in a company owned in the United Kingdom that pays dividends which track a money-market index. *Abbr* **AMPS**

AUD *abbr* Australian dollar

audit a systematic examination of the activities and status of an entity, based primarily on investigation and analysis of its systems, controls, and records

audit committee a committee of a company's board of directors, from which the company's executives are excluded, that monitors the company's finances

audited accounts a set of accounts that have been thoroughly scrutinised, checked, and approved by a team of auditors

Auditing Practices Board a body formed in 1991 by an agreement among the six members of the Consultative Committee of Accountancy Bodies, to be responsible for developing and issuing professional auditing standards in the United Kingdom and the Republic of Ireland. *Abbr* **APB**

Auditor-General an officer of an Australian state or territory government who is responsible for ensuring that government expenditure is made in accordance with legislation

auditors' fees fees paid to a company's auditors, which are approved by the shareholders at an *AGM*

auditor's report a certification by an auditor that a firm's financial records give a true and fair view of its profit and loss for the period

audit report the summary submission made by auditors of the findings of an *audit*. An audit report is usually of the financial records and accounts of a company and is a legal annual requirement in the United Kingdom. The report is filed with the Registrar of Companies along with the accounts. An audit report normally takes one of the forms approved by the accountancy professional organisations to cover all requirements imposed by law on the auditor. If reports do not support the company's records, they may be termed 'qualified'. A report is qualified if it contains any indication that the auditor has failed to satisfy himself or herself on any of the points that the law requires. The qualification may, for example, add a rider stating that the appointed auditor has had to rely on secondary information supplied by other auditors under circumstances in which it has been inappropriate to do otherwise. Qualifications may also refer to the inadequacy of information or explanations supplied, or to the fact that the auditor is not satisfied that proper books or other records are being kept.

audit risk the risk that auditors may give an inappropriate audit opinion on financial statements

audit trail the records of all the sequential stages of a transaction. An audit trail may trace the process of a purchase, a sale, a customer complaint, or the supply of goods. Tracing what happened at each stage through the records can be a useful method of problem-solving. In financial markets, audit trails may be used to ensure fairness and accuracy on the part of the dealers.

augend the number added to an *addend* in order to make a sum

Aussie Mac an informal name for a mortgage-backed certificate issued in Australia by the National Mortgage Market Corporation. The corporation has been issuing such certificates since 1985.

austerity budget a budget imposed on a country by its government with the aim of reducing the national deficit by cutting consumer spending

Austrade the Australian Trade Commission, a federal government body responsible for promoting Australian products abroad and attracting business to Australia. It currently has 108 offices in 63 countries.

Australia and New Zealand Closer Economic Relations Trade Agreement an accord between Australia and New Zealand designed to facilitate the exchange of goods between the two countries. It was signed on 1 January 1983. *Abbr* **ANZCERTA**

Australian Accounting Standards Board a body that is responsible for setting and monitoring accounting standards in Australia. It was established under Corporations Law in 1988, replacing the Accounting Standards Review Board. *Abbr* **AASB**

Australian Chamber of Commerce and Industry a national council of business organisations in Australia. It represents around 350,000 businesses and its members include state chambers of commerce as well as major national employer and industry associations. *Abbr* **ACCI**

Australian Communications Authority a government body responsible for regulating practices in the communications industries. It was set up in 1997 as a result of the merger of the Australian Telecommunications Authority and the Spectrum Management Agency. *Abbr* **ACA**

Australian Industrial Relations Commission an administrative tribunal responsible for settling industrial disputes by conciliation and for setting and modifying industrial awards. It was established in 1988 to replace the Arbitration Commission and other specialist tribunals. *Abbr* **AIRC**

Australian Prudential Regulation Authority a federal government body responsible for ensuring that financial institutions are able to meet their commitments. *Abbr* **APRA**

Australian Securities and Investments Commission an Australian federal government body responsible for regulating Australian businesses and the provision of financial products and services to consumers. It was established in 1989, replacing the Australian Securities Commission. *Abbr* **ASIC**

Australian Stock Exchange the principal market for trading shares and other securities in Australia. It was formed in 1987 as a result of the amalgamation of six state stock exchanges and has offices in most state capitals. *Abbr* **ASX**

Australian Taxation Office a statutory body responsible for the administration of the Australian federal government's taxation system. It is based in Canberra and is also responsible for the country's superannuation system. *Abbr* **ATO**

authorisation the process of assessing a financial transaction, confirming that it does not raise the account's debt above its limit, and allowing the transaction to proceed. This would be undertaken, for example, by a credit card issuer. A positive authorisation results in an authorisation code being generated and the relevant funds being set aside. The available credit limit is reduced by the amount authorised.

authorised capital the money made by a company from the sale of authorised ordinary and preference shares. It is measured by multiplying the number of authorised shares by their par value.

authorised share a share that a company is authorised to issue

authorised share capital the type, class, number, and amount of the shares which a company may issue, as empowered by its memorandum of association. *Also known as* **nominal share capital**, **registered share capital**

authorised signatory the most senior issuer of authorisation certificates in an organisation, recognised by a signatory authority and designated in a signatory certificate

authority to purchase a bill drawn up and presented with shipping documentation to the purchaser's bank, allowing the bank to purchase the bill

AUTIF *abbr* Association of Unit Trusts and Investment Funds

Automated Direct Debit Amendments and Cancellation Service in the United Kingdom, a *BACS* service that allows paying banks to inform direct debit payees of a change of instruction, for example, an amendment to a customer's account details or a request to cancel the instructions. *Abbr* **ADDACS**

Automated Order Entry System in the United States, a system that allows small orders to bypass the floor brokers and go straight to the specialists on the exchange floor

automated screen trading an electronic trading system for the sale and purchase of securities. Customers' orders are entered via a keyboard, a computer system matches and executes the deals, and prices and deals are shown on monitors, thus dispensing with the need for face-to-face contact on a trading floor.

automated teller machine *see* **ATM**

automatic debit (*US*) = *standing order*

automatic rollover on the London Money Market, the automatic reinvestment of a maturing fixed term deposit for a further identical fixed term, an arrangement that can be cancelled at any time

Auto Pact the informal name for the Agreement Concerning Automotive Products between Canada and the United States, by which duties were reduced on imported cars for US car makers assembling vehicles in Canada. Subsequent provisions of the North American Free Trade Agreement reduced its effect.

availability float money that is available to a company because cheques that it has written have not yet been charged against its accounts

AVCs *abbr* additional voluntary contributions

average accounting return the percentage return realised on an asset, as measured by its book value, after taxes and depreciation

average adjuster a person who calculates how much of an insurance is to be borne by each party

average adjustment the calculation of the share of cost of damage to or loss of a ship

average collection period the mean time required for a firm to liquidate its accounts receivable, measured from the date each receivable is posted until the last payment is received.
EXAMPLE Its formula is:

Accounts receivable / Average daily sales =
Average collection period

For example, if accounts receivable are £280,000, and average daily sales are 7,000, then:

$$280,000 / 7,000 = 40$$

average cost of capital the average of what a company is paying for the money it borrows or raises by selling stock

average nominal maturity the average length of time until a unit trust's financial instruments mature

average option an option whose value depends on the average price of a commodity during a particular period of time

avoidable costs the specific costs of an activity or sector of a business which would be avoided if that activity or sector did not exist

award wage (*ANZ*) a rate of pay set by an industrial court or tribunal for a particular occupation

B

BAA *abbr* British Accounting Association

Baby Bell (*US*) one of the regional phone companies that was established after the demise of AT & T in 1984. Nynex and Southwestern Bell are two of the Baby Bells. (*slang*)

back duty tax relating to a past period that has not been paid because of the taxpayer's failure to disclose relevant information through negligence or fraud. If back duty is found to be payable, the relevant authorities may instigate an investigation and penalties or interest may be charged on the amount.

back-end loading the practice of charging a redemption fee or deferred sales charge if the holder of an investment decides to sell it. This is used as a discouragement to selling. *See also front-end loading*

backflush costing a method of costing, associated with a JIT production system, which applies cost to the output of a process. Costs do not mirror the flow of products through the production process, but are attached to output produced (finished goods stock and cost of sales), on the assumption that such backflushed costs are a realistic measure of the actual costs incurred.

backlog depreciation the additional depreciation required when an asset is revalued to make up for the fact that previous depreciation had been calculated on a now out-of-date valuation

back office the administrative staff of a company who do not have face-to-face contact with the company's customers

back pay pay that is owed to an employee for work carried out before the current payment period and is either overdue or results from a backdated pay increase

back-to-back loan an arrangement in which two companies in different countries borrow offsetting amounts in each other's currency that each repays at a specified future date in its domestic currency. Such a loan, often between a company and its foreign subsidiary, eliminates the risk of loss from exchange rate fluctuations.

back-up a period in which bond yields rise and prices fall, or a sudden reversal in a stock market trend

back-up credit credit provided by banks for a eurocurrency note

back-up withholding withholding tax that a payer sends to the Internal Revenue Service in the United States so that somebody receiving income cannot avoid all taxes on that income

BACS an electronic bulk clearing system generally used by banks and building societies for low-value and/or repetitive items such as standing orders, direct debits, and automated credits such as salary payments. It was formerly known as the Bankers Automated Clearing Services.

BADC *abbr* Business Accounting Deliberation Council of Japan

bad debt a debt which is or is considered to be uncollectable and is, therefore, written off either as a charge to the profit and loss account or against an existing doubtful debt provision

bad debt provision an accounting estimate of the amount of debts thought likely to have to be written off

bad debt reserve an amount of money that a company sets aside to cover bad debts

bad debts recovered money formerly classified as *bad debts* and therefore written off that has since been recovered either wholly or in part

badwill negative goodwill (*slang*)

bailment the delivery of goods from the owner to another person on the condition that they will eventually be returned

balance 1. the state of an account, for example, a debit or a credit balance, indicating whether money is owed or owing **2.** in double-entry bookkeeping, the amount required to make the debit and credit figures in the books equal each other **3.** the difference between the totals of the debit and credit entries in an account

balance billing the practice of requesting payment from a receiver of a service such as medical treatment for the part of the cost not covered by the person's insurance

balance brought down an amount entered in an account at the end of a period to balance income and expenditure

balanced budget a budget in which planned expenditure on goods and services and debt income can be met by current income from taxation and other central government receipts

balanced fund a unit trust that invests in a variety of types of companies and financial instruments to reduce the risk of loss through poor performance of any one type

balanced investment strategy the practice of investing in a variety of types of companies and financial instruments to reduce the risk of loss through poor performance of any one type

balanced scorecard a system that measures and manages an organisation's progress towards strategic objectives. Introduced by Robert Kaplan and David Norton in 1992, the balanced scorecard incorporates not only financial indicators but also three other perspectives: customer, internal business,

and learning/innovation. The scorecard shows how these measures are interlinked and affect each other, enabling an organisation's past, present, and potential performance to be tracked and managed.

balanced scorecard approach an approach to the provision of information to management in order to assist strategic policy formulation and achievement to build the long-term value of the business. It emphasises the need to provide the user with a set of information that addresses all relevant areas of performance in an objective and unbiased fashion. The information provided may include financial and non-financial elements and cover areas such as profitability, customer satisfaction, internal efficiency, and innovation. The term originates from the best-selling business book *The Balanced Scorecard*, written by Robert Kaplan and David Norton and published by Harvard Business School Press in 1996. Their approach applies the concept of shareholder value analysis, and is based on the premise that the traditional measures used by managers to see how well their organisations are performing, such as business ratios, productivity, unit costs, growth, and profitability, are only a part of the picture. Traditional measures are seen as providing a narrowly focused snapshot of how an organisation performed in the past, and give little indication of likely future performance. In contrast, the Balanced Scorecard (BSC) offers a measurement and management system that links strategic objectives to comprehensive performance indicators.

balance off to add up and enter the totals for both sides of an account at the end of an accounting period in order to determine the balance

balance of payments a list of a country's credit and debit transactions with international financial institutions and foreign countries over a specific period. *Abbr* **BOP**

balance of payments capital account items in a country's balance of payments which refer to capital investments made in or by other countries

balance of payments current account a record of imports and exports of goods and services and the flows of money between countries arising from investments

balance of payments deficit a situation where a country buys more from other countries than it sells as exports

balance of payments on capital account a system of recording a country's investment transactions with the rest of the world during a given period, usually one year. Among the included transactions are the purchase of physical and financial assets, intergovernmental transfers, and the provision of economic aid to developing nations.

balance of payments on current account a system of recording a country's imports and exports of goods and services during a period, usually one year

balance of payments surplus a situation where a country sells more to other countries than it buys from them

balance of trade the difference between a country's exports and imports of goods and services. *Abbr* **BOT**

balance sheet a financial report stating the total assets, liabilities, and owners' equity of an organisation at a given date, usually the last day of the accounting period. The format of a company's balance sheet is strictly defined by the 1985 Companies Act. The debit side of the balance sheet states assets, while the credit side states liabilities and equity, and the two sides must be equal, or balance.

EXAMPLE

ASSETS	£
Current:	
Cash	8,200
Securities	5,000
Receivables	4,500
Inventory & supplies	6,300
Fixed:	
Land	10,000
Structures	90,000
Equipment (less depreciation)	5,000
Intangibles/other	
TOTAL ASSETS	129,000

LIABILITIES	£
Payables	7,000
Taxes	4,000
Misc.	3,000
Bonds & notes	25,000
TOTAL LIABILITIES	39,000
SHAREHOLDERS' EQUITY (stock, par value shares × outstanding)	80,000
RETAINED EARNINGS	10,000
TOTAL LIABILITIES AND SHAREHOLDERS' EQUITY	129,000

Assets include cash in hand and cash anticipated (receivables), inventories of supplies and materials, properties, facilities, equipment, and whatever else the company uses to conduct business. Assets also need to reflect depreciation in the value of equipment such as machinery that has a limited expected useful life.

Liabilities include pending payments to suppliers and creditors, outstanding current and long-term debts, taxes, interest payments, and other unpaid expenses that the company has incurred.

Subtracting the value of aggregate liabilities from the value of aggregate assets reveals the value of owners' equity. Ideally, it should be positive. Owners' equity consists of capital invested by owners over the years and profits (net income) or internally generated capital, which is referred to as 'retained earnings'; these are funds to be used in future operations. *Abbr* **B/S**

balance sheet audit a limited audit of the items on a company's balance sheet in order to confirm that it complies with the relevant standards and requirements. Such an audit involves checking the value, ownership, and existence of assets and liabilities and ensuring that they are correctly recorded.

balance sheet date the date, usually the end of a financial or accounting year, when a company's balance sheet is drawn up

balance sheet equation *see account-ing equation*

balance sheet total in the United Kingdom, the total of assets shown at the bottom of a balance sheet and used to classify a company according to size

balancing figure a number added to a series of numbers to make the total the same as another total. For example, if a debit total is higher than the credit total in the accounts, the balancing figure is the amount of extra credit required to make the two totals equal.

balloon loan a loan repaid in regular instalments with a single larger final payment

balloon payment the final larger payment on a balloon loan

ballpark an informal term for a rough, estimated figure. The term was derived from the approximate assessment of the number of spectators that might be made on the basis of a glance around at a sporting event.

BALO Bulletin des Annonces Légales Obligatoires: a French government publication that includes financial statements of public companies

BAN *abbr* bond anticipation note

bang for the buck *(US)* a return on investment *(slang)*

bank a commercial institution that keeps money in accounts for individuals or organisations, makes loans, exchanges currencies, provides credit to businesses, and offers other financial services

bank base rate the basic rate of interest on which the actual rate a bank charges on loans to its customers is calculated

bank bill 1. a bill of exchange issued or accepted by a bank **2.** *(US)* a bank-note

bank card a plastic card issued by a bank and accepted by merchants in payment for transactions. The most common types are *credit cards* and *debit cards*. Bank cards are governed by an internationally recognised set of rules for the authorisation of their use and the clearing and settlement of transactions.

bank certificate a document, often requested during an audit, that is signed by a bank official and confirms the balances due from a company on a specific date

bank charge an amount charged by a bank to its customers for services provided, for example, for servicing customer accounts or arranging foreign currency transactions or letters of credit, but excluding interest

bank confirmation verification of a company's balances requested by an auditor from a bank

bank credit the maximum credit available to an individual from a particular bank

bank discount the charge made by a bank to a company or customer who pays a note before it is due

bank discount basis the expression of yield that is used for US Treasury bills, based on a 360-day year

bank draft *see banker's draft*

bank-eligible issue US Treasury obligations that commercial banks may buy

banker somebody who owns or is a senior executive of a bank

banker's acceptance *see banker's credit*

banker's cheque *see banker's draft*

banker's credit a financial instrument, typically issued by an exporter or importer for a short term, that a bank guarantees. *Also known as banker's acceptance*

banker's draft a bill of exchange payable on demand and drawn by one bank on another. Regarded as being equivalent to cash, the draft cannot be returned unpaid. *Also known as bank draft, banker's cheque. Abbr* **B/D**

bankers' hours short hours of work. The term refers to the relatively short time that a bank is open in some countries. (*slang*)

banker's order an instruction by a customer to a bank to pay a specific amount at regular intervals, usually monthly or annually, until the order is cancelled

banker's reference a written report issued by a bank regarding a particular customer's creditworthiness

bank fee a charge included in most lease transactions that is either paid in advance or is included in the gross capitalised cost. The fee usually covers administrative costs such as the costs of obtaining a credit report, verifying insurance coverage, and checking the lease documentation.

Bank for International Settlements *see BIS*

bank giro *see giro (sense 1)*

bank guarantee a commitment made by a bank to a foreign buyer that the bank will pay an exporter for goods shipped if the buyer defaults

bank holding company a company that owns one or more banks as part of its assets

Banking Code a voluntary code of best practice for the banking and financial services industry, which is developed and revised by the *British Bankers' Association*

banking insurance fund in the United States, a fund maintained by the Federal Deposit Insurance Corporation to provide deposit insurance for banks other than savings and savings and loan banks

Banking Ombudsman an official of the Australian or New Zealand government responsible for dealing with complaints relating to banking practices

banking passport a document used to provide somebody with a false identity for banking transactions in another country

banking products goods and services produced by banks for customers, such as statements, direct debits, and standing orders

banking syndicate a group of investment banks that jointly underwrite and distribute a new security offering

banking system a network of commercial, savings, and specialised banks that provide financial services including accepting deposits and providing loans and credit, money transmission and investment facilities

bank investment contract a contract that specifies what a bank will pay its investors

bankmail an agreement by a bank not to finance any rival's attempt to take over the same company that a particular customer is trying to buy (*slang*)

bank mandate a written order to a bank, asking them to open an account and allowing someone to sign cheques on behalf of the account holder, giving specimen signatures and other relevant information

Bank of Canada rate the minimum interest rate charged by the Bank of Canada to major financial institutions borrowing from it, effectively setting national interest rates

Bank of England the central bank of the United Kingdom, established in 1694. Originally a private bank, it became public in 1946 and increased its independence from government in 1997 when it was granted sole responsibility for setting base interest rates.

bank overdraft borrowings from a bank on a current account, repayable on demand. The maximum permissible overdraft is normally agreed with the bank prior to the facility being made available, and interest, calculated on a daily basis, is charged on the amount borrowed, and not on the agreed maximum borrowing facility.

bank reconciliation a detailed statement reconciling, at a given date, the cash balance in an entity's cash book with that reported in a bank statement

EXAMPLE

Bank Reconciliation Statement

Cash book balance	£	£
Cash book balance o/d		(1,205)
Bank charges not in cash book	(110)	
Dividends collected by the bank, not in cash book	113	3
Updated cash book balance		**(1,202)**
Cheques drawn, not presented to bank	4,363	
Cheques received, not yet credited by bank	(1,061)	3,302
Bank statement balance		**2,100**

bank reserve ratio a standard established by a central bank governing the relationship between the amount of money that other banks must keep on hand and the amount that they can lend. By raising and lowering the ratio, the central bank can decrease or increase the money supply.

bank reserves the money that a bank has available to meet the demands of its depositors

bankroll the money used as finance for a project

bankrupt a person who has been declared by a court of law as unable to meet his or her financial obligations

bankruptcy the condition of being unable to pay debts, with liabilities greater than assets. There are two types of bankruptcy: involuntary bankruptcy, where one or more creditors bring a petition against the debtor; and voluntary bankruptcy, where the debtor files a petition claiming inability to meet his or her debts.

bank statement a record, sent by a bank to its customer, listing transactions since the date of the previous statement

bank term loan a loan from a bank that has a term of at least one year

bar or **outside the bar** one million pounds sterling (*slang*)

bar-bell a portfolio which concentrates on very long-term and very short-term bonds only

barefoot pilgrim (*US*) an unsophisticated investor who has lost everything trading in securities (*slang*)

bargain a transaction on a stock market (*slang*)

bargaining chip something that can be used as a concession or inducement in negotiation

bargain tax date the date of a transaction on a stock market

barometer stock a widely held security such as a blue chip that is regarded as an indicator of the state of the market

barren money money that is unproductive because it is not invested

barrier option an option that includes automatic trading in other options when a commodity reaches a specified price

barrier to entry any impediment to the free entry of new competitors into a market

barrier to exit any impediment to the exit of existing competitors from a market

barter the direct exchange of goods or services between two parties without the use of money as a medium

base currency the currency used for measuring the return on an investment

base date the reference date from which an index number such as the *retail price index* is calculated

base interest rate in the United States, the minimum interest rate that investors will expect for investing in a non-Treasury security

base pay *(US)* = *basic pay*

base rate the interest rate at which the Bank of England lends to other banks and which they in turn charge their customers

base rate tracker mortgage a mortgage whose interest rate varies periodically, usually annually, so as to remain a specified amount above a particular standard rate

base year the year from which an index is calculated

basic balance the balance of current account and long-term capital accounts in a country's balance of payments

basic pay a guaranteed sum of money given to an employee in payment for work, disregarding any fringe benefits, allowances, or extra rewards from an *incentive scheme*. *US term* ***base pay***

basic rate the percentage of income that the majority of workers in the United Kingdom pay to the Inland Revenue

basic rate tax the main or first rate of income tax, currently 22%, levied on taxable income after the lowest, or starting, rate, and running until the higher rate threshold is reached

basic wage the minimum rate of pay set by an industrial court or tribunal for a particular occupation

basic wage rate the wages paid for a specific number of hours work per week, excluding overtime payments and any other incentives

basis of apportionment a physical or financial unit used to apportion costs equitably to cost centres

basis of assessment a method of deciding in which year financial transactions should be assessed for taxation

basis period the period during which transactions occur, used for the purpose of deciding when they should be assessed for taxation

basis point one hundredth of 1%, used in relation to changes in bond interest rates. Thus a change from 7.5% to 7.4% is 10 basis points.

basis risk the risk that price variations in the cash or futures market will diminish revenue when a futures contract is liquidated, or the risk that changes in interest rates will affect the re-pricing of interest-bearing liabilities

basis swap the exchange of two financial instruments, each with a variable interest calculated at a different rate

basket case a company or individual considered to be in such dire circumstances as to be beyond help (*slang*)

basket of currencies a group of selected currencies used in establishing a standard of value for another unit of currency

batch a group of similar articles which maintains its identity throughout one or more stages of production and is treated as a cost unit

batch costing a form of specific order costing in which costs are attributed to batches of products

batch-level activities activities which vary directly with the number of batches of output produced, and which are independent of the number of units within a batch. Set-up costs are batch-level activities. *See also **hierarchy of activities***

bath
   take a bath (*US*) to suffer a serious financial loss (*slang*)

baud a unit used to measure speed of data transmission, equal to one data unit per second

BBA *abbr* British Bankers' Association

BC *abbr* budgetary control

BCC *abbr* British Chambers of Commerce

BCCS *abbr* Board of Currency Commissioners

B/D *abbr* banker's draft

bean counter a derogatory term for an accountant, especially one who works in a large organisation (*slang*)

bear somebody who anticipates unfavourable business conditions, especially somebody who sells stocks or commodities expecting their prices to fall, often with the intention of buying them back cheaply later. *See also **bull***
   taking a bear position acting on the assumption that the market is likely to fall

bear covering the point in a market at which dealers who sold stock short now buy back (at lower prices) to cover their positions

bearer bond a negotiable bond or security whose ownership is not registered by the issuer, but is presumed to lie with whoever has physical possession of the bond

bearer instrument a financial instrument such as a cheque or bill of exchange that entitles the person who presents it to receive payment

bearer security a share or bond that is owned by the person who possesses it. For example, a Eurobond can change hands without registration and so protect the owner's anonymity.

bearish relating to unfavourable business conditions or selling activity in anticipation of falling prices. *See also **bullish***

bear market a market in which prices are falling and in which a dealer is more likely to sell securities than to buy them. *See also **bull market***

bear raid *see **raid***

bear spread a combination of purchases and sales of options for the same commodity or stock with the intention of making a profit when the price falls. *See also **bull spread***

bear tack a downwards movement in the value of a stock, part of the market, or the market as a whole

bed and breakfast deal a transaction in which somebody sells shares at the end of one trading day and repurchases them at the beginning of the next. This is usually done to formally establish the profit or loss accrued to these shares for tax or reporting purposes.

before-tax profit margin the amount by which net income before tax exceeds expenditure

beginning inventory (*US*) = *opening stock*

behavioural accounting an approach to the study of accounting that emphasises the psychological and social aspects of the profession in addition to the more technical areas

behavioural implications the ways in which humans affect, and are affected by, the creation, existence, and use of accounting information

bell cow a product that sells well and makes a reasonable profit (*slang*)

bells and whistles special features attached to a derivatives instrument or securities issue that are intended to attract investors or reduce issue costs (*slang*)

bellwether a security whose price is viewed by investors as an indicator of future developments or trends

belly
   go belly up (*US*) to fail financially or go bankrupt (*slang*)

below-the-line 1. used to describe entries in a company's profit and loss account that show how the profit is distributed, or where the funds to finance the loss originate. *See also* **above-the-line** (*sense 1*) **2.** in macroeconomics, used to describe a country's capital transactions. *See also* **above-the-line** (*sense 2*)

belt and braces man a very cautious lender who asks for extra collateral as well as guarantees for a loan

benchmark accounting policy one of a choice of two possible policies within an International Accounting Standard. The other policy is marked as an 'allowed alternative', although there is no indication of preference.

benchmark index an influential index for a particular market or activity

benchmark interest rate the lowest interest rate that US investors will accept on securities other than Treasury bills

beneficial interest an arrangement where someone is allowed to occupy or receive rent from a house without owning it

beneficial owner somebody who receives all the benefits of a stock such as dividends, rights, and proceeds of any sale but is not the registered owner of the stock

beneficiary bank a bank that handles a gift such as a bequest

benefit something that improves the profitability or efficiency of an organisation or reduces its risk, or any non-monetary reward given to employees, for example, paid holidays or employer contributions to pensions

benefit–cost ratio = *cost-benefit analysis*

Benford's Law a law proposed in 1938 by Dr Frank Benford, a physicist at the General Electric Company, which shows that in sets of random numbers, it is more likely that the set will begin with the number 1 than with any other number

bequest a gift that has been left to somebody in a will

Berhad a Malay term for 'private'. Companies can use 'Sendirian Berhad' or 'Sdn Bhd' in their name instead of 'plc'. *Abbr* **Bhd**

Berne Union *see International Union of Credit and Investment Insurers*

beta a numerical measure of the change in value of something such as a stock

beta coefficient an indication of the level of risk attached to a share. A high beta coefficient indicates that a share is likely to be more sensitive to market movements.

beta factor the measure of the volatility of the return on a share relative to the market. If a share price were to rise or fall at double the market rate, it would have a beta factor of 2.0. Conversely, if the share price moved at half the market rate, the beta factor would be 0.5. The beta factor is defined mathematically as a share's covariance with the market portfolio divided by the variance of the market portfolio.

beta rating a means of measuring the volatility (or risk) of a stock or fund in comparison with the market as a whole.
     The beta of a stock or fund can be of any value, positive or negative, but usually is between +0.25 and +1.75. Stocks of many utilities have a beta of less than 1. Conversely, most high-tech NASDAQ-based stocks have a beta greater than 1; they offer a higher rate of return but are also risky.
     Both alpha and beta ratings should be readily available upon request from investment firms, because the figures appear in standard performance reports. It is always best to ask for them, because beta calculations can involve mathematical complexities. *See also alpha rating*

BFH Bundesfinanzhof: in Germany, the supreme court for issues concerning taxation

Bhd *abbr* Berhad

bid 1. an offer to buy all or a majority of the capital shares of a company in an attempted takeover **2.** the highest price a prospective buyer for a good or service is prepared to pay

bid-ask quote a statement of the prices that are being offered and asked for a security or option contract

bid-ask spread the difference between the buying and the selling prices of a traded commodity or a financial instrument

bid bond a guarantee by a financial institution of the fulfilment of an international tender offer

bid costs costs incurred during the takeover of a company by professionals brought in to advise the purchasing company, for example, lawyers, accountants, and bankers

bidding war a competition between prospective buyers for the same stock or security

bid form in the United States, a form containing details of an offer to underwrite municipal bonds

bid market a market for bids (the price at which a dealer will buy shares)

bid-offer spread the difference between the highest price that a buyer is prepared to offer and the lowest price that a seller is prepared to accept

bid price the price a stock exchange dealer will pay for a security or option contract

bid-to-cover ratio a number that shows how many more people wanted to buy US Treasury bills than actually did buy them

bid up 1. to bid for something merely to increase its price **2.** to make successive increases to the *bid price* for a security so that unopened orders do not remain unexecuted

Big Bang radical changes to practices on the London Stock Exchange implemented in October 1986. Fixed commission charges were abolished, leading to an alteration in the structure of the market, and the right of member firms to act as market makers as well as agents was also abolished. (*slang*)

big bath the practice of making a particular year's poor income statement look even worse by increasing expenses and selling assets. Subsequent years will then appear much better in comparison. (*slang*)

Big Board the New York Stock Exchange (*slang*) See also **Little Board**

Big Four 1. (*ANZ*) Australia's four largest banks: the Commonwealth Bank of Australia, Westpac Banking Corporation, National Australia Bank, and ANZ Bank **2.** the United Kingdom's four largest banks: Barclays, Lloyds TSB, HSBC, and NatWest

Big GAAP the *Generally Accepted Accounting Principles* that apply to large companies (*slang*)

Big Three before the merger of Chrysler and Mercedes in 1998, a phrase used to refer to the three largest car manufacturers in the United States: Chrysler, Ford, and General Motors

bilateral clearing the system of annual settlements of accounts between certain countries, where accounts are settled by the central banks

bilateral credit credit allowed by banks to other banks in a clearing system to cover the period while cheques are being cleared

bilateral facility a loan by one bank to one borrower

bilateral monopoly a market in which there is a single seller and a single buyer

bilateral netting the settling of contracts between two banks to give a new position

bilateral trade trade between two countries who give each other specific privileges such as favourable import quotas that are denied to other trading partners

bill 1. an invoice **2.** to send an invoice

bill broker somebody who buys and sells promissory notes and bills of exchange

bill discount the interest rate that the Bank of England charges banks for short-term loans. This establishes a de facto floor for the interest rate that banks charge their customers, usually a fraction above the discount rate.

bill discounting rate the amount by which the price of a US Treasury bill is reduced to reflect expected changes in interest rates

billing cycle the period of time, often one month, between successive requests for payment

bill of entry a statement of the nature and value of goods to be imported or exported, prepared by the shipper and presented to a customs house

bill of exchange 1. a document containing instructions to pay a specified person a particular amount on a specified date or on request **2.** a negotiable instrument, drawn by one party on another, for example, by a supplier of goods on a customer, who by accepting (signing) the bill, acknowledges the debt which may be payable immediately (a *sight draft*) or at some future date (a *time draft*). The holder of the bill can thereafter use an accepted time draft to pay a bill to a third party, or can discount it to raise cash.

bill of goods a consignment of goods, or a statement of their nature and value

bill of lading a document prepared by a consignor by which a carrier acknowledges the receipt of goods and which serves as a document of title to the goods consigned

bill of materials a specification of the materials and parts required to make a product

bill of sale a document confirming the transfer of goods or services from a seller to a buyer

bill payable a bill of exchange or promissory note payable

bill receivable a bill of exchange or promissory note receivable

bin card a record of receipts, issues, and balances of the quantity of an item of stock handled by a store

binder a document that an insurance company issues to a customer to serve as a temporary insurance certificate until the issue of the policy itself. Also called *cover note*

biological assets farm animals and plants classified as assets. International Accounting Standards require that they are recorded on balance sheets at market value. Once they have been slaughtered or harvested, the assets become **agricultural produce**.

BiRiLiG Bilanzrichtliniengesetz: the 1985 German accounting directives law

BIS *abbr* Bank for International Settlements: a bank that promotes co-operation between central banks, provides facilities for international financial operations, and acts as agent or trustee in international financial settlements. The 17-member board of directors consists of the governors of the central banks of Belgium, Canada, France, Germany, Italy, Japan, the Netherlands, Sweden, Switzerland, the United Kingdom, and the United States.

black
    in the black making a profit, or having more assets than debt (*slang*)

black economy economic activity that is not declared for tax purposes and is usually carried out in exchange for cash

black market an illegal *market*, usually for goods that are in short supply. Black market trading breaks government regulations or legislation and is particularly prevalent during times of shortage, such as rationing, or in industries that are very highly regulated, such as pharmaceuticals or armaments. *Also known as* **shadow market**

black market economy 1. a system of illegal trading in officially controlled goods **2.** an illicit secondary currency market that has rates markedly different from those in the official market

Black Monday either of two Mondays, 28 October 1929 or 19 October 1987, that were marked by the largest stock market declines of the 20th century. Although both market crashes originated in the United States, they were immediately followed by similar market crashes around the world.

black money money circulating in the *black economy* in payment for goods and services

Black Tuesday 29 October 1929, when values of stocks fell precipitously

blanket bond an insurance policy that covers a financial institution for losses caused by the actions of its employees

blended rate an interest rate charged by a lender that is between an old rate and a new one

blind entry 1. (*ANZ*) a document issued by a supplier that stipulates the amount charged for goods or services as well as the amount of GST payable **2.** a bookkeeping entry that records a debit or credit but fails to show other essential information

blind pool a limited partnership in which the investment opportunities the general partner plans to pursue are not specified

blind trust a trust that manages somebody's business interests, with contents that are unknown to the beneficiary. People assuming public office use such trusts to avoid conflicts of interest.

blocked account a bank account from which funds cannot be withdrawn for any of a number of reasons, for example, bankruptcy proceedings, liquidation of a company, or government order when freezing foreign assets

blocked currency a currency that people cannot easily trade for other currencies because of foreign exchange control

blocked funds money that cannot be transferred from one place to another, usually because of *exchange controls* imposed by the government of the country in which the funds are held

block grant money that the government gives to local authorities to fund local services

blockholder an individual or institutional investor who holds a large number of shares of stock or a large monetary value of bonds in a given company

block investment (*ANZ*) the purchase or holding of a large number of shares of stock or a large monetary value of bonds in a given company

block trade the sale of a large round number of stocks or amount of bonds

blow-off top a rapid increase in the price of a financial stock followed by an equally rapid drop in price (*slang*)

blowout (*US*) the rapid sale of the whole of a new stock issue

Blue Book national statistics of personal incomes and spending patterns in the United Kingdom, published annually

blue chip a description of an equity or company which is of the highest quality and in which an investment would be considered as low risk with regard to both dividend payments and capital values

blue-chip stocks ordinary shares of stock in a company that is considered to be well established, highly successful, and reliable, and is traded on a stock market

Blue List (*US*) a daily list of municipal bonds and their ratings, published by Standard & Poor's

blue-sky law a US state law that regulates investments to prevent investors from being defrauded

blue-sky securities stocks and bonds that have no value, being worth the same as a piece of 'blue sky' (*slang*)

BO *abbr* branch office

board *see **board of directors***

board dismissal the dismissal and removal from power of an entire board or ***board of directors***

Board of Currency Commissioners the sole currency issuing authority in Singapore, established in 1967. *Abbr* **BCCS**

Board of Customs and Excise in the United Kingdom, the government department responsible for administering and collecting indirect taxes, such as customs and excise duties and Value Added Tax. It also prepares UK overseas trade statistics.

board of directors the people selected to sit on an authoritative standing committee or governing body, taking responsibility for the management of an organisation. Members of the board of directors are officially chosen by shareholders, but in practice they are usually selected on the basis of the current board's recommendations. The board usually includes major shareholders as well as directors of the company. *Also known as* **board**

Board of Inland Revenue in the United Kingdom, the government department responsible for the administration and collection of the main direct taxes, such as income tax. Its duties include appointing tax inspectors, advising on new legislation, and providing statistical information. *Also known as* **Inland Revenue** (*see* **standard rate**)

board of trustees a committee or governing body that takes responsibility for managing, and holds in trust, funds, assets, or property belonging to others, for example, charitable or pension funds or assets

board seat a position of membership of a board, especially a **board of directors**

board secretary *see* **company secretary**

body corporate an association, such as a company or institution, that is legally authorised to act as if it were one person

body of creditors the creditors of a company or individual treated as a single creditor in dealing with the debtor

body of shareholders the shareholders of a company treated as a single shareholder in dealing with the company

bogey (*US*) a benchmark, often the Standard & Poor's 500 Index, against which unit trust managers or portfolio managers measure their performance (*slang*)

boilerplate (*US*) a standard version of a contract that can be used inter-changeably from contract to contract (*slang*)

bona fide used to describe a sale or purchase that has been carried out in good faith, without collusion or fraud

bona vacantia the goods of a person who has died intestate and has no traceable living relatives. In the United Kingdom, these goods become the property of the state.

bond 1. a promise to repay with interest on specified dates money that an investor lends a company or government **2.** a certificate issued by a company or government that promises repayment of borrowed money at a set rate of interest on a particular date **3.** (*ANZ*) a sum of money paid as a deposit, especially on rented premises **4.** (*S Africa*) a mortgage bond

bond anticipation note a loan that a government agency receives to provide capital that will be repaid from the proceeds of bonds that the agency will issue later. *Abbr* **BAN**

bond covenant part of a bond contract whereby the lender promises not to do certain things, for example, borrow beyond a particular limit

bond discount the difference between the face value of a bond and the lower price at which it is issued

bonded warehouse a warehouse that holds goods awaiting duty or tax to be paid on them

bond equivalent yield the interest rate that an investor would have to receive on a bond to profit as much as from investment in another type of security. *Also known as* **equivalent bond yield**

bond fund a unit trust that invests in bonds

bondholder an individual or institution owning bonds issued by a government or company. Bondholders are entitled to payments of the interest as due and the return of the *principal* when the bond matures.

bond indenture a document that specifies the terms of a bond

bond indexing the practice of investing in bonds in such a way as to match the yield of a designated index

bond issue additional shares of stock in a company given by the company to existing shareholders in proportion to their holding

bond market a market in which government or municipal bonds are traded

bond premium the difference between the face value of a bond and a higher price at which it is issued

bond quote a statement of the current market price of a bond

bond rating the rating of the reliability of a company or government or local authority which has issued a bond. The highest rating is AAA.

bond swap an exchange of some bonds for others, usually to gain tax advantage or to diversify a portfolio

bond value the value of an *asset* or *liability* as recorded in the accounts of an individual or organisation

bond-washing the practice of selling a bond before its dividend is due and buying it back later in order to avoid paying tax

bond yield the annual return on a bond (the rate of interest) expressed as a percentage of the current market price of the bond. Bonds can tie up investors' money for periods of up to 30 years, so knowing their yield is a critical investment consideration.
EXAMPLE Bond yield is calculated by multiplying the face value of the bond by its stated annual rate of interest, expressed as a decimal.

For example, buying a new ten-year £1,000 bond that pays 6% interest will produce an annual yield amount of £60:

$$1{,}000 \times 0.060 = 60$$

The £60 will be paid as £30 every six months. At the end of ten years, the purchaser will have earned £600, and will also be repaid the original £1,000. Because the bond was purchased when it was first issued, the 6% is also called the 'yield to maturity'.

This basic formula is complicated by other factors. First is the 'time-value of money' theory: money paid in the future is worth less than money paid today. A more detailed computation of total bond yield requires the calculation of the present value of the interest earned each year. Second, changing interest rates have a marked impact on bond trading and, ultimately, on yield. Changes in interest rates cannot affect the interest paid by bonds already issued, but they do affect the prices of new bonds.

bonus a financial incentive given to employees in addition to their *basic pay* in the form of a one-off payment or as part of a bonus scheme

bonus dividend a one-off extra dividend in addition to the usual twice-yearly payment

bonus issue the capitalisation of the reserves of a company by the issue of additional shares to existing stakeholders, in proportion to their holdings. Such shares are normally fully paid-up with no cash called for from the shareholders.

bonus shares 1. *see scrip issue* **2.** in the United Kingdom, extra shares paid by the government as a reward to founding shareholders who did not sell their initial holding within a certain number of years

book-building the research done among potential institutional investors to determine the optimum offering price for a new issue of stock

book cost the price paid for a stock, including any commissions

book-entry an accounting entry indicated in a record somewhere but not represented by any document

book inventory the number of items in stock according to accounting records. This number can be validated only by a physical count of the items.

bookkeeper a person who is responsible for maintaining the financial records of a business

bookkeeping the activity or profession of recording the money received and spent by an individual, business, or organisation

bookkeeping barter the direct exchange of goods between two parties without the use of money as a medium, but using monetary measures to record the transaction

book of original entry *see book of prime entry*

book of prime entry a chronological record of a business's transactions arranged according to type, for example, cash or sales. The books are then used to generate entries in a double-entry bookkeeping system. *Also called* **book of original entry**

books of account collectively, the ledgers and journals used in the preparation of financial statements

books of prime entry a first record of transactions, such as sales or purchases, from which either details or totals, as appropriate, are transferred to the ledgers

book-to-bill ratio the ratio of the value of orders that a company has received to the amount for which it has billed its customers

book transfer a transfer of ownership of a security without physical transfer of any document that represents the instrument

book value the value of a company's stock according to the company itself, which may differ considerably from market value.

EXAMPLE Book value is calculated by subtracting a company's liabilities and the value of its debt and preference shares from its total assets. All of these figures appear on a company's balance sheet.
For example:

	£
Total assets	1,300
Current liabilities	−400
Long-term liabilities, preference shares	−250
Book value	**= 650**

Book value per share is calculated by dividing the book value by the number of shares in issue. If our example is expressed in millions of pounds and the company has 35 million shares outstanding, book value per share would be £650 million divided by 35 million:

650 / 35 = £18.57 book value per share

Book value represents a company's net worth to its shareholders. When compared with its market value, book value helps reveal how a company is regarded by the investment community. A market value that is notably higher than book value indicates that investors have a high regard for the company. A market value that is, for example, a multiple of book value suggests that investors' regard may be unreasonably high. *Also known as* **carrying amount, carrying value**

book value per share the value of one share of a stock according to the company itself, which may differ considerably from the market value

boom a period of time during business activity increases significantly, with the result that demand for products grows, as do prices, salaries, and employment

BOP *abbr* balance of payments

border tax adjustment the application of a domestic tax on imported goods while exempting exported goods from the tax in an effort to make the exported goods' price competitive both nationally and internationally

borrowing costs expenses, for example, interest payments, incurred from taking out a loan or any other form of borrowing. In the United States, such costs are included in the total cost of the asset whereas in the United Kingdom, and in International Accounting Standards, this is optional.

Boston Box a model used for analysing a company's potential by plotting *market share* against growth rate. The Boston Box was conceived by the Boston Consulting Group in the 1970s to help in the process of assessing in which businesses a company should invest and of which it should divest itself. A business with a high market share and high growth rate is a **star**, and one with a low market share and low growth rate is a **dog**. A high market share with low growth rate is characteristic of a *cash cow*, which could yield significant but short-term gain, and a low market share coupled with high growth rate produces a **question mark company**, which offers a doubtful return on investment. To be useful, this model requires accurate assessment of a business's strengths and weaknesses, which may be difficult to obtain.

Boston Consulting Group matrix a representation of an organisation's product or service offerings which shows the value of product sales (depicted by the area of a circle) expressed in relation to the growth rate of the market served and the market share held. The objective of the matrix is to assist in the allocation of funds to projects.

BOT *abbr* balance of trade

bottleneck an activity within an organisation which has a lower capacity than preceding or subsequent activities, thereby limiting throughput. Bot-

tlenecks are often the cause of a build-up of work in progress and of idle time.

bottom fisher an investor who searches for bargains among stocks that have recently dropped in price (*slang*)

bottom line 1. the net profit or loss that a company makes at the end of a given period of time, used in the calculation of the earnings-per-share business ratio **2.** work that produces net gain for an organisation

bottom-of-the-harbour scheme (*ANZ*) a tax avoidance strategy that involves stripping a company of assets and then selling it a number of times so that it is hard to trace

bottom out to reach the lowest level in the downward trend of the market price of securities or commodities before the price begins an upward trend again

bottom-up relating to an approach to investing that seeks to identify individual companies that are fundamentally sound and whose shares will perform well regardless of general economic or industry-group trends

bottom-up budgeting *see participative budgeting*

bought day book a book used to record purchases made on credit, that is, for which cash is not paid immediately

bought-in goods components and sub-assemblies that are purchased from an outside supplier instead of being made within the organisation

bought ledger a book in which all of a company's expenditure is logged

bounce to refuse payment of a cheque because the account for which it is written holds insufficient money (*slang*) *Also known as* **dishonour**

bounced cheque a draft on an account that a bank will not honour, usually because there are insufficient funds in the account

bourse a European stock exchange, especially the one in Paris

boutique investment house *see niche player*

box spread an arbitrage strategy that eliminates risk by buying and selling the same thing

bracket creep (*US*) the way in which a gradual increase in income moves somebody into a higher tax bracket

Brady bond a bond issued by an emerging nation that has US Treasury bonds as collateral. It is named after Nicholas Brady, banking reformer and former Secretary of the Treasury.

branch accounts the books of account or *financial statements* for the component parts of a business, especially those that are located in a different region or country from the main enterprise

branch office a bank or other financial institution that is part of a larger group and is located in a different part of a geographical area from the parent organisation. *Abbr* **BO**

branch tax a South African tax imposed on non-resident companies that register a branch rather than a separate company

breadth-of-market theory the theory that the health of a market is measured by the relative volume of items traded that are going up or down in price

breakeven analysis a method for determining the point at which fixed and variable production costs are equalled by sales revenue and where neither a profit nor a loss is made. Usually illustrated graphically through the use of a *breakeven chart*, breakeven analysis can be used to aid decision-making, set product prices, and determine the effects of changes in production or sales volume on costs and profits.

breakeven chart a chart which indicates approximate profit or loss at different levels of sales volume within a limited range

breakeven point the point or level of financial activity at which expenditure equals income, or the value of an investment equals its cost so that the result is neither a profit nor a loss. *Abbr* **BEP**

breaking-down time the period required to return a workstation to a standard condition after completion of an operation

breakout a rise in a security's price above its previous highest price, or a drop below its former lowest price, taken by technical analysts to signal a continuing move in that direction

break-up value the combined market value of a firm's assets if each were sold separately as contrasted with selling the firm as an ongoing business. Analysts look for companies with a large break-up value relative to their market value to identify potential takeover targets.

Bretton Woods an agreement signed at a conference at Bretton Woods in the United States in July 1944 that set up the *IMF* and the *IBRD*

bridge financing borrowing that the borrower expects to repay with the proceeds of later larger loans. *See also takeout financing*

bridge loan (*US*) = *bridging loan*

bridging the obtaining of a short-term loan to provide a continuing source of financing in anticipation of receiving an intermediate- or long-term loan. Bridging is routinely employed to finance the purchase or construction of a new building or property until an old one is sold.

bridging loan a temporary loan providing funds until further money is received, for example, for buying one property while trying to sell another. *US term* **bridge loan**

bring forward to carry a sum from one column or page to the next

British Accounting Association an organisation whose aim is to promote accounting education and research in the United Kingdom. The BAA has more than 800 members, a large proportion of whom work in higher education institutions. Founded in 1947, the BAA also organises conferences and publishes *The British Accounting Review*. *Abbr* **BAA**

British Bankers' Association a not-for-profit trading association for the financial services and banking industry. The Association was established in 1919 and has 295 members as well as numerous associate members. It aims to address a variety of industry issues, including the development and revision of the voluntary *Banking Code*, which aims to set standards of best practice. *Abbr* **BBA**

British Chambers of Commerce a national network of accredited *chambers of commerce*. The BCC represents over 135,000 members in the United Kingdom. *Abbr* **BCC**

brochure a booklet or pamphlet that contains descriptive information or advertising, for example, in relation to a product or property for sale, or an available service

broker a person who acts as a financial agent in arranging a deal, sale, or contract

brokerage 1. a company whose business is buying and selling stocks and bonds for its clients **2.** the business of being a broker **3.** a fee paid to somebody who acts as a financial agent for somebody else

brokerage rebates the percentage of the commission paid to a broker which is returned to the customer as an incentive to do more business

brokered market a market in which brokers bring buyers and sellers together

broker loan rate the interest rate that banks charge brokers on money that they lend for purchases on margin

B/S *abbr* balance sheet

B share (*ANZ*) a share in a unit trust that has no front-end sales charge but carries a redemption fee, or back-end load, payable only if the share is redeemed. This load, called a CDSC, or contingent deferred sales charge, declines every year until it disappears, usually after six years.

BTI *abbr* Business Times Industrial index

bubble economy an unstable boom based on speculation in shares, often followed by a financial crash. This happened, for example, in the 1630s in the Netherlands and in the 1720s in England.

bucket shop (*US*) a firm of brokers or dealers that sells shares of questionable value

bucket trading an illegal practice in which a stockbroker accepts a customer's order but does not execute the transaction until it is financially advantageous to the broker but at the customer's expense

budget a quantitative statement, for a defined period of time, which may include planned revenues, expenses, assets, liabilities, and cash-flows. A budget provides a focus for an organisation, as it aids the co-ordination of activities, allocation of resources, direction of activity, and facilitates control. Planning is achieved by means of a fixed master budget, whereas control is generally exercised through the comparison of actual costs with a flexible budget.

Budget the UK government's annual spending plan, which is announced to the House of Commons by the Chancellor of the Exchequer. The government is legally obliged to present economic forecasts twice a year, and since the 1997 general election the main Budget is presented in the Spring while a Pre-Budget Report is given in the Autumn. This outlines government spending plans prior to the main Budget, and also reports on progress since the main Budget.

budget account a bank account set up to control a person's regular expenditures, for example, the payment of insurance premiums, mortgage, utilities, or telephone bills. The annual expenditure for each item is paid into the account in equal monthly instalments, bills being paid from the budget account as they become due.

budgetary relating to a detailed plan of financial operations, with estimates of both revenue and expenditures for a specific future period

budgetary control the establishment of budgets relating the responsibilities of executives to the requirements of a policy, and the continuous comparison of actual with budgeted results, either to secure by individual action the objectives of that policy or to provide a basis for its revision. *Abbr* **BC**

budget centre a section of an entity for which control may be exercised and budgets prepared

budget committee the group within an organisation responsible for drawing up budgets that meet departmental requirements, ensuring they comply with policy, and then submitting them to the board of directors

budget cost allowance the budgeted cost ascribed to the level of activity achieved in a budget centre in a control period. It comprises variable costs in direct proportion to volume achieved and fixed costs as a proportion of the annual budget. *Also known as* **flexed budget**

budget deficit the extent by which expenditure exceeds revenue. *Also known as* **deficit**

budget director the person in an organisation who is responsible for running the budget system

budgeted capacity an organisation's available output level for a budget period according to the budget. It may be expressed in different ways, for example, in machine hours or standard hours.

budgeted revenue the income that an organisation expects to receive in a budget period according to the budget

budget lapsing withdrawal of unspent budget allowance due to the expiry of the budget period

budget management the comparison of actual financial results with the estimated expenditures and revenues for the given time period of a budget and the taking of corrective action as necessary

budget manual a detailed set of documents providing guidelines and information about the budget process. A budget manual may include: a calendar of budgetary events; specimen budget forms; a statement of budgetary objective and desired results; a listing of budgetary activities; original, revised, and approved budgets; and budget assumptions regarding inflation, interest rates etc.

budget period the period for which a budget is prepared and used, which may then be subdivided into control periods

budget slack the intentional over-estimation of expenses and/or under-estimation of revenues in the budgeting process

budget surplus the extent by which revenue exceeds expenditure. *Also known as surplus*

budget variance the difference between the financial value of something (such as cost or revenue) as estimated for in the budget, and the actual financial value

buffer inventory the products or supplies of an organisation maintained on hand or in transit to stabilise variations in supply, demand, production, or lead time

buffer stock a stock of materials, or of work in progress, maintained in order to protect user departments from the effect of possible interruptions to supply

Building Societies Ombudsman an official whose duty is to investigate complaints by members of the public against building societies. All building societies belong to the Building Societies Ombudsman Scheme.

building society a financial institution that offers interest-bearing savings accounts, the deposits being reinvested by the society in long-term loans, primarily mortgage loans for the purchase of property

bulk handling the financing of receivables in bulk to reduce processing costs

bulk storage the shares of client-owned stock held at a brokerage

bull somebody who anticipates favourable business conditions, especially somebody who buys particular stocks or commodities in anticipation that their prices will rise, often with the expectation of selling them at a large profit at a later time. *See also bear*

bulldog bond a bond issued in sterling in the UK market by a non-British corporation

bullet bond a Eurobond which is only redeemed when it is mature. A bullet bond is used in payments between central banks and also acts as currency backing.

bullet loan a loan that involves specified payments of interest until maturity, when the principal is repaid

bullish conducive to or characterised by buying stocks or commodities in anticipation of rising prices. *See also bearish*

bull market a market in which prices are rising and in which a dealer is more likely to be a buyer than a seller. *See also bear market*

bull spread a combination of purchases and sales of options for the same commodity or stock intended to produce a profit when the price rises. *See also bear spread*

bundle a package of financial products or services offered to a customer

buoyant market a market which sees plenty of trading activity and in which prices are rising, rather than falling

Business Accounting Deliberation Council in Japan, a committee controlled by the Ministry of Finance that is responsible for drawing up regulations regarding the consolidated financial statements of listed companies. *Abbr BADC*

Business Activity Statement a standard document used in Australia to report the amount of *GST* and other taxes paid and collected by a business. *Abbr BAS*

business card a small card printed with somebody's name, job title, business address, and contact numbers or e-mail address

business cluster a group of small firms from similar industries that team up and act as one body. Creating a business cluster enables firms to enjoy economies of scale usually only available to bigger competitors. Marketing costs can be shared and goods can be bought more cheaply. There are also networking advantages, in which small firms can share experiences and discuss business strategies.

business combinations (*US*) acquisitions or mergers involving two or more enterprises

Business Council of Australia a national association of chief executives, designed as a forum for the discussion of matters pertaining to business leadership in Australia. *Abbr* **BCA**

business cycle a regular pattern of fluctuation in national income, moving from upturn to downturn in about five years

business entity concept the concept that financial accounting information relates only to the activities of the business entity and not to the activities of its owner(s)

business interruption insurance a policy indemnifying an organisation for loss of profits and continuing fixed expenses when some insurable disaster, for example, a fire, causes the organisation to stop or reduce its activities. *Also known as* **consequential loss policy**

business name in the United Kingdom, the legal term for the name under which an organisation operates

business plan a document describing the current activities of a business, setting out its aims and objectives, and how they are to be achieved over a set period of time. A business plan may cover the activities of an organisation or a group of companies, or it may deal with a single department within the organisation. In the former case, it is sometimes referred to as a corporate plan. The sections of a business plan usually include a market analysis describing the target market, customers, and competitors, an operations plan describing how products and services will be developed and produced, and a financial section providing profit, budget, and cash-flow forecasts, annual accounts, and financial requirements. Businesses may use a business plan internally as a framework for implementing strategy and improving performance or externally to attract investment or raise capital for development plans. A business plan may form part of the overall planning process, or corporate planning, within an organisation and be used for the implementation of corporate strategy.

business property relief in the United Kingdom, a reduction in the amount liable for inheritance tax on certain types of business property

business rates in the United Kingdom, a tax on businesses calculated on the value of the property occupied. Although the rate of tax is set by central government, the tax is collected by the local authority.

business risk the uncertainty associated with the unique circumstances of a particular company, for example, the introduction of a superior technology, as it might affect the price of that company's securities

business segment a distinguishable part of a business or enterprise that is subject to a different set of risks and returns from any other part. Listed companies are required to declare in their annual reports certain information, for example, sales, profits, and assets, for each segment of an enterprise.

business strategy a long-term approach to implementing a firm's business plans to achieve its business objectives

Business Times Industrial index an index of 40 Singapore and Malaysian shares. *Abbr* **BTI**

business transfer relief the tax advantage gained when selling a business for shares in stock of the company that buys it

business unit a part of an organisation that operates as a distinct function, department, division, or stand-alone business. Business units are usually treated as a separate *profit centre* within the overall, owning business.

bust up to split up a company or a division of a company into smaller units

bust-up proxy proposal an overture to a company's shareholders for a *leveraged buyout* in which the acquirer will sell some of the company's assets in order to repay the debt used to finance the takeover

butterfly spread a complex option strategy based on simultaneously purchasing and selling calls at different exercise prices and maturity dates, the profit being the premium collected when the options are sold. Such a strategy is most profitable when the price of the underlying security is relatively stable.

buy and hold an investment strategy based on retaining securities for a long time

buy and write an investment strategy involving buying stock and selling options to eliminate the possibility of loss if the value of the stock goes down

buy-back the repurchase of bonds or shares, as agreed by contract

buy-down the payment of principal amounts that reduce the monthly payments due on a mortgage

buyer 1. somebody who is in the process of buying something or who intends to buy something **2.** somebody whose job is to choose and buy goods, merchandise, services, or media time or space for a company, factory, shop, or advertiser

buyer's market a situation in which supply exceeds demand, prices are relatively low, and buyers therefore have an advantage

buy in to buy stock in a company so as to have a controlling interest. This is often done by or for executives from outside the company.

buying economies of scale a reduction in the cost of purchasing raw materials and components or of borrowing money due to the increased size of the purchase

buying manager *see purchasing manager*

buy on close a purchase at the end of the trading day

buy on opening a purchase at the beginning of the trading day

buy out 1. to purchase the entire stock of, or controlling financial interest in, a company **2.** to pay somebody to relinquish his or her interest in a property or other enterprise

buy-out 1. the purchase and *takeover* of an ongoing business. It is more formally known as an *acquisition* (*see merger*). If a business is purchased by managers or staff, it is known as a *management buy-out*. **2.** the purchase of somebody else's entire stock ownership in a firm. It is more formally known as an *acquisition* (*see merger*). **3.** an option to transfer benefits of an occupational pension scheme on leaving a company

buy stop order an order to buy stock when its price reaches a specified level

BV *abbr* besloten venootschap: the Dutch term for a limited liability company

by-bidder somebody who bids at an auction solely to raise the price for the seller

bylaws (*US*) rules governing the internal running of a corporation, such as the number of meetings, the appointment of officers, and so on. UK term *articles of association*

bypass trust a trust that leaves money in a will in trust to people other than the prime beneficiary in order to gain tax advantage

by-product output of some value that is produced incidentally in manufacturing something else. *See also **joint products***

C

CA *abbr* chartered accountant *or* certified accountant

c/a *abbr* current account

C/A *abbr* capital account

Cadbury Report the report of the Cadbury Committee (conducted in December 1992) on the Financial Aspects of Corporate Governance. It was established to consider the following issues in relation to financial reporting and accountability, and to make recommendations on good practice: the responsibilities of executive and non-executive directors for reviewing and reporting on performance to shareholders and other financially interested parties; and the frequency, clarity, and form in which information should be provided; the case for audit committees of the board, including their composition and role; the principal responsibilities of the auditors and the extent and value of the audit; the links between shareholders, boards, and auditors; and any other relevant matters. The report established a Code of Best Practice, and has been influential in the United Kingdom and overseas. *See also* **Corporate Governance Combined Code**

cage (*US*) the part of a broking firm where the paperwork involved in the buying and selling of shares is processed (*slang*)

calendar variance a variance which occurs if a company uses calendar months for the financial accounts but uses the number of actual working days to calculate overhead expenses in the cost accounts

call 1. an option to buy stock. *Also known as* **call option** (*see* **exercise price**) **2.** a request made to the holders of partly paid-up share capital for the payment of a predetermined sum due on the share capital, under the terms of

the original subscription agreement. Failure on the part of the shareholder to pay a call may result in the forfeiture of the relevant holding of partly paid shares.

callable a financial instrument with a call provision in its indenture

called-up share capital the amount which a company has required shareholders to pay on shares issued

call money money that brokers use for their own purchases or to help their customers buy on margin

call off a system whereby inventory is held at the customer's premises, to be invoiced only on use

call option *see* **call**

call payment an amount that a company demands in partial payment for stock such as a rights issue that is not paid for at one time

call provision a clause in an indenture that lets the issuer of a bond redeem it before the date of its maturity

call purchase a transaction where either the seller or purchaser can fix the price for future delivery

calls in arrears money called up for shares, but not paid at the correct time. The shares may be forfeited or else a special calls in arrears account is set up to debit the sums owing.

call up *see* **call**

Canadian Institute of Chartered Accountants in Canada, the principal professional accountancy body that is responsible for setting accounting standards. *Abbr* **CICA**

cancellation price the lowest value possible in any one day of a unit trust

cap an upper limit such as on a rate of interest for a loan

CAPA *abbr* Confederation of Asian and Pacific Accountants: an umbrella organisation for a number of Asia-Pacific accountancy bodies

capacity usage variance the difference in gain or loss in a given period compared to budgeted expectations, caused because the hours worked were longer or shorter than planned

capacity utilisation 1. a measure of the plant and equipment of a company or an industry that is actually being used to produce goods or services. Capacity utilisation is usually measured over a specific period of time, for example, the average for a month, or at a given point in time, for example, on a given date. It can be expressed as a ratio, where utilisation = actual output divided by design capacity. This measure is used in both capacity planning, and capacity requirements planning processes. **2.** the output of an economy, firm, or plant divided by its output when working at full capacity

Caparo case in England, a court decision taken by the House of Lords in 1990 that auditors owe a duty of care to present (not prospective) shareholders as a body but not as individuals

CAPEX *abbr* capital expenditure

capital money that can be invested by an individual or organisation in order to make a profit

capital account the sum of a company's capital at a particular time. *Abbr* **C/A**

capital adequacy ratio an amount of money which a bank has to have in the form of shareholders' capital, shown as a percentage of its assets. This has been agreed internationally at 8%.

capital allowance the tax advantage that a company is granted for money that it spends on fixed assets

capital allowances in the United Kingdom and Ireland, an allowance against income or corporation tax available to businesses or sole traders who have purchased plant and machinery for business use. The rates are set annually and vary according to the type of fixed asset purchased, for example, whether it is machinery or buildings. This system effectively removes subjectivity from the calculation of depreciation for tax purposes.

capital appreciation the increase in a company's or individual's wealth

capital appreciation fund a unit trust that aims to increase the value of its holdings without regard to the provision of income to its owners

capital asset property that a company owns and uses but which the company does not buy or sell as part of its regular trade

capital asset pricing model a theory which predicts that the expected risk premium for an individual stock will be proportional to its beta, such that: expected risk premium on a stock = beta × expected risk premium in the market. Risk premium is defined as the expected incremental return for making a risky investment rather than a safe one. *Abbr* **CAPM**

capital bonus a bonus payment by an insurance company which is produced by capital gain

capital budget a subsection of a company's master budget that deals with expected capital expenditure within a defined period. *Also known as **capital expenditure budget**, **capital investment budget***

capital budgeting the process concerned with decision-making with respect to the following issues: the choice of specific investment projects; the total amount of capital expenditure to commit; and the method of financing the investment portfolio

capital commitment the estimated amount of capital expenditure that is contracted for, but not yet provided for, and authorised by the directors of a company but not yet contracted for

capital commitments expenditure on assets which has been authorised by directors, but not yet spent at the end of a financial period

capital consumption in a given period, the total depreciation of a national economy's fixed assets based on replacement costs

capital controls regulations placed by a government on the amount of capital residents may hold

capital cost allowance a tax advantage in Canada for the depreciation in value of capital assets

capital costs expenses on the purchase of fixed assets

capital deepening the process whereby increasingly capital-intensive production results when a country's *capital stock* increases but the numbers employed fall or remain constant

capital employed the funds used by an entity for its operations. This can be expressed in various ways depending upon the purpose of the computation. For example, for operations evaluation, capital employed may be defined as the total value of non-current assets plus working capital, whereas for investor evaluation, owners' capital plus reserves may be used.

capital expenditure the cost of acquiring, producing, or enhancing fixed assets. *Abbr* **CAPEX**

capital expenditure budget *see capital budget*

capital expenditure proposal a formal request for authority to undertake capital expenditure. This is usually supported by the case for expenditure

in accordance with capital investment appraisal criteria. Levels of authority must be clearly defined and the reporting structure of actual expenditure must be to the equivalent authority level.

capital flight the transfer of large sums of money between countries to seek higher rates of return or to escape a political or economic disturbance

capital formation the process of adding to the stock of a country's *real capital* by investment in fixed assets

capital funding planning the process of selecting suitable funds to finance long-term assets and working capital

capital gain the financial gain made upon the disposal of an asset. The gain is the difference between the cost of its acquisition and net proceeds upon its sale.

capital gains distribution a sum of money that, for example, a unit trust pays to its owners in proportion to the owners' share of the organisation's capital gains for the year

capital gains expenses expenses incurred in buying or selling assets, which can be deducted when calculating a capital gain or loss

capital gains reserve in Canada, a tax advantage for money not yet received in payment for something that has been sold

capital gains tax a tax on the difference between the gross acquisition cost and the net proceeds when an asset is sold. In the United Kingdom, this tax also applies when assets are given or exchanged, although each individual has an annual capital gains tax allowance that exempts gains within that tax year below a stated level. In addition, certain assets may be exempt, for example, a person's principal private residence and transfers of assets between spouses, and the tax may not be levied on the absolute gain. An adjustment is made for inflation and the length of time that the asset has been held. There are also concessions on the sale of a business at retirement. *Abbr* **CGT**

capital gearing the amount of fixed-cost debt that a company has for each of its ordinary shares

capital goods stocks of physical or financial assets that are capable of generating income

capital growth an increase in the value of assets in a fund, or of the value of shares

capital inflow the amount of capital that flows into an economy from services rendered abroad

capital instruments the means that an organisation uses to raise finance, for example, the issue of shares or debentures

capital-intensive using a greater proportion of capital, as opposed to labour

capital investment *see* ***capital expenditure***

capital investment appraisal the application of a set of methodologies (generally based on the discounting of projected cash flows) whose purpose is to give guidance to managers with respect to decisions as to how best to commit long-term investment funds. *See also* ***discounted cash flow***

capital investment budget *see* ***capital budget***

capitalisation 1. the amount of money invested in a company, or the worth of the bonds and stocks of a company **2.** the conversion of a company's reserves into capital through a scrip issue

capitalisation issue a proportional issue of free shares to existing shareholders. *US term* **stock split**

capitalisation rate the rate at which a company's *reserves* are converted into capital by way of a ***capitalisation issue***

capitalisation ratio the proportion of a company's value represented by debt, stock, assets, and other items.
EXAMPLE A company whose long-term debt totals £5,000 and whose owners hold equity worth £3,000 would have a capitalisation ratio of:

5,000 / (5,000 + 3,000) = 5,000 / 8,000 = .625 capitalisation ratio

By comparing debt to total capitalisation, these ratios provide a glimpse of a company's long-term stability and ability to withstand losses and business downturns.

A company's capitalisation ratio can be expressed in two ways:

= Long-Term Debt / Long-Term Debt + Owners' Equity

and

= Total Debt / Total Debt + Preferred + Common Equity

Both expressions of the ratio are also referred to as **component percentages**, since they compare a firm's debt with either its total capital (debt plus equity) or its equity capital. They readily indicate how reliant a firm is on debt financing.

Capitalisation ratios need to be evaluated over time, and compared with other data and standards. Care should be taken when comparing companies in different industries or sectors. The same figures that appear to be low in one industry can be very high in another.

capitalise 1. to provide ***capital*** for a business **2.** to include money spent on the purchase of an ***asset*** as an element in a ***balance sheet***

capitalism an economic and social system in which individuals can maximise profits because they own the means of production

capitalist an investor of capital in a business

capital levy a tax on fixed assets or property

capital loss a loss made through selling a *capital asset* for less than its market price

capital maintenance concept a concept used to determine the definition of profit, that provides the basis for different systems of inflation accounting

capital market a financial market dealing with securities that have a life of more than one year

capital project management control of a project that involves expenditure of an organisation's monetary resources for the purpose of creating capacity for production. Capital project management often involves the organisation of major construction or engineering work. **Capital projects** are usually large scale, complex, need to be completed quickly, and involve capital investment. Different techniques have evolved for capital project management from those used for normal *project management*, including methods for managing the complexity of such projects, and for analysing return on investment afterwards.

capital property under Canadian tax law, assets that can depreciate in value or be sold for a capital gain or loss

capital ratio a company's income expressed as a fraction of its tangible assets

capital rationing 1. the restriction of new investment by a company **2.** a restriction on an organisation's ability to invest capital funds, caused by an internal budget ceiling being imposed

by management (**soft capital rationing**), or by external limitations being applied to the company, as when additional borrowed funds cannot be obtained (**hard capital rationing**)

capital reconstruction the act of placing a company into voluntary liquidation and then selling its assets to another company with the same name and same shareholders, but with a larger capital base

capital redemption reserve an account required to prevent a reduction in capital, where a company purchases or redeems its own shares out of distributable profits

capital reduction the retirement or redemption of capital funds by a company

capital reorganisation the act of changing the capital structure of a company by amalgamating or dividing existing shares to form shares of a higher or lower nominal value

capital reserves a former name for *undistributable reserves*

capital resource planning the process of evaluating and selecting long-term assets to meet strategies

capital shares shares in a unit trust which rise in value as the capital value of the units rises, but do not receive any income. The other form of shares in a split-level investment trust are income shares, which receive income from the investments, but do not rise in value.

capital stock the stock authorised by a company's charter, representing no ownership rights

capital structure the relative proportions of equity capital and debt capital within a company's balance sheet

capital sum a lump sum of money that an insurer pays, for example, on the death of the insured person

capital surplus the value of all of the stock in a company that exceeds the par value of the stock

capital tax a tax levied on the *capital* owned by a company, rather than on its spending. See *capital gains tax*

capital transactions transactions affecting non-current items such as fixed assets, long-term debt, or share capital, rather than revenue transactions

capital transfer tax in the United Kingdom, a tax on the transfer of assets that was replaced in 1986 by inheritance tax

capital turnover the value of annual sales as a multiple of the value of the company's stock

capital widening the process whereby capital-intensive production is reduced as a result of an increase in a country's *capital stock* and the number of people employed

CAPM *abbr* capital asset pricing model

capped rate an interest rate on a loan that may change, but cannot be greater than an amount fixed at the time when the loan is taken out by a borrower

captive finance company an organisation that provides credit and is owned or controlled by a commercial or manufacturing company, for example, a retailer that owns its store card operation or a car manufacturer that owns a company for financing the vehicles it produces

captive insurance company an insurance company that has been established by a parent company to underwrite all its insurance risks and those of its subsidiaries. The benefit is that the premiums paid do not leave the organisation. Many captive insurance companies are established offshore for tax purposes.

cardholder an individual or company that has an active credit card account with an *issuer* with which transactions can be initiated

card-issuing bank *see issuer*

card-not-present merchant account an account that permits e-merchants to process credit card transactions without the purchaser being physically present for the transaction

caring economy an economy based on amicable and helpful relationships between businesses and people

carriage inwards delivery expenses incurred through the purchase of goods

carriage outwards delivery expenses incurred through the sale of goods

carrier's note *see delivery note*

carrying amount *see book value*

carrying cost any expense associated with holding stock for a given period, for example, from the time of delivery to the time of dispatch. Carrying costs will include storage and insurance.

carrying value *see book value*

carry-over the stock of a commodity held at the beginning of a new financial year

carry-over day the first day of trading on a new account on the London Stock Exchange

cartel an alliance of business companies formed to control production, competition, and prices

cash *money* in the form of banknotes and coins that are legal tender. This includes cash in hand, deposits repayable on demand with any bank or other financial institution, and deposits denominated in foreign currencies.

cash account 1. a brokerage account that permits no buying on margin **2.** a record of receipts and payments of cash, cheques, or other forms of money transfer

cash accounting 1. an accounting method in which receipts and expenses are recorded in the accounting books in the period when they actually occur. *See also* **accrual concept 2.** in the United Kingdom, a system for Value Added Tax that enables the taxpayer to account for tax paid and received during a given period, thus allowing automatic relief for bad debts

cash advance a loan on a credit card account

cash at bank the total amount of money held at the bank by an individual or company

cash available to invest the amount, including cash on account and balances due soon for outstanding transactions, that a client has available for investment with a broker

cashback a sales promotion technique offering customers a cash refund after they buy a product

cash basis the bookkeeping practice of accounting for money only when it is actually received or spent

cash bonus an unscheduled dividend that a company declares because of unexpected income

cashbook a book in which all cash payments and receipts are recorded. In a double-entry bookkeeping system, the balance at the end of a given period is included in the trial balance and then transferred to the balance sheet itself.

cash budget a detailed budget of estimated cash inflows and outflows incorporating both revenue and capital items

cash contract a contract for actual delivery of a commodity

cash conversion cycle the time between the acquisition of a raw material and the receipt of payment for the finished product. *Also known as* *cash cycle*

cash cow a product characterised by a high market share but low sales growth, whose function is seen as generating cash for use elsewhere within an organisation

cash crop a crop, for example, tobacco, that can be sold for cash, usually by a developing country

cash cycle *see* *cash conversion cycle*

cash deficiency agreement a commitment to supply whatever additional cash is needed to complete the financing of a project

cash discount a discount offered to a customer who pays for goods or services with cash, or who pays an invoice within a particular period

cash dividend a share of a company's current earnings or accumulated profits distributed to shareholders

cash equivalents short-term investments that can be converted into cash immediately and that are subject to only a limited risk. There is usually a limit on their duration, for example, three months.

cash float notes and coins held by a retailer for the purpose of supplying customers with change

cash flow the movement through an organisation of money that is generated by its own operations, as opposed to borrowing. It is the money that a business actually receives from sales (the cash inflow) and the money that it pays out (the cash outflow).

cash-flow accounting *see cash-flow statement*

cash-flow coverage ratio the ratio of income to cash obligations

cash-flow forecast a prediction of the amount of money that will move through an organisation. This is an important tool for monitoring its solvency. *See also cash budget*

cash flow per common share the amount of cash that a company has for each of its ordinary shares

cash-flow risk the risk that a company's available cash will not be sufficient to meet its financial obligations

cash-flow statement a record of a company's cash inflows and cash outflows over a specific period of time, typically a year.
EXAMPLE It reports funds on hand at the beginning of the period, funds received, funds spent, and funds remaining at the end of the period. Cash flows are divided into three categories: cash from operations; cash-investment activities; and cash-financing activities. Companies with holdings in foreign currencies use a fourth classification: effects of changes in currency rates on cash.
A standard direct cash-flow statement looks like this:

CRD Ltd
Statement of Cash Flows
For year ended 31 December 20__

CASH FLOWS FROM OPERATIONS

	£
Operating Profit	82,000
Adjustments to net earnings	
Depreciation	17,000
Accounts receivable	(20,000)
Accounts payable	12,000
Inventory	(8,000)
Other adjustments to earnings	4,000
Net cash flow from operations:	**87,000**

CASH FLOWS FROM INVESTMENT ACTIVITIES

	£
Purchases of marketable securities	(58,000)
Receipts from sales of marketable securities	45,000
Loans made to borrowers	(16,000)
Collections on loans	11,000
Purchases of plant and land and property assets	(150,000)
Receipts from sales of plant and land and property assets	47,000
Net cash flow from investment activities:	**(− 121,000)**

CASH FLOWS FROM FINANCING ACTIVITIES

	£
Proceeds from short-term borrowings	51,000
Payments to settle short-term debts	(61,000)
Proceeds from issuing bonds payable	100,000
Proceeds from issuing capital stock	80,000
Dividends paid	(64,000)
Net cash flow from financing activities:	**106,000**
Net change in cash during period:	**72,000**
Cash and cash equivalents, beginning of year	27,000
Cash and cash equivalents, end of year	99,000

cash fraction a small amount of cash paid to a shareholder to make up the full amount of part of a share which has been allocated in a *share split*

cash-generating unit the smallest identifiable group of assets that generates cash inflows and outflows that can be measured

cashier's check a bank's own cheque, drawn on itself and signed by the cashier or other bank official

cashless pay the payment of a weekly or monthly wage through the electronic transfer of funds directly into the bank account of an employee

cashless society a society in which all bills and debits are paid by electronic money media, for example, bank and credit cards, direct debits, and online payments

cash loan company (*S Africa*) a micro-lending business that provides short-term loans without collateral, usually at high interest rates

cash management models sophisticated cash-flow forecasting models which assist management in determining how to balance the cash needs of an organisation. Cash management models might help in areas such as optimising cash balances; in the management of customer, supplier, investor, and company investment needs; in the decision whether to invest or buy back shares, or in the decision as to the optimum method of financing working capital.

cash market the gilt-edged securities market where purchases are paid for almost immediately, as opposed to the futures market

cash offer an offer to buy a company for cash rather than for stock

cash payments journal a chronological record of all the payments that have been made from a company's bank account

cash ratio the ratio of a company's liquid assets such as cash and securities divided by total liabilities. *Also known as **liquidity ratio***

cash receipts journal a chronological record of all the receipts that have been paid into a company's bank account

cash sale 1. *see **cash settlement** 2.* a sale in which payment is made immediately in cash rather than put on credit

cash settlement 1. an immediate payment on an options contract with-out waiting for expiry of the normal, usually five-day, settlement period **2.** the completion of a transaction by paying for securities

cash surrender value the amount of money that an insurance company will pay to terminate a policy at a particular time if the policy does not continue until its normal expiry date

catastrophe bond a bond with a very high interest rate which may be worth less or give a lower rate of interest if a disaster occurs, whether it be natural or otherwise

category killer (*US*) a major organisation that puts out of business smaller or more specialised companies in a given field by offering goods or services at a lower price, or by using its brand to attract more consumer interest (*slang*)

cats and dogs (*US*) shares with dubious sales histories (*slang*)

cause and effect diagram a diagram that aids the generation and sorting of the potential causes of variation in an activity or process

CBI *abbr* Confederation of British Industry

CC *abbr* (*S Africa*) close corporation

CCA *abbr* current-cost accounting

CCAB *abbr* Consultative Committee of Accountancy Bodies

ccc *abbr* cwmni cyfyngedig cyhoeddus: the Welsh term for a public limited company

CD *abbr* certificate of deposit

CDSC *abbr* contingent deferred sales charge

CEIC *abbr* closed-end investment company

central bank the bank of a country that controls its credit system and its money supply

centralisation the gathering together, at a corporate headquarters, of specialist functions such as finance, personnel, and information technology. Centralisation is usually undertaken in order to effect economies of scale and to standardise operating procedures throughout the organisation. Centralised management can become cumbersome and inefficient, and may produce communication problems. Some organisations have shifted towards decentralisation to try to avoid this.

centralised purchasing the control by a central department of all the purchasing undertaken within an organisation. In a large organisation centralised purchasing is often located within the headquarters. Centralisation has the advantages of reducing duplication of effort, pooling volume purchases for discounts, enabling more effective inventory control, consolidating transport loads to achieve lower costs, increasing skills development in purchasing personnel, and enhancing relationships with *suppliers*.

central purchasing purchasing organised by a company's main office on behalf of all its departments or branches

centre a department, area, or function to which costs and/or revenues are charged

certainty equivalent method an approach to dealing with risk in a capital budgeting context. It involves expressing risky future cash flows in terms of the certain cash flow which would be considered, by the decision-maker, as their equivalent.

certificate a document representing partial ownership of a company that states the number of shares that the document is worth and the names of the company and the owner of the shares

certificate of deposit a negotiable instrument which provides evidence of a fixed-term deposit with a bank. Maturity is normally within 90 days, but can be longer. *Abbr* **CD**

certificate of incorporation in the United Kingdom, a written statement by the Registrar of Companies confirming that a new company has fulfilled the necessary legal requirements for incorporation and is now legally constituted

certificate of tax deducted a document issued by a financial institution showing that tax has been deducted from interest payments on an account

certificate to commence business in the United Kingdom, a written statement issued by the Registrar of Companies confirming that a public limited company has fulfilled the necessary legal requirements regarding its authorised minimum share capital

certified accountant an accountant trained in industry, the public service, or in the offices of practising accountants, who is a member of the *Association of Chartered Certified Accountants*. Although they are not *chartered accountants*, they fulfil much the same role and they are qualified to audit company records. *Abbr* **CA**

certified public accountant (*US*) an accountant trained in industry, the public service, or in the offices of practising accountants, who is a member of the *American Institute of Certified Public Accountants*. Although they are not *chartered accountants*, they fulfil much the same role and they are qualified to audit company records. *Abbr* **CPA**

cessation the discontinuation of a business for tax purposes or of its trading on the stock market

CGT *abbr* capital gains tax

CH *abbr* Companies House

chairman's report *or* **chairman's statement** a statement included in the annual report of most large companies in which the chair of the board of directors gives an often favourable overview of the company's performance and prospects

chamber of commerce an organisation of local businesspeople who work together to promote trade in their area and protect common interests. The *British Chambers of Commerce* acts as a national association for accredited members.

Chancellor of the Exchequer the United Kingdom's chief finance minister, based at *HM Treasury* in London. The office of Chancellor dates back to the 13th century. A very senior government position, some of the most famous names in British politics have served as Chancellor, including William Gladstone and Lloyd George.

changeover time the period required to change a workstation from a state of readiness for one operation to a state of readiness for another

channel stuffing the artificial boosting of sales at the end of a financial year by offering distributors and dealers incentives to buy a greater quantity of goods than they actually need (*slang*)

CHAPS *abbr* Clearing House Automated Payment System: a method for the rapid electronic transfer of funds between participating banks on behalf of large commercial customers, where transfers tend to be of significant value

Chapter 11 the US Bankruptcy Reform Act (1978) that entitles enterprises experiencing financial difficulties to apply for protection from creditors and thus have an opportunity to avoid bankruptcy

charge a legal interest in land or property created in favour of a creditor to ensure that the amount owing is paid off

chargeable asset an asset which will produce a capital gain when sold. Assets which are not chargeable include family homes, cars, and some types of investments, such as government stocks.

chargeable gain a *profit* from the sale of an *asset* that is subject to *capital gains tax*

chargeable transfer in the United Kingdom, gifts that are liable to inheritance tax. Under UK legislation, individuals may gift assets to a certain value during their lifetime without incurring any liability to inheritance tax. These are regular transfers out of income that do not affect the donor's standard of living. Additionally, individuals may transfer up to £3,000 a year out of capital. If this exemption is not used in one year, or is only partially used, then the unused allowance may be carried forward to the next year providing the full exemption is then used. Each person may also make small annual gifts of up to £250 per donee. Additionally a parent may give up to £5,000 on the occasion of an offspring's marriage, while a grandparent or more remote ancestor may give up to £2,500, and any other person up to £1,000. Other outright gifts during a lifetime to an individual, and certain types of trust, are known as **potentially exempt transfers**: there is no inheritance tax to be paid on these at the time of the gift, but a liability arises if the donor dies within seven years, with that liability decreasing the longer the donor survives. If the donor dies within seven years of the gift, then **potentially exempt transfers** become chargeable transfers for inheritance tax purposes.

charge account a facility with a retailer that enables the customer to buy goods or services on credit rather than pay in cash. The customer may be required to settle the account within a month to avoid incurring interest on the credit. *Also known as* **credit account**

charge and discharge accounting formerly, a bookkeeping system in which a person charges himself or herself with receipts and credits himself or herself with payments. This system was used extensively in medieval times before the advent of double-entry bookkeeping.

charge card a credit card for which a fee is payable but which does not allow the user to take out a loan. Users must pay off the total sum or a proportion of the total sum charged at the end of each month.

chargee **1.** a person who holds a charge over a property **2.** a person who has the right to force a debtor to pay

charitable contribution a donation by a company to a charity

charity accounts the accounting records of a charitable institution, that include a statement of financial activities rather than a profit and loss account. In the United Kingdom, the accounts should conform to the requirements stipulated in the Charities Act (1993).

chartered accountant in the United Kingdom, a qualified professional accountant who is a member of the Institute of Chartered Accountants. Chartered accountants are qualified to audit company accounts and some hold management positions in companies. *Abbr* **CA**

Chartered Association of Certified Accountants the former name of the Association of Chartered Certified Accountants

chartered company *or* **chartered entity** in the United Kingdom, an organisation formed by the grant of a royal charter. The charter authorises the entity to operate and states the powers specifically granted.

chartered entity *see* **chartered company**

Chartered Institute of Management Accountants *see* **CIMA**

Chartered Institute of Public Finance and Accountancy *see* **CIPFA**

Chartered Institute of Taxation in the United Kingdom, an organisation for professionals in the field of taxation, formerly the Institute of Taxation

charter value the value of a bank being able to continue to do business in the future, reflected as part of its share price

charting the use of charts to analyse stock market trends and to forecast future rises or falls

chartist an analyst who studies past stock market trends, the movement of share prices, and changes in the accounting ratios of individual companies. The chartist's philosophy is that history repeats itself: using charts and graphs, he or she uses past trends and repetitive patterns to forecast the future. Although the chartist approach is considered narrower than that of a traditional analyst, it nevertheless has a good following.

chart of accounts a comprehensive and systematically arranged list of the named and numbered accounts applicable to an enterprise. Originally devised in Germany, it provides a standard list of account codes for assets, liabilities, capital, revenue, and expenses. It is still used in Germany on a voluntary basis and was adopted as part of the French general accounting plan after the Second World War.

chattel mortgage money lent against the security of an item purchased, but not against property

cheap money low interest rates, used as a government strategy to stimulate an economy either at the initial signs of, or during, a recession

check (*US*) = *cheque*

check digit the last digit of a string of computerised reference numbers, used to validate a transaction

cheque a bill of exchange drawn on a bank, payable on demand

cheque register a control record of cheques issued or received

Chinese wall the procedures enforced within a securities firm to prevent the exchange of confidential information between the firm's departments so as to avoid the illegal use of inside information

chose in action a personal right which can be enforced or claimed as if it were property, such as a patent, copyright, debt, or cheque

chose in possession a physical item which can be owned, such as a piece of furniture

churn to encourage an investor to change stock frequently because the broker is paid every time there is a change in the investor's portfolio (*slang*)

churn rate a measure of the frequency and volume of trading of stocks and bonds in a brokerage account

CICA *abbr* Canadian Institute of Chartered Accountants

CIMA *abbr* Chartered Institute of Management Accountants: an organisation that is internationally recognised as offering a financial qualification for business, focusing on strategic business management. Founded in 1919 as the Institute of Cost and Works Accountants, it has offices worldwide, supporting over 128,000 members and students in 156 countries.

CIPFA *abbr* Chartered Institute of Public Finance and Accountancy: in the United Kingdom, one of the leading professional accountancy bodies and the only one that specialises in the public services, for example, local government, public service bodies, and national audit agencies, as well as major accountancy firms. It is responsible for the education and training of professional accountants and for their regulation through the setting and monitoring of professional standards. CIPFA also provides a range of advisory, information, and consultancy services to public service organisations. As such, it is the leading independent commentator on managing accounting for public money.

circuit breaker a rule created by the major US stock exchanges and the *Securities and Exchange Commission* by which trading is halted during times of extreme price fluctuations (*slang*)

circular flow of income a model of a country's economy showing the flow of resources when consumers' wages and salaries are used to buy goods and so generate income for manufacturing firms

circularisation of debtors the sending of letters by a company's auditors to debtors in order to verify the existence and extent of the company's assets

circular letter of credit a letter of credit sent to all branches of the bank which issues it

circulating capital = *working capital*

circulation of capital the movement of capital from one investment to another

City Code on Takeovers and Mergers in the United Kingdom, a code issued on behalf of the Panel on Takeovers and Mergers that is designed principally to ensure fair and equal treatment of all shareholders in relation to takeovers. The Code also provides an orderly framework within which take-overs are conducted. It is not concerned with the financial or commercial advantages or disadvantages of a take-over, nor with those issues, such as competition policy, which are the responsibility of the government. The Code represents the collective opinion of those professionally involved in the field of takeovers on how fairness to shareholders can be achieved in prac-tice.

claim an official request for money, usually in the form of compensation, from an individual or organisation

claims adjuster *(US)* = *loss adjuster*

class action a civil law action taken by a group of individuals who have a common grievance against an indi-vidual, organisation, or legal entity

classical economics a theory focusing on the functioning of a market econ-omy and providing a rudimentary explanation of consumer and producer behaviour in particular markets. The theory postulates that, over time, the economy would tend to operate at full employment because increases in sup-ply would create corresponding increases in demand.

classical system of corporation tax a system in which companies and their owners are liable for *corporation tax* as separate entities. A company's taxed income is therefore paid out to share-holders who are in turn taxed again. This system operates in the United States and the Netherlands. It was replaced in the United Kingdom in 1973 by an *imputation system*.

classification the arrangement of items in logical groups having regard to their nature (subjective classification) or purpose (objective classification). *See also* **code**

classified stock *(US)* a company's *common stock* divided into classes such as Class A and Class B

class of assets the grouping of similar assets into categories. This is done be-cause under International Accounting Standards Committee rules, *tangible assets* and *intangible assets* cannot be revalued on an individual basis, only for a class of assets.

clean float a floating exchange rate that is allowed to vary without any intervention from the country's monet-ary authorities

clean opinion *or* **clean report** an aud-itor's report that is not qualified

clean surplus concept the idea that a company's income statement should show the totality of gains and losses, without any of them being taken dir-ectly to equity

clearing bank a bank that deals with other banks through a clearing house

clearing house an institution that set-tles accounts between banks

Clearing House Automated Pay-ment System *see* **CHAPS**

clearing system the system of settling accounts among banks

clear title *see* **good title**

clickable corporation a company that operates on the Internet

clicks and mortar used to describe a hybrid business involved in e-com-merce and also in marketing its prod-ucts through a traditional store or otherwise incurs the cost of physical structures such as warehouses. The term is based on bricks-and-mortar.

clicks-and-mortar *or* **clicks-and-bricks** combining a traditional bricks-and-mortar organisation with the click technology of the Internet. A clicks-and-mortar organisation has both a vir-tual and a physical presence. Examples include retailers with physical shops on the high street and also websites where their goods can be bought online.

clicks-and-mortar business a hybrid business involved in e-commerce and also in marketing its products through a traditional retail outlet or otherwise incurring the cost of physical structures such as warehouses

clientele effect the preference of an investor or group of investors for buying a particular type of security

Clintonomics the policy of former US President Clinton's Council of Economic Advisors to intervene in the economy to correct market failures and redistribute income

CLOB International in Singapore, a mechanism for buying and selling foreign shares, especially Malaysian shares

clock
   clean somebody's clock (*US*) a rule created by the major US stock exchanges and the SEC to halt trading during times of extreme price fluctuations (*slang*)

clock card a document on which is recorded the starting and finishing time of an employee, for example, by insertion into a time-recording device, for ascertaining total actual attendance time.
   Where an employee also clocks on and off different jobs within total attendance time, such cards are referred to as **job cards**.

close company *or* **closed company** a company in which five or fewer people control more than half the voting shares, or in which such control is exercised by any number of people who are also directors

close corporation *or* **closed corporation** 1. (*US*) a public corporation in which all of the voting stock is held by a few shareholders, for example, management or family members. Although it is a public company, shares would not normally be available for trading because of a lack of liquidity. 2. (*S*

Africa) a business registered in terms of the Close Corporations Act of 1984, consisting of not more than ten members who share its ownership and management. *Abbr* **CC**

closed economy an economic system in which little or no external trade takes place

closed-end credit a loan, plus any interest and finance charges, that is to be repaid in full by a specified future date. Loans that have property or motor vehicles as collateral are usually closed-end. *See also* **open-ended credit**

closed-end fund *or* **closed-end investment company** a unit trust that has a fixed number of shares. *See also* **open-ended fund**

closed-end investment company *see* **open-ended investment company**, **closed-end fund**. *Abbr* **CEIC**

closed-end mortgage a mortgage in which no prepayment is allowed. *See also* **open-ended mortgage**. *Also known as* **closed mortgage**

closed loop system a control system which includes a provision for corrective action, taken on either a feed-forward or a feedback basis

closed mortgage *see* **closed-end mortgage**

closely-held corporation a company whose shares are publicly traded but held by very few people

closely-held shares shares that are publicly traded but held by very few people

Closer Economic Relations Agreement *see* **Australia and New Zealand Closer Economic Relations Trade Agreement**

closing balance 1. the amount in credit or debit in a bank account at the end of a business day 2. the difference between credits and debits in a ledger at the end of one accounting period that is carried forward to the next

closing bell (*US*) the end of a trading session at a stock or commodities exchange

closing entries in a double-entry bookkeeping system, entries made at the very end of an accounting period to balance the expense and revenue ledgers

closing price the price of the last transaction for a particular security or commodity at the end of a trading session

closing quote the last bid and offer prices recorded at the close of a trading session

closing rate the exchange rate of two or more currencies at the close of business of a balance sheet date, for example, at the end of the financial year

closing-rate method a technique for translating the figures from a set of financial statements into a different currency using the *closing rate*. This method is often used for the accounts of a foreign subsidiary of a parent company.

closing sale a sale that reduces the risk that the seller has through holding a greater number of shares or a longer term contract

closing stock a business's remaining stock at the end of an accounting period. It includes finished products, raw materials, or work in progress and is deducted from the period's costs in the balance sheets.

CN *abbr* credit note

CNC *abbr* Conseil National de la Comptabilité

CNCC *abbr* Compagnie Nationale des Commissaires aux Comptes

COB *abbr* Commission des Opérations de Bourse

CoCoA *abbr* continuously contemporary accounting

code a system of symbols designed to be applied to a classified set of items to give a brief, accurate reference, facilitating entry, collation, and analysis. For example, in costing systems, composite symbols are commonly used. In the composite symbol 211.392 the first three digits might indicate the nature of the expenditure (subjective classification), and the last three digits might indicate the cost centre or cost unit to be charged (objective classification).

co-financing the joint provision of money for a project by two or more parties

COGS *abbr* cost of goods sold

cohesion fund the main financial instrument for reducing economic and social disparities within the European Union by providing financial help for projects in the fields of the environment and transport infrastructure

coin analysis the quantities and denominations of banknotes and coins required to pay employees on a payroll

COLA *abbr* cost-of-living adjustment

collar a contractually imposed lower limit on a financial instrument

collateral property or goods used as security against a loan and forfeited to the lender if the borrower defaults

collateralise to secure a loan by pledging assets. If the borrower defaults on loan repayments, the pledged assets can be taken by the lender.

collateral trust certificate a bond for which shares in another company, usually a subsidiary, are used as collateral

collecting bank a bank into which a person has deposited a cheque, and which has the duty to collect the money from the account of the writer of the cheque

collection ratio the average number of days it takes a firm to convert its accounts receivable into cash.

Ideally, this period should be decreasing or constant. A low figure means the company collects its outstanding receivables quickly. Collection ratios are usually reviewed quarterly or yearly.

Calculating the collection ratio requires three figures: total accounts receivable, total credit sales for the period analysed, and the number of days in the period (annual, 365; six months, 182; quarter, 91). The formula is:

Accounts receivable / total credit sales for the period × number of days in the period

EXAMPLE If total receivables are £4,500,000, total credit sales in a quarter are £9,000,000, and number of days is 91, then:

4,500,000 / 9,000,000 × 91 = 45.5

Thus, it takes an average 45.5 days to collect receivables.

Properly evaluating a collection ratio requires a standard for comparison. A traditional rule of thumb is that it should not exceed a third to a half of selling terms. For instance, if terms are 30 days, an acceptable collection ratio would be 40 to 45 days.

Companies use collection ratio information with an *accounts receivable ageing* report. This lists four categories of receivables: 0–30 days, 30–60 days, 60–90 days, and over 90 days. The report also shows the percentage of total accounts receivable that each group represents, allowing for an analysis of delinquencies and potential bad debts. *Also known as* **days' sales outstanding**

collusive tendering the illegal practice among companies making tenders for a job of sharing inside information between themselves, with the aim of fixing the end result

combination annuity *see annuity*

combination bond a government bond for which the collateral is both revenue from the financed project and the government's credit

combined financial statement a written record covering the assets, liabilities, net worth, and operating statement of two or more related or affiliated companies

COMEX *abbr* commodity exchange

comfort letter 1. in the United States, a statement from an accounting firm provided to a company preparing for a public offering, that confirms that the unaudited financial information in the prospectus follows *Generally Accepted Accounting Principles* **2.** a letter from the parent company of a subsidiary that is applying for a loan, stating the intention that the subsidiary should remain in business

command economy an economy in which all economic activity is regulated by the government, as in the former Soviet Union or China

commerce the large-scale buying and selling of goods and services, usually applied to trading between different countries

commerce integration the blending of Internet-based commerce capabilities with the *legacy systems* of a traditional business to create a seamless transparent process

commerce server a networked computer that contains the programs required to process transactions via the Internet, including dynamic inventory databases, shopping cart software, and online payment systems

commerce service provider an organisation or company that provides a service to a company to facilitate some aspect of electronic commerce, for example, by functioning as an Internet *payment gateway*. *Abbr* **CSP**

commercial relating to the buying and selling of goods and services

commercial bank a bank that primarily provides financial services to businesses. *See also* **merchant bank**

commercial hedger a company that holds options in the commodities it produces

commercialisation the application of business principles to something in order to run it as a business

commercial law the body of law that deals with the rules and institutions of commercial transactions, including banking, commerce, contracts, copyrights, insolvency, insurance, patents, trademarks, shipping, storage, transportation, and warehousing

commercial loan a short-term renewable loan or line of credit used to finance the seasonal or cyclical working capital needs of a company

commercial mortgage-backed securities shares which are backed by the security of a commercial mortgage

commercial paper an unsecured short-term loan note issued by companies and generally maturing within nine months

commercial property buildings and land used for the performance of business activities. Commercial property can include single offices, buildings, factories, and hotels.

commercial report an investigative report made by an organisation such as a credit bureau that specialises in obtaining information regarding a person or organisation applying for something such as credit or employment

commercial substance the economic reality that underlies a transaction or arrangement, regardless of its legal or technical denomination. For example, a

company may sell an office block and then immediately lease it back: the commercial substance may be that it has not been sold.

commercial year an artificial year treated as having 12 months of 30 days each, used for calculating such things as monthly sales data and inventory levels

commission a payment made to an intermediary, often calculated as a percentage of the value of goods or services provided. Commission is most often paid to sales staff, brokers, or agents.

Commission des Opérations de Bourse the body, established by the French government in 1968, that is responsible for supervising France's stock exchanges. *Abbr* **COB**

Commissioners of the Inland Revenue in the United Kingdom, officials responsible for hearing appeals by taxpayers against their tax assessment

commission house a firm which buys or sells something, usually commodities, for clients and charges a commission for this service

commitment accounting a method of accounting which recognises expenditure as soon as it is contracted

commitment document a contract, change order, purchase order, or letter of intent pertaining to the supply of goods and services that commits an organisation to legal, financial, and other obligations

commitment fee a fee that a lender charges to guarantee a rate of interest on a loan a borrower is soon to make. *Also known as* **establishment fee**

commitment letter (*US*) an official notice from a lender to a borrower that the borrower's application has been approved and confirming the terms and conditions of the loan

commitments basis the method of recording the expenditure of a public sector organisation at the time when it commits itself to it rather than when it actually pays for it

commitments for capital expenditure the amount a company has committed to spend on fixed assets in the future. In the United Kingdom, companies are legally obliged to disclose this amount, and any additional commitments, in their *annual report*.

committed costs costs arising from prior decisions which cannot, in the short run, be changed. Committed cost incurrence often stems from strategic decisions concerning capacity, with resulting expenditure on plant and facilities. Initial control of committed costs at the decision point is through investment appraisal techniques. *See also commitment accounting*

Committee on Accounting Procedure in the United States, one of the committees of the American Institute of Certified Public Accountants that was responsible between 1939 and 1959 for issuing accounting principles, some of which are still part of the *Generally Accepted Accounting Principles*

commodities exchange a market in which raw materials are bought and sold in large quantities as *actuals* or *futures*

commodity a good or service, for example, cotton, wool, or a laptop computer, resulting from a production process

commodity-backed bond a bond tied to the price of an underlying commodity, for example, gold or silver, often used as a hedge against inflation

commodity contract a legal document for the delivery or receipt of a commodity

commodity exchange an exchange where futures are traded, for example, the commodity exchange for metals in the United States. *Abbr* **COMEX**

commodity future a contract to buy or sell a commodity at a predetermined price and on a particular delivery date

commodity paper loans for which commodities are collateral

commodity pool a group of people who join together to trade in options

commodity pricing pricing a product or service on the basis that it is undifferentiated from all competitive offerings, and cannot therefore command any price premium above the base market price

commodity-product spread co-ordinated trades in both a commodity and a product made from it

common cost[1] a cost which is allocated to two or more cost centres within a company

common cost[2] cost relating to more than one product or service

common market an economic association, typically between nations, with the goal of removing or reducing trade barriers

common pricing the illegal fixing of the price of a good or service by several businesses so that they all charge the same price

common seal the impression of a company's official signature on paper or wax. Certain documents, such as share certificates, have to bear this seal. *Also known as company seal*

common-size financial statements statements in which all the elements are expressed as percentages of the total. Such statements are often used for making performance comparisons between companies.

common stock a stock that pays a dividend after dividends for preferred stock have been paid

common stock ratio a measure of the interest each stockholder has in the company's capital

commorientes the legal term for two or more people who die at the same time. For the purposes of inheritance law, in the event of two people dying at the same time, it is assumed that the older person died first.

Communism a classless society where private ownership of goods is abolished and the means of production belong to the community

Compagnie Nationale des Commissaires aux Comptes in France, an organisation that regulates external audit. *Abbr* **CNCC**

Companies Act Acts of Parliament that regulate the working of companies. Although the first one was passed in 1844, the 1985 Act consolidated previous legislation and incorporated directives from the European Union.

Companies House in the United Kingdom, the office of the *Registrar of Companies*. It has three main functions: the incorporation, re-registration, and striking-off of companies; the registration of documents that must be filed under company, insolvency, and related legislation; and the provision of company information to the public. *Abbr* **CH**

Companies Registration Office the office of the Registrar of Companies, an official UK organisation at which companies' records must be deposited so that they can be inspected by the public

companion bond a class of a collateral mortgage obligation that is paid off first when interest rates fall, leading to the underlying mortgages being prepaid. Conversely, the principal on these bonds will be repaid more slowly when interest rates rise and fewer mortgages are prepaid.

company a legal entity whose life is independent of that of its members. There are three ways of forming a company or corporation, namely by registration under the Companies Act, by charter, or by an Act of Parliament.

company auditor the individual or firm of accountants a company appoints to audit its annual accounts

company formation the legal procedure required in order to set up a company. In the United Kingdom, this involves filing a series of documents with the *Registrar of Companies* and signing a declaration to the effect that the requirements stipulated in the Companies Act have been met.

company law the body of legislation that relates to the formation, status, conduct, and *corporate governance* of companies as legal entities

company limited by guarantee a company in which each member undertakes to contribute (to the limit of his guarantee), on a winding-up, towards payment of the liabilities of the company. No new registrations of this nature may be made.

company limited by shares 1. a type of organisation in which each member of the company is liable only for the fully paid value of the shares they own. This is the most common form of company in the United Kingdom. **2.** a company in which the liability of members for the company's debts is limited to the amount, if any, unpaid on the shares taken up by them. *Also known as* **joint stock company**, **limited liability company**

company officers the directors of a company and the company secretary

company report a document giving details of the activities and performance of a company. Companies are legally required to produce particular reports and submit them to the competent authorities in the country of their registration. These include *annual reports* and financial reports. Other reports may cover specific aspects of an organisation's activities, for example, environmental or social impact.

company seal *see common seal*

company secretary a senior employee in an organisation with director status and administrative and legal authority. The appointment of a company secretary is a legal requirement for all limited companies. A company secretary can also be a board secretary with appropriate qualifications. In the United Kingdom, many company secretaries are members of the Institute of Chartered Secretaries and Administrators.

comparability a feature in the financial statements of two or more companies that enables an analyst to make a faithful comparison between them

comparative advantage an instance of higher, more efficient production in a particular area. A country that produces far more cars than another, for example, is said to have the comparative advantage in car production. David Ricardo originally argued that specialisation in activities in which individuals or groups have a comparative advantage will result in gains in trade.

comparative balance sheet one of two or more financial statements prepared on different dates that lend themselves to a comparative analysis of the financial condition of an organisation

comparative credit analysis an analysis of the risk associated with lending to different companies

compensated absences days when an employee is absent from work, for example, through illness or on compassionate leave, but is still paid

compensating balance 1. the amount of money a bank requires a customer to maintain in a non-interest-bearing account, in exchange for which the bank provides free services **2.** the amount of money a bank requires a customer to maintain in an account in return for holding credit available, thereby increasing the true rate of interest on the loan

compensating error in a double-entry bookkeeping system, an error that does not appear in a trial balance because it is cancelled out by another error or errors

compensating errors two or more errors which are set against each other so that the accounts still balance

compensation package (*US*) a bundle of rewards including *pay*, financial incentives, and fringe benefits offered to, or negotiated by, an employee

compensatory financing finance from the International Monetary Fund to help a country in economic difficulty

competition rivalry between companies to achieve greater *market share*. Competition between companies for customers will lead to product innovation and improvement, and ultimately lower prices. The opposite of market competition is either a *monopoly* or a **controlled economy**, where production is governed by quotas. A company that is leading the market is said to have achieved *competitive advantage*.

competitive advantage a factor giving an advantage to a nation, company, group, or individual in competitive terms. Used by Michael Porter for the title of his classic text on international corporate strategy, *The Competitive Advantage of Nations* (1990), the concept of competitive advantage derives from the ideas on *comparative advantage* of the 19th-century economist David Ricardo.

competitive bid a method of auctioning new securities whereby various underwriters offer the stock at competing prices of terms

competitive devaluation the devaluation of a currency to make a country's goods more competitive on the international markets

competitive equilibrium price the price at which the number of buyers willing to buy a good equals the number of sellers prepared to sell it

competitive position the market share, costs, prices, quality, and accumulated experience of an entity or product relative to competition

competitive pricing setting a price by reference to the prices of competitive products

competitive saw an illustration of the principle that every investment in a product, while initially improving the reported performance in relation to competitors, eventually degrades and has to be succeeded by further investment(s) to maintain the competitive position

competitor analysis or **competitor profiling** the identification and quantification of the relative strengths and weaknesses of a product or service (compared with those of competitors or potential competitors) which could be of significance in the development of a successful competitive strategy

compilation (*US*) the drawing up of a company's financial statements by an independent accountant

complete capital market a market with a security that represents each possible result

completed contract method a way of accounting for a particular con-

tractual obligation, for example, a long-term construction project, whereby the profit is not recorded until the final completion of the project, even if there has been some revenue while the project was still in progress

compliance audit an audit of specific activities in order to determine whether performance conforms with a predetermined contractual, regulatory, or statutory requirement

compliance costs expenses incurred as a result of meeting legal requirements, for example, for safety requirements or to comply with company law

compliance department a department, most often in stockbroking firms, which makes sure that the appropriate industry rules and regulations are followed and that confidentiality is maintained in cases where the same firm represents rival clients

compliance documentation documents that a share-issuing company publishes in line with regulations on share issues

compliance officer an employee of a financial organisation who ensures that regulations governing its business are observed

compliance tests investigations carried out during an audit to assess the effectiveness of a company's internal controls

composition a legal agreement between a company and its creditors that arranges for the partial payment of debts that the company is unable to settle in full

compound discount the difference between the nominal amount of a particular sum in the future and its present discounted value. So, if £150 in a year's time is worth £142 now, the compound discount is £8.

compounded annual return the net return on an investment, calculated after adding interest and deducting tax

compounding the calculation, payment, or receipt of *compound interest*

compound instrument a financial instrument that has both an equity and a liability component

compound interest interest calculated on the sum of the original borrowed amount and the accrued interest. *See also* **simple interest**

compound journal entry an entry in a journal that comprises more than individual equally matched debit and credit items

compound rate an interest rate of a loan based on its *principal*, the amount remaining to be paid, or any interest payments already received

comprehensive auditing *see* **value for money audit**

comprehensive income a company's total income for a given accounting period, taking into account all gains and losses, not only those included in a normal income statement. In the United States, comprehensive income must be declared whereas in the United Kingdom it appears in the statement of total recognised gains and losses.

comprehensive tax allocation the setting aside of money to cover deferred tax

comptroller (*US*) a company's financial director or the person responsible for the accounting of a group of companies

Comptroller and Auditor General in the United Kingdom, the head of the National Audit Office who reports back to Parliament on the audit of government departments

Comptroller of the Currency an official of the US government respon-

sible for the regulation of banks which are members of the Federal Reserve

compulsory acquisition the purchase, by right, of the last 10% of shares in an issue by a bidder at the offer price

compulsory annuity in the United Kingdom, the legal requirement that at least 75% of the funds built up in a personal pension plan have to be used to purchase an annuity by the age of 75

computer model a system for calculating investment opportunities, used by fund managers to see the right moment to buy or sell

concentration services the placing of money from various accounts into a single account

concepts principles underpinning the preparation of accounting information. *See* **fundamental accounting concepts**

conceptual framework a set of theoretical principles that underlies the practice and regulation of financial accounting. In the United States, this is expressed in the Statements of Financial Accounting Concepts issued by the Financial Accounting Standards Board. In the United Kingdom, it is expressed in the Statement of Principles issued by the Accounting Standards Board.

concession 1. a reduction in price for a particular group of people **2.** the right of a retail outlet to set up and sell goods within another establishment

concurrent engineering a means of reducing product development time and cost by managing development processes so that they can be implemented simultaneously, rather than sequentially

conditions of sale agreed ways in which a sale takes place (such as discounts and credit terms)

Confederation of Asian and Pacific Accountants a large association of accountancy bodies that operate in Asia and the Pacific Rim countries

Confederation of British Industry a corporate membership organisation which aims to promote the interests of UK business. The CBI's headquarters are in London, but it has regional offices throughout the United Kingdom, a European office in Brussels, and a US base in Washington DC. *Abbr* **CBI**

confidence indicator a number that gives an indication of how well a market or an economy will fare

confirmed letter of credit *see letter of credit*

conglomerate an entity comprising a number of dissimilar businesses

conglomerate company an organisation that owns a diverse range of companies in different industries. Conglomerates are usually *holding companies* with subsidiaries in wideranging business areas, often built up through mergers and takeovers and operating on an international scale.

conglomerate diversification the *diversification* of a *conglomerate company* through the setting up of subsidiary companies with activities in various areas

connected persons for purposes of disclosure under the UK Companies Act, certain people who are related to or connected with a member of the board of directors, including his or her spouse and children

Conseil National de la Comptabilité in France, a committee appointed by the government that is responsible for drawing up the Plan Comptable Général (General Accounting Plan)

consent letter a letter from an expert in a particular field, for example, valuation, granting permission for his or her report to be included in a company's prospectus

consequential loss policy *see business interruption insurance*

consideration 1. the monetary value of a stock market transaction before costs and taxes **2.** something of value, for example, money, that is offered by a buyer in a contract. A contract is not valid unless there is a consideration.

consignment a batch of goods dispatched together

  sent on consignment used to describe goods that have been sent to a retailer in order to be sold and remain the property of the sender until sold

consignment account a ledger that records transactions involving goods sent on consignment. It will include details of the price of the goods, the sale proceeds, the agent's fee, and any other expenses incurred.

consignment note *see delivery note*

consignment stock stock held by one party (the 'dealer') but legally owned by another (the 'manufacturer') on terms that give the dealer the right to sell the stock in the normal course of its business, or, at its option, to return it unsold to the legal owner

consistency the idea that a company should apply the same rules and standards to its accounting procedures from year to year. In the United Kingdom, any changes to the rules of recognition, presentation, and measurement must be disclosed in the annual report.

CONSOB *abbr* Commissione Nazionale per la Società e la Borsa

consol certain irredeemable UK government stocks carrying fixed coupons. They are sometimes used as a general term for an undated or irredeemable bond.

consolidated accounts *see consolidated financial statement*

consolidated balance sheet a listing of the most significant details of a company's finances

consolidated cash-flow statement a cash-flow statement for a group of enterprises and its parent company as a whole

consolidated debt the use of a large loan to eliminate smaller ones

consolidated financial statement a listing of the most significant details of the finances of a company and of all its subsidiaries. *Also known as consolidated accounts*

consolidated fund a fund of public money, especially from taxes, used by the government to make interest payments on the national debt and other regular payments

consolidated income statement an income statement for a group of enterprises and its parent company as a whole

consolidated invoice an invoice that covers all items shipped by one seller to one buyer during a particular period

consolidated loan a large loan, the proceeds of which are used to eliminate smaller ones

consolidated profit and loss account *see consolidated income statement*

consolidated tape a ticker tape that lists all transactions of the New York and other US stock exchanges

consolidated tax return a tax return that covers several companies, typically a parent company and all of its subsidiaries

consolidation 1. the uniting of two or more businesses into one company **2.** the combination of several lower-priced shares into one higher-priced one

consolidation accounting the process of adjusting and combining financial information from the individual financial statements of a parent undertaking and its subsidiary undertakings

to prepare consolidated financial statements that present financial information for the group as a single economic entity

consolidation adjustments necessary changes and deletions made to financial records when consolidating the accounts of a group of enterprises

consolidation difference the difference between the price paid for a subsidiary and the value of the assets and liabilities obtained in the purchase

consortium an association of several entities with a view to carrying out a *joint venture*

consortium relief in the United Kingdom, a corporation tax benefit for the 20 or fewer members of a consortium

constant dollar accounting *(US)* = *current purchasing power accounting*

constraint an activity, resource, or policy that limits the ability to achieve objectives. Constraints are commonly used in mathematical programming to describe a restriction which forms part of the boundary for the range of solutions to a problem, and which define the area within which the solution must lie.

construction contract a contract drawn up specifically for the construction of an asset or a group of assets

constructive obligation an obligation that arises when an organisation creates a valid expectation that it will discharge certain responsibilities

Consultative Committee of Accountancy Bodies an organisation established in 1974 that represents and encourages co-ordination between the six professional accountancy bodes in the United Kingdom and Ireland

consulting actuary an independent actuary who advises large pension funds

consumable materials materials that are used in a production process but are not part of the direct cost

consumer somebody who uses a product or service. A consumer may not be the purchaser of a product or service and should be distinguished from a customer, who is the person or organisation that purchased the product or service.

Consumer Credit Act in the United Kingdom, an act of Parliament that received Royal Assent in 1974 and is designed to protect consumers, including sole traders and partnerships, when borrowing money. *US term* ***Truth in Lending Act***

consumer price index an index of the prices of goods and services that consumers purchase, used to measure the cost of living or the rate of inflation in an economy. *Abbr* **CPI**

consumer-to-consumer commerce e-business transactions conducted between two individuals

consumption the quantity of resources that consumers use to satisfy their current needs and wants, measured by the sum of the current expenditure of the government and individual consumers

consumption tax a tax used to encourage people to buy less of a particular good or service by increasing its price. This type of tax is often levied in times of national hardship.

Contact Committee an advisory body, established by the European Union, that oversees the application of European accounting directives and feeds back to the European Commission with recommended changes to those directives

contango a situation where the price of commodities is higher for future delivery than it is for immediate delivery

contestable market a market in which there are no barriers to entry, as when there is *perfect competition*

contingencies *see* *contingent asset*, *contingent liability*

contingency plan action to be implemented only upon the occurrence of anticipated future events other than those in the accepted forward plan

contingency tax a one-off tax levied by a government to deal with a particular economic problem, for example, too high a level of imports coming into the country

contingency theory the hypothesis that there can be no universally applicable best practice in the design of organisational units or of control systems such as management accounting systems. The efficient design and functioning of such systems is dependent on an awareness by the system designer of the specific environmental factors which influence their operation, such as the organisational structure, technology base, and market situation.

contingent asset a possible asset that arises from an event in the past but whose existence will only be confirmed by one or more uncertain events in the future. Contingent assets do not need to be declared in accounts.

contingent consideration a payment by a buyer that is conditional on certain future events occurring, for example, a business hitting certain targets

contingent deferred sales charge *abbr* **CDSC**. *See* **B share**

contingent gain a possible gain that is conditional on the occurrence of a certain event in the future

contingent liability a possible liability that may or may not feature on the balance sheets on a certain date, but for which provision is made in the accounts

contingent loss a possible loss that is conditional on the occurrence of a certain event in the future

contingent rent a share of a lease payment that varies according to a factor other than time, for example, the degree of usage

continuity assumption *see going concern*

continuous budget *see rolling budget*

continuous disclosure in Canada, the practice of ensuring that complete, timely, accurate, and balanced information about a public company is made available to shareholders

continuous improvement the seeking of small improvements in processes and products, with the objective of increasing quality and reducing waste. Continuous improvement is one of the tools that underpin the philosophies of *total quality management* and lean production. Through constant study and revision of processes, a better product can result at reduced cost. Kaizen has become a foundation for many continuous improvement strategies, and for many employees it is synonymous with continuous improvement.

continuous inventory regular and consistent stocktaking throughout the financial year in order to ensure that the physical reality of the stock situation at any given time tallies with the accounting records such as bin cards. Any discrepancies will highlight errors or losses of stock and the accounts are adjusted to reflect this. Continuous inventory may preclude the need for an annual stocktake. *Also called continuous stocktaking*

continuously contemporary accounting an accounting system that measures assets and liabilities at their current cash price. Profit and loss can therefore be viewed in terms of changes in the value as all items are measured in the same way. *Abbr* **CoCoA**

continuous operation costing *or* **continuous process costing** the costing method applicable where goods or services result from a sequence of continuous or repetitive operations or processes. Costs are averaged over the units produced during the period, being initially charged to the operation or process.

continuous stocktaking = *continuous inventory*

contra a bookkeeping term meaning against, or on the opposite side. It is used where debits are matched with related credits, in the same or a different account. A common example is where a supplier is also a customer.

contra accounts entries in the accounts of two separate businesses that can be offset against each other. For example, if two companies owe money to each other, both debts can be offset and settled with one payment.

contract 1. the buying and selling of securities and other financial instruments 2. a mutually agreed, legally binding agreement between two or more parties

contract broker a broker who fulfils an order placed by somebody else

contract cost aggregated costs of a single contract; usually applies to major long-term contracts rather than short-term jobs

contract costing a form of specific order costing in which costs are attributed to individual contracts

contracting costs the expenses generated when the owner and manager of an enterprise are not the same person or persons. For example, one of the contracting costs of a listed company is the audit: it is ordered by the shareholders (owners) to check up on and monitor the appointed directors (managers).

contracting out the withdrawal of employees by an employer from the State Earnings-Related Pension Scheme and their enrolment in an occupational pension scheme that meets specified standards

contract month the month in which an option expires and goods covered by it must be delivered. *Also known as delivery month*

contract note a document with the complete description of a stock transaction

contractual savings savings in the form of regular payments into long-term investments, such as pension schemes

contra entry an entry in a bookkeeping system that cancels out a previous entry but without crossing it out

contrarian research research that advises potential purchasers to buy shares against the current trend

contrarian stockpicking the choosing of stocks and shares against the trend of the market

contributed surplus the portion of shareholders' equity that comes from sources other than earnings, for example, from the initial sale of stock above its par value

contribution sales value less variable cost of sales. Contribution may be expressed as total contribution, contribution per unit, or as a percentage of sales.

contribution centre a *profit centre* in which marginal or direct costs are matched against revenue

contribution income statement a way of presenting an income statement in which fixed costs are shown as a deduction from the total contribution. This format is often used as part of management accounting.

contribution margin a way of showing how much individual products or services contribute to net profit

contributions holiday a period during which a company stops making contributions to its pension plan because the plan is sufficiently well funded

contributory pension a pension where both the employer and employee pay into the pension fund

contributory pension scheme a pension scheme where the worker has to pay a proportion of his salary

control the ability to direct the financial and operating policies of an entity with a view to gaining economic benefits from its activities

control account a ledger account which collects the sum of the postings into the individual accounts which it controls. The balance on the control account should equal the sum of the balances on the individual accounts, which are maintained as subsidiary records.

control contract a contract that grants one organisation legal control over another which then becomes a subsidiary of the controlling company. This form of contract is not considered legal in the United Kingdom as it would disenfranchise shareholders.

control environment the overall attitude, awareness, and actions of directors and management regarding internal *controls* and their importance to the organisation

controllability concept the principle that management accounting identifies the elements or activities which management can or cannot influence, and seeks to assess risk and sensitivity factors. This facilitates the proper monitoring, analysis, comparison, and interpretation of information which can be used constructively in the control, evaluation, and corrective functions of management.

controllable cost a cost which can be influenced by its budget holder

controllable variance a difference between actual and budgeted amounts that is considered as being within the control of the budget centre manager

controlled company a company where more than 50% (or, in the United States, 25%) of the shares belong to one owner

controlled disbursement the presentation of cheques only once each day

controlled economy an economy where most business activity is directed by orders from the government

control limits quantities or values outside which managerial action is triggered

control period the fraction of the financial year, for example, a month, for which separate totals are given in a budget

control procedures the policies and procedures in addition to the *control environment* which are established to achieve an organisation's specific objectives. They include, in particular, procedures designed to prevent or to detect and correct errors.

control risk the part of an audit risk that relates to a client's internal control system

conversion 1. a trade of one convertible financial instrument for another, for example, a bond for shares 2. a trade of shares of one unit trust for shares of another in the same family 3. the offering of a new government stock issue in exchange for government stock near *redemption*

conversion costs the cost of changing raw materials into finished or semi-finished products. Conversion costs include wages, other direct production costs, and the production overheads.

conversion issue the issue of new bonds, timed to coincide with the date of maturity of older bonds, with the intention of persuading investors to reinvest

conversion price the price per share at which the holder of convertible bonds, or debentures, or preference shares, can convert them into ordinary shares.

Depending on specific terms, the conversion price may be set when the convertible asset is issued. If the conversion price is set, it will appear in the indenture, a legal agreement between the issuer of a convertible asset and the holder, that states specific terms. If the conversion price does not appear in the agreement, a conversion ratio is used to calculate the conversion price.

EXAMPLE A conversion ratio of 25:1, for example, means that 25 shares of stock can be obtained in exchange for each £1,000 convertible asset held. In turn, the conversion price can be determined simply by dividing £1,000 by 25:

$$£1,000 / 25 = £40 \text{ per share}$$

Comparison of a stock's conversion price to its prevailing market price can help decide the best course of action. If the shares of the company in question are trading at £52 per share, converting makes sense, because it increases the value of a £1,000 convertible to £1,300 (£52 × 25 shares). But if the shares are trading at £32 per share, then conversion value is only £800 (£32 × 25) and it is clearly better to defer conversion.

conversion ratio an expression of the quantity of one security that can be obtained for another, for example, shares for a *convertible bond*.

The conversion ratio may be established when the convertible is issued. If that is the case, the ratio will appear in the indenture, the binding agreement that details the convertible's terms.

EXAMPLE If the conversion ratio is not set, it can be calculated quickly: divide the par value of the convertible security (typically £1,000) by its conversion price.

£1,000 / £40 per share = 25

In this example, the conversion ratio is 25:1, which means that every bond held with a £1,000 par value can be exchanged for 25 ordinary shares.

Knowing the conversion ratio enables an investor to decide whether convertibles (or group of them) are more valuable than the ordinary shares they represent. If the stock is currently trading at 30, the conversion value is £750, or £250 less than the par value of the convertible. It would therefore be unwise to convert.

A convertible's indenture can sometimes contain a provision stating that the conversion ratio will change over the years.

Conversion ratio also describes the number of ordinary shares of one type to be issued for each outstanding ordinary share of a different type when a merger takes place.

conversion value the value a security would have if converted into shares

convertible ARM an adjustable-rate mortgage that the borrower can convert into a fixed-rate mortgage under specified terms

convertible bond a bond that the owner can convert into another asset, especially ordinary shares

convertible loan stock a loan which gives the holder the right to convert to other securities, normally ordinary shares, at a predetermined price/rate and time

convertible preference shares shares that give the holder the right to exchange them at a fixed price for another security, usually ordinary shares.

Preference shares and other convertible securities offer investors a hedge:

fixed-interest income without sacrificing the chance to participate in a company's capital appreciation.

When a company does well, investors can convert their holdings into ordinary shares that are more valuable. When a company is less successful, they can still receive interest and principal payments, and also recover their investment and preserve their capital if a more favourable investment appears.

Conversion ratios and prices are important facts to know about preference shares. This information is found on the indenture statement that accompanies all issues. Occasionally the indenture will state that the conversion ratio will change over time.

For example, the conversion price might be £50 for the first five years, £55 for the next five years, and so forth. Stock splits can affect conversion considerations. In theory, convertible preference shares (and convertible exchangeable preference shares) are usually perpetual. However, issuers tend to force conversion or induce voluntary conversion for convertible preference shares within ten years. Steadily increasing ordinary share dividends is one inducement tactic used. As a result, the conversion feature for preference shares often resembles that of debt securities. Call protection for the investor is usually about three years, and a 30- to 60-day call notice is typical.

About 50% of convertible equity issues also have a 'soft call provision'. If the ordinary share price reaches a specified ratio, the issuer is permitted to force conversion before the end of the normal protection period.

convertibles corporate bonds or preference shares which can be converted into ordinary shares at a set price on set dates

convertible security a convertible bond, warrant, or preference share

convertible share a non-equity share such as a preference share, carrying rights to convert into equity shares on predetermined terms

convertible term insurance term insurance that the policyholder can convert to fixed life assurance under particular conditions

conveyancing the legal transfer of a property from the seller to the buyer

cooling-off period 1. a period during which someone who is about to enter into an agreement may reflect on all aspects of the arrangement and change his or her mind if necessary **2.** in insurance, a period of ten days during which a person who has signed a life assurance policy may cancel it

co-proprietor a person who owns a property with one other person or more

corporate action a measure that a company takes that has an effect on the number of shares outstanding or the rights that apply to shares

corporate appraisal a critical assessment of strengths and weaknesses, opportunities and threats (commonly known as SWOT analysis) in relation to the internal and environmental factors affecting an entity in order to establish its condition prior to the preparation of the long-term plan

corporate bond a long-term bond with fixed interest issued by a corporation

corporate fraud *fraud* committed by large organisations, rather than individuals. Auditing practice around the world, but especially in the United States, has come under much scrutiny since the collapse of Enron and WorldCom in 2001 and 2002 respectively. Both companies had overstated their profits, but the auditors, Arthur Andersen, had approved the accounts in each case.

corporate governance the system by which companies are directed and controlled. Boards of directors are responsible for the governance of their companies. The shareholders' role in governance is to appoint the directors and the auditors and to satisfy themselves that an appropriate governance structure is in place. The responsibilities of the board include setting the company's strategic aims, providing the leadership to put them into effect, supervising the management of the business, and reporting to the shareholders on their stewardship. The board's actions are subject to laws, regulations, and the wishes of the shareholders in general meeting.

Corporate Governance Combined Code the successor to the Cadbury Code, established by the Hampel Committee. The code consists of a set of principles of corporate governance and detailed code provisions embracing the work of the Cadbury, Greenbury, and Hampel Committees. Section 1 of the code contains the principles and provisions applicable to UK listed companies, while section 2 contains the principles and provisions applicable to institutional shareholders in their relationships with companies.

corporate resolution a document signed by the officers of a corporation naming those persons who can sign cheques, withdraw cash, and have access to the corporation's bank account

corporate settlement the period of five business days after the date of a trade

corporate social accounting the reporting of the social and environmental impact of an entity's activities upon those who are directly associated with the entity (employees, customers, suppliers, etc) or those who are in any way affected by the activities of the entity, as well as an assessment of the cost of compliance with relevant regulations in this area

corporate spinoff a small company which has been split off from a larger, parent organisation

corporation *(US)* = *limited liability company*

corporation tax tax chargeable on companies resident in the United Kingdom or trading in the United Kingdom through a branch or agency as well as on certain unincorporated associations

corporation tax company a company in a foreign country used to reduce taxes

correspondent bank a bank which acts as an agent for a foreign bank in another country

cost 1. the amount of expenditure (actual or notional) incurred on, or attributable to, a specified thing or activity **2.** the amount of money that is paid to secure a good or service. Cost is the amount paid from the purchaser's standpoint, whereas the price is the amount paid from the vendor's standpoint. **3.** to ascertain the cost of a specific thing or activity

cost account a record of revenue and/or expenditure of a cost centre or cost unit

cost accounting the establishment of budgets, standard costs, and actual costs of operations, processes, activities, or products; and the analysis of variances, profitability, or the social use of funds. The use of the term 'costing' is not recommended except with a qualifying adjective, for example, standard costing.

cost audit the verification of cost records and accounts, and a check on adherence to prescribed *cost accounting* procedures and their continuing relevance

cost behaviour the variability of input costs with activity undertaken. A number of cost behaviour patterns are pos-

sible, ranging from **variable costs**, whose cost level varies directly with the level of activity, to *fixed costs*, where changes in output have no effect upon the cost level.

cost-benefit analysis a comparison between the cost of the resources used, plus any other costs imposed by an activity (for example, pollution, environmental damage) and the value of the financial and non-financial benefits derived

cost centre a department, function, section, or individual whose cost, overall or in part, is an accepted overhead of a business in return for services provided to other parts of the organisation. A cost centre is usually an *indirect cost* of an organisation's products or services.

cost classification the arrangement of elements of cost into logical groups with respect to their nature (fixed, variable, value adding, etc.), function (production, selling, etc.), or use in the business of the entity

cost (at cost) concept the practice of valuing assets with reference to their acquisition cost

cost control the process which ensures that actual costs do not exceed acceptable limits

cost-cutting the reduction of the amount of money spent on the operations of an organisation or on the provision of products and services. Cost-cutting measures such as budget reductions, salary freezes, and staff redundancies may be taken by an organisation at a time of *recession* or financial difficulty or in situations where inefficiency has been identified. Alternative approaches to cost-cutting include modifying organisational structures and redesigning organisational processes for greater efficiency. Excessive cost-cutting may affect *productivity* and quality or the organisation's ability to add value.

cost driver a factor that determines the cost of an activity. Cost drivers are analysed as part of *activity-based costing* and can be used in *continuous improvement* programmes. They are usually assessed together as multiple drivers rather than singly. There are two main types of cost driver: the first is a *resource driver*, which refers to the contribution of the quantity of resources used to the cost of an activity; the second is an **activity driver**, which refers to the costs incurred by the activities required to complete a particular task or project.

cost-effective offering the maximum benefit for a given level of expenditure. When limited resources are available to meet specific objectives, the cost-effective solution is the best that can be achieved for that level of expenditure and the one that provides good value for money. The term is also used to refer to a level of expenditure that is perceived to be commercially viable.

cost-effectiveness analysis a method for measuring the benefits and effectiveness of a particular item of expenditure. Cost-effectiveness analysis requires an examination of expenditure to determine whether the money spent could have been used more effectively or whether the resulting benefits could have been attained through less financial outlay.

cost estimation the determination of *cost behaviour*. This can be achieved by engineering methods, analysis of the accounts, use of statistics, or the pooling of expert views.

cost function a mathematical function relating a firm's or an industry's total cost to its output and factor costs

costing the process of determining the costs of products, services, or activities

cost management the application of management accounting concepts, methods of data collection, analysis, and presentation, in order to provide the information required to enable costs to be planned, monitored, and controlled

cost of appraisal costs incurred in order to ensure that outputs produced meet required quality standards

cost of capital the minimum acceptable return on an investment, generally computed as a hurdle rate for use in investment appraisal exercises. The computation of the optimal cost of capital can be complex, and many ways of determining this opportunity cost have been suggested.

cost of conformance the cost of achieving specified quality standards. *See also* **cost of appraisal, cost of prevention**

cost of external failure the cost arising from inadequate quality discovered after the transfer of ownership from supplier to purchaser

cost of goods sold 1. for a retailer, the cost of buying and acquiring the goods it sells to its customers **2.** for a service firm, the cost of the employee services it supplies **3.** for a manufacturer, the cost of buying the raw materials and manufacturing its finished products *abbr* **COGS**

cost of internal failure the costs arising from inadequate quality which are identified before the transfer of ownership from supplier to purchaser

cost of living the average amount spent by an individual on accommodation, food, and other basic necessities. Salaries are usually increased annually to cover rises in the cost of living.

cost-of-living adjustment (*US*) a small increase to salaries made to account for rises in the *cost of living*. *Abbr* **COLA**

cost-of-living allowance a salary supplement paid to some employees to cover rises in the *cost of living*. The specific amount of the supplement is dictated by the *cost of living index*.

cost of living index an index which indicates changes in the cost of living by comparing current prices for a variety of goods with the prices paid for them in previous years

cost of non-conformance the cost of failure to deliver the required standard of quality. *See also cost of external failure*, *cost of internal failure*

cost of prevention the costs incurred prior to or during production in order to prevent substandard or defective products or services from being produced

cost of quality the difference between the actual cost of producing, selling, and supporting products or services and the equivalent costs if there were no failures during production or usage. *See also cost of conformance*, *cost of non-conformance*

cost of sales the sum of *variable cost* (*see cost behaviour*) of sales plus factory overhead attributable to the sales

cost-plus pricing the determination of price by adding a mark-up, which may incorporate a desired *return on investment*, to a measure of the cost of the product/service

cost pool the point of focus for the costs relating to a particular activity in an activity-based costing system

cost reduction the reduction in unit cost of goods or services without impairing suitability for the use intended

cost table a database containing all the costs associated with the production of a product, broken down to include the costs of functions and/or components and sub-assemblies. Cost tables also incorporate the cost changes which would result from a number of possible changes in the input mix.

cost unit a unit of product or service in relation to which costs are ascertained

cost-volume-profit analysis the study of the effects on future profit of changes in fixed cost, variable cost, sales price, quantity, and mix

cottage industry an industry made up of small businesses, often run from the home of the proprietor

council tax a tax paid by individuals or companies to a local authority, Introduced in April 1993 as a replacement for the much maligned community charge, or 'poll tax', council tax depends on the value of the residential or commercial property occupied

counterparty (*US*) a person with whom somebody is entering into a contract

counterpurchase *see countertrade*

countertrade a variety of reciprocal trading practices. This umbrella term encompasses the direct exchange of goods for goods (or *barter*), where no cash changes hands, to more complex variations: **counterpurchase**, which involves a traditional export transaction plus the commitment of the exporter to buy additional goods or services from that country; and *buy-back*, in which the supplier of plant or equipment is paid from the future proceeds resulting from the use of the plant. Countertrade conditions vary widely from country to country and can be costly and administratively cumbersome.

country risk the risk associated with undertaking transactions with, or holding assets in, a particular country. Sources of risk might be political, economic, or regulatory instability affecting overseas taxation, repatriation of profits, nationalisation, currency instability, etc.

coupon 1. a piece of paper attached to a government bond certificate that a bondholder presents to request payment **2.** the rate of interest on a bond **3.** an interest payment made to a bondholder

clip coupons to collect periodic interest on a bond (*slang*)

coupon rate the rate of interest paid on a *bond*

covenant to agree to pay annually a specified sum of money to a person or organisation by contract. When payments are made under covenant to a charity, the charity can reclaim the tax paid by the donor.

cover the taking out of insurance by an individual or organisation in order to protect against loss, damage, risk, or liability

to operate without adequate cover to act without being completely protected by insurance

covered option an option whose owner has the shares for the option

covered warrant a futures contract for shares in a company

cover note a document that an insurance company issues to a customer to serve as a temporary insurance certificate until the issue of the policy itself. *US term* **binder**

CPA *abbr* **1.** customer profitability analysis **2.** certified public accountant

CPI *abbr* consumer price index

CPIX (*ANZ*) the *consumer price index* excluding interest costs, on the basis that these are a direct outcome of monetary policy

crash 1. a precipitous drop in value, especially of the stocks traded in a market **2.** a sudden and catastrophic downturn in an economy. The crash in the United States in 1929 is one of the most famous.

crawling peg a method of fixing exchange rates, but allowing them to move up or down slowly

creative accounting the use of accounting methods to hide aspects of a company's financial dealings in order to make the company appear more or less successful than it is in reality (*slang*) *See also* **corporate fraud**

creative destruction a way of describing the endless cycle of innovation which results in established goods, services, or organisations being replaced by new models. The term was first mentioned by Joseph Schumpeter in *Capitalism, Socialism and Democracy* (1942), but used heavily during the dotcom boom of the late 1990s and early 2000s.

credit 1. the amount of money left over when an individual or organisation has more *assets* than *liabilities*, and those liabilities are subtracted from the total of the assets **2.** the trust that a lender has in a borrower's ability to repay a loan, or a loan itself **3.** a financial arrangement between the vendor and the purchaser of a good or service by which the purchaser may buy what he or she requires, but pay for it at a later date

credit account *see* **charge account**

credit availability the amount of money that can be borrowed at a given time

credit available the amount of money that somebody can borrow at a given time

credit balance the amount of money that somebody owes on a credit account

credit bureau a company that assesses the creditworthiness of people for businesses or banks in the United States. *See also* **mercantile agency**

credit capacity the amount of money that somebody can borrow and be expected to repay

credit card a card issued by a bank or financial institution and accepted by a merchant in payment for a transaction for which the cardholder must subsequently reimburse the issuer

credit ceiling the largest amount that a lender will permit somebody to borrow, for example, on a credit card

credit committee a committee that evaluates a potential borrower's creditworthiness

credit company a company that extends credit to people

credit constraint effect the crowding out of investment by debt

credit controller a member of staff whose job is to expedite the payment of overdue invoices

credit co-operative an organisation of people who join together to gain advantage in borrowing

credit creation the collective ability of lenders to make money available to borrowers

credit crunch a situation in which money for borrowing is unavailable (*slang*)

credit derivative a financial instrument that transfers a lender's risk to a third party

credit entity a borrower or lender

credit entry an item on the asset side of a financial statement

credit exposure the risk to a lender of a borrower defaulting

credit freeze a period during which lending by banks is restricted by the government

credit-granter a person or organisation that lends money

credit history a potential borrower's record of debt repayment. Individuals or organisations with a poor credit his-

tory may find it difficult to find lenders who are willing to risk their taking out a loan.

crediting rate the interest rate paid on an insurance policy that is an investment

credit limit the highest amount that a lender will allow somebody to borrow, for example, on a credit card

credit line *see line of credit*

credit note a document stating that a shop owes somebody an amount of money and entitling the person to goods to the specified value. *Abbr* **CN**

creditor a person or an entity to whom money is owed as a consequence of the receipt of goods or services in advance of payment

creditor days the number of days on average that a company requires to pay its creditors.

To determine creditor days, divide the cumulative amount of unpaid suppliers' bills (also called trade creditors) by sales, then multiply by 365.

EXAMPLE If suppliers' bills total £800,000 and sales are £9,000,000, the calculation is:

(800,000 / 9,000,000) × 365 = 32.44 days

The company takes 32.44 days on average to pay its bills. Creditor days is an indication of a company's creditworthiness in the eyes of its suppliers and creditors, since it shows how long they are willing to wait for payment. Within reason, the higher the number the better, because all companies want to conserve cash. At the same time, a company that is especially slow to pay its bills (100 or more days, for example) may be a company having trouble generating cash, or one trying to finance its operations with its suppliers' funds. *See also debtor days*

creditor days ratio a measure of the number of days on average that a company requires to pay its creditors

To determine creditor days, divide the cumulative amount of unpaid suppliers' bills (also called trade creditors) by sales, then multiply by 365.

EXAMPLE If suppliers' bills total £800,000 and sales are £9,000,000, the calculation is:

(800,000 / 9,000,000) × 365 = 32.44 days

This means the company takes 32.44 days on average to pay its bills.

creditor nation a country that has a balance of payments surplus

creditors' committee a group that directs the efforts of creditors to receive partial repayment from a bankrupt person or organisation. *Also known as* ***creditors' steering committee***

creditors' meeting a meeting of those to whom a bankrupt person or organisation owes money

creditors' settlement an agreement on partial repayment to those to whom a bankrupt person or organisation owes money

creditors' steering committee *see creditors' committee*

credit ranking *see credit rating*

credit rating *or* **credit ranking 1.** an assessment of somebody's creditworthiness **2.** the process of assessing somebody's creditworthiness

credit rating agency *(US)* = *credit-reference agency*

credit rationing the process of making credit less easily available or subject to high interest rates

credit receipt *(US)* a document stating that a shop owes somebody an amount of money and entitling the person to goods to the specified value

credit-reference agency a company that assesses the creditworthiness of people on behalf of businesses or banks. *US term* ***credit rating agency***

credit references details of individuals, companies, or banks who have given credit to a person or company in the past, supplied as references when opening a credit account with a new supplier

credit report information about an individual or entity relevant to a decision to grant credit

credit risk the possibility that a loss may occur from the failure of another party to perform according to the terms of a contract

credit sale a sale for which the buyer need not pay immediately

credit scoring a calculation done in the process of credit rating

credit side the part of a financial statement that lists assets. In ***double-entry bookkeeping***, the right-hand side of each account is designated as the credit side.

credit squeeze a situation in which credit is not easily available or is subject to high interest rates

credit standing the reputation that somebody has with regard to meeting financial obligations

credit system a set of rules and organisations involved in making loans

credit union a co-operative savings association that lends money to members at low rates of interest

credit watch a warning that a governmental organisation's credit rating may soon fall

creditworthy regarded as being reliable in terms of meeting financial obligations

creeping takeover a takeover achieved by the gradual acquisition of small amounts of stock over an extended period of time *(slang)*

creeping tender offer an acquisition of many shares in a company by purchase, especially to avoid US restrictions on tender offers

CREST the paperless system used for settling stock transactions electronically in the United Kingdom

critical success factor an element of organisational activity which is central to its future success. Critical success factors may change over time, and may include items such as product quality, employee attitudes, manufacturing flexibility, and brand awareness.

crony capitalism a form of capitalism in which business contracts are awarded to the family and friends of the government in power rather than by open-market tender

cross a transaction in securities in which one broker acts for both parties

cross-border services accountancy services provided by an accountancy firm in one country on behalf of a client based in another country

cross-border trade trade between two countries that have a common frontier

cross default clause an offering of the same security for trading on more than one exchange

crossed cheque a cheque with two lines across it showing that it can only be deposited at a bank and not exchanged for cash

cross-hedging a form of hedging using an option on a different but related commodity, especially a currency

cross-holding a situation in which two companies hold shares in each other to prevent each from being taken over by a third party

cross-listing the practice of offering the same item for sale in more than one place

cross-rate the rate of exchange between two currencies expressed in terms of the rate of exchange between them and a third currency, for example, sterling and the peso in relation to the dollar

cross-sell to sell customers a range of products or services offered by an organisation at the same time, for example, offering insurance services while selling someone a mortgage

crowding out the effect on markets of credit produced by extraordinarily large borrowing by a national government

crown jewels an organisation's most valuable *assets*, often the motivation behind *takeover* bids

crystallisation the process whereby a floating charge relating to company assets becomes fixed to the assets to which it relates

cum with

cum rights an indication that the buyer of the shares is entitled to participate in a forthcoming rights issue

cumulative interest interest which is added annually to the *capital* originally invested

cumulative method a system in which items are added together

cumulative preference shares shares which entitle the holders to a fixed rate of dividend, and the right to have any arrears of dividend paid out of future profits with priority over any distribution of profits to the holders of ordinary share capital

cumulative preferred stock preferred stock for which dividends accrue even if they are not paid when due

currency the money in circulation in a particular country

currency band exchange rate levels between which a *currency* is allowed to move without full revaluation or devaluation

currency clause a clause in a contract which avoids problems of payment caused by exchange rate changes by fixing in advance the exchange rate for the various transactions covered by the contract

currency future an option on currency

currency hedging a method of reducing *exchange rate risk* by diversifying currency holdings and adjusting them according to changes in exchange rates

currency mismatching the practice of borrowing of money in the currency of a country where interest rates are low and depositing it in the currency of a country with higher interest rates. The potential profit from the interest rate margin may be offset by changes in the exchange rates which increase the value of the loan in the company's balance sheet.

currency note a bank note

currency risk the possibility of a loss or gain due to future changes in exchange rates

currency swap 1. an agreement to use a certain currency for payments under a contract in exchange for another currency. The organisations bound by the contract may buy one of the currencies at a more favourable rate than the other. **2.** the buying or selling of a fixed amount of a foreign currency on the *spot market*, and the selling or buying of the same amount of the same currency on the *forward market*

currency unit each of the notes and coins that are the medium of exchange in a country

current account a record of transactions between two parties, for example, between a bank and its customer, or a branch and head office. *Abbr* **c/a**

current account equilibrium a country's economic circumstances when its expenditure equals its income from trade and invisible earnings

current account mortgage a long-term loan, usually for the purchase of a property, in which the borrower pays interest on the sum loaned in monthly instalments and repays the principal in one lump sum at the end of the term. When calculating the interest payments, the lender takes into account the balance in the borrower's current and/or savings accounts. It is the borrower's responsibility to make provisions to accumulate the required capital during the period of the mortgage, usually by contributing to tax efficient investment plans such as Individual Savings Accounts or by relying on an anticipated inheritance. *See also* **mortgage**

current asset cash or other assets, such as stock, debtors, and long-term investments, held for conversion into cash in the normal course of trading

current assets cash or assets that are readily convertible to cash

current assets financing the use of current assets as collateral for a loan

current cash balance the amount, which excludes balances due soon for outstanding transactions, that a client has available for investment with a broker

current cost accounting a method of accounting which notes the cost of replacing assets at current prices, rather than valuing assets at their original cost. *Abbr* **CCA**

current earnings the annual earnings most recently reported by a company

current liabilities liabilities which fall due for payment within one year. They include that part of any long-term loan due for repayment within one year.

current principal factor the portion of the initial amount of a loan that remains to be paid

current purchasing power accounting a method of accounting in which the values of non-monetary items in the historical cost accounts are adjusted, using a general price index, so that the resulting profit allows for the maintenance of the purchasing power of the shareholders' interest in the organisation

current ratio a ratio of *current assets* to *current liabilities*, used to measure a company's liquidity and its ability to meet its short-term debt obligations.

The current ratio formula is a simple one:

Current assets / Current liabilities = Current ratio

Current assets are the ones that a company can turn into cash within 12 months during the ordinary course of business. Current liabilities are bills due to be paid within the coming 12 months.

EXAMPLE For example, if a company's current assets are £300,000 and its current liabilities are £200,000, its current ratio would be:

300,000 / 200,000 = 1.5

As a rule of thumb, the 1.5 figure means that a company should be able to get hold of £1.50 for every £1.00 it owes.

The higher the ratio, the more liquid the company. Prospective lenders expect a positive current ratio, often of at least 1.5. However, too high a ratio is cause for alarm too, because it indicates declining receivables and/or inventory—which may mean declining liquidity.

Also known as **working capital ratio**

current stock value the value of all stock in a portfolio, including stock in transactions that have not yet been settled

current value a ratio indicating the amount by which *current assets* exceed *current liabilities*

current yield the interest being paid on a bond divided by its current market price, expressed as a percentage

cushion money which allows an organisation to pay interest on its borrowings or to survive a loss of some type

cushion bond a bond that pays a high rate of interest but sells at a low premium because of the risk of its being called soon

custodial account (*US*) a bank account opened, normally by a parent or guardian, in the name of a minor who is too young to control it

custodian a *bank* whose principal function is to maintain and grow the assets contained in a trust

customer profitability analysis analysis of the revenue streams and service costs associated with specific customers or customer groups. *Abbr* **CPA**

customs broker a person or company that takes goods through customs for a shipping company

customs declaration a statement showing goods being imported on which duty will have to be paid

customs duty tax paid on goods brought into or taken out of a country

customs formalities a declaration of goods by the shipper and examination of them by the customs authorities

customs union agreement between several countries that goods can travel between them without paying duty while goods from other countries have to pay special duties

cut-off a date and procedure for isolating the flow of cash and goods, stocktaking, and the related documentation, to ensure that all aspects of a transaction are dealt with in the same financial period

cybersales sales made electronically through computers and information systems

cycle time the total time taken from the start of the production of a product or service to its completion. Cycle time includes processing time, move time, wait time, and inspection time, only the first of which creates value.

cyclical stock a stock whose value rises and falls periodically, for example, according to the seasons of the year or economic cycles

cyclical unemployment unemployment, usually temporary, caused by a lack of *aggregate demand*, for example, during a downswing in the business cycle

D

D/A *abbr* deposit account

daily price limit the amount by which the price of an *option* can rise or fall within one trading day

Daimyo bond a Japanese bearer bond that can be cleared through European clearing houses

daisy chaining an illegal financial practice whereby traders create artificial transactions in order to make a particular security appear more active than it is in reality (*slang*)

D&B *abbr* Dun & Bradstreet

data warehouse a database in which information is held not for operational purposes, but to assist in analytical tasks such as the identification of new market segments. Data warehouses provide a repository for historical data and collect, integrate, and organise data from unintegrated application systems. The data stored in a data warehouse almost certainly comes from the operational environment, but is always physically separate from it.

dawn raid a sudden, planned purchase of a large number of a company's shares at the beginning of a day's trading. Up to 15% of a company's shares can be bought in this way, and the purchaser must wait for seven days before buying any more shares. A dawn raid may sometimes be the first step towards a *takeover*.

DAX *abbr* Deutscher Aktienindex: the principal German stock exchange, based in Frankfurt

day order for dollar trading only, an order that is valid only during one trading day

days' sales outstanding *see collection ratio*

day trader somebody who makes trades with very close dates of maturity

day trading the making of trades that have very close dates of maturity

DCF *abbr* discounted cash flow

DCM *abbr* (*S Africa*) Development Capital Market

DD *abbr* **1.** direct debit **2.** due diligence

dead cat bounce a short-term increase in the value of a stock following a precipitous drop in value (*slang*)

dear money money which has to be borrowed at a high interest rate, thus restricting the borrower's expenditure

death benefit money paid to the family of someone who dies in an accident at work

debenture the written acknowledgment of a debt by a company, usually given under its seal, and normally containing provisions as to payment of interest and the terms of repayment of principal. A debenture may be secured on some or all of the assets of the company or its subsidiaries.

debenture bond 1. a certificate showing that a *debenture* has been issued **2.** (*US*) a long-term unsecured loan

debit an entry in accounts which shows an increase in *assets* or expenses or a decrease in liabilities, revenue, or capital. It is entered in the left-hand side of an account in *double-entry bookkeeping*.

debit balance the difference between debits and credits in an account where the value of *debits* is greater

debit card a card issued by a bank or financial institution and accepted by a merchant in payment for a transaction. Unlike the procedure with a *credit* *card*, purchases are deducted from the cardholder's account, as with a cheque, when the transaction takes place.

debit column the left-hand side of an account showing increases in a company's assets or decreases in its liabilities

debit entry an entry on the debit side of an account

debit note a document prepared by a purchaser notifying the seller that the account is being reduced by a stated amount, for example, because of an allowance, return of goods, or cancellation. *Abbr* **D/N**

debits and credits figures entered in a company's accounts to record increases and decreases in *assets*, expenses, liabilities, revenues, or capital

debt 1. an amount of money owed to a person or organisation 2. money borrowed by a person or organisation to finance personal or business activities

debt capacity the extent to which an entity can support and/or obtain loan finance

debt collection agency a business that secures the repayment of debts for third parties on a commission or fee basis

debt counselling a service offering advice and support to individuals who are financially stretched

debt/equity ratio the ratio of what a company owes to the value of all of its outstanding shares

debt factoring the business of buying debts at a discount. A factor collects a company's debts when due, and pays the creditor in advance part of the sum to be collected, thus 'buying' the debt.

debt financing the raising of money by borrowing it

debt forgiveness the writing off of all or part of a nation's debt by a lender

debt instrument any document used or issued for raising money, for example, a bill of exchange, bond, or promissory note

debtnocrat a senior bank official who specialises in lending extremely large sums, for example, to developing nations (*slang*)

debtor a person or entity owing money

debtor days the number of days on average that it takes a company to receive payment for what it sells.

To determine debtor days, divide the cumulative amount of accounts receivable by sales, then multiply by 365.
EXAMPLE If accounts receivable total £600,000 and sales are £9,000,000, the calculation is:

(600,000 / 9,000,000) × 365 = 24.33 days

The company takes 24.33 days on average to collect its debts.

Debtor days is an indication of a company's efficiency in collecting monies owed. Obviously, the lower the number the better. An especially high number is a telltale sign of inefficiency or worse. *See also **creditor days***

debtor nation a country whose foreign debts are larger than money owed to it by other countries

debtors' control strategies used to ensure that borrowers pay back loans on time

debt ratio the debts of a company shown as a percentage of its *equity* plus loan capital

debt rescheduling the renegotiation of debt repayments. Debt rescheduling is necessary when a company can no longer meet its debt payments. It can involve deferring debt payments, deferring payment of interest, or negotiating a new loan. It is usually undertaken as part of turnaround management to avoid business failure. Debt rescheduling is also undertaken in less developed countries that encounter national debt difficulties. Such arrangements are usually overseen by the *International Monetary Fund*.

debt/service ratio the ratio of a country's or company's borrowing to its equity or *venture capital*

decision support system a computer system whose purpose is to aid managers to make unstructured decisions, where the nature of the problem requiring resolution may be unclear. *Abbr* **DSS**

decision tree a pictorial method of showing a sequence of interrelated decisions and their expected outcomes. Decision trees can incorporate both the probabilities and values of expected outcomes, and are used in decision-making.

declaration date (*US*) the date when the directors of a company meet to announce the proposed dividend per share that they recommend be paid

declaration of dividend a formal announcement by a company's directors of the proposed dividend per share that they recommend be paid. It is subsequently put to a shareholders' vote at the company's *annual general meeting*.

declaration of solvency a document, lodged with the Registrar of Companies, that lists the assets and liabilities of a company seeking voluntary liquidation to show that the company is capable of repaying its debts within 12 months

declared value the value of goods as entered on a customs declaration

declining balance method *see accelerated depreciation*

de-diversify to sell off parts of a company or group that are not considered

directly relevant to a corporation's main area of interest

deductible the part of a commercial insurance claim that has to be met by the policyholder rather than the insurance company. A deductible of £500 means that the company pays all but £500 of the claim for loss or damage. *See also excess*

deduction at source a UK term for the collection of taxes from an organisation or individual paying an income rather than from the recipient, for example, from an employer paying wages, a bank paying interest, or a company paying dividends

deed a legal document, most commonly one that details the transfer or sale of a property

deed of arrangement a legal document which sets out the agreement between a insolvent person and his or her *creditors*

deed of assignment a legal document detailing the transfer of property from a *debtor* to a *creditor*

deed of covenant a legal document in which a person or organisation promises to pay a third party a sum of money on an annual basis. In certain countries this arrangement may have tax advantages. For example, in the United Kingdom, it is often used for making regular payments to a charity.

deed of partnership a legal document formalising the agreement and financial arrangements between the parties that make up a partnership

deed of transfer a legal document which attests to the transfer of share ownership

deed of variation in the United Kingdom, an arrangement that allows the will of a deceased person to be amended, provided certain conditions are met and the amendment is signed by all the original beneficiaries

deep-discount bond a bond offered at a large discount on the face value of the debt so that a significant proportion of the return to the investor comes by way of a capital gain on redemption, rather than through interest payments

deep-in-the-money call option a *call option* (*see exercise price*) that has become very profitable and is likely to remain so

deep-in-the-money put option a put option that has become very profitable and is likely to remain so

deep market a commodity, currency, or stock market where such is the volume of trade that a considerable number of transactions will not influence the market price

deep pocket a term used to refer to a company or an individual that provides much-needed funds for another company (*slang*)

defalcation the improper and illegal use of funds by someone who does not own them, but who has been charged with their care

default to fail to comply with the terms of a binding legal agreement, such as a contract. The term is most often used in relation to a failure to pay back a debt, such as a mortgage.

default notice a formal document issued by a lender to a borrower who is in default. *US term notice of default*

defended takeover bid a bid for a company takeover in which the directors of the target company oppose the action of the bidder

defensive stock stock that prospers predictably regardless of external circumstances such as an economic slowdown, for example, the stock of a company that markets a product everyone must have

deferred consideration instalment payments for the acquisition of new subsidiaries usually made in the form of cash and shares, where the balance due after the initial deposit depends on the performance of the business acquired

deferred coupon a *coupon* that pays no interest at first, but pays relatively high interest after a specified date

deferred credit *or* **deferred income** revenue received but not yet reported as income in the profit and loss account, for example, payment for goods to be delivered or services provided at a later date, or government grants received for the purchase of assets. The deferred credit is treated as a credit balance on the balance sheet while waiting to be treated as income. *See also accrual concept*

deferred income *see deferred credit*

deferred month a month relatively late in the term of an option

deferred ordinary share 1. a share, usually held by founding members of a company, often with a higher dividend that is only paid after other shareholders have received their dividends and, in some cases, only when a certain level of profit has been achieved **2.** a share that pays no dividend for a certain number of years after its issue date but that then ranks with the company's ordinary shares

deferred shares a special class of shares ranking for dividend after preference and ordinary shares

deficit *see budget deficit*

deficit financing the borrowing of money because expenditures will exceed receipts

deficit spending government spending financed through borrowing rather than taxation

deflation a reduction in the general level of prices sustained over several months, usually accompanied by declining employment and output

deflationary fiscal policy a government policy that raises taxes and reduces public expenditure in order to reduce the level of *aggregate demand* in the economy

deflationary gap a gap between *GDP* and the potential output of the economy

deflator the amount by which a country's *GDP* is reduced to take into account *inflation*

degearing a reduction in a company's loan capital in relation to the value of its ordinary shares plus reserves. *See also financial leverage*

degressive tax a tax whose payments depend on an individual's salary. Those on smaller salaries pay a lower percentage of their income than those with larger salaries.

delayed settlement processing a procedure for storing authorised transaction settlements online until after the merchant has shipped the goods to the purchaser

del credere agent an agent who agrees to sell goods on commission and pay the principal even if the buyer defaults on payment. To cover the risk of default, the commission is marginally higher than that of a general agent.

delinquent (*US*) used to refer to an individual who or an organisation which is late in paying an account

delist (*US*) to remove a company from the list of companies whose stocks are traded on an exchange

delivery month *see contract month*

delivery note a document containing details of the quantity and specifications of accompanying goods. A signed copy of the delivery note often acts as proof of delivery. An **advice note** contains similar information, but is sent to inform a third party of delivery. *Also known as carrier's note, consignment note, despatch note*

demand forecasting the activity of estimating the quantity of a product or service that consumers will purchase. Demand forecasting involves techniques including both informal methods, such as educated guesses, and quantitative methods, such as the use of historical sales data or current data from test markets. Demand forecasting may be used in making pricing decisions, in assessing future capacity requirements, or in making decisions on whether to enter a new market.

demerge to split up an organisation into a number of separate parts

demonetise to withdraw a coin or note from a country's currency

demurrage compensation paid to a customer when shipment of a good is delayed at a port or by customs

departmental accounts revenue and expenditure statements for departments of an entity. These usually take the form of a trading and profit and loss account for each department, or operating accounts for service departments.

departmental budget *see functional budget*

deposit an amount of money paid into a bank, given as a partial payment, or given as security

deposit account an account which pays interest but on which notice usually has to be given to withdraw money. *Abbr* **D/A**. See *savings account*

depositary a person who or organisation which has placed money or documents for safekeeping with a *depository*

depository a bank or organisation with whom money or documents can be left for safekeeping

deposit protection insurance that depositors have against loss

deposit receipt *see deposit slip*

deposit slip a US term for the slip of paper that accompanies money or cheques being paid into a bank account. *Also called* **deposit receipt**

depreciable cost an expense which may be set against the profits of more than one accounting period

depreciation 1. an allocation of the *cost* of an *asset* over a period of time for accounting and tax purposes. Depreciation is charged against earnings, on the basis that the use of capital assets is a legitimate cost of doing business. Depreciation is also a non-cash expense that is added into net income to determine cash-flow in a given accounting period.

To qualify for depreciation, assets must be items used in the business that wear out, become obsolete, or lose value over time from natural causes or circumstances, and they must have a useful life beyond a single tax year. Examples include vehicles, machines, equipment, furnishings, and buildings, plus major additions or improvements to such assets. Some intangible assets can also be included under certain conditions. Land, personal assets, stock, leased or rented property, and a company's employees cannot be depreciated.

Straight-line depreciation is the most straightforward method. It assumes that the net cost of an asset should be written off in equal amounts over its life. The formula used is:

(Original cost – scrap value) / Useful life (years)

EXAMPLE If a vehicle cost £30,000 and can be expected to serve the business for seven years, its original cost would be divided by its useful life:

(30,000 – 2,000) / 7 = 4,000 per year

The £4,000 becomes a depreciation expense that is reported on the company's year-end income statement under 'operation expenses'.

In theory, an asset should be depreciated over the actual number of years that it will be used, according to its actual drop in value each year. At the end of each year, all the depreciation claimed to date is subtracted from its cost in order to arrive at its **book value**, which would equal its market value. At the end of its useful business life, any undepreciated portion would represent the salvage value for which it could be sold or scrapped.

For tax purposes, some accountants prefer to use **accelerated depreciation** to record larger amounts of depreciation in the asset's early years in order to reduce tax bills as soon as possible. In contrast to the straight-line method, the **declining balance method** assumes that the asset depreciates more in its earlier years of use. The table below compares the depreciation amounts that would be available, under these two methods, for a £1,000 asset that is expected to be used for five years and then sold for £100 as scrap.

Straight-line Method

Year	Annual Depreciation	Year-end Book Value
1	£900 × 20% = £180	£1,000 – £180 = £820
2	£900 × 20% = £180	£820 – £180 = £640
3	£900 × 20% = £180	£640 – £180 = £460
4	£900 × 20% = £180	£460 – £180 = £280
5	£900 × 20% = £180	£280 – £180 = £100

Declining-balance Method

Year	Annual Depreciation	Year-end Book Value
1	£1,000 × 40% = £400	£1,000 – £400 = £600
2	£600 × 40% = £240	£600 – £240 = £360
3	£360 × 40% = £144	£360 – £144 = £216
4	£216 × 40% = £86.40	£216 – £86.40 = £129.60
5	£129.60 × 40% = £51.84	£129.60 – £51.84 = £77.76

The depreciation method to be used for a particular asset is fixed at the time that the asset is first placed in service. Whatever rules or tables are in effect for that year must be followed as long as the asset is owned.

Depreciation laws and regulations change frequently over the years as a result of government policy changes, so a company owning property over a long period may have to use several different depreciation methods.

2. a reduction of a currency's value in relation to the value of other currencies

depression a prolonged slump or downturn in the business cycle, marked by a high level of unemployment

deprival value a basis for asset valuation based on the maximum amount which an organisation would be willing to pay rather than forgo the asset. *Also known as* **value to the business, value to the owner**

derivative a security, such as an option, the price of which has a strong correlation with an underlying financial instrument

Derivative Trading Facility a computer system and associated network operated by the Australian Stock Exchange to facilitate the purchase and sale of exchange-traded options. *Abbr* **DTF**

designated account an account opened and held in one person's name, but which also features another person's name for extra identification purposes

despatch note *see delivery note*

Deutscher Aktienindex *see DAX*

devaluation a reduction in the official fixed rate at which one currency exchanges for another under a fixed-rate regime, usually to correct a balance of payments deficit

developing country a country, often a producer of primary goods such as cotton or rubber, which cannot generate investment income to stimulate growth and which possesses a national income that is vulnerable to change in commodity prices

Development Capital Market (*S Africa*) a sector on the *JSE* Securities Exchange for listing smaller developing companies. Criteria for listing in the Development Capital Market sector are less stringent than for the main board listing. *Abbr* **DCM**

Diagonal Street (*S Africa*) an informal term for the financial centre of Johannesburg or, by extension, South Africa

differential cost the difference in total cost between alternatives, calculated to assist decision-making. *Also known as* **incremental cost**

differential costing a costing method which shows the difference in costs which results from different levels of activity, such as the cost of making one thousand or ten thousand extra units of a product

differential tariff a tariff on goods or services which varies according to their class or source

digital cash an anonymous form of *digital money* that can be linked directly to a bank account or exchanged for physical money. As with physical cash, there is no way to obtain information about the buyer from it, and it can be transferred by the seller to pay for subsequent purchases. *Also known as* **e-cash**

digital certificate 1. an electronic document issued by a recognised authority that validates a purchaser. It is used much as a driving licence or passport is used for identification purposes in a traditional business transaction. **2.** an electronic document from a certifying agent that contains information identifying someone, that person's public key, and other data for electronic transactions

digital coins a form of electronic payment authorised for instant transactions that facilitates the purchase of items priced in small denominations of *digital cash*. Digital coins are transferred from customer to merchant for a transaction such as the purchase of a newspaper using a *smart card* for payment.

digital coupon a voucher or similar form that exists electronically, for example, on a website, and can be used to reduce the price of goods or services

digital economy an economy in which the main productive functions are in electronic commerce, for example, trade on the Internet

digital goods merchandise that is sold and delivered electronically, for example, over the Internet

digital money a series of numbers with an intrinsic value in some physical currency. Online digital money requires electronic interaction with a bank to conduct a transaction; offline digital money does not. Anonymous digital money is synonymous with *digital cash*. Identified digital money carries with it information revealing the identities of those involved in the transaction. *Also known as* **e-money**, **electronic money**

digital timestamp an electronic signal that verifies the time of day at which an electronic order is received or completed

digital wallet 1. software on the hard drive of an online shopper from which the purchaser can pay for the transaction electronically. The wallet can hold in encrypted form such items as credit card information, digital cash or coins, a digital certificate to identify the user, and standardised shipping information.

Also known as **electronic wallet 2.** a collection of digital cash

dilution 1. the reduction in value of shares when additional shares in the company are issued without any increase in the company's assets **2.** a reduction in the earnings and voting power per share caused by an increase or potential increase in the number of shares in issue. For the purpose of calculating diluted earnings per share, the net profit attributable to ordinary shareholders and the weighted average number of shares outstanding should be adjusted for the effects of all dilutive potential ordinary shares.

dilution levy an extra charge levied by fund managers on investors buying or selling units in a fund, to offset any potential effect on the value of the fund of such sales or purchases

dilution of equity a situation in which the ordinary share capital of a company has been increased but without an increase in the assets, with the end result that each share is worth less than before

direct cost a variable cost directly attributable to production. Items that are classed as direct costs include materials used, labour deployed, and marketing budget. Amounts spent will vary with output. *See also* **indirect cost**

direct debit a direct claim on an individual or organisation by a creditor, and paid by the individual's or organisation's bank. Variations in period claims are admissible. *Abbr* **DD**

direct labour cost percentage rate an *overhead absorption rate* based on direct labour cost

direct labour hour rate an *overhead absorption rate* based on direct labour hours

director's dealing the purchase or sale of a company's stock by one of its directors

direct product profitability used primarily within the retail sector, DPP involves the attribution of costs other than the purchase price (for example, distribution, warehousing, retailing) to each product line. Thus a net profit, as opposed to a gross profit, can be identified for each product. The cost attribution process uses a variety of measures (for example, warehousing space or transport time) to reflect the resource consumption of individual products.

direct tax a tax on income or capital that is paid directly rather than added to the price of goods or services

dirty float a floating exchange rate that cannot float freely because a country's central bank intervenes on foreign exchange markets to alter its level

dirty price the price of a debt instrument that includes the amount of accrued interest that has not yet been paid

disbursing agent *see paying agent*

discharged bankrupt a person who has been released from being bankrupt because he or she has paid all outstanding debts

disclosure of shareholding a public announcement of a shareholding in a company. The Stock Exchange must be informed if someone owns or buys 5% of the shares in a listed company.

discount 1. a reduction in the price of goods or services in relation to the standard price. A discount is a selling technique that is used, for example, to encourage customers to buy in large quantities or to make payments in cash. It can also be used to improve sales of a slow-moving line. The greater the purchasing power of the buyer, the greater the discounts that can be negotiated. Some companies inflate original list prices to give the impression that discounts offer value for money; conversely too many genuine discounts

may harm profitability. **2.** the difference between the share price of an investment trust and its *net asset value*

discount allowed the amount by which the seller agrees to reduce his or her price to the customer

discount broker a broker who charges relatively low fees because he or she provides restricted services

discounted bond a bond that is sold for less than its face value because its yield is not as high as that of other bonds

discounted cash flow the discounting of the projected net cash flows of a capital project to ascertain its present value. The methods commonly used are: yield, or *internal rate of return* (IRR), in which the calculation determines the return in the form of a percentage; *net present value* (NPV), in which the discount rate is chosen and the present value is expressed as a sum of money; and discounted payback, in which the discount rate is chosen and the payback is the number of years required to repay the original investment. *See also* *capital investment appraisal*. *Abbr* **DCF**

discounted dividend model a method of calculating a stock's value by reducing future dividends to the present value. *Also known as* *dividend discount model*

discounted value the difference between the face value of a share and its lower market price

discount loan a loan that amounts to less than its face value because payment of interest has been subtracted

discount rate the rate charged by a central bank on any loans it makes to other banks

discount received the amount by which the purchaser receives a reduction in price from the seller

discount security a security that is sold for less than its face value in lieu of bearing interest

discretionary account a securities account in which the broker has the authority to make decisions about buying and selling without the customer's prior permission

discretionary cost a cost whose amount within a time period is determined by, and is easily altered by, a decision taken by the appropriate budget holder. Marketing, research, and training are generally regarded as discretionary costs. Control of discretionary costs is through the budgeting process.

discretionary management an arrangement between a stockbroker and his or her client whereby the stockbroker makes all investment decisions. It is the opposite of an *advisory management* arrangement.

discretionary order a security transaction in which a broker controls the details, such as the time of execution

discretionary trust a trust where the trustees decide how to invest the income and when and how much income should be paid to the beneficiaries

discriminating monopoly a company able to charge different prices for its output in different markets because it has power to influence prices for its goods

diseconomies of scale a situation in which increased production increases, rather than decreases, unit costs

disequilibrium price the price of a good set at a level at which demand and supply are not in balance

dishonour to refuse payment of a cheque because the account for which it is written holds insufficient money. *Also known as **bounce***

disinflation the elimination or reduction of inflation or inflationary pressures in an economy by fiscal or monetary policies

dispensation a legal arrangement between an employer and the Inland Revenue in which business expenses paid to an employee are not declared for tax

disposable income income that is left for spending after tax and other deductions

dispute benefit *see **strike pay***

disqualification a court order which forbids a person from being a director of a company. A variety of offences, even those termed as 'administrative', can result in some being disqualified for up to five years.

distrain to seize *assets* belonging to a person or organisation in order to pay off a debt

distressed property property purchased with the aid of a loan on which repayments have stopped and the borrower has defaulted

distribution cost the cost of warehousing saleable products and delivering them to customers

distributions any income arising from a bond fund or an equity

District Bank one of the 12 banks that make up the *Federal Reserve System*. Each District Bank is responsible for all banking activity in its area.

diversification a strategy to increase the variety of business, service, or product types within an organisation. Diversification can be a growth strategy, taking advantage of market opportunities, or it may be aimed at reducing risk by spreading interests over different areas. It can be achieved through *acquisition* or through internal research and development, and it can involve managing two, a few, or many different areas of interest. Diversification can also be a corporate strategy of investment in acquisitions within a broad portfolio range by a large *holding company*. One distinct type is **horizontal diversification**, which involves expansion into a similar product area, for example, a domestic furniture manufacturer producing office furniture. Another is **vertical diversification**, in which a company moves into a different level of the supply chain, for example, a manufacturing company becoming a retailer. A well-known example of diversification is the move of Bic, the ball-point pen manufacturer, into the production of disposable razors.

diversified investment company a unit trust with a variety of types of investments

diverted hours the available hours of nominally direct workers who are diverted to indirect activities, for example, the cleaning of machines, and are therefore charged as indirect labour. This contrasts with the hours worked by indirect workers, whose entire time is charged as indirect.

divestment proportional or complete reduction in an ownership stake in an organisation

dividend an amount payable to shareholders from profits or other distributable reserves. Dividends are normally paid in cash, but *scrip dividends*, paid by the issue of additional shares, are permissible. Listed companies normally pay two dividends per year, an interim dividend, based on interim profits reported during the accounting period, and a final dividend, based on the final audited accounts and approved at the *Annual General Meeting*.

dividend clawback an agreement that dividends will be reinvested as part of the financing of a project

dividend cover the number of times a company's dividends to ordinary shareholders could be paid out of its net after-tax profits. This measures the likelihood of dividend payments being sustained, and is a useful indication of sustained profitability.

If the figure is 3, a firm's profits are three times the level of the dividend paid to shareholders.

Dividend cover is calculated by dividing earnings per share by the dividend per share:

Earnings per share / dividend per share = dividend cover

EXAMPLE If a company has earnings per share of £8, and it pays out a dividend of 2.1, dividend cover is:

8 / 2.1 = 3.80

An alternative formula divides a company's net profit by the total amount allocated for dividends. So a company that earns £10 million in net profit and allocates £1 million for dividends has a dividend cover of 10, while a company that earns £25 million and pays out £10 million in dividends has a dividend cover of 2.5:

10,000,000 / 1,000,000 = 10 and 25,000,000 / 10,000,000 = 2.5

A dividend cover ratio of 2 or higher is usually adequate, and indicates that the dividend is affordable. A dividend cover ratio below 1.5 is risky, and a ratio below 1 indicates a company is paying the current year's dividend with retained earnings from a previous year: a practice that cannot continue indefinitely. On the other hand, a high dividend cover figure may disappoint an investor looking for income, since the figure suggests directors could have declared a larger dividend. *See also payout ratio*

dividend discount model *see discounted dividend model*

dividend growth model a financial model which can be used to value companies based on assumptions about their current and future dividend payments

dividend limitation a provision in a bond limiting the dividends that may be paid

dividend mandate an authorisation by a shareholder to the company in which he or she has a holding to pay dividends directly into his or her bank account

dividend per share total amounts declared as dividends per share. The dividend per share is actually paid in respect of a financial year. Special rules apply if equity shares are issued during the year.

dividend reinvestment plan a plan that provides for the reinvestment of dividends in the shares of the company paying the dividends. *Abbr* **DRIP**

dividend rights rights to receive dividends

dividends-received deduction a tax advantage on dividends that a company receives from a company it owns

dividend yield dividends expressed as a percentage of a share's price

D/N *abbr* debit note

documentary credit an arrangement, used in the finance of international transactions, whereby a bank undertakes to make a payment to a third party on behalf of a customer

dogs of the Dow (*US*) the stocks in the Dow Jones Industrial Average that pay the smallest dividends as a percentage of their prices (*slang*)

dollar area an area of the world where the US dollar is the main trading currency

dollar cost averaging (*US*) = *pound cost averaging*

dollar roll (*US*) an agreement to sell a stock and buy it later for a specified price

dollars-and-cents (*US*) considering money as the determining factor

domicilium citandi et executandi (*S Africa*) the address where a summons or other official notice should be served if necessary, which must be supplied by somebody applying for credit or entering into a contract

dominant influence influence that can be exercised to achieve the operating and financial policies designed by the holder of the influence, notwithstanding the rights or influence of any other party

dormant account a bank account which is no longer used by the account holder

dormant company a company which has not made any transactions during a specified accounting period

double-entry bookkeeping the most commonly used system of *bookkeeping*, based on the principle that every financial transaction involves the simultaneous receiving and giving of value, and is therefore recorded twice

double indemnity a provision in an insurance policy that guarantees payment of double its face value on the accidental death of the holder

double taxation the taxing of something twice, usually the combination of corporation tax and tax on the dividends that shareholders earn

double taxation agreement an agreement between two countries intended to avoid a situation in which income is subject to taxation in both

double taxation relief a reduction of tax payable in one country by the amount of tax on income, profits, or capital gains already paid in another country

doubtful debts provision an amount charged against profit and deducted from debtors to allow for the estimated non-recovery of a proportion of the debts. *See also* **bad debt**

Dow Jones Averages an index of the prices of selected stocks on the New York Stock Exchange compiled by Dow Jones & Company, Inc

downgrade 1. to reduce the forecast for a **share 2.** to reduce the credit rating for a **bond**

downsizing organisational restructuring involving outsourcing activities, replacing permanent staff with contract employees, and reducing the number of levels within the organisational hierarchy, with the intention of making the organisation more flexible, efficient, and responsive to its environment

Dow Theory the theory that stock market prices can be forecast on the basis of the movements of selected industrial and transport stocks

draft a written order to pay a particular sum from one account to another, or to a person. *See also* **sight draft**, **time draft**

drawee the individual or institution to whom a bill of exchange or cheque is addressed

drawing account an account that permits the tracking of withdrawals

DRIP *see* **dividend reinvestment plan**

drop a bundle to spend or lose a lot of money, especially on the stock market (*slang*)

drop lock the automatic conversion of a debt instrument with a floating rate to one with a fixed rate when interest rates fall to an agreed percentage

DSO *abbr* days' sales outstanding. *See* **collection ratio**

DTF *abbr* (ANZ) Derivative Trading Facility

dual currency bond a bond that pays interest in a currency other than the one used to buy it

dual economy an economy in which the manufacturing and service sectors are growing at different rates

dual pricing a form of transfer pricing in which the two parties to a common transaction use different prices

dual trading the practice of acting as agent for both a broker's firm and its customers

due diligence the examination of a company's accounts prior to a potential *takeover* by another organisation. This assessment is often undertaken by an independent third party. *Abbr* **DD**

due-on-sale clause a provision requiring a homeowner to pay off a mortgage upon sale of the property

dumping the selling of a commodity on a foreign market at a price below its *marginal cost*, either to dispose of a temporary surplus or to achieve a monopoly by eliminating competition

Dun & Bradstreet an international organisation that sources credit information from companies and their creditors which it then makes available to subscribers. *Abbr* **D&B**

duopoly a market in which only two sellers of a good exist. If one decides to alter the price, the other will respond and influence the market's response to the first decision.

Dutch auction an auction in which the lot for sale is offered at an initial price which, if there are no takers, is then reduced until there is a bid

dynamic pricing pricing that changes in line with patterns of demand

dynamic programming an operational research technique used to solve multi-stage problems in which the decisions at one stage are the accepted assumptions applicable to the next stage

E

EAA *abbr* European Accounting Association

e-alliance a partnership forged between organisations in order to achieve business objectives, for enterprises conducted over the Web. There has been a surge in such alliances since the Internet took off in the mid-1990s, and studies show that the most successful have been those involving traditional offline businesses and online entities—the *clicks-and-mortar* strategy—such as that between Amazon.com and Toys 'R' Us. Toys 'R' Us had the physical infrastructure and brand, while Amazon.com had the online infrastructure and experience of making e-commerce work.

E&O *abbr* errors and omissions

E&OE *abbr* errors and omissions excepted

early withdrawal the removal of money from a deposit account before the due date. Early withdrawal often incurs a penalty that the account holder must pay.

earned income money generated by an individual's or an organisation's labour, for example, wages, salaries, fees, royalties, and business profits. *See also **unearned income***

earning potential 1. the amount of money a person should be able to earn in his or her professional capacity **2.** the amount of dividend that a share potentially can produce

earnings 1. a sum of money gained from paid employment, usually quoted before tax, including any extra rewards such as fringe benefits, allowances, or incentives. *Also known as **pay*** **2.** income or profit from a business, quoted gross or net of tax, which may be retained and distributed in part to the shareholders

earnings before interest and taxes *abbr* **EBIT**. *See **operating income***

earnings before interest, tax, depreciation, and amortisation *see **EBITDA***

earnings cap the top limit of earnings which can be used in calculating a retirement pension paid from an occupational pension scheme

earnings credit an allowance which reduces bank charges on checking accounts

earnings per share a financial ratio that measures the portion of a company's profit allocated to each outstanding ordinary share. It is the most basic measure of the value of a share, and also is the basis for calculating several other important investment ratios.

EPS is calculated by subtracting the total value of any preference shares from net income (earnings) for the period in question, then dividing the resulting figure by the number of shares outstanding during that period.

Net income – Dividends on any preference shares / Average number of shares outstanding

Companies usually use a weighted average number of shares outstanding over the reporting period, but shares outstanding can either be 'primary' or 'fully diluted'. Primary EPS is calculated using the number of shares that are currently held by investors in the market and able to be traded. Diluted EPS is the result of a complex calculation that determines how many shares would be outstanding if all exercisable warrants and options were converted into shares at the end of a quarter.

EXAMPLE Suppose that a company has granted a large number of share options to employees. If these options are capable of being exercised in the near future, that could significantly alter the number of shares in issue and thus the

EPS–even though the net income is the same. Often in such cases, the company might quote the EPS on the existing shares and the fully diluted version. *Abbr* **EPS**

earnings-related contributions contributions to social security which rise as the worker's earnings rise

earnings report *(US)* = *published accounts*

earnings retained *see retained profits*

earnings surprise a considerable difference in size between a company's actual and anticipated earnings

earnings yield money earned by a company during a year, expressed as a percentage of the price of one of its shares

earn-out arrangement a procedure whereby owner/managers selling an organisation receive a portion of their consideration linked to the financial performance of the business during a specified period after the sale. The arrangement gives a measure of security to the new owners, who pass some of the financial risk associated with the purchase of a new enterprise to the sellers.

EASDAQ *abbr* European Association of Securities Dealers Automated Quotations: a stock exchange for technology and high-growth companies based in Europe and modelled on **NASDAQ** in the United States. EASDAQ has offices in London and Brussels.

eased used in stock market reports to describe a market that has experienced a slight fall in prices

easy market a market in which fewer people are buying, with the effect that prices are lower than hoped

easy money *see cheap money*

easy money policy a government policy which aims to expand the economy by making money more easily accessible to the public. This is done by strategies such as lowering interest rates and offering easy access to credit.

EBIT *abbr* earnings before interest and taxes

EBITDA *abbr* earnings before interest, tax, depreciation, and amortisation: the earnings generated by a business's fundamental operating performance, frequently used in accounting ratios for comparison with other companies. Interest on borrowings, tax payable on those profits, depreciation, and amortisation are excluded on the basis that they can distort the underlying performance.

It is calculated as follows:

Revenue – Expenses (excluding tax and interest, depreciation, etc) = EBITDA

It is important to note that EBITDA ignores many factors that impact on true cash flow, such as working capital, debt payments, and other fixed expenses. Even so, it may be useful for evaluating firms in the same industry with widely different capital structures, tax rates, and depreciation policies.

EBRD *abbr* European Bank for Reconstruction and Development: the bank, which was established in 1991, developed programmes to tackle a range of issues. These included: the creation and strengthening of infrastructure; industry privatisation; the reform of the financial sector, including the development of capital markets and the privatisation of commercial banks; the development of productive competitive private sectors of small and medium-sized enterprises in industry, agriculture, and services; the restructuring of industrial sectors to put them on a competitive basis; and encouraging foreign investment and cleaning up the environment. The EBRD had 41 original members: the European Commission, the European Investment Bank, all the EEC countries, and all the countries of Eastern Europe except Albania, which finally became a member in October 1991, followed by all the republics of the former USSR in March 1992.

e-business a company that conducts business on the Internet

e-cash *see digital cash*

ECB *abbr* European Central Bank: the financial institution that replaced the European Monetary Institute (EMI) in 1998 and which is responsible for carrying out EU monetary policy and administering the euro

e-commerce the exchange of goods, information products, or services via an electronic medium such as the Internet. Originally limited to buying and selling, it has evolved to include such functions as customer service, marketing, and advertising. *Also known as electronic commerce, web commerce*

econometric model a way of representing the relationship between economic variables as an equation or set of equations with statistically precise parameters linking the variables

econometrics the branch of *economics* concerned with using mathematical models to describe relationships in an economy, for example, between wage rates and levels of employment

Economic and Monetary Union *see EMU*

economic assumption an assumption built into an economic model, for example, that output will grow at 2.5% in the next tax year

Economic Development Board an organisation established in 1961 that aims to promote investment in Singapore by providing various services and assistance schemes to foreign and local companies. *Abbr* **EDB**

economic goods services or physical objects that can command a price in the market

economic growth an increase in the national income of a country created by the long-term productive potential of its economy

economic indicator a statistic that may be important for a country's long-term economic health, for example, rising prices or falling exports

economic life the conditions of trade and manufacture in a country that contribute to its prosperity or poverty

economic miracle the rapid growth after 1945 in countries such as Germany and Japan, where in ten years economies shattered by the Second World War were regenerated

economic order quantity the most economic stock replenishment order size, which minimises the sum of stock ordering costs and stockholding costs. EOQ is used in an 'optimising' stock control system. *Abbr* **EOQ**

economic paradigm a basic unchanging economic principle

Economic Planning and Advisory Council a committee of businesspeople and politicians appointed to advise the Australian government on economic issues

economic pressure a condition in a country's economy in which economic indicators are unfavourable

economics the study of the consumption, distribution, and production of wealth in a society

economic sanctions restrictions on trade with a country in order to influence its political situation or to make its government change its policy

economic surplus the difference between an economy's output and the costs incurred, for example, wages, raw material costs, and depreciation

economic theory of the firm the theory that states that the only duty that a company has to those external to it is financial. The economic theory of the firm holds that shareholders should be the prime beneficiaries of an organisation's activities. The theory is associated with top-down leadership and *cost-cutting* through rationalisation and *downsizing*. With immediate share price dominating management activities, economic theory has been criticised as being too short term, as opposed to the longer-term thinking behind *stakeholder theory*.

economic value added a way of judging financial performance by measuring the amount by which the earnings of a project, an operation, or a company exceed or fall short of the total amount of capital that was originally invested by its owners.

EVA is conceptually simple: from net operating profit, subtract an appropriate charge for the opportunity cost of all capital invested in an enterprise—the amount that could have been invested elsewhere. It is calculated using this formula:

Net operating profit less applicable taxes – Cost of capital = EVA

EXAMPLE If a company is considering building a new plant, and its total weighted cost over ten years is £80 million, while the expected annual incremental return on the new operation is £10 million, or £100 million over ten years, then the plant's EVA would be positive, in this case £20 million:

£100 million – £80 million = £20 million

An alternative but more complex formula for EVA is:

(% Return on invested capital – % Cost of capital) × original capital invested = EVA

EVA is frequently linked with shareholder value analysis, and an objective of EVA is to determine which business units best utilise their assets to generate returns and maximise shareholder value; it can be used to assess a company, a business unit, a single plant, office, or even an assembly line. This same technique is equally helpful in evaluating new business opportunities. *Abbr* **EVA**

economic welfare the level of prosperity in an economy, as measured by employment and wage levels

economies of scale reductions in unit average costs caused by increasing the scale of production

economies of scope reductions in unit average costs caused by the simultaneous production of a number of related products, permitting benefits such as the sharing of joint costs over a larger volume than would otherwise be possible

economist somebody who studies the consumption, distribution, and production of wealth in a society

economy the distribution of wealth in a society and the means by which that wealth is produced and consumed

economy efficiency principle the principle that if an economy is efficient, no one can be made better off without somebody else being made worse off

ecopreneur an entrepreneur who is concerned with environmental issues

EDB *abbr* Economic Development Board

e-economy an economy that is characterised by extensive use of the Internet and information technology

effective annual interest rate *see* *APR*

effective annual rate the average interest rate paid on a deposit for a period of a year. It is the total interest received over 12 months expressed as a percentage of the principal at the beginning of the period.

effective date the date when an action, such as an issuance of new stock, is effective

effectiveness the utilisation of resources such that the output of the activity achieves the desired result

effective price the price of a share adjusted to take into account the effects of a rights issue. *See also rights issue*

effective spread the difference between the price of a newly issued share and what the underwriter pays, adjusted for the effect of the announcement of the offering

effective strike price the price of an option at a specified time, adjusted for fluctuation since the initial offering

effective tax rate the average tax rate applicable to a given transaction, whether it is income from work undertaken, the sale of an asset, or a gift, taking into account personal allowances and scales of tax. It is the amount of money generated by the transaction divided by the additional tax payable because of it.

effective yield *see gross yield to redemption*

efficiency the achievement of goals in an economical way. Efficiency involves seeking a good balance between economy in terms of resources such as time, money, space, or materials, and the achievement of an organisation's aims and objectives. A distinction is often made between technical and economic efficiency. **Technical efficiency** means producing maximum output with a minimum input, while economic efficiency means the production and distribution of goods at the lowest possible cost. In management, a further distinction is often made between efficiency and effectiveness, with the latter denoting performance in terms of achieving objectives.

efficiency ratio a way of measuring the proportion of operating revenues spent on overhead expenses.

Often identified with banking and financial sectors, the efficiency ratio indicates a management's ability to keep overhead costs low. In banking, an acceptable efficiency ratio was once in the low 60s. Now the goal is 50, while better performing banks boast ratios in the mid-40s. Low ratings usually indicate a higher return on equity and earnings.

This measurement is also used by mature industries, such as steel manufacture, chemicals, or car production, that must focus on tight cost controls to boost profitability because growth prospects are modest.

The efficiency ratio is defined as operating overhead expenses divided by turnover.

EXAMPLE If operating expenses are £100,000, and turnover is £230,000, then:

100,000 / 230,000 = 0.43 efficiency ratio

However, not everyone calculates the ratio in the same way. Some institutions include all non-interest expenses, while others exclude certain charges and intangible asset amortisation.

A different method measures efficiency simply by tracking three other measures: accounts payable to sales, days' sales outstanding, and stock turnover. This indicates how fast a company is able to move its merchandise. A general guide is that if the first two of these measures are low and the third is high, efficiency is probably high; the reverse is likewise true.

To find the stock turnover ratio, divide total sales by total stock.

If net sales are £300,000, and stock is £140,000, then:

300,000 / 140,000 = 2.14 stock turnover ratio

To find the accounts payable to sales ratio, divide a company's accounts payable by its annual net sales. A high ratio suggests that a company is using its suppliers' funds as a source of cheap financing because it is not operating efficiently enough to generate its own funds.

If accounts payable are £50,000, and total sales are £300,000, then:

50,000 / 300,000 = 0.16 × 100 = 16%
accounts payable to sales ratio

efficiency variance the difference between the standard cost of making a product and actual costs of production. A separate variance can be calculated for materials, labour, and overheads.

efficient capital market a market in which share prices reflect all the information available to the market about future economic trends and company profitability

efficient markets hypothesis the hypothesis that the stock market responds immediately to all available information, with the effect that an individual investor cannot, in the long run, expect to obtain greater than average returns from a diversified portfolio of shares. There are three forms: the weak form, a market in which security prices instantaneously reflect all information on past price and volume changes in the market; the semi-strong form, a market in which security prices reflect all publicly available information; and the strong form, a market in which security prices reflect instantaneously all information available to investors, whether publicly available or otherwise. *Abbr* **EMH**

EFT *abbr* electronic funds transfer

EIB *abbr* European Investment Bank: a financial institution whose main task is to further regional development within the EU by financing capital projects, modernising or converting undertakings, and developing new activities

either-way market a currency market with identical prices for buying and selling, especially for the euro

elasticity the measure of the sensitivity of one variable to another.
  In practical terms, elasticity indicates the degree to which consumers respond to changes in price. It is obviously important for companies to consider such relationships when contemplating changes in price, demand, and supply.

Demand elasticity measures how much the quantity demanded by a customer changes when the price of a product or service is increased or lowered. This measurement helps companies to find out whether demand will remain constant despite price changes. Supply elasticity measures the impact on supply when a price is changed.
  The general formula for elasticity is:

Elasticity = % change in x / % change in y

In theory, x and y can be any variable. However, the most common application measures price and demand.
EXAMPLE If the price of a product is increased from £20 to £25, or 25%, and demand in turn falls from 6,000 to 3,000, elasticity would be calculated as:

−50% / 25% = −2

A value greater than 1 means that demand is strongly sensitive to price, while a value of less than 1 means that demand is not price-sensitive.

electronic cheque a payment system in which fund transfers are made electronically from the buyer's current account to the seller's bank account. *US term* ***electronic check***

electronic commerce *see* ***e-commerce***

electronic funds transfer 1. a payment system that processes financial transactions between two or more parties or institutions **2.** the system used by banking organisations for the movement of funds between accounts and for the provision of services to the customer. *Abbr* **EFT**

electronic funds transfer at point of sale the payment for goods or services by a bank customer using a card that is swiped through an electronic reader on the till, thereby transferring the cash from the customer's account to the retailer's or service provider's account

electronic money *see* ***digital money***

electronic payment system a means of making payments over an electronic network such as the Internet

electronic retailer *see e-retailer*

electronic shopping the process of selecting, ordering, and paying for goods or services over an electronic network such as the Internet. *Also known as online shopping*

electronic trading the buying and selling of investment instruments using computers

electronic wallet *see digital wallet*

elements of cost the constituent parts of costs according to the factors upon which expenditure is incurred, namely, material, labour, and expenses

elephant a very large financial institution, such as a bank, which makes trades in high volumes, thereby increasing prices (*slang*)

eligible paper 1. in the United Kingdom, bills of exchange or securities accepted by the Bank of England as security for loans to discount houses **2.** in the United States, first-class paper (such as a bill of exchange or a cheque) acceptable for rediscounting by the Federal Reserve System. *See also lender of last resort*

eligible reserves the sum of the cash held by a US bank plus the money it holds at its local Federal Reserve Bank

Eligible Termination Payment a sum paid to an employee when he or she leaves a company, that can be transferred to a concessionally taxed investment account, such as an Approved Deposit Fund. *Abbr* **ETP**

embargo a government order which stops a type of trade, such as exports to, or imports from, a specified country

embedded option an option that is included in a bond

embezzlement the illegal practice of using money entrusted to an individual's care by a third party for personal benefit

emergency credit credit given by the US Federal Reserve to an organisation which has no other means of borrowing capital

emerging market a country that is becoming industrialised

EMH *abbr* efficient markets hypothesis

emoluments wages, salaries, fees, or any other monetary benefit derived from employment

e-money *see digital money*

employee share scheme a plan to give, or encourage employees to buy, a stake in the company that employs them by awarding free or discounted shares. Employee share schemes may be available to some or all employees, and schemes approved by the Inland Revenue enjoy tax advantages. Types of scheme include employee share ownership plans, *share options*, *save as you earn*, and employee share ownership trusts. Among the potential benefits are improved employee commitment and productivity, but the success of a scheme may depend on linking it to employee performance and the performance of the share price.

employee stock fund in the United States, a fund from which money is taken to buy shares of a company's stock for its employees

employee stock ownership plan a plan conforming to US tax law for the company-assisted purchase of a company's stock by its employees. *Abbr* **ESOP**

employer's contribution money paid by an employer towards a worker's pension

EMS *abbr* European Monetary System: the first stage of economic and monetary union of the EU, which came into force in March 1979, giving stable, but adjustable, exchange rates

EMU *abbr* Economic and Monetary Union, or European Monetary Union: the timetable for EMU was outlined in the Maastricht Treaty in 1991. The criteria were that national debt must not exceed 60% of GDP; budget deficit should be 3% or less of GDP; inflation should be no more than 1.5% above the average rate of the three best-performing economies of the EU in the previous 12 months; and applicants must have been members of the **ERM** for two years without having re-aligned or devalued their currency.

encash to exchange a cheque for cash

encumbrance a liability, such as a mortgage or charge, which is attached to a property or piece of land

endorse to sign a bill or cheque on the back to show that its ownership is being passed to another person or company

endowment assurance life cover that pays a specific sum of money on a specified date, or earlier in the event of the policyholder's death. Part of the premium paid is for the life cover element, while the remainder is invested in property and stocks and shares (either a 'with-profits' or 'without-profits' policy) or, in the case of a unit-linked policy, is used to purchase units in a life fund. The sum the policyholder receives at the end of the term depends on the size of the premiums and the performance of the investments. *See also* **term assurance**

endowment fund a unit trust that supports a non-profit institution

endowment mortgage a long-term loan, usually for the purchase of a property, in which the borrower makes two monthly payments, one to the lender to cover the interest on the loan, and the other as a premium paid into an endowment assurance policy. At the end of the loan's term, the proceeds from the endowment policy are used to repay the principal. *See also* **mortgage**

endowment policy an insurance policy that pays a set amount to the policyholder when the policy matures, or to a beneficiary if the policyholder dies before it matures

engagement letter a letter, usually required by an accounting body's professional standards, sent by an accountant to a client setting out the work the accountant is to do and further administrative matters, such as any limit on the accountant's liability

engineered cost a cost which varies in proportion to a measure of activity. Direct materials and royalty payments are engineered costs. Control is through flexible budgeting or standard costing.

entail a legal condition which passes ownership of a property only to specified persons

enterprise investment scheme a UK scheme to promote investment in unquoted companies which allows qualifying gains to be exempt from capital gains tax

enterprise zone an area in which the government offers financial incentives, such as tax relief, to encourage new business activities. *Abbr* **EZ**

entertainment expenses costs, reimbursable by an employer, that are incurred by an employee in hosting social events for clients or suppliers in order to obtain or maintain their custom or goodwill

entitlement offer an offer that cannot be transferred to anyone else

entity an economic unit that has a separate, distinct identity, for example, an industrial or commercial company, charity, or fund

entrapment restrictions placed on an organisation due to the limitations of its existing resource base and management competencies, which prevent it from responding to changes in its environment

entrepreneur somebody who sets up a business or enterprise. An entrepreneur typically demonstrates effective application of a number of enterprising attributes such as creativity, initiative, risk-taking, problem-solving ability, and autonomy, and will often risk his or her own capital to set up a business.

environmental impact assessment a study, undertaken during the planning phase before an investment is made or an operation started, to consider any potential environmental effects

EOQ *abbr* economic order quantity

EPAC *abbr* (*ANZ*) Economic Planning and Advisory Council

equal pay the principle and practice of paying men and women in the same organisation at the same rate for like work, or work that is rated as of equal value. Work is assessed either through an organisation's job evaluation scheme or by the judgment of an independent expert appointed by an industrial tribunal. Although many countries have legislation on equal pay, a gap still exists between men's pay and women's pay and is attributed to sexual discrimination in job evaluation and payment systems.

equilibrium price the price at which the supply of and the demand for a good are equal. Suppliers increase prices when demand is high and reduce prices when demand is low.

equilibrium quantity the quantity that regulates supply and demand. Suppliers increase quantity when demand is high and reduce quantity when demand is low.

equilibrium rate of interest the rate at which the expected interest rate in a market equals the actual rate prevailing

equipment trust certificate a bond sold for a 20% down payment and collateralised by the equipment purchased with its proceeds

equity the issued ordinary share capital plus reserves, statutory and otherwise, which represent the investment in a company by the ordinary *shareholders*

equity capital the amount of a company's capital owned by the *shareholders*

equity claim a claim on earnings that remain after debts are satisfied

equity contribution agreement an agreement to provide equity under specified circumstances

equity dilution the reduction in the percentage of a company represented by each share for an existing shareholder who has not increased his or her holding in the issue of new ordinary shares

equity dividend cover an accounting ratio, calculated by dividing the distributable profits during a given period by the actual dividend paid in that period, that indicates the likelihood of the dividend being maintained in future years. *See also* **capital reserves**

equity financing an investment that combines a life insurance policy and a unit trust

equity floor an agreement for one party to pay another whenever some indicator of a stock market's value falls below a specified limit

equity gearing the ratio between a company's borrowings and its *equity*

equity multiplier (*US*) a measure of a company's worth, expressed as a multiple of each dollar of its stock's price

equity share capital a company's issued share capital less capital which carries preferential rights. Equity share capital normally comprises ordinary shares.

equity sweetener an incentive to encourage people to lend a company money. The sweetener takes the form of a warrant that gives the lender the right to buy shares at a later date and at a specified price.

equivalent annual cash flow the value of an annuity required to provide an investor with the same return as some other form of investment

equivalent bond yield *see bond equivalent yield*

equivalent taxable yield the value of a taxable investment required to provide an investor with the same return as some other form of investment

equivalent units notional whole units representing uncompleted work. They are used to apportion costs between work in progress and completed output, and in performance assessment.

e-retailer a business that uses an electronic network such as the Internet to sell its goods or services. *Also known as electronic retailer, e-tailer*

erf (*S Africa*) a plot of rural or urban land, usually no larger than a small-holding

ERM *abbr* Exchange Rate Mechanism: a system to maintain exchange rate stability used in the past by member states of the European Community

ERR *abbr* expected rate of return

error account an account for the temporary placement of funds involved in a financial transaction known to have been executed in error

error rate the number of mistakes per thousand entries or per page

errors and omissions mistakes from incorrect record-keeping or accounting. *Abbr* **E&O**

ESC *abbr* European Social Charter: a charter adopted by the European Council of the EU in 1989. The 12 rights it contains are: freedom of movement, employment, and remuneration; social protection; improvement of living and working conditions; freedom of association and collective bargaining; worker information; consultation and participation; vocational training; equal treatment of men and women; health and safety protection in the workplace; pension rights; integration of those with disabilities; protection of young people.

escalator clause a clause in a contract which allows for regular price increases for a product or service to cover projected cost increases

escrow an agreement between two parties which holds that something, such as a good, document, or amount of money, should be held for safekeeping by a third party until certain conditions are fulfilled

escrow account an account where money is held in *escrow* until certain conditions are met, for example, a contract is signed, or a consignment of goods safely delivered

essential industry an industry regarded as crucial to a country's economy and often supported financially by a government by way of tariff protection and tax breaks

establishment fee *see commitment fee*

estate 1. a substantial area of land that normally includes a large house such as a stately home **2.** a deceased person's net assets

estimate 1. an approximate calculation of an uncertain value. An estimate may be a reasonable guess based on knowledge and experience or it may be calculated using more sophisticated techniques designed to forecast projected costs, profits, losses, or value. **2.** an approximate price quoted for work to be undertaken by a business

estoppel a rule of evidence whereby someone is prevented from denying or asserting a fact in legal proceedings

e-tailer *see e-retailer*

e-tailing the practice of doing business over an electronic network such as the Internet

ethical fund a fund which invests in companies that follow certain moral standards, for example, companies which do not manufacture weapons, do not trade with certain countries, or only use environmentally acceptable sources of raw materials

ethical index an index of shares in companies that follow certain moral standards

ethical investment investment only in companies whose policies meet the ethical criteria of the investor. *Also known as* **socially-conscious investing**

Ethical Investment Research Service an organisation which does research into companies and recommends those which follow certain ethical standards

ETP *abbr* Eligible Termination Payment

EU *abbr* European Union: a social, economic, and political organisation of European countries whose aim is integration for all member nations. It has been so called since November 1993 under the Maastricht Treaty, before which it was known as the European Community (EC), and before that as the European Economic Community. *Also called* **single market**

EUREX *abbr* Eureka Research Expert System: EUREX was established by Eureka (European Research and Co-ordination Agency) in 1985 on a French initiative for non-military industrial research in advanced technologies in Europe

euro the currency of 12 member nations of the European Union. The euro was introduced in 1999, when the first 11 countries to adopt it joined together in an Economic and Monetary Union and fixed their currencies' exchange rate to the euro. Notes and coins were brought into general circulation in January 2002, although banks and other financial institutions had before that time carried out transactions in euros.

Eurobank a US bank that handles transactions in foreign European currencies

Eurobond a bond specified in the currency of one country and sold to investors from another country. *Also known as* **global bond**

Euro-commercial paper short-term uncollateralised loans obtained by companies in foreign countries

Eurocredit intermediate-term notes used by banks to lend money to governments and companies

Eurocurrency money deposited in one country but denominated in the currency of another country

Eurodeposit a short-term deposit of Eurocurrency

Eurodollar a US dollar deposited in a European bank or other bank outside the United States

Euroequity issue a note issued by banks in several countries

Euroland the area of Europe comprising those countries that have adopted the euro

Euro-note a note in the Eurocurrency market

European Accounting Association an organisation for accounting academics. Founded in 1977 and based in

Brussels, the EAA aims to be a forum for European research in the subject. It holds an annual congress and since 1992 has published a journal, *European Accounting Review*. *Abbr* **EAA**

European Association of Securities Dealers Automated Quotations *see EASDAQ*

European Bank for Reconstruction and Development *see EBRD*

European Central Bank *see ECB*

European Economic Community *or* **European Community** *see EU*

European Investment Bank *see EIB*

European Monetary System *see EMS*

European Monetary Union *see EMU*

European option an option that the buyer can exercise only on the day that it expires. *See also* **American option**

European Social Charter *see ESC*

European-style option *see European option*

European Union *see EU*

Euroyen bond a Eurobond denominated in yen

EVA *abbr* economic value added

evergreen loan a series of loans providing a continuing stream of capital for a project

ex 'without', as in *ex dividend*, where security purchases do not include rights to the next dividend payment, and *ex-rights*, where rights attaching to share ownership, such as a scrip issue, are not transferred to a new purchaser

ex-all having no right in any transaction that is pending with respect to shares, such as a split, or the issue of dividends

ex ante before the event. An ex ante budget, or standard, is set before a period of activity commences, and is based on the best information available at that time on expected levels of cost, performance, etc.

excess 1. the part of an insurance claim that has to be met by the policyholder rather than the insurance company. An excess of £50 means that the company pays all but £50 of the claim for loss or damage. *See also* **deductible 2.** in a financial institution, the amount by which assets exceed liabilities

excess liquidity cash held by a bank above the normal requirement for that bank

excess profits tax a tax levied by a government on a company that makes extraordinarily large profits in times of unusual circumstances, for example, during a war. An excess profits tax was imposed in both the United States and the United Kingdom during the Second World War.

excess reserves reserves held by a financial institution that are higher than those required by the regulatory authorities. As such reserves may indicate that demand for loans is low, banks often sell their excess reserves to other institutions.

exchange¹ 1. the conversion of one type of security for another, for example, the exchange of a bond for shares **2.** a *market* where goods, services, or financial instruments are bought and sold

exchange² 1. to trade one currency for another **2.** to barter

exchange controls the regulations by which a country's banking system controls its residents' or resident companies' dealings in foreign currencies and gold

exchange equalisation account the Bank of England account that sells and buys sterling for gold and foreign currencies to smooth out fluctuations in the exchange rate of the pound

exchange offer an offer to trade one security for another

exchange rate the rate at which one country's currency can be exchanged for that of another country

Exchange Rate Mechanism *see ERM*

exchange rate parity the relationship between the value of one currency and another

exchange rate risk the risk of suffering loss on converting another currency to the currency of a company's own country.

Exchange rate risks can be arranged into three primary categories. (1.) Economic exposure: operating costs will rise due to changes in rates and make a product uncompetitive in the world market. Little can be done to reduce this routine business risk that every enterprise must endure. (2.) Translation exposure: the impact of currency exchange rates will reduce a company's earnings and weaken its balance sheet. To reduce translation exposure, experienced corporate fund managers use a range of techniques known as *currency hedging*. (3.) Transaction exposure: there will be an unfavourable move in a specific currency between the time when a contract is agreed and the time it is completed, or between the time when a lending or borrowing is initiated and the time the funds are repaid. Transaction exposure can be eased by *factoring*: transferring title to foreign accounts receivable to a third-party factoring house.

Although there is no definitive way of forecasting exchange rates, largely because the world's economies and financial markets are evolving so rapidly, the relationships between exchange rates, interest rates, and inflation rates can serve as leading indicators of changes in risk. These relationships are as follows. Purchasing Power Parity theory (PPP): while it can

be expressed differently, the most common expression links the changes in exchange rates to those in relative price indices in two countries:

Rate of change of exchange rate = Difference in inflation rates

International Fisher Effect (IFE): this holds that an interest-rate differential will exist only if the exchange rate is expected to change in such a way that the advantage of the higher interest rate is offset by the loss on the foreign exchange transactions. Practically speaking, the IFE implies that while an investor in a low-interest country can convert funds into the currency of a high-interest country and earn a higher rate, the gain (the interest-rate differential) will be offset by the expected loss due to foreign exchange rate changes. The relationship is stated as:

Expected rate of change of the exchange rate = Interest-rate differential

Unbiased Forward Rate Theory: this holds that the forward exchange rate is the best unbiased estimate of the expected future spot exchange rate.

Expected exchange rate = Forward exchange rate

exchange rate spread the difference between the price at which a broker or other intermediary buys and sells foreign currency

Exchequer in the United Kingdom, the government's account at the Bank of England into which all revenues from taxes and other sources are paid

Exchequer stocks UK government stocks used to finance government expenditure

excise duty a tax on goods such as alcohol or tobacco produced and sold within a particular country

excise licence a licence issued (against payment) to allow someone to trade in products which are subject to excise duty, such as making wine

exclusive economic zone a zone in a country in which particular economic conditions apply. The Special Economic Zone (SEZ) in China, where trade is conducted free of state control, is an example.

ex dividend used to refer to bonds or shares which, when they are sold, do not provide the buyer with the right to a dividend

execution only used to describe a stock market transaction undertaken by an intermediary who acts on behalf of a client without providing advice. *See also active fund management, discretionary management*

executive pension plan in the United Kingdom, a pension scheme for senior executives of a company. The company's contributions are a tax-deductible expense but are subject to a cap. The plan does not prevent the executive being a member of the company's group pension scheme although the executive's total contributions must not exceed a certain percentage of his or her salary.

executive share option scheme a UK term for an arrangement whereby certain directors and employees are given the opportunity to purchase shares in the company at a fixed price at a future date. In certain jurisdictions, such schemes can be tax efficient if certain local tax authority conditions are met.

executor a person appointed under a will to ensure the deceased's estate is distributed according to the terms of the will

exempt gift a gift that is not subject to US gift tax

exempt investment fund in the United Kingdom, a collective investment, usually a unit trust, for investors who have certain tax privileges, for example, charities or contributors to pension plans

exemption an amount per family member that an individual can subtract when reporting income to be taxed

exempt purchaser an institutional investor who may buy newly issued securities without filing a prospectus with a securities commission

exempt security a security that is not subject to a provision of law such as margin or registration requirements

exempt supply an item or service on which VAT is not levied, for example, the purchase of, or rent on, property and financial services

exercise notice an option-holder's notification to the option's writer of his or her desire to exercise the option

exercise of warrants the use of a warrant to purchase stock

exercise price the price at which an option to purchase or to sell shares or other items, such as **call options** or *put options*, may be exercised

exercise value the amount of profit that can be realised by cashing in an option

ex gratia as an act of favour, without obligation

Eximbank *abbr* Export-Import Bank: a US bank founded in 1934 that provides loans direct to foreign importers of US goods and services

exit charge a charge sometimes made by a trust when selling units in a unit trust or when selling out of a PEP

exit P/E ratio the *price/earnings ratio* when a company changes hands

expected rate of return the projected percentage return on an investment, based on the weighted probability of all possible rates of return.

It is calculated by the following formula:

$$E[r] = \Sigma sP(s)rs$$

where E[r] is the expected return, P(s) is the probability that the rate rs occurs, and rs is the return at s level.

EXAMPLE The following example illustrates the principle which the formula expresses.

The current price of ABC Ltd stock is trading at £10. At the end of the year, ABC shares are projected to be traded:

25% higher if economic growth exceeds expectations—a probability of 30%

12% higher if economic growth equals expectations—a probability of 50%

5% lower if economic growth falls short of expectations—a probability of 20%

To find the expected rate of return, simply multiply the percentages by their respective probabilities and add the results:

$$(30\% \times 25\%) + (50\% \times 12\%) + (25\% \times -5\%) = 7.5 + 6 + -1.25 = 12.25\% \text{ ERR}$$

A second example:

if economic growth remains robust (a 20% probability), investments will return 25%

if economic growth ebbs, but still performs adequately (a 40% probability), investments will return 15%

if economic growth slows significantly (a 30% probability), investments will return 5%

if the economy declines outright (a 10% probability), investments will return 0%

Therefore:

$$(20\% \times 25\%) + (40\% \times 15\%) + (30\% \times 5\%) + (10\% \times 0\%) = 5\% + 6\% + 1.5\% + 0\% = 12.5\% \text{ ERR.}$$

Abbr **ERR**. *See also* **capital asset pricing model**

expected return the average profit that can be expected from a risky investment, expressed as a percentage

expected value the financial forecast of the outcome of a course of action multiplied by the probability of achieving that outcome. The probability is expressed as a value ranging from 0 to 1.

expenditure switching government action to divert domestic spending from one sector to another, for example, from imports to home-produced goods

expense 1. a cost incurred in buying goods or services **2.** a charge against a company's profit

expense account money which businesspeople are allowed by their companies to spend on travelling and entertaining clients in connection with business

expenses personal costs incurred by an employee in carrying out activities for an organisation that are reimbursed by the employer

exploding bonus a bonus offered to recent graduates that encourages them to sign for a job as quickly as possible as it reduces in value with every day of delay (*slang*)

exponent the number indicating the power to which a base number is to be raised

Export-Import Bank *see Eximbank*

export-led growth growth in which a country's main source of income is from its export trade

ex post after the event. An ex post budget, or standard, is set after the end of a period of activity, when it can represent the optimum achievable level of performance in the conditions which were experienced. Thus the budget can be flexed, and standards can reflect factors such as unanticipated changes in technology and in price levels. This approach may be used in conjunction with sophisticated cost and revenue modelling to determine how far both the plan and the achieved results differed from the performance that would have been expected in the circumstances which were experienced.

ex-rights for sale without rights, for example, voting or conversion rights.

The term can be applied to transactions such as the purchase of new shares.

ex-rights date the date when a stock first trades ex-rights

extendable bond a bond whose maturity can be delayed by either the issuer or the holder

extendable note a note whose maturity can be delayed by either the issuer or the holder

extended fund facility a credit facility of the *IMF* that allows a country up to eight years to repay money it has borrowed from the Fund

Extensible Business Reporting Language *abbr* XBRL

external account an account held at a United Kingdom-based bank by a customer who is an overseas resident

external audit a periodic examination of the books of account and records of an entity conducted by an independent third party (an auditor) to ensure that they have been properly maintained, are accurate and comply with established concepts, principles, and accounting standards, and give a true and fair view of the financial state of the entity. *See also* **internal audit**

external debt the part of a country's debt that is owed to creditors who are not residents of the country

external finance money that a company obtains from investors, for example, by loans or by issuing stock

external funds money that a business obtains from a third party rather than from its own resources

external growth business growth as a result of a merger, a takeover, or through a partnership with another organisation

extraordinary item an *item* included in a company's accounts that is not likely to occur again, such as an acquisition or a sale of assets. These items are not taken into account when a company's operating profit is calculated.

extraordinary resolution in the United Kingdom, an exceptional issue that is put to the vote at a company's general meeting, for example, a change to the company's articles of association. *Also known as* **special resolution**

EZ *abbr* enterprise zone

F

face value the value written on a financial instrument

facility-sustaining activities activities undertaken to support the organisation as a whole, which cannot be logically linked to individual units of output. *Accounting* is a facility-sustaining activity. *See also* **hierarchy of activities**

factored goods goods purchased for resale

factoring the sale of debts to a third party (the factor) at a discount, in return for prompt cash. A factoring service may be with recourse, in which case the supplier takes the risk of the debt not being paid, or without recourse when the factor takes the risk. *See also* **invoice discounting**

factor market a market in which factors of production are bought and sold, for example, the capital market or the labour market

fair value the amount for which an *asset* (or liability) could be exchanged in an arm's length transaction between informed and willing parties, other than in a forced or liquidation sale

fallen angel a stock that was once very desirable but has now dropped in value (*slang*)

falling knife a share whose price has fallen at an alarming rate over a short time period

false accounting the criminal offence of changing, destroying, or hiding accounting records for a dishonest purpose, such as to gain money

false market a market in shares caused by persons or companies conspiring to buy or sell and so influence the share price to their advantage

Fannie Mae (*US*) *see FNMA*

far month the latest month for which there is a futures contract for a particular commodity. *See also* **nearby month**

FASB *abbr* (*US*) Financial Accounting Standards Board: a body responsible for establishing the standards of financial reporting and accounting for US companies in the private sector. The Securities and Exchange Commission (SEC) performs a comparable role for public companies.

FASTER a computer-based clearing, settlement, registration, and information system operated by the New Zealand Stock Exchange. *Abbr of* **Fully Automated Screen Trading and Electronic Registration**

fat cat a derogatory term used to describe a chief executive of a large company or organisation who secures extremely large pay, pension, and termination packages, often causing concern among shareholders

FCA *abbr* Fellow of the Institute of Chartered Accountants in England and Wales

FCCA *abbr* Fellow of the Association of Chartered Certified Accountants

FCM *see* **futures commission merchant**

FCMA *abbr* Fellow of the Chartered Institute of Management Accountants

FDI *see* **foreign direct investment**

feasible region the area contained within all of the constraint lines shown on a graphical depiction of a linear programming problem. All feasible combinations of output are contained within, or located on, the boundaries of the feasible region.

Fed *abbr* Federal Reserve System

Federal Funds deposits held in reserve by the US *Federal Reserve System*

Federal income tax (*US*) money deducted from employees' salaries in order to fund federal services and projects

Federal National Mortgage Association *see FNMA*

Federal Reserve bank a bank that is a member of the US *Federal Reserve System*

Federal Reserve Board (*US*) a body of seven governors appointed by Congress on the nomination of the President that supervises the US *Federal Reserve System* and formulates monetary policy. Appointees to the Board of Governors serve for 14 years. *Abbr* **FRB**

Federal Reserve note a note issued by the US *Federal Reserve System* to increase the availability of money temporarily

Federal Reserve System the central banking system of the United States, founded in 1913 by an Act of Congress. The Board of Governors, made up of seven members, is based in Washington DC and 12 Reserve Banks are located in major cities across the United States. *Abbr* **Fed**

Federation of Small Businesses a not-for-profit membership organisation representing the interests of small businesses in the United Kingdom. The FSB was established in 1974 and has over 174,000 members. *Abbr* **FSB**

Fed pass the addition of reserves to the US *Federal Reserve System* in order to increase credit availability

Fedwire the US *Federal Reserve System*'s electronic system for transferring funds

feedback control the measurement of differences between planned outputs and actual outputs achieved, and the modification of subsequent action

and/or plans to achieve future required results

feedforward control the forecasting of differences between actual and planned outcomes, and the implementation of action, before the event, to avoid such differences

feeding frenzy a period of frantic buyer activity in a market (*slang*)

fee work work on a project carried out by independent workers or contractors, rather than employees of an organisation

Fellow of the Association of Chartered Certified Accountants *abbr* **FCCA**

Fellow of the Chartered Institute of Management Accountants *abbr* **FCMA**

Fellow of the Institute of Chartered Accountants in England and Wales *abbr* **FCA**

FET *abbr* federal excise tax

fiat money coins or notes which are not worth much as paper or metal but which are said by the government to have some value

fictitious assets assets, such as prepayments, which do not have a resale value, but which are entered as assets on a company's balance sheet

FID *abbr* (*ANZ*) Financial Institutions Duty

fiduciary deposit a bank deposit which is managed for the depositor by the bank

FIFO *abbr* first in first out: a method of stock control in which the stock of a given product first placed in store is used before more recently produced or acquired goods or materials

FIF Tax *abbr* (*ANZ*) Foreign Investment Funds Tax

filing date the date by which income tax returns must be lodged with the Inland Revenue

fill or kill to carry out a client's order immediately or else the order is cancelled. *Abbr* **FOK**

final average monthly salary (*US*) = *pensionable earnings*

final closing date the last date for the acceptance of a *takeover* bid, when the bidder has to announce how many shareholders have accepted his or her offer

final demand a last reminder from a supplier to a customer to pay an outstanding debt. Suppliers often begin legal proceedings if a final demand is ignored.

final discharge the final payment on the amount outstanding on a debt

final dividend the dividend paid at the end of a year's trading. The final dividend must be approved by a company's shareholders.

finance the money needed by an individual or company to pay for something, for example, a project or stocks

Finance and Leasing Association an organisation representing firms engaged in business finance and the leasing of equipment and cars

finance bill an act passed by a legislature to provide money for public spending

finance company a business that lends money to people or companies against collateral, especially to enable purchases by hire purchase

finance house a financial institution

finance lease a lease that is treated as though the lessee had borrowed money and bought the leased assets. *US term* *capital lease*

financial relating to finance

Financial Accountant a qualified accountant, a member of the Institute of Financial Accountants, who advises on accounting matters or who works as the financial director of a company

financial accounting the classification and recording of the monetary transactions of an entity in accordance with established concepts, principles, accounting standards, and legal requirements and their presentation, by means of profit and loss accounts, balance sheets, and cash flow statements, during and at the end of an accounting period

Financial Accounting Standards Board (*US*) *see FASB*

financial advisor somebody whose job is to give advice about investments

financial aid monetary assistance given to an individual, organisation, or nation. International financial aid, that is, from one country to another, is often used to fund educational, health-related, or other humanitarian activities.

financial analyst *see investment analyst*

financial control the control of divisional performance by setting a range of financial targets and the monitoring of actual performance towards these targets

financial distress the condition of being in severe difficulties over money, especially being close to bankruptcy

financial economies of scale financial advantages gained by being able to do things on a large scale

financial engineering the conversion of one form of financial instrument into another, such as the swap of a fixed-rate instrument for a floating-rate one

financial institution an organisation such as a bank, building society, pension fund, or insurance company which invests large amounts of money in securities

Financial Institutions Duty (*ANZ*) a tax on monies paid into financial institutions imposed by all state governments in Australia except for that of Queensland. Financial institutions usually pass the tax on to customers. *Abbr* **FID**

financial instrument any contract that gives rise to both a financial asset of one entity and a financial liability or equity instrument of another entity. Financial instruments include both primary financial instruments, such as bonds, debtors, creditors, and shares, and derivative financial instruments whose value derives from the underlying assets.

financial intermediary an institution which accepts deposits or loans from individuals and lends money to clients. Banks, building societies, and hire purchase companies are all financial intermediaries.

financial leverage the use of debt finance to increase the return on equity by deploying borrowed funds in such a way that the return generated is greater than the cost of servicing the debt. If the reverse is true, and the return on deployed funds is less than the cost of servicing the debt, the effect of financial leverage is to reduce the return on equity. *Also known as* **gearing**

financial liability any liability that is a contractual obligation to deliver either cash or another financial asset to another entity, or to exchange financial instruments with another entity under conditions that are potentially unfavourable

financial management the management of all the processes associated with the efficient acquisition and

deployment of both short- and long-term financial resources

Financial Ombudsman an organisation responsible for investigating and resolving complaints involving money from members of the public against a company, institution, or other organisation. The Ombudsman is not a governmental body, but it does operate under an Act of Parliament in the form of the Financial Services and Markets Act 2000.

financial planning planning the acquisition of funds to finance anticipated activities

Financial Planning Association of Australia a national organisation representing companies and individuals working in the Australian financial planning industry. Established in 1992, the Association is responsible for monitoring standards among its members. *Abbr* **FPA**

Financial Reporting Review Panel a UK review panel established to examine contentious departures from accounting standards by large companies

Financial Reporting Standards Board (*ANZ*) a peak body that is responsible for setting and monitoring accounting standards in New Zealand. *Abbr* **FRSB**

financial risk the possibility of loss in an investment or speculation

Financial Services Authority an independent non-governmental body formed in 1997 following reforms in the regulation of financial services. Banking and investment services supervision was merged into the remit of the previous regulator, the Securities and Investments Board (SIB), which then changed its name to become the Financial Services Authority. The FSA's four statutory objectives were specified by the Financial Services and Markets Act 2000: maintaining market confidence; increasing public knowledge of the finance system; ensuring appropriate protection for consumers; and reducing financial crime. *Abbr* **FSA**

financial statements summaries of accounts to provide information for interested parties. The most common financial statements are: trading and profit and loss account; profit and loss appropriation account; balance sheet; cash flow statement; report of the auditors; statement of total recognised gains and losses; and reconciliation of movements in shareholders' funds. *See annual report*

financial supermarket a company which offers a variety of financial services. For example, a bank may offer loans, mortgages, pensions, and insurance alongside its existing range of normal banking services.

financial year 1. the twelve-month period for which a company produces accounts. A financial year is not necessarily the same as a calendar year. *Abbr* **FY 2.** for corporation tax purposes, the period from 1st April of a given year to 31st March of the following year

financing gap a gap in funding for institutions such as the *IMF* caused by cancelling the debts of poorer countries such as those in West Africa

finder's fee a fee paid to a person who finds a client for another person or company, for example, someone who introduces a new client to a stockbroking firm

FIRB *abbr* (ANZ) Foreign Investment Review Board

firm sale a sale which does not allow the purchaser to return the goods

first in first out *see* **FIFO**

first-round financing the first infusion of capital into a project

fiscal relating to financial matters, especially in respect of governmental collection, use, and regulation of money through taxation

fiscal balance a taxation policy that keeps a country's employment and taxation levels in balance

fiscal drag the effect that inflation has on taxation in that, as earnings rise, the amount of tax collected increases without a rise in tax rates

fiscal policy the central government's policy on lowering or raising taxation or increasing or decreasing public expenditure in order to stimulate or depress *aggregate demand*

fixed annuity *see annuity*

fixed asset a long-term asset of a business, such as a machine or building, that will not usually be traded

fixed assets register a record of individual tangible fixed assets

fixed budget a budget which is normally set prior to the start of an accounting period, and which is not changed in response to subsequent changes in activity or costs/revenues. Fixed budgets are generally used for planning purposes.

fixed charge a form of protection given to secured creditors relating to specific assets of a company. The charge grants the holder the right of enforcement against the identified asset (in the event of default on repayment) so that the creditor may realise the asset to meet the debt owed. Fixed charges rank first in order of priority in receivership or liquidation.

fixed cost a cost that does not change according to sales volumes, unlike variable costs. Fixed costs are usually overheads, such as rent and utility payments. *See also cost behaviour*

fixed deduction a deduction agreed by the Inland Revenue and a group of employees, which covers general expenditure on clothes or tools used in the course of employment

fixed exchange rate system a system of currency exchange in which there is no change of rate

fixed-interest loan a loan whose rate of interest does not change

fixed-price agreement an agreement where a company provides a service or a product at a price which stays the same for the whole period of the agreement

fixed-rate loan a loan with an interest rate that is set at the beginning of the term and remains the same throughout

fixtures and fittings the objects in a property which are sold with the property, both those which cannot be removed and those which can. Fixtures and fittings are a category of *fixed assets*.

flame to express an inappropriately strong or vulgar opinion about something in an Internet posting or e-mail message (*slang*)

flat tax a tax levied at one fixed rate whatever an individual's income

flat yield curve a *yield curve* with the same interest rates for long-term bonds as for short-term bonds

flexed budget a budget which changes in response to changes in sales turnover and output. *See* **budget cost allowance**

flexible budget a budget which, by recognising different **cost behaviour** patterns, is designed to change as volume of activity changes

flexible exchange rate system a system of currency exchange in which rates change from time to time

flexible manufacturing system an integrated, computer-controlled production system which is capable of producing any of a range of parts, and of switching quickly and economically between them. *Abbr* **FMS**

flight of capital the rapid movement of *capital* out of a country because of lack of confidence in that country's economic future

float 1. to sell shares or bonds, for example, to finance a project **2.** the period between presentation of a cheque as payment and the actual payment to the payee, or the financial advantage this time represents to the drawer **3.** a small cash balance maintained to facilitate low-value cash transactions. Records of these transactions should be maintained as evidence of expenditure, and periodically a float or petty cash balance will be replenished to a predetermined level.

floating asset an asset which it is assumed will be consumed during the company's normal trading cycle and then replaced by the same type of asset

floating charge a form of protection given to secured creditors which relates to assets of the company that are changing in nature. Often current assets like stock or debtors are the subject of this type of charge. In the event of default on repayment, the chargeholder may take steps to enforce the charge so that it *crystallises* and becomes attached to the current assets to which it relates. Floating charges rank after certain other prior claims in receivership or liquidation.

floating debenture a debenture secured on all of a company's *assets* which runs until the company is wound up

floating debt a short-term borrowing that is repeatedly refinanced

floating rate an interest rate that is not fixed and which changes according to fluctuations in the market

floor a lower limit on an interest rate, price, or the value of an asset

floor broker *see* **pit broker**

floor limit the highest sale through a credit card that a retailer can accept without having to obtain authorisation from the issuing bank

flotation the financing of a company by selling shares in it or a new debt issue, or the offering of shares and bonds for sale on the stock exchange

flow on a pay increase awarded to one group of workers as a result of a pay rise awarded to another group working in the same field

FMA *abbr* Fund Managers' Association. *See* **Investment Management Association**

FMS *abbr* flexible manufacturing system

FNMA *abbr* (*US*) Federal National Mortgage Association: the largest source of housing finance in the United States, the FNMA trades in mortgages guaranteed by the Federal Housing Finance Board. Created in 1938, the FNMA is a shareholder-owned private company and its stock is traded on the New York Stock Exchange. It has two principal regulators; the Department for Housing and Urban Development (HUD) aims to make sure that liquidity in the residential mortgage finance market is increased, while the Office of Federal Housing Enterprise Oversight (OFHEO) monitors soundness of accounting practice and financial safety. *Also known as* **Fannie Mae**

FOK *abbr* fill or kill

Forbes 500 a list of the 500 largest public companies in the United States, ranked according to various criteria by *Forbes* magazine

forced sale a sale which takes place as the result of a court order or because it represents the only reasonable way for a company or individual to avoid a financial crisis

force majeure an occurrence, such as a strike, war, or storm, that is beyond the control of the parties who have signed a contract to obtain or supply a product or service

forecast a prediction of future events and their quantification for planning purposes

foreign bill a bill of exchange that is not payable in the country where it is issued

foreign currency the currency or interest-bearing bonds of a foreign country

foreign currency translation the restatement of the foreign currency accounts of overseas subsidiaries and associated companies into the domestic currency of the country in which the group is incorporated, for the purpose of producing consolidated group accounts

foreign debt hard-currency debt owed to a foreign country in payment for goods and services

foreign direct investment the establishment of new overseas facilities, or the expansion of existing overseas facilities, by an investor. FDI may be inward (domestic investment by overseas companies) or outward (overseas investment by domestic companies). *Abbr* **FDI**

foreign dividend in the United Kingdom, a dividend paid by another country, possibly subject to special rules under UK tax codes

foreign draft a cheque that is not both drawn and payable in the same country

foreign equity market the market in one country for equities of companies in other countries

foreign exchange the currencies of other countries, or dealings in these

foreign exchange option a contract which, for a fee, guarantees a worst-case exchange rate for the future purchase of one currency for another. Unlike a *forward transaction*, the option does not obligate the buyer to deliver a currency on the settlement date unless the buyer chooses to. These options protect against unfavourable currency movements while preserving the ability to participate in favourable movements.

foreign income dividend a dividend paid from earnings in other countries

Foreign Investment Funds Tax (*ANZ*) a tax imposed by the Australian government on unrealised gains made by Australian residents from offshore investments. It was introduced in 1992 to prevent overseas earnings being taxed at low rates and never brought to Australia. *Abbr* **FIF Tax**

Foreign Investment Review Board (*ANZ*) a non-statutory body that regulates and advises the federal government on foreign investment in Australia. It was set up in 1976. *Abbr* **FIRB**

foreign reserve the currency of other countries held by an organisation, especially a country's central bank

foreign tax credit a tax advantage for taxes that are paid to or in another country

forensic accounting the use of accounting records and documents in order to determine the legality or otherwise of past activities

forfaiting the purchase of financial instruments such as bills of exchange or letters of credit on a non-recourse basis by a forfaiter, who deducts interest (in the form of a discount) at an agreed rate for the period covered by the notes. The forfaiter assumes the responsibility for claiming the debt from the importer (buyer) who initially accepted the

financial instrument drawn by the seller of the goods. Traditionally, forfaiting is fixed-rate, medium-term (one- to five-year) finance.

forfeit clause a clause in a contract which states that goods or a deposit will be taken away if the contract is not fulfilled by one of the signees

Fortune 500 a list of the 500 largest industrial companies in the United States, compiled annually by *Fortune* magazine

forward contract a private futures contract for delivery of a commodity

forward cover the purchase for cash of the quantity of a commodity needed to fulfil a futures contract

forward delivery delivery of a good or service at some date in the future which has been agreed between the buyer and seller

forwarding agent a person or company that arranges shipping and customs documents for clients

forward interest rate an interest rate specified for a loan to be made at a future date

forward margin the difference between the current (or spot) price and the forward price

forward market a market for the buying of foreign currency, shares, or commodities for delivery at a later date at a certain price

forward pricing the establishment of the price of a share in a unit trust based on the next asset valuation

forward rate an estimate of what an interest rate will be at a specified future time

forward transaction an agreement to buy one currency and sell another on a date sometime beyond two business days. This allows an exchange rate on a given day to be locked in for a future payment or receipt, thereby eliminating exchange rate risk.

founders' shares *see deferred shares*

fourth market trading carried out directly without brokers, usually by large institutions

FPA *abbr* Financial Planning Association of Australia

fractional certificate a certificate for part of a *share*

fractional currency the paper money that is in denominations smaller than one unit of a standard national currency

franked investment income the total of dividends received plus their associated tax credit

franked payment dividends plus tax credits paid by a company to shareholders

franked payments the total of dividends paid plus their associated tax credit

fraud the use of dishonesty, deception, or false representation in order to gain a material advantage or to injure the interests of others. Types of fraud include false accounting, theft, third party or investment fraud, employee collusion, and computer fraud. *See also corporate fraud*

FRB *abbr* (*US*) Federal Reserve Board

free cash flow cash flow from operations after deducting interest, tax, dividends, and ongoing capital expenditure, but excluding capital expenditure associated with strategic acquisitions and/or disposals

free coinage a government's minting of coins from precious metals provided by citizens

free enterprise the trade carried on in a free-market economy, where resources are allocated on the basis of supply and demand

free gold gold held by a government but not pledged as a reserve for the government's currency

free market a market in which supply and demand are unregulated, except by the country's competition policy, and rights in physical and intellectual property are upheld

free period the period of grace allowed to credit card holders before payment for credit card purchases is demanded

free reserves the part of a bank's reserves which are above the statutory level and so can be used for various purposes as the bank wishes

free-standing additional voluntary contributions plan a separate pension plan taken out by an individual in addition to a company pension scheme

free stock stock on hand or on order which has not been scheduled for use

freeze-out the exclusion of minority *shareholders* in a company that has been taken over. A freeze-out provision may exist in a *takeover* agreement, which permits the acquiring organisation to buy the non-controlling shares held by small shareholders. A fair price is usually set, and the freeze-out may take place at a specified time, perhaps two to five years after the takeover. A freeze-out can still take place, even if provision for it is not made in a corporate charter, by applying pressure on minority shareholders to sell their shares to the acquiring company.

frictional unemployment a situation in which people are temporarily out of the labour market. They could be seeking a new job, incurring search delays as they apply, attending interviews, and relocating.

friction-free market a market in which there is little differentiation between competing products, so that the customer has exceptional choice

front-end loading the practice of taking the commission and administrative expenses from the early payments made to an investment or insurance plan. *See also* **back-end loading**

frozen account a bank account whose funds cannot be used or withdrawn because of a court order

FRSB *abbr* (*ANZ*) Financial Reporting Standards Board

FSA *abbr* Financial Services Authority

FSB *abbr* Federation of Small Businesses

FTSE 100 *abbr* FTSE 100 Share Index

FTSE 100 Share Index an index, established in 1984, that is based on the share prices of the 100 most highly capitalised public companies in the United Kingdom. *Abbr* **FTSE 100**

FTSE 250 *abbr* FTSE 250 Index

FTSE 250 Index an index of medium-capitalised companies not included in the FTSE 100 Index. It represents over 17% of UK market capitalisation. *Abbr* **FTSE 250**

FTSE 30 *abbr* FTSE 30

FTSE 30 Share Index an index showing the share prices of 30 influential companies on the London Stock Exchange. Although in existence since 1935, the 30 Share Index is now one of the less popular indices. *Abbr* **FTSE 30**

FTSE All-Share *abbr* FTSE All-Share Index

FTSE All-Share Index an average of the share prices of all the companies listed on the London Stock Exchange. As this encompasses over 1,000 companies, this index is often used as a reli-

able barometer of the performance of different companies. This index aggregates the FTSE 100, FTSE 250, and FTSE Small Cap indices. *Abbr* **FTSE All-Share**

FTSE Small Cap *abbr* FTSE Small Cap Index

FTSE Small Cap Index an index which indicates the performance of companies with the smallest market capitalisation, representing roughly 2% of market capitalisation in the United Kingdom. *Abbr* **FTSE Small Cap**

FTSE TMT *abbr* FTSE TMT Index

FTSE TMT Index an index which indicates the performance of companies in three key business areas: technology, media, and telecommunications

full bank a local or foreign bank permitted to engage in the full range of domestic and international services

full coupon bond a bond whose interest rate is competitive in the current market

full-service banking a type of banking that offers a whole range of services including mortgages, loans, and pensions

full-service broker a broker who manages portfolios for clients, and gives advice on shares and financial questions in general

fully diluted earnings per share *earnings per share* calculated over the whole number of shares on the assumption that convertible shares have been converted to ordinary shares

fully diluted earnings per (common) share earnings on a share that take into account commitments to issue more shares, for example, as a result of convertibles, share options, or warrants

fully distributed issue an issue of shares sold entirely to investors rather than held by dealers

functional analysis an analysis of the relationships between product functions, their perceived value to the customer, and their cost of provision

functional budget a budget of income and/or expenditure applicable to a particular function. A function may refer to a department or a process. Functional budgets frequently include the following: production cost budget (based on a forecast of production and plant utilisation); marketing cost budget; sales budget; personnel budget; purchasing budget; and research and development budget. *Also known as departmental budget*

fund accounting the preparation of financial statements for an *entity* which is a fund. Such statements are usually on a cash basis and are most commonly found in the public sector.

fundamental accounting concepts broad basic assumptions which underlie the periodic financial accounts of business entreprises. *See concepts*

fundamental analysis analysis of external and internal influences on the operations of a company with a view to assisting in investment decisions. Information accessed might include fiscal/monetary policy, financial statements, industry trends, competitor analysis, etc. *See also technical analysis*

funded debt long-term debt or debt that has a maturity date in excess of one year. Funded debt is usually issued in the public markets or in the form of a private placement to qualified institutional investors.

funding risk the risk that an entity will encounter difficulty in realising assets or otherwise raising funds to meet commitments associated with financial instruments

fund manager somebody who manages the investments of a unit trust or large financial institution

Fund Managers' Association *abbr* **FMA**

fund of funds (*S Africa*) a registered unit trust that invests in a range of underlying unit trusts; subscribers own units in the fund of funds, not in the underlying unit trusts

fungible interchangeable and indistinguishable for business purposes from other items of the same type

funny money an unusual type of financial instrument created by a company

future a contract to deliver a commodity at a future date. *Also known as futures contract*

future option a contract in which somebody agrees to buy or sell a commodity, currency, or security at an agreed price for delivery in the future. *Also known as futures option*

futures commission merchant somebody who acts as a broker for futures contracts. *Abbr* **FCM**

futures contract *see future*

futures exchange an exchange on which futures contracts are traded

futures market 1. a market for buying and selling securities, commodities, or currencies that tend to fluctuate in price over a period of time. The market's aim is to reduce the risk of uncertainty about future prices. **2.** an exchange-traded market for the purchase or sale of a standard quantity of an underlying item such as currencies, commodities, or shares, for settlement at a future date at an agreed price

futures option *see future option*

future value the value that a sum of money will have in the future, taking into account the effects of inflation, interest rates, or currency values.

EXAMPLE Future value calculations require three figures: the sum in question, the percentage by which it will increase or decrease, and the period of time.

In this example, these figures are £1,000, 11%, and two years.

At an interest rate of 11%, the sum of £1,000 will grow to £1,232 in two years:

£1,000 × 1.11 = £1,110 (first year) × 1.11 = £1,232 (second year, rounded to whole pounds)

Note that the interest earned in the first year generates additional interest in the second year, a practice known as compounding. When large sums are in question, the effect of compounding can be significant.

At an inflation rate of 11%, by comparison, the sum of £1,000 will shrink to £812 in two years:

£1,000 / 1.11 = £901 (first year) / 1.11 = £812 (second year, rounded to whole pounds)

In order to avoid errors, it is important to express the percentage as 1.11 and multiply and divide by that figure, instead of using 11%; and to calculate each year, quarter, or month separately. *See also* **present value**

futuristic planning planning for that period which extends beyond the planning horizon in the form of future expected conditions which may exist in respect of the entity, products/services, and environment, but which cannot usefully be expressed in quantified terms. An example would be working out the actions needed in a future with no motor cars.

FY *abbr financial year*

G

G10 *abbr* Group of Ten

G7 the group of seven major industrial nations established in 1985 to discuss the world economy, consisting of Canada, France, Germany, Italy, Japan, the United Kingdom, and the United States

G8 the group of eight major industrial nations consisting of the *G7* plus Russia

GAAP *abbr* Generally Accepted Accounting Principles

GAB *abbr* General Arrangements to Borrow: a fund financed by the *Group of Ten* that is used when the IMF's own resources are insufficient, for example, when there is a need for large loans to one or more industrialised countries

gap analysis a method of improving a company's financial performance by reducing the gap between current results and long-term objectives

garage 1. a UK term meaning to transfer assets or liabilities from one financial centre to another to take advantage of a tax benefit **2.** the annex to the main floor of the New York Stock Exchange (*slang*)

garbatrage (*US*) stocks that rise because of a takeover but are not connected to the target company (*slang*)

GAS *abbr* Government Accountancy Service

GATT *abbr* General Agreement on Tariffs and Trade: a treaty signed in Geneva in 1947 that aimed to foster multilateral trade and settle trading disputes between adherent countries. Initially signed by 23 nations, it started to reduce trade tariffs and, as it was accepted by more and more countries, tackled other barriers to trade. It was replaced on 1 January 1995 by the World Trade Organization.

gazump in the period between agreeing verbally to sell to one buyer but before the agreement becomes legally binding, to accept a higher offer from another buyer. Gazumping is normally associated with the property market, although it can occur in any market where the prices are rising rapidly.

gazunder in the period between agreeing verbally to buy at one price but before the agreement is legally binding, to offer a lower price. Gazundering is normally associated with the property market, although it can occur in any market where the prices are falling rapidly.

GDP *abbr* gross domestic product: the total flow of services and goods produced by an economy over a quarter or a year, measured by the aggregate value of services and goods at market prices

GDP per capita *GDP* divided by the country's population so as to achieve a figure per head of population

GEAR *abbr* (*S Africa*) Growth, Employment, and Redistribution: the macroeconomic reform programme of the South African government, intended to foster economic growth, create employment, and redistribute income and opportunities in favour of the poor

geared investment trust an investment trust that borrows money in order to increase its portfolio. When the market is rising, shares in a geared investment trust rise faster than those in an ungeared trust, but they fall faster when the market is falling.

gearing *see financial leverage*

gearing ratios ratios that indicate the level of risk taken by a company as a result of its capital structure. A number of different ratios may be calculated, for example, debt ratio (total debt divided by total assets), debt-to-equity or leverage ratio (total debt divided by total equity), or interest cover (earnings before interest and tax divided by interest paid). Gearing is most frequently used to measure the return on shareholders' investment from assets, and is calculated as borrowed capital divided by equity capital. This ratio is one of the most difficult to manage because it needs to be kept in balance. If it is high then the return to equity shareholders will also be high, but the risk to shareholders and fixed interest lenders is greater. *US term* **leverage ratios**

geisha bond *see* *shogun bond*

General Agreement on Tariffs and Trade *see GATT*

General Arrangements to Borrow *see GAB*

general audit an examination of all books and accounts belonging to a company

General Commissioners a body of unpaid individuals appointed by the Lord Chancellor in England, Wales, and Northern Ireland, and the Secretary of State for Scotland in Scotland, to hear appeals on tax matters

general fund a unit trust with investments in a variety of stocks

general ledger a book that lists all of the financial transactions of a company

Generally Accepted Accounting Principles a summary of best practice in respect of the form and content of financial statements, the form and content of auditors' reports, and best practice and acceptable alternatives in respect of accounting policies and disclosures adopted for the preparation of financial information. GAAP does not have any statutory or regulatory authority in the United Kingdom, unlike in a number of other countries where the term is in use, such as the United States, Canada, and New Zealand. *Abbr* **GAAP**

general obligation bond a municipal or state bond issued to finance public undertakings, such as road-building, which is repaid out of general funds

general undertaking an agreement signed by all the directors of a company applying for Stock Exchange listing, which promises that they will work within the regulations of the Stock Exchange

gensaki the Japanese term for a bond sale incorporating a repurchase agreement at a later date

gentleman's agreement a verbal agreement between two parties who trust each other

gift-leaseback the practice of giving somebody a property and then leasing it back, usually for tax advantage or charitable purposes

gift with reservation a gift with some benefit retained for the donor, for example, the legal transfer of a dwelling when the donor continues in residence

gilt *see* *gilt-edged security*

gilt-edged security 1. a security issued by the UK government that pays a fixed rate of interest on a regular basis for a specific period of time until the redemption date when the principal is returned. The name of the security, for example, Exchequer 10½% 2005 (abbreviated to Ex 10½% '05) or Treasury 11¾% 2003–07 (abbreviated to Tr 11¾% '03–'07) indicates the rate and redemption date. Thought to have originated in the 17th century to help fund the war with France, today they form a large part of the National Debt. *Also known as* **gilt**. *See also* **index-linked gilt** **2.** a US term used to describe a security issued by a blue-chip company, which is therefore considered very secure

gilt repos the market in agreed sales and repurchase of gilt-edged securities, launched in 1996 by the Bank of

England to make gilts more attractive to overseas investors

gilt strip a zero-coupon bond created by unbundling the interest payments from a gilt-edged security so that it produces a single cash payment at maturity

gilt unit trust in the United Kingdom, a unit trust where the underlying investments are gilt-edged securities

Ginnie Mae *(US) see* **GNMA**

giro 1. a European term for the transfer of money from one bank account to another. *Also known as* **bank giro 2.** a benefit paid by the state *(slang)*

glamour stock *(US)* a fashionable security with an investment following

Glass-Steagall Act a US law that enforces the separation of the banking and brokerage industries

global bank a bank that is active in the international markets and that has a presence in several continents

global bond *see* **Eurobond**

global bond issue an issue of bonds that incorporates a settlement mechanism allowing for the transfer of titles between markets

global co-ordinator the lead manager of a global offering who is responsible for overseeing the entire issue and is usually supported by regional and national co-ordinators

global custody a financial service, usually only available to institutional investors, that includes the safekeeping of securities certificates issued in markets across the world, the collection of dividends, dealing with tax, valuation of investments, foreign exchange, and the settlement of transactions

global hedge *see* **macrohedge**

global offering the offering of securities in several markets simultaneously, for example, in Europe, the Far East, and North America

GM *abbr* gross margin

GNI *abbr* gross national income. *See* **GNP**

GNMA *abbr* Government National Mortgage Association: a US-owned corporation that issues mortgage-backed bonds. *Also known as* **Ginnie Mae**

gnomes of Zurich a derogatory term for Swiss bankers and currency dealers (who have a reputation for secrecy), often used when unknown speculators cause havoc in the currency markets

GNP *abbr* gross national product: GDP plus domestic residents' income from investment abroad less income earned in the domestic market accruing to foreigners abroad. *Also known as* **GNI**.

GNP per capita *GNP* divided by the country's population so as to achieve a figure per head of population

goal congruence in a control system, the state which leads individuals or groups to take actions which are in their self-interest and also in the best interest of the entity. Goal incongruence exists when the interests of individuals or of groups associated with an entity are not in harmony.

go-go fund a unit trust that trades heavily and predominantly in high-return, high-risk investments

going concern an actively trading company

going concern concept the assumption that an entity will continue in operational existence for the foreseeable future. The assumption that a particular entity is a going concern can now be tested by statistical models for firms operating in well-defined business areas. *See also* **Z score**

going short selling an asset one does not own with the intention of acquiring it at a later date at a lower price for delivery to the purchaser. *See also **bear***

gold bond a bond for which gold is collateral, often issued by mining companies

gold card a gold-coloured credit card, generally issued to customers with above average incomes, that may include additional benefits, for example, an overdraft at an advantageous interest rate, and may have an annual fee

gold certificate a document that shows ownership of gold

golden handcuffs a financial incentive paid to encourage employees to remain in an organisation and dissuade them from leaving for a rival business or to start their own company (*slang*)

golden handshake a sum of money given to a senior executive on his or her involuntary departure from an employing organisation as a form of severance pay. A golden handshake can be offered when an executive is required to leave before the expiration of his or her contract, for example, because of a *merger* or corporate restructuring. It is intended as compensation for loss of office. It can be a very large sum of money, but often it is not related to the perceived performance of the executive concerned. (*slang*)

golden hello a welcome package for a new employee that may include a *bonus* and share options. A golden hello is designed as an incentive to attract employees. Some of the contents of the welcome package may be contingent on the performance of the employee.

golden parachute a clause inserted in the contract of employment of a senior employee that details a financial package payable if the employee is dismissed. A golden parachute provides an executive with a measure of financial

security and may be payable if the employee leaves the organisation following a *takeover* or *merger*, or is dismissed as a result of poor performance. *Also known as **golden umbrella***

golden share a controlling shareholding retained by a government in a company that has been privatised after having been in public ownership

golden umbrella *see **golden parachute***

gold fix the daily setting of the gold price in London and Zurich

gold fixing a system whereby the world price for gold is set twice a day in US dollars in Paris, Zurich, and London on the Gold Exchange

gold reserve gold coins or bullion held by a central bank to support a paper currency and provide security for borrowing

gold standard a system in which a currency unit is defined in terms of its value in gold

good for the day used to describe instructions to a broker that are valid only for the day given

good for this week/month used to describe instructions to a broker that are valid only for the duration of the week/month given. *Abbr **GTW/GTM***

Goods and Services Tax 1. a government-imposed consumption tax, currently of 10%, added to the retail cost of goods and services in Australia. *Abbr **GST 2.** a former Canadian tax on goods and services. It was a value-added tax and was replaced by the *harmonised sales tax*. *Abbr **GST***

goods received note a record of goods at the point of receipt

good 'til cancel relating to an order to buy or sell a security that is effective until an investor cancels it, up to a maximum of 60 days. *Abbr **GTC***

good title the legally unquestionable title to property. *Also known as **clear title***

goodwill an intangible asset of a company that includes factors such as reputation, contacts, and expertise, for which a buyer of the company may have to pay a premium.

EXAMPLE Goodwill becomes an intangible asset when a company has been acquired by another. It then appears on a balance sheet in the amount by which the price paid by the acquiring company exceeds the net tangible assets of the acquired company. In other words:

Purchase price – net assets = goodwill

If, for example, an airline is bought for £12 billion and its net assets are valued at £9 billion, £3 billion of the purchase would be allocated to goodwill on the balance sheet. The treatment of goodwill in accounts is determined by FRS10, 'Goodwill and Intangible Assets', issued by the Accounting Standards Board of the Institute of Chartered Accountants in England and Wales.

go private to revert from being a public limited company quoted on a stock exchange to a private company without a stock market listing

go public 1. to float the shares of a *company* on a stock exchange, thereby changing the company status to that of a *public limited company* **2.** to put shares in a private company on the market as a means of raising funds

Government Accountancy Service part of *HM Treasury*, a service whose remit is to ensure that best accounting practice is observed and conducted across the whole of the Civil Service. *Abbr* **GAS**

Government National Mortgage Association (*US*) *see* **GNMA**

government securities/stock securities or stock issued by a government, for example, US Treasury bonds or UK gilt-edged securities

graduated payments mortgage (*US*) a low start mortgage. *Abbr* **GPM**

graduated pension scheme a pension scheme where the benefit is calculated as a percentage of the salary of each person in the scheme

graduated tax a tax that increases in line with an individual's income

granny bond *see **index-linked savings certificate***

grant of probate in the United Kingdom, a document issued by the Probate Court that pronounces the validity of a will and upholds the appointment of the executor(s)

grantor a person who sells an option

graveyard market 1. a UK term for a market for shares that are infrequently traded either through lack of interest or because they are of little or no value **2.** a bear market where investors who dispose of their holdings are faced with large losses, as potential investors prefer to stay liquid until the market shows signs of improving

gravy train any type of business activity in which an individual or an organisation makes a large *profit* without much effort

greater fool theory the investing strategy that assumes it is wise to buy a stock that is not worth its current price. The assumption is that somebody will buy it from you later for an even greater price.

Green chips small companies with potential for growth

green day (*US*) a profitable day

greenmail the purchase of enough of a company's shares to threaten it with takeover, so that the company is forced to buy back the shares at a higher price to avoid the takeover (*slang*)

green pound the fixed European Currency Unit (ECU) in which prices of agricultural goods in the European Union are set

green shoe or **greenshoe option** an option offered by a company raising the capital for the issue of further shares to cover a shortfall in the event of over-allocation. It gets its name from the Green Shoe Manufacturing Company which was the first to include the feature in a public offering. (*slang*)

green taxes taxes levied to discourage behaviour that will be harmful to the environment

grey knight *see knight*

grey wave used to describe a company that is thought likely to have good prospects in the distant future. It gets its name from the fact that investors are likely to have grey hair before they see their expectations fulfilled (slang).

gross total, before consideration of taxes

gross borrowings the total of all monies borrowed by a company, such as overdrafts and long-term loans, but without deducting cash in bank accounts and on deposit

gross domestic product *see GDP*

gross earnings total earnings before tax and other deductions

gross income yield the yield of an investment before tax is deducted

gross interest the interest earned on a deposit or security before the deduction of tax. *See also* **net interest**

gross lease a lease that does not require the lessee to pay for things the owner usually pays for. *See also* **net lease**

gross margin 1. the differential between the interest rate paid by a borrower and the cost of the funds to the lender. *Abbr* **GM 2.** the differential between the manufacturing cost of a unit of output and the price at which it is sold

gross national product *see GNP*

gross profit the difference between an organisation's sales revenue and the cost of goods sold. Unlike **net profit**, gross profit does not include distribution, administration, or finance costs. *Also known as* **trading profit**

gross profit margin *see profit margin*

gross receipts the total revenue received by a business

gross redemption yield *see* **gross yield to redemption**

gross turnover total *turnover* including discounts, such as VAT

gross yield the share of income return derived from securities before the deduction of tax

gross yield to redemption the total return to an investor if a fixed interest security is held to maturity, in other words, the aggregate of gross interest received and the capital gain or loss at redemption, annualised. *Also known as* **gross redemption yield**. *US term* **yield to maturity**

group a parent company and all its subsidiaries

group certificate (*ANZ*) a document provided by an employer that records an employee's income, income tax payments, and superannuation contributions during the previous financial year

group investment an investment made by more than one person

group life assurance a life assurance policy that covers a number of people, for example, members of an association or club, or a group of employees at a company

Group of Seven *see G7*

Group of Ten the group of ten countries who contribute to the General Arrangements to Borrow fund: Belgium, Canada, France, Germany, Italy, Japan, the Netherlands, Sweden, the United States, and the United Kingdom. Switzerland joined in 1984. *Also known as* **Paris Club**. *See also* **GAB**. *Abbr* **G10**

Growth, Employment, and Redistribution *see GEAR*

growth and income fund a unit trust that tries to maximise growth of capital while paying significant dividends

growth capital funding that allows a company to accelerate its growth. For new start-up companies, growth capital is the second stage of funding after *seed capital*.

growth company a company whose contribution to the economy is growing because it is increasing its workforce or earning increased foreign exchange for its exported goods

growth equity an equity that is thought to have good investment prospects

growth fund a unit trust that tries to maximise growth of capital without regard to dividends

growth industry an industry that has the potential to expand at a faster rate than other industries

growth rate the rate of an economy's growth as measured by its technical progress, the growth of its labour force, and the increase in its *capital stock*

growth share 1. a share that offers investors the prospect of longer-term earnings, rather than a quick return **2.** a share that has been rising greatly in value, relative to its industry or to the market as a whole

growth stock stock that offers investors the prospect of longer-term earnings, rather than a quick return

GST *abbr* Goods and Services Tax

GTC *abbr* good 'til cancel

guarantee a promise made by a third party, or guarantor, that he or she will be liable if one of the parties to a contract fails to fulfil their contractual obligations. A guarantee may be acceptable to a bank as security for borrowing provided the guarantor has sufficient financial means to cover his or her potential liability.

guaranteed bond in the United States, a bond on which the principal and interest are guaranteed by a company other than the one that issues them, or a stock in which the dividends are similarly guaranteed. *See also* **guaranteed stocks**

guaranteed fund a fixed-term investment where a third party promises to repay the investors' principal in full should the investment fall below the initial sum invested

guaranteed income bond a bond issued by a UK life assurance company designed to provide an investor with a fixed rate of income for a specified period of time. Changes to the regulations now permit only those policies with an independent third party guarantee to receive this denomination.

guaranteed investment certificate an investment instrument issued by an insurance company that guarantees interest but not the principal originally invested

guaranteed stocks in the United Kingdom, bonds issued by nationalised industries that incorporate an explicit guarantee from the government. *See also guaranteed bond*

guarantor a person or organisation that guarantees repayment of a loan if the borrower defaults or is unable to pay

guardian ad litem a person who acts on behalf of a minor who is a defendant in a court case

gun jumping (*US*) an informal US alternative name for *insider trading*

H

haggle to negotiate a price with a buyer or seller by the gradual raising of offers and lowering of asking prices until a mutually agreeable price is reached

hammering the market used to describe a situation where there is intense selling (*slang*)

handling charge money to be paid for packing, invoicing, or dealing with goods which are being shipped

hand signals the signs used by traders on the trading floors at exchanges for futures and options to overcome the problem of noise

hang-out loan the amount of a loan that is still outstanding after the termination of the loan

Hang Seng index an index of the prices of selected shares on the Hong Kong Stock Exchange

hara-kiri swap an interest rate swap made without a profit margin

hard capital rationing *see capital rationing*

hard commodities metals and other solid raw materials. *See also commodity, soft commodities*

hard currency a currency that is traded in a foreign exchange market and for which demand is persistently high relative to its supply. *See also soft currency*

hard landing the rapid decline of an economy into recession and business stagnation after a sustained period of growth

harmonised sales tax a Canadian tax on goods and services. It is a value-added tax that replaced the Goods and Services Tax. *Abbr* **HST**

harvesting strategy a reduction in or cessation of marketing for a product prior to it being withdrawn from sale, resulting in an increase in profits on the back of previous marketing and advertising campaigns

head and shoulders used to describe a graph plotting a company's share price that resembles the silhouette of a person's head and shoulders. Analysts see this as an early indication of a market fall.

headline rate of inflation a measure of inflation that takes account of home owners' mortgage costs

head tax a tax paid by all inhabitants of a country, regardless of their income

health warning a warning message printed on advertisements for investments, stating that the value of investments can fall as well as rise. This is a legal requirement in the United Kingdom. (*slang*)

heavy share price a price on the London Stock Exchange which is over £10.00 per share, and so discourages the small investor from buying. If the company wants to encourage more people to buy its shares, it may take steps to reduce the share price by splitting or issuing bonus shares.

hedge a transaction to reduce or eliminate an exposure to risk

hedge fund a unit trust that takes considerable risks, including heavy investment in unconventional instruments, in the hope of generating great profits

hedging against inflation investing in order to avoid the impact of inflation, thus protecting the purchasing power of capital. Historically, equities have generally outperformed returns from savings accounts in the long term and beaten the Retail Price Index. They are thus considered as one of the best hedges against inflation, although it is important to bear in mind that no stock market investment is without risk.

held order an order that a dealer does not process immediately, often because of its great size

heritage industry an industry centred on the efficient business management of a country's historical monuments, with the aim of encouraging tourism and boosting the local economy

hidden asset an *asset* which is shown in a company's accounts as being worth much less than its true market value

hidden reserves illegal reserves which are not declared in the company's balance sheet

hidden tax a tax that is not immediately apparent. For example, while a consumer may be aware of a tax on retail purchases, a tax imposed at the wholesale level, which consequently increases the cost of items to the retailer, will not be apparent.

hierarchy of activities the classification of activities according to the level within the organisation to which they relate, for example, product level activities, batch level activities, product sustaining activities, or facility sustaining activities

higher-rate tax in the United Kingdom, the highest of the three bands of income tax. Most countries have bands of income tax with different rates applicable to income within each band.

high finance the lending, investing, and borrowing of very large sums of money organised by financiers

high-flier *or* **high-flyer** a heavily traded stock that increases in value quickly over a short period

high gearing a situation in which a company has a high level of borrowing compared to its share price

high/low method a method of estimating cost behaviour by comparing the total costs associated with two different levels of output. The difference in costs is assumed to be caused by variable costs increasing, allowing the unit variable cost to be calculated. From this, since total cost is known, the fixed cost can be derived.

high-premium convertible debenture a convertible bond sold at a high premium that offers a competitive rate of interest and has a long term

high yielder a security that has a higher than average yield and is consequently often a higher risk investment

hire purchase a method of paying for a product or service in which the buyer pays by a series of instalments over a period of time. *US term* **instalment plan**. *Abbr* **HP**

historical cost the original acquisition cost of an asset, unadjusted for subsequent price level or value changes

historical cost accounting a system of accounting in which all values are based on the historical costs incurred. This is the basis prescribed in the Companies Act for published accounts.

historical pricing the basing of current prices on prior period prices, perhaps uplifted by a factor such as *inflation*

historical summary in the United Kingdom, an optional synopsis of a company's results over a period of time, often five or ten years, featured in the annual accounts

historic pricing the establishment of the price of a share in a unit trust on the basis of the most recent values of its holdings

HMCE *abbr* HM Customs and Excise

HM Customs and Excise the UK government department responsible for collecting revenue in the form of taxes (including VAT) and customs duties. It also aims to reduce and prevent tax fraud and the illegal importing and smuggling of drugs, alcohol, and tobacco into the United Kingdom. *Abbr* **HMCE**

HMT *abbr* HM Treasury

HM Treasury the UK government department responsible for managing the country's public revenues. While the incumbent prime minister holds the title of First Lord of the Treasury, the department is run on a day-to-day basis by the *Chancellor of the Exchequer*.

hockey stick a performance curve typical of businesses in their early stages that descends then rises sharply in a straight line, creating a shape similar to that of a hockey stick (*slang*)

holder the person who is in possession of a bill of exchange or promissory note

holding company a parent organisation that owns and controls other companies. In the United Kingdom, a holding company has to own over half of the nominal share capital in companies that are then deemed to be its subsidiaries. A holding company may have no other business than the holding of shares of other companies.

holding cost the cost of retaining an asset, generally stock. Holding cost includes the cost of financing the asset in addition to the cost of physical storage.

home loan a mortgage

home run 1. a very great achievement **2.** an investment that produces a high rate of return in a short time

honorarium a token sum given in recognition of the recipient's performance of specific, non-onerous duties. An honorarium may take the form of an annual retainer.

horizontal merger *see* **merger**

horizontal spread a purchase of two options that are identical except for their dates of maturity

horse-trading hard bargaining that results in one party giving the other a concession

hostile bid a takeover bid that is opposed by the target company. *See also* **greenmail, knight**

hostile takeover *see* **takeover**

hot card a credit card that has been stolen

hot file a list of stolen credit cards

hot issue a new security that is expected to trade at a significant premium on its issue price. *See also* **hot stock**

hot money 1. money that has been obtained by dishonest means. *See also* **money laundering 2.** money that is moved at short notice from one financial centre to another to secure the best possible return

hot stock a share, usually a new issue, that rises quickly on the stock market. *See also* **hot issue**

HP *abbr* hire purchase

HST *abbr* harmonised sales tax

human resource accounting the identification, recording, and reporting of the investment in, and return from the employment of, the personnel of an organisation

hurdle rate a rate of return which a capital investment proposal must achieve if it is to be accepted. Set by reference to the cost of the capital, the hurdle rate may be increased above the basic cost of capital to allow for different levels of risk.

hybrid a combination of financial instruments, for example, a bond with warrants attached, or a range of cash and derivative instruments designed to mirror the performance of a financial market

hybrid annuity *see annuity*

hybrid financial instrument a financial instrument such as a convertible bond that has characteristics of multiple types of instruments, often convertible from one to another

hyperinflation a very rapid growth in the rate of inflation so that money loses value and physical goods replace currency as a medium of exchange. This happened in Latin America in the early 1990s, for example.

hypothecate to use a property as collateral for a loan

I

IAS *abbr* (*ANZ*) Instalment Activity Statement

IASC *abbr* International Accounting Standards Committee

IB *abbr* investment bank

IBOR *abbr* Inter Bank Offered Rate: the rate of interest at which banks lend to each other on the interbank market

IBR *abbr* Inter Bank Rate. *See* **IBOR**

IBRC *abbr* Insurance Brokers Registration Council: in the United Kingdom, a statutory body established under the Insurance Brokers Registration Act of 1977 that was deregulated following the establishment of the Financial Services Authority and the General Insurance Services Council. Its complaints and administration functions passed to the Institute of Insurance Brokers.

IBRD *abbr* International Bank for Reconstruction and Development: a United Nations organisation that provides funds, policy guidance, and technical assistance to facilitate economic development in its poorer member countries

ICAEW *abbr* Institute of Chartered Accountants in England and Wales

ICAI *abbr* Institute of Chartered Accountants in Ireland

Icarus factor the tendency of managers or executives to embark on over-ambitious projects which then fail. In Greek mythology, Icarus made himself wings of wax and feathers to attempt to escape from Crete, but flew too near the sun and drowned in the sea after the wax melted. (*slang*)

ICAS *abbr* Institute of Chartered Accountants of Scotland

ICC *abbr* International Chamber of Commerce: an organisation that represents business interests to governments, aiming to improve trading conditions and foster private enterprise

ICSA *abbr* Institute of Chartered Secretaries and Administrators: an organisation that aims to promote the efficient administration of commerce, industry, and public affairs. Founded in 1891 and granted a royal charter in 1902, it represents the interests of its members to government, publishes journals and other materials, promotes the standing of its members, and provides educational support and qualifying schemes.

IDA *abbr* International Development Association: an agency administered by the IBRD to provide assistance on concessionary terms to the poorest developing countries. Its resources consist of subscriptions and general replenishments from its more industrialised and developed members, special contributions, and transfers from the net earnings of the IBRD.

IDR *abbr* International Depository Receipt

IEA *abbr* International Energy Authority: an autonomous agency within the OECD whose objectives include improving global energy co-operation, developing alternative energy sources, and promoting relations between oil-producing and oil-consuming countries

IFA *abbr* Institute of Financial Accountants

IFC *abbr* International Finance Corporation: a United Nations organisation promoting private sector investment in developing countries to reduce poverty and improve the quality of people's lives. It finances private sector projects that are profit-oriented and environmentally and socially sound, and helps to foster development. The IFC has a staff of 2,000 professionals around the world who seek profitable and creative solutions to complex business issues.

IHT *abbr* inheritance tax

IIB *abbr* Institute of Insurance Brokers: in the United Kingdom, the professional body for insurance brokers and the caretaker for the deregulated Insurance Brokers Registration Council's complaints scheme

ILG *abbr* index-linked gilt

illegal parking a stock market practice that involves a broker or company purchasing securities in another company's name though they are guaranteed by the real investor (*slang*)

illiquid 1. used to describe a person or business that lacks cash or assets such as securities that can readily be converted into cash **2.** used to refer to an asset that cannot be easily converted into cash

IMA *abbr* **1.** (*ANZ*) Investment Management Agreement **2.** Investment Management Association

IMF *abbr* International Monetary Fund: the organisation that industrialised nations have established to reduce trade barriers and stabilise currencies, especially those of less industrialised nations

immediate holding company a company with one or more subsidiaries but which is itself a subsidiary of another company (the holding company)

impact day the day when the terms of a new issue of shares are announced

impaired capital a company's capital that is worth less than the par value of its stock

impairment of capital the extent to which the value of a company is less than the par value of its stock

imperfect competition a situation that exists in a market when there are strong barriers to the entry of new competitors

impersonal account any account other than a personal account, being classified as either a real account, in which property is recorded, or a nominal account, in which income, expenses, and capital are recorded. *See also account, personal account*

import duty a tax on goods imported into a country. Although it may simply be a measure for raising revenue, it can also be used to protect domestic manufacturers from overseas competition.

import penetration the situation in which one country's imports dominate the market share of those from other industrialised countries. This is the case, for example, with high-tech imports to the United States from Japan.

import surcharge an extra duty levied on imported goods in an attempt to limit imports in general and to encourage local manufacture

imposed budget a budget allowance which is set without permitting the ultimate budget holder to have the opportunity to participate in the budgeting process. *Also known as top-down budget*

imprest account a UK term for a record of the transactions of a type of petty cash system. An employee is given an advance of money, an imprest, for incidental expenses and when most of it has been spent, he or she presents receipts for the expenses to the accounts department and is then reimbursed with cash to the total value of the receipts.

imprest system a method of controlling cash or stock: when the cash or stock has been reduced by disbursements or issues, it is restored to its original level

imputation system a system in which recipients of dividends gain tax advantage for taxes paid by the company that paid the dividends

incentive scheme a programme set up to give benefits to employees to reward them for improved commitment and performance and as a means of motivation. An incentive scheme is designed to supplement *basic pay* and fringe benefits. A **financial incentive scheme** may offer share options or a cash bonus, whereas a **non-financial incentive scheme** offers benefits such as additional paid holidays. Awards from incentive schemes may be made on an individual or team basis.

incentive stock option in the United States, an employee stock option plan that gives each qualifying employee the right to purchase a specific number of the corporation's shares at a set price during a specific time period. Tax is only payable when the shares are sold.

incestuous share dealing share dealing by companies within a group in the shares of the other companies within that group. The legality of such transactions depends on the objective of the deals.

inchoate instrument a negotiable instrument that is incomplete because, for example, the date or amount is missing. The person to whom it is delivered has the prima facie authority to complete it in any way he or she considers fit.

incidence of tax used to indicate where the final burden of a tax lies. For example, although a retailer pays any sales tax to the tax collecting authority, the tax itself is ultimately paid by the customer.

income 1. money received by a company or individual **2.** money received from savings or investments, for example, interest on a deposit account or dividends from shares. This is also known as unearned income. **3.** money generated by a business

income and expenditure account a financial statement for non-profit entities such as clubs, associations, and charities. It shows the surplus or deficit, being the excess of income over expenditure or vice versa, for a period and is drawn up on the same accruals basis as a profit and loss account.

income bond a bond that a company repays only from its profits

income distribution 1. the UK term for the payment to investors of the income generated by a collective investment, less management charges, tax, and expenses. It is distributed in proportion to the number of units or shares held by each investor. *US term **income dividend*** **2.** the distribution of income across a particular group, such as a company, region, or country. It shows the various wage levels and gives the percentage of individuals earning at each level.

income dividend *(US)* = *income distribution*

income gearing the ratio of the interest a company pays on its borrowing shown as a percentage of its pre-tax profits

income-linked gilt a bond issued by the United Kingdom whose principal and interest track the retail price index

income redistribution a government policy to redirect income to a targeted sector of a country's population, for example, by lowering the rate of tax paid by low-income earners

income shares shares in an investment trust which receive income from the investments, but do not benefit from the rise in capital value of the investments. The other form of shares in a split-level investment trust are capital shares, which increase in value as the value of the investments rises, but do not receive any income.

income shares/stock 1. ordinary shares sought because of their relatively high yield as opposed to their potential to produce capital growth **2.** fixed interest securities acquired for their relatively high yield as opposed to their potential to produce capital growth **3.** certain funds, for example, investment trusts, that issue split level funds where holders of the income element receive all the income (less expenses, charges, and tax), while holders of the capital element receive only the capital gains (less expenses, charges, and tax)

income smoothing a UK term for a form of creative accounting that involves the manipulation of a company's financial statements to show steady annual profits rather than large fluctuations

incomes policy a government policy that seeks to restrain increases in wages or prices by regulating the permitted level of increase

income statement see *trading, profit and loss account*

income stream the income received by a company from a particular product or activity

income tax a tax levied directly on the income of a person and paid to the government. *Abbr* **IT**

income tax allowance a proportion of a person's income that is not subject to tax. Allowances are announced each year by the *Chancellor of the Exchequer* in the *Budget*.

income tax return a form used for reporting income and computing the tax due on it

income unit a unit in a unit trust that makes regular payments to its unit holders

income units units in a unit trust from which the investor receives dividends in the form of income (as opposed to accumulation units, from which the dividend is left to accumulate as new units)

income yield the actual percentage yield of government stocks, the fixed interest being shown as a percentage of the market price

incomplete records an accounting system which is not double-entry bookkeeping. Various degrees of incompleteness can occur, for example, *single-entry* bookkeeping, in which usually only a cash book is maintained.

incorporation the legal process of creating a corporation or company. All incorporated entities have a legal status distinct from that of their owners and most have limited liability.

incorporeal chattels intangible properties, such as patents or copyrights

incremental analysis analysis of the changes in costs and revenues caused by a change in activity. Normally the technique is used where a significant volume change occurs, causing changes to both variable and fixed costs, and possibly to selling prices. Incremental or differential costs and revenues are compared to determine the financial effect of the activity change.

incremental budgeting a method of setting budgets in which the prior period budget is used as a base for the current budget, which is set by adjusting the prior period budget to take account of any anticipated changes

incremental cost see *differential cost*

indemnity an agreement by one party to make good the losses suffered by another. *See also* **indemnity insurance,** *letter of indemnity*

indemnity insurance an insurance contract in which the insurer agrees to cover the cost of losses suffered by the insured party. Most insurance contracts take this form except personal accident and life assurance policies where fixed sums are paid as compensation, rather than reimbursement, for a loss that cannot be quantified in monetary terms.

indenture a formal agreement showing the terms of a *bond issue*

independent authenticator a company that has the authority, either from the government or a controlling body, to issue certificates of authentication when they are sure that a company is who it claims to be

index 1. a standard that represents the value of stocks in a market, particularly a figure such as the *Hang Seng*, FTSE 100, or Nikkei average **2.** an amount calculated to represent the relative value of a group of things

index arbitrage the buying or selling of a basket of stocks against an index option or future

indexation the linking of a rate to a standard index of prices, interest rates, share prices, or similar items

indexed portfolio a portfolio of shares in all the companies which form the basis of a stock exchange index

index fund a unit trust composed of companies listed in an important stock market index in order to match the market's overall performance. *See also managed fund. Also known as index-tracker, tracker fund*

index futures a futures contract trading in one of the major stock market indices, such as the *FTSE 100 Share Index. See also Dow Jones Averages*

index-linked bond a security where the income is linked to an index, such as a financial index. *See also index-linked gilt, index-linked savings certificate*

index-linked gilt an inflation-proof UK government bond, first introduced for institutional investors in 1981 and then made available to the general public in 1982. It is inflation-proof in two ways: the dividend is raised every six months in line with the Retail Price Index and the original capital is repaid in real terms at redemption, when the indexing of the repayment is undertaken. The nominal value of the stock, however, does not increase with inflation. Like other gilts, ILGs are traded on the market. Price changes are principally dependent on investors' changing perceptions of inflation and real yields. *Abbr* **ILG**

index-linked savings certificate a National Savings Certificate issued by the UK National Savings organisation with a return linked to the rate of inflation. *Also known as granny bond*

index number a weighted average of a number of observations of an economic attribute such as retail prices expressed as a percentage of a similar weighted average calculated at an earlier period

index tracker a fund which follows closely one of the stock market indices, such as the *FTSE 100 Share Index*

index-tracker *see index fund*

index tracking an investment technique whereby a portfolio is maintained in such a way as to match the growth in a stock market index

indicated dividend the forecast total of all dividends in a year if the amount of each dividend remains as it is

indicated yield the yield that an indicated dividend represents

indication price an approximation of the price of a security as opposed to its firm price

indicative price the price shown on a screen-based system for trading securities such as the UK Stock Exchange Automated Quotations system. The price is not firm, as the size of the bargain will determine the final price at which market makers will actually deal.

indirect cost a fixed or overhead cost that cannot be attributed directly to the production of a particular item and is incurred even when there is no output. Indirect costs may include the *cost centre* functions of finance and accounting, information technology, administration, and personnel. *See also direct cost*

individual retirement account *(US) see IRA*

Individual Savings Account *see ISA*

Individual Voluntary Arrangement a legally binding arrangement between debtors and creditors by which debtors offer the creditors the best deal they can afford by realising their assets, thus avoiding the expense of bankruptcy proceedings

industrial production the output of a country's productive industries. Until the 1960s, this commonly related to iron and steel or coal, but since then lighter engineering in motor car or robotics manufacture has taken over.

industrial revenue bond a bond that a private company uses to finance construction

industrial-sector cycle a business cycle that reflects patterns of an old economy rather than the new electronic economy

ineligible bills bills of exchange which cannot be discounted by a central bank

infant industry an industry in the early stages of development

inflation 1. a sustained increase in a country's general level of prices that devalues its currency, often caused by excess demand in the economy **2.** a general increase in the price level over time. *See also hyperinflation*

inflation accounting the adjustment of a company's accounts to reflect the effect of inflation and provide a more realistic view of the company's position

inflationary characterised by excess demand or high costs creating an excessive increase in the country's money supply

inflationary gap a gap that exists when an economy's resources are utilised and *aggregate demand* is more than the full-employment level of output. Prices will rise to remove the excess demand.

inflationary spiral a situation in which, repeatedly, in inflationary conditions, excess demand causes producers to raise prices and workers to demand wage rises to sustain their living standards

inflation-proof pension a pension which will rise to keep pace with inflation

inflation-proof security *(US)* a security that is indexed to inflation

inflation rate the rate at which general price levels increase over a period of time

inflation tax an incomes policy that taxes companies that grant pay rises above a particular level

info rate a money market rate quoted by dealers for information only

informal economy the economy that runs in parallel to the formal economy but outside the reach of the tax system, most transactions being paid for in cash or goods

infotainment television programmes that deal with serious issues or current affairs in an entertaining way

inheritance tax tax payable on wealth or property worth above a certain amount and inherited after the death of someone. The current threshold is £250,000, and the estate is liable for 40% tax on the excess amount.

initial offer the first offer that a company makes to buy the shares of another company

initial public offering the first instance of making particular shares available for sale to the public. *Abbr* **IPO**

injunction a court order forbidding an individual or organisation from doing something

inland bill a UK term for a bill of exchange that is payable and drawn in the same country

Inland Revenue *see* *Board of Inland Revenue*

Inland Revenue Department (*ANZ*) the New Zealand government body responsible for the administration of the national taxation system. *Abbr* **IRD**

input tax *see* *VAT*

input tax credit (*ANZ*) an amount paid as *Goods and Services Tax* on supplies purchased for business purposes, which can be offset against Goods and Services Tax collected

inside information information that is of advantage to investors but is only available to people who have personal contact with a company

inside quote a range of prices for a security, from the highest offer to buy to the lowest offer to sell

insider somebody intending to buy shares using access to privileged or confidential information that is not available to general investors

insider dealing *see* *insider trading*

insider trading *or* **insider dealing** profitable, usually illegal, trading in securities carried out using privileged information

insolvency the inability to pay debts when they become due. Insolvency will apply even if total assets exceed total liabilities, if those assets cannot be readily converted into cash to meet debts as they mature. Even then, insolvency may not necessarily mean business failure. *Bankruptcy* may be avoided through *debt rescheduling* or turnaround management.

inspector of taxes in the United Kingdom, an official who reports to the *Board of Inland Revenue* and is responsible for issuing tax returns and assessments, agreeing tax liabilities, and conducting appeals on matters of tax

instalment one of two or more payments or repayments for the purchase of an initial public offering

Instalment Activity Statement (*ANZ*) a standard form used in Australia to report *Pay-As-You-Go* instalment payments on investment income. *Abbr* **IAS**

instalment credit the UK term for a loan that is repaid with fixed regular instalments, and with a rate of interest fixed for the duration of the loan. *US term* **instalment loan**

instalment loan (*US*) = *instalment credit*

instalment plan (*US*) = *hire purchase*

instalment purchase a financing arrangement in which the buyer pays by a series of instalments over a period of time

instant access account an account which pays interest, but from which the account holder can withdraw money when he or she needs it

Institute of Chartered Accountants in England and Wales the largest professional accountancy body in Europe, providing qualification by examinations, ensuring high standards of education and training, and supervising professional conduct. *Abbr* **ICAEW**

Institute of Chartered Accountants in Ireland the oldest and largest professional body for accountants in Ireland, the ICAI was founded in 1888. Its many aims include promoting best practice in chartered accountancy and maintaining high standards of professionalism among its members. It publishes a journal, *Accountancy Ireland*, and has offices in Dublin and Belfast. *Abbr* **ICAI**

Institute of Chartered Accountants of Scotland the world's oldest professional body for accountants, based in Edinburgh. *Abbr* **ICAS**

Institute of Chartered Secretaries and Administrators *see ICSA*

Institute of Directors an individual membership association whose stated aim is to 'serve, support, represent, and set standards for directors'. Founded in 1903 by Royal Charter, the IoD has approximately 55,000 members and is an independent, non-political body. It is based in London, but also has offices in Belfast, Birmingham, Bristol, Edinburgh, Manchester, and Nottingham. *Abbr* **IoD**

Institute of Financial Accountants a professional body, established in 1916, which aims to set technical and ethical standards in UK financial accountancy. *Abbr* **IFA**

Institute of Financial Services the trading name of the Chartered Institute of Bankers

Institute of Insurance Brokers *see IIB*

institutional buyout the takeover of a company by a financial institution, which backs a group of managers who will run it

institutional investor an institution that makes investments

instrument 1. a generic term for either securities or derivatives. *See also financial instrument, negotiable instrument* **2.** an official or legal document **3.** a means to an end, for example, a government's expenditure and taxation in its quest for reducing unemployment

insurable risk *see risk*

insurance 1. an arrangement in which individuals or companies pay another company to guarantee them compensation if they suffer loss resulting from risks such as fire, theft, or accidental damage **2.** in financial markets, hedging or any other strategy that reduces risk while permitting participation in potential gains

insurance agent in the United States, an individual who sells the insurance policies of a particular company

Insurance and Superannuation Commission (*ANZ*) an Australian federal government body responsible for regulating the superannuation and insurance industries. *Abbr* **ISC**

insurance broker a person or company that acts as an intermediary between companies providing insurance and individuals or companies who need insurance

Insurance Brokers Registration Council *see IBRC*

Insurance Council of Australia an independent body representing the interests of businesses involved in the insurance industry. It was set up in

1975 and currently represents around 110 companies. *Abbr* **ICA**

insurance intermediary an individual or firm that provides advice on insurance or assurance and can arrange policies. *See also* ***IBRC, IIB***

insurance policy a document that sets out the terms and conditions for providing insurance cover against specified risks

insurance premium tax a tax on household, motor vehicle, travel, and other general insurance

insured covered by a contract of insurance

insured account (*US*) an account with a bank or savings institution that belongs to a federal or private insurance organisation

insurer the underwriter of an insurance risk

intangible asset an asset such as intellectual property or ***goodwill*** that is not physical. *Also known as* ***invisible asset***

integrated accounts a set of accounting records which provides both financial and cost accounts using a common input of data for all accounting purposes

intellectual capital knowledge which can be used to create value. Intellectual capital includes: human resources, the collective skills, experience, and knowledge of employees; intellectual assets, knowledge which is defined and codified such as a drawing, computer program, or collection of data; and intellectual property, intellectual assets which can be legally protected, such as patents and copyrights.

intellectual property the ownership of rights to ideas, designs, and inventions, including copyrights, ***patents***, and trademarks. Intellectual property is protected by law in most countries, and

the World Intellectual Property Organisation is responsible for harmonising the law across different countries and promoting the protection of intellectual property rights.

Inter Bank Offered Rate *see IBOR*

Inter Bank Rate *abbr* **IBR**

interchangeable bond a bond whose owner can change it at will between bearer and book-entry form

intercommodity spread a combination of purchase and sale of options for related commodities with the same delivery date

intercompany pricing the setting of prices by companies within a group to sell products or services to each other, rather than to external customers

interdependency concept the principle that management accounting, in recognition of the increasing complexity of business, must access both external and internal information sources from interactive functions such as marketing, production, personnel, procurement, and finance. This assists in ensuring that the information is adequately balanced.

interest the rate that a lender charges for the use of money that is a loan

interest arbitrage transactions in two or more financial centres in order to make an immediate profit by exploiting differences in interest rates. *See also* ***arbitrage***

interest assumption the expected rate of return on a portfolio

interest charged the cost of borrowing money, expressed as an absolute amount, or, as a percentage interest rate. *See also* ***annual percentage rate, nominal interest rate, real interest rate***

interest cover the amount of earnings available to make interest payments after all operating and non-operating income and expenses—except interest and income taxes—have been accounted for.

Interest cover is regarded as a measure of a company's creditworthiness because it shows how much income there is to cover interest payments on outstanding debt.

It is expressed as a ratio, comparing the funds available to pay interest—earnings before interest and taxes, or EBIT—with the interest expense. The basic formula is:

**EBIT / interest expense =
Interest coverage ratio**

EXAMPLE If interest expense for a year is £9 million, and the company's EBIT is £45 million, the interest coverage would be:

45 million / 9 million = 5:1

The higher the number, the stronger a company is likely to be. A ratio of less than 1 indicates that a company is having problems generating enough cash flow to pay its interest expenses, and that either a modest decline in operating profits or a sudden rise in borrowing costs could eliminate profitability entirely. Ideally, interest coverage should at least exceed 1.5; in some sectors, 2.0 or higher is desirable.

Variations of this basic formula also exist. For example, there is:

**Operating cash flow + interest + taxes /
interest = Cash-flow interest
coverage ratio**

This ratio indicates the firm's ability to use its cash flow to satisfy its fixed financing obligations. Finally, there is the fixed-charge coverage ratio, which compares EBIT with fixed charges:

**EBIT + lease expenses / interest + lease
expense = Fixed-charge coverage ratio**

'Fixed charges' can be interpreted in many ways, however. It could mean, for example, the funds that a company is obliged to set aside to retire debt, or dividends on preferred stock.

interest-elastic investment an investment with a rate of return that varies with interest rates

interest-inelastic investment an investment with a rate of return that does not vary with interest rates

interest in possession trust a trust that gives one or more beneficiaries an immediate right to receive any income generated by the trust's assets. It can be used for property, enabling the beneficiary either to enjoy the rent generated by the property or to reside there, or as a life policy, a common arrangement for inheritance tax planning.

interest-only mortgage a long-term loan, usually for the purchase of a property, in which the borrower only pays interest to the lender during the term of the mortgage, with the principal being repaid at the end of the term. It is thus the borrower's responsibility to make provisions to accumulate the required capital during the period of the mortgage, usually by contributing to tax efficient investment plans such as Individual Savings Accounts or by relying on an anticipated inheritance. *See also **mortgage***

interest rate the amount of interest charged for borrowing a sum of money over a specified period of time

interest rate cap an upper limit on a rate of interest, for example, in an adjustable-rate mortgage

interest rate collar a combination of an interest rate floor and an interest rate cap for the same loan

interest rate effect the mechanism by which interest rates adjust so that investment is equal to savings in an economy

interest rate exposure the risk of a loss associated with movements in the level of interest rates. *See also **bond***

interest rate floor a lower limit on a rate of interest, for example, in an adjustable-rate mortgage

interest rate future *see future*

interest rate guarantee 1. an interest rate cap, collar, or cap and collar **2.** a tailored indemnity protecting the purchaser against future changes in interest rates

interest rate option *see option*

interest rate parity theory a method of predicting foreign exchange rates based on the hypothesis that the difference between the interest rates in two countries should offset the difference between the spot rates and the forward foreign exchange rates over the same period

interest rate risk *(US)* the risk of a loss associated with movements in the level of interest rates. = *interest rate exposure*

interest rate swap an exchange of two debt instruments with different rates of interest, made to tailor cash flows to the participants' different requirements

interest sensitive used to describe assets, generally purchased with credit, that are in demand when interest rates fall but considered less attractive when interest rates rise

interest yield the annual rate of interest earned on a security, excluding the effect of any increase in price to maturity

interfirm comparison systematic and detailed comparison of the performance of different companies generally operating in a common industry. Companies participating in such a scheme normally provide standardised, and therefore comparable, information to the scheme administrator, who then distributes to participating members only the information supplied by participants. Normally the information distributed is in the form of ratios, or in a format which prevents the identity of individual scheme members from coming to light.

interim certificate a document certifying partial ownership of stock that is not totally paid for at one time

interim dividend a dividend whose value is determined on the basis of a period of time of less than a full fiscal year

interim financial statement a financial statement that covers a period other than a full financial year. Although UK companies are not legally obliged to publish interim financial statements, those listed on the London Stock Exchange are obliged to publish a half-yearly report of their activities and a profit and loss account which may either be sent to shareholders or published in a national newspaper. In the United States, the practice is to issue quarterly financial statements.

interim financing financing by means of bridging loans

interim statement a financial statement relating to a period of time of less than a full fiscal year

interlocking accounts a system in which cost accounts are kept distinct from the financial accounts, the two sets of accounts being kept continuously in agreement by the use of control accounts or reconciled by other means. *Also known as* **non-integrated accounts**

intermarket spread a combination of purchase and sale of options for the same commodity with the same delivery date on different markets

intermediary somebody who makes investments for others

internal audit an audit of a company undertaken by its employees. *See also* **external audit**

internal check the procedures designed to provide assurance that everything which should be recorded has been recorded; errors or irregularities are identified; assets and liabilities exist and are correctly recorded

internal cost analysis an examination of an organisation's value-creating activities to determine sources of profitability and to identify the relative costs of different processes. Internal cost analysis is a tool for analysing the *value chain*. Principal steps include identifying those processes that create value for the organisation, calculating the cost of each value-creating process against the overall cost of the product or service, identifying the cost components for each process, establishing the links between the processes, and working out the opportunities for achieving relative cost advantage.

internal growth organic growth created within a business, for example, by inventing new products and so increasing its market share, producing products that are more reliable, offering a more efficient service than its competitors, or being more aggressive in its marketing. *See also **external growth***

internal rate of return in a discounted cash-flow calculation, the rate of interest that reduces future income streams to the cost of the investment; practically speaking, the rate that indicates whether or not an investment is worth pursuing. EXAMPLE Let's assume that a project under consideration costs £7,500 and is expected to return £2,000 per year for five years, or £10,000. The IRR calculated for the project would be about 10%. If the cost of borrowing money for the project, or the return on investing the funds elsewhere, is less than 10%, the project is probably worthwhile. If the alternative use of the money will return 10% or more, the project should be rejected, since from a financial perspective it will break even at best.

Typically, managements require an IRR equal to or higher than the cost of capital, depending on relative risk and other factors.

The best way to compute an IRR is by using a spreadsheet (such as Excel) or financial calculator.

If using Excel, for example, select the IRR function. This requires the annual cash-flows to be set out in columns and the first part of the IRR formula requires the cell reference range of these cash-flows to be entered. Then a guess of the IRR is required. The default is 10%, written 0.1.

If a project has the following expected cash-flows, then guessing IRR at 30% returns an accurate IRR of 27%, indicating that if the next best way of investing the money gives a return of −20%, the project should go ahead.

Now	−2,500
Year 1	1,200
Year 2	1,300
Year 3	1,500

IRR can be misleading, especially as significant costs will occur late in the project. The rule of thumb 'the higher the IRR the better' does not always apply. For the most thorough analysis of a project's investment potential, some experts urge using both IRR and net present value calculations, and comparing their results. *Abbr* **IRR**

Internal Revenue Code (*US*) the complex series of federal tax laws

Internal Revenue Service *see IRS*

International Accounting Standards Board an independent and privately funded accounting standards setting organisation, based in London. The Board, whose members come from nine countries and a range of backgrounds, is committed to developing a single set of high quality, understandable, and enforceable global standards that require transparent and comparable information in general purpose financial statements. It also works with national accounting standard setters to achieve convergence in accounting standards around the world. *Abbr* **IASB**

International Accounting Standards Committee an organisation based in London that works towards achieving global agreement on accounting standards. *Abbr* **IASC**

International Bank for Reconstruction and Development *see IBRD*

International Centre for Settlement of Investment Disputes one of the five institutions that comprise the World Bank Group. It was established in 1966 to undertake the role previously undertaken in a personal capacity by the President of the World Bank in assisting in mediation or conciliation of investment disputes between governments and private foreign investors. The overriding consideration in its establishment was that a specialist institution could help to promote increased flows of international investment. Although ICSID has close links to the World Bank, it is an autonomous organisation. *Abbr* **ICSID**

International Chamber of Commerce *see ICC*

International Depository Receipt the equivalent of an **American depository receipt** in the rest of the world, an IDR is a negotiable certificate issued by a bank that indicates ownership of stock. *Abbr of* **IDR**

International Development Association *see IDA*

International Energy Authority *see IEA*

International Finance Corporation *see IFC*

international fund a unit trust that invests in securities both inside and outside a country

International Fund for Agricultural Development a specialised United Nations agency with a mandate to combat hunger and rural poverty in developing countries. Established as an international financial institution in 1977 following the 1974 World Food Conference, it has financed projects in over 100 countries and independent territories, to which it has committed US$7.7 billion in grants and loans. It has three sources of finance (contributions from members, loan repayments, and investment income) and an annual commitment level of approximately US$450 million.

International Monetary Fund *see IMF*

International Organization of Securities Commissions an organisation of securities commissions from around the world, based in Madrid. Its objectives are to promote high standards of regulation, exchange information, and establish standards for and effective surveillance of international securities transactions. *Abbr* **IOSCO**

International Securities Market Association the self-regulatory organisation and trade association for the international securities market. Its primary role is to oversee the fast-changing marketplace through the issuing of rules and recommendations relating to trading and settlement practices. Established in 1969, the organisation has over 600 members from 51 countries. *Abbr* **ISMA**

International Union of Credit and Investment Insurers an organisation that works for international acceptance of sound principles of export credit and foreign investment insurance. Founded in 1934, the London-based Union has 51 members in 42 countries who play a role of central importance in world trade, both as regards exports and foreign direct investments. *Also known as* **Berne Union**

Internet commerce the part of *e-commerce* that consists of commercial transactions conducted over the Internet

Internet merchant a businessman or businesswoman who sells a product or service over the Internet

Internet payment system any mechanism for fund transfer from customer to merchant or business to business via the Internet. There are many payment options available, including credit card payment, credit transfer, electronic cheques, direct debit, smart cards, prepaid schemes, loyalty scheme points-based approaches, person-to-person payments, and mobile phone schemes.

Getting the online payment system right is critical to the success of e-commerce. Currently, the most common form of online consumer payment is by credit card (90% in the United States; 70% in Europe). The most common business-to-business payments, however, are still offline—probably because such transactions often involve large sums of money.

Good online payment systems share key characteristics: ease of use; robustness and reliability; proper authentication (to combat fraud); efficient integration with the vendor's own internal systems; security and assurance procedures which check that the seller gets the money and the buyer gets the goods.

interstate commerce commerce that involves more than one US state and is therefore subject to regulation by Congress. See also **intrastate commerce**

intervention government action to manipulate market forces for political or economic purposes

intervention mechanism any of the methods used by central banks in maintaining exchange rate parities, such as the buying or selling of foreign currency

in the money used to refer to an option with **intrinsic value**

in-the-money option an option whose underlying transaction shows a profit. See **out-of-the-money option**

intrastate commerce commerce that occurs within a single state of the United States. See also **interstate commerce**

intrinsic value the difference between the exercise price of an option and its market value

introducing broker a broker who cannot accept payment from customers

inventory (US) the total of an organisation's commercial assets

inventory turnover an accounting ratio of the number of times **inventory** is replaced during a given period. The ratio is calculated by dividing net sales by average inventory over a given period. Values are expressed as times per period, most often a year, and a higher figure indicates a more efficient manufacturing operation. Also known as **stock turns**

EXAMPLE It is calculated as follows:

Cost of goods sold / Inventory

If COGS is £2 million, and inventory at the end of the period is £500,000, then:

2,000,000 / 500,000 = 4.

inverse floating rate note a note whose interest rate varies inversely with a **benchmark interest rate**

inverted market a situation in which near-term futures cost more than long-term futures for the same commodity

inverted money a situation in which near-term futures cost more than long-term futures for the same commodity

inverted yield curve a yield curve with lower interest rates for long-term bonds than for short-term bonds. See also **yield curve**

investment any application of funds which is intended to provide a return by way of interest, dividend, or capital appreciation

investment analyst an employee of a stock-exchange company who researches other companies and identifies investment opportunities for clients. *Also known as financial analyst*

investment appraisal analysis of the future profitability of capital purchases as an aid to good management

investment bank 1. a bank that specialises in providing funds to corporate borrowers for start-up or expansion. *Abbr* **IB 2.** (*US*) = *merchant bank*. *Abbr* **IB**

investment bill a bill of exchange that is an investment

investment bond in the United Kingdom, a product where the investment is paid as a single premium into a life assurance policy with an underlying asset-backed fund. The bondholder receives a regular income until the end of the bond's term when the investment—the current value of the fund—is returned to the bondholder.

investment borrowing the borrowing of funds intended to encourage a country's economic growth or to support the development of particular industries or regions by adding to physical or human capital

investment centre a *profit centre* with additional responsibilities for capital investment, and possibly for financing, and whose performance is measured by its return on investment

investment club a group of people who join together to make investments in securities

investment committee (*US*) a group of employees of an investment bank who evaluate investment proposals

investment company (*US*) a company that pools for investment the money of several investors by means of unit trusts

investment dealer (*Canada*) a securities broker

investment fund a savings scheme that invests its clients' funds in corporate start-up or expansion projects

Investment Management Agreement (*ANZ*) a contract between an investor and an investment manager required under SIS legislation. *Abbr* **IMA**

Investment Management Association the trade body for the UK investment industry, formed in February 2002 following the merger of the Association of Unit Trusts and Investment Funds (AUTIF) and the Fund Managers' Association. *Abbr* **IMA**

investment manager see *fund manager*

investment portfolio see *portfolio*

investment properties either commercial buildings (for example, shops, factories, or offices) or residential dwellings (for example, houses or apartments) that are purchased by businesses or individuals for renting to third parties

investment revaluation reserve the capital reserve where changes in the value of a business's investment properties are disclosed when they are revalued

investment tax credit (*US*) a tax advantage for investment, available until 1986 in the United States

investment trust an association of investors that invests in securities

investomer a customer of a business who is also an investor (*slang*)

investor a person or organisation that invests money in something, especially in shares of publicly owned corporations

invisible asset *see intangible asset*

invisible earnings foreign currency earned by a country in providing services, such as banking and tourism, rather than in selling goods

invisible exports the profits, dividends, interest, and royalties received from selling a country's services abroad

invisible imports the profits, dividends, interest, and royalties paid to foreign service companies based in a country

invisibles items such as financial and leisure services, as opposed to physical goods, that are traded by a country

invisible trade trade in items such as financial and other services that are listed in the current account of the balance of payments

invoice 1. a document that a supplier sends to a customer detailing the cost of products or services supplied and requesting payment **2.** a document prepared by a supplier showing the description, quantities, prices, and values of goods delivered or services rendered. To the supplier this is a sales invoice; to the purchaser the same document is a purchase invoice.

invoice date the date on which an invoice is issued. The invoice date may be different from the delivery date.

invoice discounting the selling of invoices at a discount for collection by the buyer

invoice register a list of purchase invoices recording the date of receipt of the invoice, the supplier, the invoice value, and the person to whom the invoice has been passed to ensure that all invoices are processed by the accounting system

invoicing the process of issuing invoices

involuntary liquidation preference a payment that a company must make to holders of its preference shares if it is forced to sell its assets when facing bankruptcy

inward investment investment by a government or company in its own country or region, often to stimulate employment or develop a business infrastructure

IoD *abbr* Institute of Directors

IOSCO *abbr* International Organization of Securities Commissions

IOU a rendition in letters of 'I owe you' that can be used as legal evidence of a debt, although it is most commonly used by an individual as a reminder that small change has been taken, for example, from a float

IPO *abbr* initial public offering

IRA *abbr* (*US*) individual retirement account: a pension plan, designed for individuals without a company pension scheme, that allows annual sums, subject to limits dependent upon employment income, to be set aside from earnings tax free. Individuals with a company pension may invest in an IRA, but only from their net income. IRAs, including the Education IRA, designed as a way of saving for children's education, may invest in almost any financial security except property.

IRD (*ANZ*) *abbr* Inland Revenue Department

IRD number (*ANZ*) a numeric code assigned to all members of the New Zealand workforce for the purpose of paying income tax

IRR *abbr* internal rate of return

irredeemable bond a government bond which has no date of maturity and which therefore provides interest but can never be redeemed at full value

irrevocable letter of credit *see letter of credit*

IRS *abbr* Internal Revenue Service: in the United States, the branch of the federal government charged with collecting the majority of federal taxes

ISA *abbr* Individual Savings Account: a portfolio created according to rules that exempt its proceeds, including dividends and capital gains, from taxes. It was launched in 1999 with the intention that it would be available for at least ten years. Individuals may invest up to £7,000 each year, £3,000 of which may be invested in a savings account and £1,000 in life assurance. Either the remaining £3,000, or the entire £7,000, may be invested in the stock market. A 'maxi' ISA is an investment of up to the maximum amount, whether divided or entirely in the stock market, that has been purchased from one provider only. A 'mini' ISA is one of the three individual components which may be purchased from different providers. Investors may therefore have up to three 'minis', but only one 'maxi'.

ISCID *abbr* International Centre for Settlement of Investment Disputes

ISDA *abbr* International Swaps and Derivatives Association

ISMA *abbr* International Securities Market Association

ISO 9000 a quality system standard which requires complying organisations to operate in accordance with a structure of written policies and procedures that are designed to ensure the consistent delivery of a product or service to meet customer requirements

issuance costs the underwriting, legal, and administrative fees required to issue a debt. These fees are significant when issuing debt in the public markets, such as bonds. However, other types of debt, such as private placements or bank loans, are cheaper to issue because they require less underwriting, legal, and administrative support.

issue a set of stocks or bonds that a company offers for sale at one time

issue by tender *see sale by tender*

issued capital an amount of capital which is formed of money paid for shares issued to shareholders

Issue Department the department of the Bank of England that is responsible for issuing currency

issued price the price of shares in a new company when they are offered for sale for the first time

issued share capital the type, class, number, and amount of the shares held by shareholders

issued shares those shares that comprise a company's authorised capital that has been distributed to investors. They may be either fully paid or partly paid shares.

issue price the price at which securities are first offered for sale

issuer a financial institution that issues payment cards, such as credit or debit cards, pays out to the merchant's account, and bills the customer or debits the customer's account. The issuer guarantees payment for authorised transactions using the payment card. *Also known as* **card-issuing bank**, **issuing bank**

issuer bid an offer made by an issuer for its own securities when it is disappointed by the offers of others

issuing bank *see issuer*

issuing house in the United Kingdom, a financial institution that specialises in the flotation of private companies. *See also* **investment bank**, **merchant bank**

IT *abbr* income tax

item a single piece of information included in a company's accounts

J

Jensen's measure *see* *risk-adjusted return on capital*

jikan in Japan, the priority rule relating to transactions on the Tokyo Stock Exchange whereby the earlier of two buy or sell orders received at the same price prevails

job a customer order or task of a relatively short duration

jobber's turn formerly, a term used on the London Stock Exchange for a *spread*

jobbing backwards a UK term for the analysis of an investment transaction with a view to learning from mistakes rather than apportioning blame

job card *see* *clock card*

job costing a form of specific order costing in which costs are attributed to individual jobs

job cost sheet a detailed record of the amount, and cost, of the labour, material, and overhead charged to a specific job

job lot a miscellaneous assortment of items, including securities, that are offered as a single deal

joint account an account, for example one held at a bank or by a broker, that two or more people own in common and have access to

joint and several liability a legal liability that applies to a group of individuals as a whole and each member individually, so that if one member does not meet his or her liability, the shortfall is the shared responsibility of the others. Most guarantees given by two or more individuals to secure borrowing are joint and several. It is a typical feature of most partnership agreements.

joint cost the cost of a process which results in more than one main product

joint float a group of currencies which maintains a fixed internal relationship and moves jointly in relation to another currency

joint life annuity an annuity that continues until both parties have died. They are attractive to married couples as they ensure that the survivor has an income for the rest of his or her life.

joint products two or more products produced by the same process and separated in processing, each having a sufficiently high saleable value to merit recognition as a main product. *See also* *by-product*

joint return a tax return filed jointly by a husband and wife

joint stock bank a term that was formerly used for a commercial bank (one that is a partnership), rather than a High Street bank (one that is a public limited company)

joint venture a project undertaken by two or more persons/entities joining together with a view to profit, often in connection with a single operation. *Abbr* **JV**

journal a record of original entry, into which transactions are normally transferred from source documents. The journal may be subdivided into: sales journal/day book for credit sales; purchases journal/day book for credit purchases; cash book for cash receipts and payments; and the journal proper for transactions which could not appropriately be recorded in any of the other journals.

JSE *abbr* Johannesburg Stock Exchange: the former unofficial name of the JSE Securities Exchange

judgment creditor in a legal action, the individual or business who has brought the action and to whom the court orders the judgment debtor to pay the money owed. In the event of the *judgment debtor* not conforming to the court order, the judgment creditor must return to the court to request that the judgment be enforced.

judgment debtor in a legal action, the individual or business ordered to pay the *judgment creditor* the money owed

jumbo mortgage (*US*) a mortgage that is too large to qualify for favourable treatment by a US government agency

junior capital capital in the form of shareholders' equity, which is repaid only after secured loans (or senior capital) have been paid if the firm goes into liquidation

junior debt a debt that has no claim on a debtor's assets, or less claim than another debt. *See also senior debt. Also known as subordinated debt*

junior mortgage a mortgage whose holder has less claim on a debtor's assets than the holder of another mortgage. *See also senior mortgage*

junk bond[1] a high-yielding bond issued on a low-grade security. The issue of junk bonds has most commonly been linked with takeover activity.

junk bond[2] a bond with high return and high risk (*slang*)

just-in-time production a production system which is driven by demand for finished products, whereby each component on a production line is produced only when needed for the next stage

just-in-time purchasing a purchasing system in which material purchases are contracted so that the receipt and usage of material coincide to the maximum extent possible

JV *abbr* joint venture

K

K *abbr* a thousand

kaizen budget a budget into which is incorporated the expectation of continuous performance improvement throughout the budget period

kakaku yusen in Japan, the price priority system operated on the Tokyo Stock Exchange whereby a lower price takes precedence over a higher price for a sell order, and vice versa for a buy order. *See also jikan*

kangaroo an Australian share traded on the London Stock Exchange (*slang*)

Kansas City Board of Trade a commodities exchange, established in 1856, that specialises in futures and options contracts for red winter wheat, the Value Line© Index, natural gas, and the ISDEX© Internet Stock Index

Keidanren the Japanese abbreviation for the Japan Federation of Economic Organizations. Established in 1946, it aims to work towards a resolution of the major problems facing the Japanese and international business communities and to contribute to the sound development of their economies. The equivalent of the Confederation of British Industry, its members include over 1,000 of Japan's leading corporations (including over 50 foreign companies) and over 100 industry-wide groups representing such major sectors as manufacturing, trade, distribution, finance, and energy.

Keough Plan a pension subject to tax advantage in the United States for somebody who is self-employed or has an interest in a small company. *See also stakeholder pension*

kerb market a stock market that exists outside the stock exchange. The term originates from markets held in the street.

Keynesian economics the economic teachings and doctrines associated with John Maynard Keynes

kickback a sum of money paid illegally in order to gain concessions or favours (*slang*)

kicker an addition to a standard security that makes it more attractive, for example, options and warrants (*slang*) *See also bells and whistles, sweetener (sense 2)*

kill to stop, as in the request 'kill that order' (*slang*)

killerbee somebody, especially a banker, who helps a company avoid being taken over

killing a considerable profit on a transaction (*slang*)

kite 1. a fraudulent financial transaction, for example, a bad cheque that is dated to take advantage of the time interval required for clearing **2.** to write bad cheques in order to take advantage of the time interval required for clearing

    fly a kite to use a fraudulent financial document such as a bad cheque

kiwibond a Eurobond denominated in New Zealand dollars

knight a term borrowed from chess strategy to describe a company involved in the politics of a *takeover* bid. There are three main types of knight. A **white knight** is a company that is friendly to the board of the company to be acquired. If the white knight gains control, it may retain the existing *board of directors*. A **black knight** is a former white knight that has disagreed with the board of the company to be acquired and has set up its own hostile bid. A **grey knight** is a white knight that does not have the confidence of the company to be acquired.

knock-for-knock used to describe a practice between insurance companies whereby each will pay for the repairs to the vehicle it insures in the event of an accident

knock-out option an option to which a condition relating to the underlying security or commodity's present price is attached so that it effectively expires when it goes out of the money

know-how fund a fund created by the UK government to provide technical training and advice to countries of Eastern Europe

Krugerrand a South African coin consisting of one ounce of gold, first minted in 1967, bearing the portrait of 19th century statesman and South African president Paul Kruger on the obverse

L

labour-intensive involving large numbers of workers or high labour costs

lagging indicator (*US*) a measurable economic factor, for example, corporate profits or unemployment, that changes after the economy has already moved to a new trend, which it can confirm but not predict

land bank the land that a builder or developer has that is available for development

land banking (*US*) the practice of buying land that is not needed immediately, but with the expectation of using it in the future

landed costs costs of goods which have been delivered to a port, unloaded, and passed through customs

landing order a permit which allows an importer to unload goods into a bonded warehouse without paying customs duty

land tax a form of wealth tax imposed in Australia on the value of residential land. The level and conditions of the tax vary from state to state.

lapping (*US*) = *teeming and lading*

lapse the termination of an option without trade in the underlying security or commodity

lapse rights rights, such as those to a specified premium, owned by the person who allows an offer to lapse

last survivor policy an assurance policy covering the lives of two or more people. The sum assured is not paid out until all the policyholders are deceased. *See also **joint life annuity***

last trading day the last day when stock exchange trading takes place in an account, or the last day when futures trading takes place relating to a certain delivery month

launder to pass the profits of illegal activities, such as tax evasion, into the normal banking system via apparently legitimate businesses

laundering the process of making money obtained illegally appear legitimate by passing it through banks or businesses

law of diminishing returns a rule stating that as one factor of production is increased, while others remain constant, the extra output generated by the additional input will eventually fall. The law of diminishing returns therefore means that extra workers, extra capital, extra machinery, or extra land may not necessarily raise output as much as expected. For example, increasing the supply of raw materials to a production line may allow additional output to be produced by using any spare capacity workers have. Once this capacity is fully used, however, continually increasing the amount of raw material without a corresponding increase in the number of workers will not result in an increase of output.

law of supply and demand *see **supply and demand***

LBO *abbr* leveraged buyout

L/C *abbr* letter of credit

LCH *abbr* London Clearing House

LCM *abbr* lower of cost or market

LDC *abbr* less developed country

lead in an insurance policy from Lloyd's, the first named underwriting syndicate

lead bank the main bank in a loan syndicate

leading economic indicator a factor, such as private-sector wages, that is used as a reference for public-sector wage claims

leading indicator an indicator, such as manufacturing order books, which shows a change in economic trends earlier than other indicators

lead manager the financial institution with overall responsibility for a new issue including its co-ordination, distribution, and related administration

leads and lags in businesses that deal in foreign currencies, the practice of speeding up the receipt of payments (leads) if a currency is going to weaken, and slowing down the payment of costs (lags) if a currency is thought to be about to strengthen, in order to maximise gains and reduce losses

lead time the time interval between the start of an activity or process and its completion, for example, the time between ordering goods and their receipt, or between starting manufacturing of a product and its completion

lead underwriter *(US)* = *lead manager*

LEAPS *abbr* long-term equity anticipation securities: options that expire between one and three years in the future

learning curve the mathematical expression of the phenomenon that when complex and labour-intensive procedures are repeated, unit labour times tend to decrease at a constant rate. The learning curve models mathematically this reduction in unit production time.

leaseback *see sale and leaseback*

ledger 1. a book in which account transactions are recorded **2.** a collection of accounts, or book of accounts. Credit sales information is recorded, for example, by debtor, in the sales ledger. **3.** a collection of accounts, maintained by transfers from the books of original entry. The ledger may be subdivided as follows: the sales ledger/debtors' ledger contains all the personal accounts of customers; the purchases ledger/creditors' ledger contains all the personal accounts of suppliers; the private ledger contains accounts relating to the proprietor's interest in the business such as capital and drawings; the general ledger/nominal ledger contains all other accounts relating to assets, expenses, revenue, and liabilities.

legacy system an existing computer system that provides a strategic function for a specific part of a business. Inventory management systems, for example, are legacy systems.

legal tender banknotes and coins that have to be accepted within a given jurisdiction when offered as payment of a debt. *See also* **limited legal tender**

lemon an investment that is performing poorly (*slang*)

lender of last resort a central bank that lends money to banks that cannot borrow elsewhere

less developed countries countries which are not economically advanced and borrowed heavily from commercial banks in the 1970s and 1980s to finance their industrial development, and so created an international debt crisis

less developed country a country whose economic development is held back by the lack of the natural resources needed to produce goods demanded on world markets. *Abbr* **LDC**

lessee the person who has the use of a leased asset

lessor the person who provides the asset being leased

letter of allotment a document that says how many shares have been allotted to a shareholder

letter of comfort a letter from a holding company addressed to a bank where one of its subsidiaries wishes to borrow money. The purpose of the letter is to support the subsidiary's application to borrow funds and offer reassurance— although not a guarantee—to the bank that the subsidiary will remain in business for the foreseeable future, often with an undertaking to advise the bank if the subsidiary is likely to be sold. *US term **letter of moral intent***

letter of credit a letter issued by a bank that can be presented to another bank to authorise the issue of credit or money. *Abbr* **L/C**. *Also known as **irrevocable letter of credit***

letter of indemnity a statement that a share certificate has been lost, destroyed, or stolen and that the shareholder will indemnify the company for any loss that might result from its reappearance after the company has issued a replacement to the shareholder

letter of intent a document in which an individual or organisation indicates an intention to do something, for example, buy a business, grant somebody a loan, or participate in a project. The intention may or may not depend on certain conditions being met and the document is not legally binding. *See also **letter of comfort***

letter of licence a letter from a creditor to a debtor who is having problems repaying money owed, giving the debtor a certain period of time to raise the money and an undertaking not to bring legal proceedings to recover the debt during that period

letter of moral intent *(US)* = *letter of comfort*

letter of renunciation a form used to transfer an allotment

letters patent a official document which gives someone the exclusive right to make and sell something which he or she has invented

level term assurance a life assurance policy in which an agreed lump sum is paid if the policyholder dies before a certain date. A joint form of this life cover is popular with couples who have children.

leverage a method of corporate funding in which a higher proportion of funds is raised through borrowing than share issue

leveraged bid a takeover bid financed by borrowed money, rather than by an issue of shares

leveraged buyout a takeover using borrowed money, with the purchased company's assets as collateral. *Abbr* **LBO**

leveraged required return the rate of return from an investment of borrowed money needed to make the investment worthwhile

leverage ratios *(US)* = *gearing ratios*

liability a debt that has no claim on a debtor's assets, or less claim than another debt

liability insurance insurance against legal liability that the insured might incur, for example, from causing an accident

liability management any exercise carried out by a business with the aim of controlling the effect of liabilities on its profitability. This will typically involve controlling the amount of risk undertaken, and ensuring that there is sufficient liquidity and that the best terms are obtained for any funding needs.

LIBID *abbr* London Inter Bank Bid Rate

LIBOR *abbr* London Inter Bank Offered Rate

licence a contractual arrangement, or a document representing this, in which one organisation gives another the rights to produce, sell, or use something in return for payment

licensing the transfer of rights to manufacture or market a particular product to another individual or organisation through a legal arrangement or contract. Licensing usually requires that a fee, commission, or royalty is paid to the licensor.

licensing agreement an agreement permitting a company to market or produce a product or service owned by another company. A licensing agreement grants a licence in return for a fee or royalty payment. Items licensed for use can include patents, trademarks, techniques, designs, and expertise. This kind of agreement is one way for a company to penetrate overseas markets in that it provides a middle path between direct export and investment overseas.

life annuity an annuity that pays a fixed amount per month until the holder's death

life assurance insurance that pays a specified sum to the insured person's beneficiaries after the person's death. *US term* **life insurance**. *Also known as* **life cover**

life assured the person or persons covered by a life assurance policy. The *life office* pays out on the death of the policyholder.

lifeboat (*S Africa*) a low-interest emergency loan made by a central bank to rescue a commercial bank in danger of becoming insolvent

life cover *see* **life assurance**

life-cycle costing the maintenance of physical asset cost records over the life of an entire asset, so that decisions concerning the acquisition, use, or disposal of the assets can be made in a way that achieves the optimum asset usage at the lowest possible cost to the entity. The term may be applied to the profiling of cost over a product's life, including the pre-production stage (**terotechnology**), and to both company and industry life cycles.

life-cycle savings motive a reason that a household or individual has for saving or spending during the course of their life, as, for example, spending when starting a family or saving when near retirement

life insurance US *see* **life assurance**

life interest a situation where someone benefits from a property for the entirety of his or her lifetime

life office a company that provides *life assurance*

life policy a life assurance contract

lifestyle business a typically small business run by individuals who have a keen interest in the product or service offered, for example, handmade greetings cards or jewellery, antique dealing or restoring. Such businesses tend to operate during hours that suit the owners, and generally provide them with a comfortable living.

lifetime transfer *see* *chargeable transfer*

lifetime value a measure of the total value to a supplier of a customer's business over the duration of their transactions.

In a consumer business, customer lifetime value is calculated by analysing the behaviour of a group of customers who have the same recruitment date. The revenue and cost for this group of customers is recorded, by campaign or season, and the overall contribution for that period can then be worked out. Industry experience has shown that the benefits to a business of increasing lifetime value can be enormous. A 5% increase in customer retention can create a 125% increase in profits; a 10% increase in retailer retention can translate to a 20% increase in sales; and extending customer life cycles by three years can treble profits per customer.

LIFFE *abbr* London International Financial Futures and Options Exchange

LIMEAN *abbr* London Inter Bank Mean Rate

limit an amount above or below which a broker is not to conclude the purchase or sale of a security for the client who specifies it

limit down the most that the price of an option may fall in one day on a particular market

Limited used to indicate that a UK company is a limited company when placed at the end of the company's name

limited by guarantee *see* *public limited company*

limited company a company where each shareholder is responsible for the company's debts only to the amount that he or she has invested in the company. Limited companies must be formed by at least two directors. *See also private company, public limited company. Abbr* **Ltd**

limited legal tender in some jurisdictions, low denomination notes and all coins that may only be submitted up to a certain sum as legal tender in any one transaction

limited liability the restriction of an owner's loss in a business to the amount of capital he or she has invested in it

limited liability company a company in which a number of people provide finance in return for shares. The principle of limited liability limits the maximum loss a shareholder can make if the company fails. *US term* ***corporation***

limited market a market in which dealings for a specific security are dif-

ficult to transact, for example, because it has only limited appeal to investors or, in the case of shares, because institutions or family members are unlikely to sell them

limited partnership a registered business in which the liability of the partners is limited to the amount of capital they have each provided for the business, and in the running of which the partners may not take part

limiting factor anything which limits the activity of an entity. An entity seeks to optimise the benefit it obtains from the limiting factor. Examples are a shortage of supply of a resource, or a restriction on sales demand at a particular price.

limit up the most that the price of an option may rise in one day on a particular market

linear programming the use of a series of linear equations to construct a mathematical model. The objective is to obtain an optimal solution to a complex operational problem, which may involve the production of a number of products in an environment in which there are many constraints.

line item budget the traditional form of budget layout showing, line by line, the costs of a cost object analysed by their nature (salaries, occupancy, maintenance, etc.)

line of credit an agreed finance facility that allows a company or individual to borrow money. *Also known as* ***credit line***

liquid asset ratio the ratio of liquid assets to total assets

liquid assets cash, and other assets readily convertible into cash

liquidate to close a company by selling its assets, paying off any outstanding debts, distributing any remaining profits to the shareholders, and then ceasing trading

liquidated damages an amount of money somebody pays for breaching a contract

liquidation the winding-up of a company, a process during which assets are sold, liabilities settled as far as possible, and any remaining cash returned to the members. Liquidation may be voluntary or compulsory.

liquidation value the amount of money that a quick sale of all of a company's assets would yield

liquidator the person appointed by a company, its creditors, or its shareholders to sell the assets of an insolvent company. The proceeds of the sale are used to discharge debts to creditors, with any surplus distributed to shareholders.

liquidity a condition in which assets are held in a cash or near cash form

liquidity agreement an agreement to allow conversion of an asset into cash

liquidity preference a choice made by people to hold their wealth in the form of cash rather than bonds or stocks

liquidity ratio *see cash ratio*

liquidity risk the risk that an entity will encounter difficulty in realising assets or otherwise raising funds to meet commitments associated with financial instruments. *Also called fund-ing risk*

liquidity trap a central bank's inability to lower interest rates once investors believe rates can go no lower

liquid market a market in which an ample number of shares is being traded

list broker a person or organisation that makes the arrangements for one company to use another company's direct mail list

listed company a company whose shares trade on a stock exchange

listed securities shares which can be bought or sold on a stock exchange and which appear on its official list

listing *see listed company, listing requirements*

Listing Agreement a document which a company signs when being listed on the London Stock Exchange, in which the company promises to abide by Stock Exchange regulations

listing requirements the conditions that have to be met before a security can be traded on a recognised stock exchange. Although exact requirements vary from one exchange to another, the two main ones are that the issuing company's assets should exceed a minimum amount and that the required information about its finances and business should have been published.

Little Board the American Stock Exchange (*slang*) *See also Big Board*

lively market an active stock market which sees many shares being bought or sold

living wage a level of *pay* that provides just enough income for normal day-to-day subsistence

Lloyd's broker an agent who represents a client who wants insurance and who arranges this insurance for him through a Lloyd's underwriting syndicate

LME *abbr* London Metal Exchange

load an initial charge in some investment funds. *See also load fund*

load fund a unit trust that charges a fee for the purchase or sale of shares. *See also no-load fund*

loading (*ANZ*) a payment made to workers over and above the basic wage in recognition of special skills or unfavourable conditions, for example, for overtime or shiftwork

loan a borrowing either by a business or a consumer where the amount borrowed is repaid according to an agreed schedule at an agreed interest rate, typically by regular instalments over a set period of years. However, the principal may be repayable in one instalment. *See also balloon loan, fixed-rate loan, interest-only mortgage, variable interest rate*

loanable funds theory the theory that interest rates are determined solely by supply and demand

loanback the ability of a holder of a pension fund to borrow money from it

loan capital debentures and other long-term loans to a business

loan committee a committee which examines applications for special loans, such as higher loans than normally allowed by a bank

loan constant ratio the total of annual payments due on a loan as a fraction of the amount of the principal

Loan Council (*ANZ*) an Australian federal body, made up of treasurers from the states and the Commonwealth of Australia that monitors borrowing by state governments

loan loss reserves the money a bank holds to cover losses through defaults on loans that it makes

loan participation the grouping together by several banks to share a very large loan to one single customer

loan production cycle the period that begins with an application for a loan and ends with the lending of money

loan schedule a list of the payments due on a loan and the balance outstanding after each has been made

loan shark somebody who lends money at excessively, often illegally high rates of interest

loan stock bonds and debentures

loan to value ratio the ratio of the amount of a loan to the value of the collateral for it

loan value the amount that a lender is willing to lend a borrower

local authority bond a loan raised by a local authority in the form of a fixed-interest bond, repayable at a certain date. Local authority bonds are similar to US *treasury bonds*.

local authority deposits money deposited with a local authority to earn interest for the depositor

London Bullion Market the world's largest market for gold, where silver is also traded. It is a wholesale market, where the minimum trades are generally 1,000 ounces for gold and 50,000 ounces for silver. Members typically trade with each other and their clients on a principal-to-principal basis so that all risks, including those of credit, are between the two parties to the transaction.

London Chamber of Commerce and Industry in the United Kingdom, the largest chamber of commerce that aims 'to help London businesses succeed by promoting their interests and expanding their opportunities as members of a worldwide business network'. *See also ICC*

London Clearing House an organisation that acts on behalf of its members as a central counterparty for contracts traded on the London International Financial Futures and Options Exchange, the International Petroleum Exchange, and the London Metal Exchange. When the LCH has registered a trade, it becomes the buyer to every member who sells and the seller to every member who buys, ensuring good financial performance. To protect it against the risks assumed as central counterparty, the LCH establishes margin requirements. *See also* **margining**. *Abbr* **LCH**

London Commodity Exchange *see London International Financial Futures and Options Exchange*

London Inter Bank Bid Rate on the UK money markets, the rate at which banks will bid to take deposits in Euro-currency from each other. The deposits are for terms from overnight up to five years. *Abbr* **LIBID**

London Inter Bank Mean Rate the average of the London Inter Bank Offered Rate and the London Inter Bank Bid Rate, occasionally used as a reference rate. *Abbr* **LIMEAN**

London Inter Bank Offered Rate on the UK money markets, the rate at which banks will offer to make deposits in Euro-currency from each other, often used as a reference rate. The deposits are for terms from overnight up to five years. *Abbr* **LIBOR**

London International Financial Futures and Options Exchange 1. an exchange for trading financial futures and options. Established in 1982, it offered contracts on interest rates denominated in most of the world's major currencies until 1992, when it merged with the London Traded Options Market, adding equity options to its product range. In 1996 it merged with the London Commodity Exchange, adding a range of soft commodity and agricultural commodity contracts to its financial portfolio. From November 1998, trading gradually migrated from the floor of the exchange to screen-based trading. *Abbr* **LIFFE**

London Metal Exchange one of the world's largest non-ferrous metal exchanges that deals in aluminium, tin, and nickel. The primary roles of the exchange are hedging, providing official international reference prices, and appropriate storage facilities. Its origins can be traced back to 1571, though in its present form it dates from 1877. *Abbr* **LME**

London Traded Options Market *see London International Financial Futures and Options Exchange*

long having more shares than are promised for sale

long-dated bond a bond issued by the United Kingdom with a maturity at least 15 years in the future

long-dated gilt *see gilt-edged security*

long position a situation in which dealers hold securities, commodities, or contracts, expecting prices to rise

longs government stocks which will mature more than 15 years after the date of purchase

long-term balance of payments a record of movements of capital relating to overseas investments and the purchase of companies overseas

long-term bond a bond that has at least ten years before its redemption date, or, in some markets, a bond with more than seven years until its redemption date

long-term debt loans that are due after at least one year

long-term equity anticipation securities *see LEAPS*

long-term financing forms of funding such as loans or stock issue that do not have to be repaid immediately

long-term lease a lease of at least ten years

long-term liabilities forms of debt such as loans that do not have to be repaid immediately

lookback option an option whose price the buyer chooses from all of the prices that have existed during the option's life

loss a financial position in which the *costs* of an activity exceed the *income* derived from it

loss adjuster a professional person acting on behalf of an insurance company to assess the value of an insurance claim. *Also known as **claims adjuster***

loss assessor in the United Kingdom, a person appointed by a insurance policyholder to assist with his or her claim. *See also **loss adjuster***

loss leader a product or service that is sold at a *loss* in order to attract more customers to an organisation

lost time record a record of the time a machine or employee is not producing, usually stating reasons and responsibilities. Lost time can include waiting time and maintenance.

lot 1. the minimum quantity of a commodity that may be purchased on an exchange, for example, 1,000 ounces of gold on the London Bullion Market **2.** an item or a collection of related items being offered for sale at an auction **3.** (*US*) a group of shares held or traded together, usually in units of 100 **4.** (*US*) a piece of land that can be sold

lottery the random method of selecting successful applicants for something, occasionally used when a new *share issue* is oversubscribed

lower of cost or market a method used by manufacturing and supply firms when accounting for their homogeneous stocks that involves valuing them either at their original cost or the current market price, whichever is lower. *Abbr* **LCM**

low start mortgage a long-term loan, usually for the purchase of a property, in which the borrower only pays the interest on the loan for the first few years, usually three. After that, the repayments increase to cover the interest and part of the original loan, as in a *repayment mortgage*. Low start mortgages are popular with first-time buyers as the lower initial costs may free up funds for furnishings or home improvements. *See also **mortgage***

loyalty bonus in the United Kingdom in the 1980s, a number of extra shares, calculated as a proportion of the shares originally subscribed, given to original subscribers of privatisation issues providing the shares were held continually for a given period of time

Ltd *abbr* limited company

lump sum 1. used to describe a loan that is repayable with one instalment at the end of its term. *See also **balloon loan**, **interest-only mortgage** **2.** an amount of money received in one payment, for example, the sum payable to the beneficiary of a life assurance policy on the death of the policyholder

luxury tax a tax on goods or services that are considered non-essential

M

machine hour rate an *overhead absorption rate* based on machine hours

macroeconomics the branch of economics that studies national income and the economic systems of national economies

macroeconomy the broad sectors of a country's economic activity, for example, the financial or industrial sectors, that are aggregated to form its economic system as a whole

macrohedge a hedge that pertains to an entire portfolio. *See also* **microhedge**. *Also known as* **global hedge**

mainstream corporation tax formerly the balance of corporation tax due after deducting ACT. *See also* *Advance Corporation Tax*

maintenance bond a bond that provides a guarantee against defects for some time after a contract has been fulfilled

majority shareholder a shareholder with a controlling interest in a company. *See also* *minority interest*

managed bonds *see* *diversified investment company*

managed currency fund a unit trust that makes considered investments in currencies

managed derivatives fund a fund which uses mainly futures and options instead of investing in the underlying securities

managed economy an economy directed by a government rather than the free market

managed float the position when the exchange rate of a country's currency is influenced by government action in the foreign exchange market

managed fund a unit trust that makes considered investments. *See also* *index fund*

managed futures fund *see* *managed derivatives fund*

managed rate a rate of interest charged by a financial institution for borrowing that is not prescribed as a margin over base rate but is set from time to time by the institution

management accountant a person who contributes to a management's decision-making processes by, for example, collecting and processing data relating to a business's costs, sales, and the profitability of individual activities

management accounting the application of the principles of accounting and financial management to create, protect, preserve, and increase value so as to deliver that value to the stakeholders of profit and not-for-profit enterprises, both public and private. Management accounting is an integral part of management, requiring the identification, generation, presentation, interpretation, and use of information relevant to formulating business strategy; planning and controlling activities; decision-making; efficient resource usage; performance improvement and value enhancement; safeguarding tangible and intangible assets; and corporate governance and internal control.

management buy-out the purchase of an existing business by an individual manager or management group from within that business. *Abbr* **MBO**

management control all of the processes used by managers to ensure that organisational goals are achieved and procedures adhered to, and that the organisation responds appropriately to changes in its environment

managing agent a person who runs the day-to-day activities of a Lloyd's syndicate

managing for value an approach to building the long-term value of a business. The term is most frequently used by businesses that are implementing the *balanced scorecard* and emphasises the need to make financial and commercial decisions that build the value of the business for its shareholders.

M&A *abbr* mergers and acquisitions

mandatory bid an offer to purchase the shares of a company which has to be made when a shareholder acquires 30% of that company's shares

mandatory quote period a period of time during which prices of securities must be displayed in a market

manufacturing account a financial statement which shows production costs only, as opposed to a trading account which shows sales and costs of sales. A manufacturing account will include direct materials and labour costs and the production overheads.

Marché des Options Négotiables de Paris in France, the traded options market. *Abbr* **MONEP**

Marché International de France in France, the international futures and options exchange

margin 1. the difference between the cost and the selling price of a product or service **2.** (*ANZ*) a payment made to workers over and above the basic wage in recognition of special skills

margin account an account with a broker who lends money for investments

marginal analysis the study of the way small changes in an economic variable will affect an economy

marginal cost 1. the amount by which the costs of a firm will be increased if its output is increased by one more unit, or if one more customer is served.

If the price charged is greater than the marginal cost, then the revenue gain will be greater than the added cost. That, in turn, will increase profit, so the expansion in production or service makes economic sense and should proceed. The reverse is also true: if the price charged is less than the marginal cost, expansion should not go ahead.

The formula for marginal cost is:

Change in cost / change in quantity

EXAMPLE If it costs a company £260,000 to produce 3,000 items, and £325,000 to produce 3,800 items, the change in cost would be:

£325,000 – £260,000 = £65,000

The change in quantity would be:

3,800 – 3,000 = 800

When the formula to calculate marginal cost is applied, the result is:

£65,000 / 800 = £81.25

If the price of the item in question were £99.95, expansion should proceed.

Relying on marginal cost is not failsafe, however; putting more products on a market can drive down prices and thus cut margins. Moreover, committing idle capacity to long-term production may tie up resources that could be directed to a new and more profitable opportunity. An important related principle is contribution: the cash gained (or lost) from selling an additional unit.

2. the part of the cost of one unit of product or service which would be avoided if that unit were not produced, or which would increase if one extra unit were produced

marginal costing the accounting system in which variable costs are charged to cost units and fixed costs of the period are written off in full against the aggregate contribution. Its special value is in recognising cost behaviour, and hence assisting in decision-making. *Also known as* **variable costing**

marginal costs and benefits the losses or gains to an individual or household arising from a small change in a variable, such as food consumption or income received

marginal lender a lender who will make a loan only at or above a particular rate of interest

marginal private cost the cost to an individual of a small change in the price of a variable, for example, petrol

marginal revenue the revenue generated by additional units of production

marginal tax rate the rate of tax payable on a person's income after business expenses have been deducted

margin call a broker's demand that an investor repay amounts, over a specified maximum for that investor, used for buying on margin

margining the system by which the London Clearing House (LCH) controls the risk associated with a London International Financial Futures and Options Exchange clearing member's position on a daily basis. To achieve this, clearing members deposit cash or collateral with the LCH in the form of initial and variation margins. The initial margin is the deposit required on all open positions (long or short) to cover short-term price movements and is returned to members by the LCH when the position is closed. The variation margin is the members' profits or losses, calculated daily from the marked-to-market-close value of their position (whereby contracts are revalued daily for the calculation of variation margin), and credited to or debited from their accounts.

marital deductions the part of an estate which, after a death, is not subject to estate tax because it goes to the spouse of the deceased

mark-down a reduction in the selling price of damaged or slow-selling goods

marked cheque a certified cheque (*slang*)

marked price the original displayed price of a product in a shop. In a sale, customers may be offered a saving on the marked price.

market 1. a group of people or organisations unified by a common need **2.** a gathering of sellers and purchasers to exchange commodities **3.** the rate at which financial commodities or securities are being sold

market based pricing setting a price based on the value of the product in the perception of the customer. *Also known as perceived value pricing*

market bubble a stock market phenomenon in which values in a particular sector become inflated for a short period. If the bubble bursts, share prices in that sector collapse.

market economist a person who specialises in the study of financial structures and the return on investments in the stock market

market economy an economy in which a *free market* in goods and services operates

marketeer a small company that competes in the same market as larger companies. Examples of marketeers are restaurants, travel agents, computer software providers, garages, and insurance brokers.

market forces influences on sales which bring about a change in prices

market if touched an order to trade a security if it reaches a specified price. *Abbr* **MIT**

marketing cost the cost of researching potential markets and promoting a product or service

market leader *see market share*

market logic the prevailing forces or attitudes that determine a company's success or failure on the stock market

market maker 1. somebody who works in a stock exchange to facilitate trade in one particular company **2.** a broker or bank that maintains a market for a security that does not trade on any exchange

market-neutral funds hedge funds which are not related to general market movements but which are used to find opportunities to arbitrage temporary slight changes in the relative values of particular financial assets

market order an order to trade a security at the best price the broker can obtain

market-oriented economy an economy in which prices tell households and firms the value of individual resources

market price in economics, the theoretical price at which supply equals demand

market risk risk that cannot be diversified away, also known as systematic risk. **Non-systematic** or **unsystematic risk** applies to a single investment or class of investments, and can be reduced or eliminated by diversification.

market risk premium the extra return required from a share to compensate for its risk compared with the average risk of the market

market sentiment the mood of those participating in exchange dealings that can range from absolute euphoria to downright gloom and despondency and tends to reflect recent company results, economic indicators, and comments by politicians, analysts, or opinion formers. Optimism increases demand and therefore prices, while pessimism has the opposite effect.

market share one entity's sales of a product or service in a specified market expressed as a proportion of total sales by all entities offering that product or service to the market. It can be viewed as a planning tool and a performance assessment ratio.

market size the largest number of shares that a market will handle in one trade of a particular security

market valuation 1. the value of a portfolio at market prices **2.** the opinion of an expert professional as to the current worth of a piece of land or property

market value the price that buyers are willing to pay for a good or service

marking down the reduction by market makers in the price at which they are prepared to deal in a security, for example, because of an adverse report by an analyst, or the announcement or anticipated announcement of a profit warning by a company

mark-up the addition to the cost of goods or services which results in a selling price. The mark-up may be expressed as a percentage or as an absolute monetary amount.

massaging the adjustment of financial figures to create the impression of better performance (*slang*)

master budget the budget into which all subsidiary budgets are consolidated, normally comprising budgeted profit and loss account, budgeted balance sheet, and budgeted cash-flow statement. These documents, and the supporting subsidiary budgets, are used to plan and control activities for the following year.

master limited partnership a partnership of a type that combines tax advantages and advantages of liquidity

matador bond a foreign bond in the Spanish domestic market (*slang*)

matched bargain the linked sale and repurchase of the same security. *See also bed and breakfast deal*

matching convention the basis for preparing accounts which says that profits can only be recognised if sales are fully matched with costs accrued during the same period

material facts 1. information that has to be disclosed in a prospectus. *See also listing requirements* **2.** in an insurance contract, information that the insured has to reveal at the time that the policy is taken out, for example, that a house is located on the edge of a crumbling cliff. Failure to reveal material facts can result in the contract being declared void.

material information *see material news*

material news price sensitive developments in a company, for example, proposed acquisitions, mergers, profit warnings, and the resignation of directors, that most stock exchanges require a company to announce immediately prior to the exchange. *US term material information*

material requirements planning (MRP I) a system that converts a production schedule into a listing of the materials and components required to meet that schedule, so that adequate stock levels are maintained and items are available when needed

materials requisition 1. a document which authorises the issue from a store of a specified quantity of materials. *Also known as stores requisition* **2.** a document, raised by a production/ user department, authorising the issue from stores of a specified quantity of material. Any surplus material issued should be returned to stores accompanied by a materials returned note.

materials returned note a record of the return to stores of unused material

materials transfer note a record of the transfer of material between stores, cost centres, or cost units

mature economy an economy that is no longer developing or growing rapidly

maturity the stage at which a financial instrument, such as a bond, is due for repayment

maturity date the date when an *option* expires

maturity yield *see yield*

MAXI ISA an ISA for somebody who uses only one firm to handle all ISA funds. *See MINI ISA*

maximax criterion an approach to decision-making under uncertainty in which an 'optimistic' view of the possible outcome is adopted. The favoured strategy is therefore to implement the course of action which leads to the highest possible profit, irrespective of (a) the probability of that profit actually being achieved, and (b) the outcome if it is not successful. A risk-taker may make decisions on this basis.

maximin criterion an approach to decision-making under uncertainty in which a 'pessimistic' view of the possible outcome is adopted. The favoured strategy is therefore to implement the course of action whose worst possible outcome generates the highest profit. This basis for decision-making characterises risk-averse decision-makers.

MBIA *abbr* Municipal Bond Insurance Association: a group of insurance companies that insure high-rated municipal bonds

mean reversion the tendency of a variable such as price to return towards its average value after approaching an extreme position

Medicare a US health insurance programme in which the government pays part of the cost of medical care and hospital treatment for people over 65

medium *see gilt-edged security*

medium-dated gilt *see gilt-edged security*

medium of exchange anything that is used to pay for goods. Nowadays, this usually takes the form of money (bank-notes and coins), but in ancient societies, it included anything from cattle to shells.

medium-term bond a bond that has at least five but no more than ten years before its redemption date. *See also long-term bond*

meltdown an incidence of substantial losses on the stock market. Black Monday (19 October 1987) was described as Meltdown Monday in the press the following day.

member bank a bank that is a member of the US Federal Reserve System

member firm a firm of brokers or market makers that is a member of the London Stock Exchange

member of a company in the United Kingdom, a shareholder whose name is recorded in the register of members

members' voluntary liquidation in the United Kingdom, a special resolution passed by the members of a solvent company for the winding-up of the organisation. Prior to the resolution the directors of the company must make a declaration of solvency. Should the appointed liquidator have grounds for believing that the company is not solvent, the winding-up will be treated as compulsory liquidation. *See also voluntary liquidation*

memorandum of association an official company document, registered with the *Registrar of Companies*. A memorandum of association sets out company name, status, address of the registered office, objectives of the company, statement of *limited liability*, amount of guarantee, and the amount of authorised share capital. The *articles of association* is a related document.

mercantile relating to trade or commercial activity

mercantile agency a company that evaluates the creditworthiness of potential corporate borrowers. *See also credit bureau*

mercantile paper *see commercial paper*

mercantilism the body of economic thought developed between the 1650s and 1750s, based on the belief that a country's wealth depended on the strength of its foreign trade

merchant account an account established by an e-merchant at a financial institution or *merchant bank* to receive the proceeds of credit card transactions

merchant bank a bank that does not accept deposits but only provides services to those who offer securities to investors and also to those investors. *US term investment bank*

merger the union of two or more organisations under single ownership, through the direct **acquisition** by one organisation of the net assets or liabilities of the other. A merger can be the result of a friendly *takeover*, which results in the combining of companies on an equal footing. After a merger, the legal existence of the acquired organisation is terminated. There is no standard definition of a merger, as each union is different, depending on what is expected from the merger, and on the negotiations, strategy, stock and assets, human resources, and shareholders of the players. Four broad types of mergers are recognised. A **horizontal merger** involves firms from the same industry, while a **vertical merger** involves firms from the same supply chain. A **circular merger** involves firms with different products but similar distribution channels. A *conglomerate company* is produced by the union of firms with few or no similarities in production or marketing but that come together to create a larger economic base and greater profit potential. *Also known as* **acquisition,** *one-to-one merger. See also* **consolidation,** *joint venture, partnership*

merger accounting a method of accounting which regards the business combination as the acquisition of one company by another. The identifiable assets and liabilities of the company acquired are included in the consolidated balance sheet at their fair value at the date of acquisition, and its results included in the profit and loss account from the date of acquisition. The difference between the fair value of the consideration given and the fair values of the net assets of the entity acquired is accounted for as *goodwill*.

mergers and acquisitions a blanket term covering the main ways in which organisations change hands. *Abbr* **M&A**

microcash a form of electronic money with no denominations, permitting sub-denomination transactions of a fraction of a penny or cent

microeconomic incentive a tax benefit or subsidy given to a business to achieve a particular objective, such as increased sales overseas

microeconomics the branch of economics that studies the contribution of groups of consumers or firms, or of individual consumers, to a country's economy

microeconomy the narrow sectors of a country's economic activity that influence the behaviour of the economy as a whole, for example, consumer choices

microhedge a hedge that relates to a single asset or liability. *See also* **macrohedge**

micromerchant a provider of goods or services on the Internet in exchange for electronic money

micropayment a payment protocol for small amounts of electronic money, ranging from a fraction of a cent or penny to no more than ten US dollars or euros

middle price a price, halfway between the bid price and the offer price, that is generally quoted in the press and on information screens

MIGA *abbr* Multilateral Investment Guarantee Agency

MINI ISA an ISA for somebody who uses up to three firms for handling the components of the ISA. *See MAXI ISA*

minimax regret criterion an approach to decision-making under uncertainty in which the opportunity cost (regret) associated with each possible course of action is measured, and the decision-maker selects the activity which minimises the maximum regret, or loss. Regret is measured as the difference between the best and worst possible payoff for each option.

minimum lending rate 1. (*US*) an interest rate charged by a central bank, which serves as a floor for loans in a country **2.** the lowest rate of interest formerly charged by the Bank of England to discount houses, now replaced by the base rate

minimum quote size the smallest number of shares that a market must handle in one trade of a particular security

minimum subscription the smallest number of shares or securities that may be applied for in a new issue

minority used to describe a situation where less than 50% of an organisation's shares or common stock are available for trading on a stock exchange. This may occur when a parent company has sold off a proportion of the shares in a subsidiary company.

minority interest the nominal value of shares held in a subsidiary undertaking by members other than the parent company or its nominees plus the appropriate portion of the accumulated reserves, including the share premium account

minority ownership ownership of less than 50% of a company's ordinary shares, which is not enough to control the company

mirror fund an investment trust where the manager also runs a unit trust with the same objectives

MIT *abbr* market if touched

mixed account an account containing both long and short positions

mixed economy an economy in which both public and private enterprises participate in the production and supply of goods and services

MMC *abbr* Monopolies and Mergers Commission

MMDA *abbr* money market deposit account

model risk the possibility that a computer model used when investing may have a flaw which makes it function badly in extreme market conditions

modified accounts *see abbreviated accounts*

modified ACRS a system used in the United States for computing the depreciation of some assets acquired after 1985 in a way that reduces taxes. The ACRS applies to older assets. *See also accelerated cost recovery system*

modified book value *see adjusted book value*

modified cash basis the bookkeeping practice of accounting for short-term assets on a cash basis and for long-term assets on an accrual basis

momentum investor an investor who buys shares which seem to be moving upwards

MONEP *abbr* Marché des Options Négotiables de Paris

monetarism an economic theory that states that inflation is caused by increases in a country's money supply

monetary relating to or involving money, cash, or assets

monetary aggregate a way of measuring the spending power in an economy

monetary assets a generic term for accounts receivable, cash, and bank balances: assets that are realisable at the amount stated in the accounts. Other assets, for example, facilities and machinery, inventories, and marketable securities will not necessarily realise the sum stated in a business's balance sheet.

monetary base the stock of a country's coins, notes, and bank deposits with the central bank

monetary base control the restricting of the amount of *liquid assets* in an economy through government control

monetary items monetary assets (such as cash and debtors) and monetary liabilities (such as overdraft and creditors) whose values stay the same in spite of inflation

monetary policy government economic policy concerning a country's rate of interest, its exchange rate, and the amount of money in the economy

monetary reserve the foreign currency and precious metals that a country holds, usually in a central bank

monetary system the set of government regulations concerning a country's monetary reserves and its holdings of notes and coins

monetary targets figures which are given as targets by the government when setting out its budget for the forthcoming year

monetary unit the standard unit of a country's currency

monetary working capital adjustment an adjustment in current cost accounting to the historical cost balance sheet to take account of the effect of inflation on the value of debtors, creditors, and stocks of finished goods. *Abbr* **MWCA**

monetise to establish a currency as a country's legal tender

money a medium of exchange that is accepted throughout a country as payment for goods and services and as a means of settling debts

money at call money loaned for which repayment can be demanded without notice. It is used by commercial banks placing money on very short-term deposit with discount houses.

money at call and short notice
1. advances made by banks to other financial institutions, or corporate and personal customers, that are repayable either upon demand (call) or within 14 days (short notice) **2.** balances in an account that are either available upon demand (call) or within 14 days (short notice)

money broker an intermediary who works on the money market

moneyer somebody who is authorised to coin money

money laundering the process of making money obtained illegally appear legitimate by passing it through banks or businesses

moneylender a person who lends money for interest

money market 1. a country's financial centre, where foreign currency and domestic and foreign bills are bought and sold **2.** the wholesale market for short-term debt instruments and money market instruments. New York is the major money market centre followed by London and Tokyo. **3.** the short-term wholesale market for securities maturing in one year, such as certificates of deposit, treasury bills, and commercial paper

money market account an account with a financial institution that requires a high minimum deposit and pays a rate of interest related to the wholesale money market rates and so is generally higher than retail rates. Most institutions offer a range of term accounts, with either a fixed rate or variable rate, and notice accounts, with a range of notice periods at variable rates.

money market fund a unit trust that invests in short-term debt securities

money market instruments short-term (usually under 12 months) assets and securities, such as certificates of deposit, and commercial paper and treasury bills, that are traded on money markets

money national income GDP measured using money value, not adjusted for the effect of inflation

money of account a monetary unit that is used in keeping accounts but is not necessarily an actual currency unit

money order a written order to pay somebody a sum of money, issued by a bank or post office

money purchase pension a pension plan to which both employer and employee make contributions

money purchase pension scheme in the United Kingdom, a pension plan where the fund that is built up is used to purchase an annuity. The retirement income that the beneficiary receives therefore depends on his or her contributions, the performance of the investments those contributions are used to buy, the annuity rates, and the type of annuity purchased at retirement.

money-purchase plan in the United States, a pension plan (a defined benefit plan) in which the participant contributes part and the firm contributes at the same or a different rate

money substitute any goods used as a medium of exchange because of the degree of devaluation of a country's currency

money supply the stock of *liquid assets* in a country's economy that can be given in exchange for services or goods

Monopolies and Mergers Commission in the United Kingdom, a commission that was replaced by the Competition Commission in April 1999. *Abbr* **MMC**

monopoly 1. a *market* in which there is only one supplier **2.** a situation in which one person or entity controls the entire market in the supply of a product or service

moral hazard the risk that the existence of a contract will cause behavioural changes in one or both parties to the contract, as where asset insurance causes less care to be taken over the safeguarding of the assets

moratorium a period of delay, for example, additional time agreed by a creditor and a debtor for recovery of a debt

more bang for your buck (US) a better return on your investment (*slang*)

mortgage 1. a financial lending arrangement whereby an individual borrows money from a bank or another lending institution in order to buy property or land. The original amount borrowed, the *principal*, is then repaid with interest to the lender over a fixed number of years. **2.** a borrowing arrangement whereby the lender is granted a legal right to an asset, usually a property, should the borrower default on the repayments. Mortgages are usually taken out by individuals who wish to secure a long-term loan to buy a home. *See also* **current account mortgage, endowment mortgage, interest-only mortgage, low start mortgage, repayment mortgage**

mortgage-backed security a security for which a mortgage is collateral

mortgage banker somebody who owns or is a senior executive of a bank that trades in mortgages

mortgage bond (US) a debt secured by land or property

mortgage broker a person or company that acts as an agent between people seeking mortgages and organisations that offer them

mortgage constant the ratio of the annual interest payments on a mortgage to its principal

mortgage debenture a debenture in which the loan is secured against a company's *fixed assets*

mortgage discount a percentage discount of a mortgage's principal when the mortgage is sold

mortgagee a person or organisation that lends money to a borrower under a mortgage agreement. *See also* **mortgagor**

mortgage equity analysis a computation of the difference between the value of a property and the amount owed on it in the form of mortgages

mortgage famine a situation where there is not enough money available to offer mortgages to house buyers

mortgage insurance insurance that provides somebody holding a mortgage with protection against default

mortgage lien a claim against a property that is mortgaged

mortgage life assurance insurance that provides somebody holding a mortgage with protection in case of the debtor's death. *US term* ***mortgage life insurance***

mortgage life insurance (*US*) = *mortgage life assurance*

mortgage note a note that documents the existence and terms of a mortgage

mortgage pool a group of mortgages with similar characteristics packaged together for sale

mortgage portfolio a group of mortgages held by a mortgage banker

mortgage rate the interest rate charged on a mortgage by a lender

mortgage tax a tax on mortgages

mortgagor somebody who has taken out a mortgage to borrow money. *See also* ***mortgagee***

most distant futures contract a futures option with the latest delivery date. *See also* ***nearby futures contract***

move time the time taken in moving a product between locations during the production process. *See also* ***cycle time***

MRP II *abbr* manufacturing resource planning: a computer-based manufacturing, inventory planning and control system that broadens the scope of production planning by involving other functional areas that affect production decisions. Manufacturing resource planning evolved from material requirements planning to integrate other functions in the planning process. These functions may include engineering, marketing, purchasing, production scheduling, business planning, and finance.

MSB *abbr* mutual savings bank

multicurrency relating to a loan that gives the borrower a choice of currencies

multicurrency clause a provision allowing a borrower to change European currency after a rollover date

multifunctional card a plastic card that may be used for two or more purposes, for example, as a cash card, a cheque card, and a debit card

Multilateral Investment Guarantee Agency one of the five institutions that comprise the World Bank Group. MIGA was created in 1988 to promote foreign direct investment into emerging economies with the objective of improving people's lives and reducing poverty. This is fulfilled by the Agency offering political risk insurance to investors and lenders and by assisting developing countries to attract and retain private investment. *Abbr* **MIGA**

multilateral netting a method of grouping sums from various sources into one currency. It is used by groups of banks trading in several currencies at the same time.

multinational business *or* **multinational company** a company that operates internationally, usually with subsidiaries, offices, or production facilities in more than one country

multinational corporation *see* *multinational business*

multiple application the submission of more than one share application for a new issue which is expected to be over-subscribed. In most jurisdictions, this practice is illegal.

multiple exchange rate a two-tier rate of exchange used in certain countries where the more advantageous rate may be for tourists or for businesses proposing to build a factory

multitasking the practice of performing several different tasks simultaneously (*slang*)

muni *or* **muni-bond** *see municipal bond*

municipal bond in the United States, a security issued by states, local governments, and municipalities to pay for special projects such as motorways

municipal bond fund a unit trust that invests in municipal bonds

Municipal Bond Insurance Association *full form of MBIA*

municipals *see municipal bond*

mutual used to describe an organisation that is run in the interests of its members and that does not have to pay dividends to its shareholders, so surplus profits can be ploughed back into the business. In the United Kingdom, building societies and friendly societies were formed as mutual organisations, although in recent years many have demutualised, either by becoming public limited companies or by being bought by other financial organisations, resulting in members receiving cash or share windfall payments. In the United States, **mutual associations**, a type of savings and loan association, and state-chartered mutual savings banks are organised in this way.

mutual association (*US*) *see mutual*

mutual company a company that is owned by its customers who share in the profits

mutual fund (*US*) = *unit trust*

mutual insurance an insurance company that is owned by its policyholders who share the profits and cover claims with their pooled premiums

mutual recognition directive a directive of the European Union that each country's accountancy firms and cross-border services should be recognised by other member states

mutual savings bank in the United States, a state-chartered savings bank run in the interests of its members. It is governed by a local board of trustees, not the legal owners. Some of these banks have recently begun offering accounts and services that are typical of commercial banks. *Abbr* **MSB**

MWCA *abbr* Monetary Working Capital Adjustment

N

naked debenture *see debenture*

naked option an option in which the underlying asset is not owned by the seller, who risks considerable loss if the price of the asset falls

naked position a holding of unhedged securities

naked writer a writer of an option who does not own the underlying shares

name an individual who is a member of Lloyd's of London

NAO *abbr* National Audit Office

narrow market a market where the trading volume is low. A characteristic of such a market is a wide spread of bid and offer prices.

narrow range securities *see trustee investment*

NASD *abbr* National Association of Securities Dealers

NASDAQ *abbr* National Association of Securities Dealers Automated Quotation system: a screen-based quotation system supporting market-making in US-registered equities. NASDAQ International has operated from London since 1992.

NASDAQ Composite Index a specialist US share price index covering shares of high-technology companies

National Association of Investors Corporation *(US)* a US organisation that fosters investment clubs

National Association of Securities Dealers in the United States, the self-regulatory organisation for securities dealers that develops rules and regulations, conducts regulatory reviews of members' business activities, and designs and operates marketplace ser-

vices facilities. It is responsible for the regulation of the NASDAQ Stock Market as well as the extensive US over-the-counter securities market. Established in 1938, it operates subject to the Securities Exchange Commission oversight and has a membership that includes virtually every US broker or dealer doing securities business with the public. *Abbr* **NASD**

National Audit Office an independent non-governmental body which examines public spending. The NAO audits the accounts of government agencies and departments, reporting back to Parliament with the results. An officer of the House of Commons, the Comptroller and Auditor General, runs the NAO. It has offices in London, Newcastle, Cardiff, and Blackpool. *Abbr* **NAO**

national bank 1. a bank owned or controlled by the state that acts as a bank for the government and implements its monetary policies **2.** *(US)* a bank that operates under federal charter and is legally required to be a member of the Federal Reserve System

national debt the total borrowing of a country's central government that is unpaid

national demand the total demand of consumers in an economy

National Guarantee Fund a supply of money held by the Australian Stock Exchange which is used to compensate investors for losses incurred when an exchange member fails to meet its obligations

national income the total earnings from a country's production of services and goods in a particular year

national income accounts economic statistics that show the state of a nation's economy over a given period of time, usually a year. *See also* **gross domestic product**, **gross national product**

National Insurance a compulsory state social insurance scheme to which employees and employers contribute. *Abbr* **NI**

National Insurance contributions payments made by both employers and employees to the government. The contributions, together with other government receipts, are used to finance state pensions and other benefits such as unemployment benefit. *Abbr* **NIC**

National Insurance number a unique number allocated to each UK citizen at the age of 16. It allows the Inland Revenue and the Department for Work and Pensions to record contributions and credit to each person's National Insurance account.

National Market System in the United States, an inter-exchange network system designed to foster greater competition between domestic stock exchanges. Legislated for in 1975, it was implemented in 1978 with the Intermarket Trading System that electronically links eight markets: American, Boston, Cincinnati, Chicago, New York, Pacific, Philadelphia, and the NASD over-the-counter market. It allows traders at any exchange to seek the best available price on all other exchanges that a particular security is eligible to trade on. *Abbr* **NMS**

national product the distribution of a country's production of services and goods in a particular year

National Savings in the United Kingdom, a government agency accountable to the Treasury that offers a range of savings products directly to the public or through post offices. The funds raised finance the national debt.

National Savings Bank in the United Kingdom, a savings scheme established in 1861 as the Post Office Savings Bank and now operated by National Savings. *Abbr* **NSB**

National Savings Certificate in the United Kingdom, either a fixed-interest or an index-linked certificate issued for two or five year terms by National Savings with returns that are free of income tax. *Abbr* **NSC**

National Society of Accountants (*US*) a non-profit organisation of some 17,000 professionals who provide accounting, tax preparation, financial and estate planning, and management advisory services to an estimated 19 million individuals and business clients. Most of the NSA's members are individual practitioners or partners in small to mid-size accounting and tax firms. *Abbr* **NSA**

NAV *abbr* net asset value

NBFI *abbr* (*ANZ*) non-bank financial institution

NBV *abbr* net book value

NCUA *abbr* National Credit Union Administration

NDP *abbr* net domestic product

nearby futures contract a futures option with the earliest delivery date. *See also* **most distant futures contract**

nearby month the earliest month for which there is a futures contract for a particular commodity. *Also known as* **spot month**. *See also* **far month**

near money assets that can quickly be turned into cash, for example, some types of bank deposit, short-dated bonds, and certificates of deposit

negative amortisation an increase in the *principal* of a loan due to the inadequacy of payments to cover the interest

negative carry interest that is so high that the borrowed money does not return enough profit to cover the cost of borrowing

negative cash-flow a cash-flow with higher outgoings than income

negative equity a situation in which a fall in prices leads to a property being worth less than was paid for it

negative gearing the practice of borrowing money to invest in property or shares and claiming a tax deduction on the difference between the income and the interest repayments

negative income tax (*US*) payments such as tax credits made to households or individuals to make their income up to a guaranteed minimum level

negative pledge clause a provision in a bond that prohibits the issuer from doing something that would give an advantage to holders of other bonds

negative yield curve a representation of interest rates that are higher for short-term bonds than they are for long-term bonds

negotiable certificate of deposit 1. a certificate of deposit with a very high value that can be freely traded **2.** a credit instrument available in Singapore since 1974

negotiable instrument 1. a financial instrument that can be freely traded **2.** a document of title which can be freely traded, such as a bill of exchange or other certificate of debt

negotiable order of withdrawal a cheque drawn on an account that bears interest

negotiable security a security that can be freely traded

negotiate to transfer financial instruments such as bearer securities, bills of exchange, cheques, and promissory notes, for consideration to another person

negotiated budget a budget in which budget allowances are set largely on the basis of negotiations between budget holders and those to whom they report

negotiated commissions commissions that result from bargaining between brokers and their customers, typically large institutions

negotiated issue *see negotiated offering*

negotiated market a market in which each transaction results from negotiation between a buyer and a seller

negotiated offering a public offering, the price of which is determined by negotiations between the issuer and a syndicate of underwriters. *Also known as negotiated issue*

negotiated sale a public offering, the price of which is determined by negotiations between the issuer and a single underwriter

nest egg assets, usually other than a pension plan or retirement account, that have been set aside by an individual for his or her retirement (*slang*)

net adjusted present value the present value of an investment in excess of the purchase price

net advantage of refunding the amount realised by refunding debt

net advantage to leasing the amount by which leasing something is financially better than borrowing money and purchasing it

net advantage to merging the amount by which the value of a merged enterprise exceeds the value of the pre-existing companies, minus the cost of the merger

net assets the amount by which the value of a company's assets exceeds its liabilities

net asset value a sum of the values of all that a unit trust owns at the end of a trading day. *Abbr* **NAV**

NetBill a micropayment system developed at Carnegie Mellon University for purchasing digital goods over the Internet. After the goods are delivered in encrypted form to the purchaser's computer, the money is debited from the purchaser's prefunded account and the goods are decrypted for the purchaser's use.

net book value the historical cost of an asset less any accumulated depreciation or other provision for diminution in value, for example, reduction to net realisable value, or asset value which has been revalued downwards to reflect market conditions. *Also known as written-down value. Abbr* **NBV**

net borrowings the total of all borrowings less the cash in bank accounts and on deposit

net capital the amount by which net assets exceed the value of assets not easily converted to cash

net cash balance the amount of cash that is on hand

net change on the day the difference between the opening price of a share at the beginning of a day's trading and the closing price at the end

NetCheque a trademark for an electronic payment system developed at the University of Southern California to allow users to write electronic cheques to each other

net current assets the amount by which the value of a company's current assets exceeds its current liabilities

net dividend the value of a dividend after the recipient has paid tax on it

net domestic product the figure produced after factors such as depreciation have been deducted from *GDP*

net errors and omissions the net amount of the discrepancies that arise in calculations of balances of payments

net export function a mathematical relationship that shows the level of a country's exports at various levels of its overall income

net fixed assets the value of fixed assets after depreciation

net foreign factor income income from outside a country, constituting the amount by which a country's gross national product exceeds its gross domestic product

net income 1. an organisation's income less the costs incurred to generate it **2.** gross income less tax **3.** a salary or wage less tax and other statutory deductions, for example, National Insurance contributions

net interest gross interest less tax

net lease a lease that requires the lessee to pay for things that the owner usually pays for. *See also* **gross lease**

net liquid funds an organisation's cash plus its marketable investments less its short-term borrowings, such as overdrafts and loans

net margin the percentage of revenues that is profit

net operating income the amount by which income exceeds expenses, before considering taxes and interest

net operating margin net operating income as a percentage of revenues

net pay *see take-home pay*

net position the difference between an investor's long and short positions in the same security

net present value 1. the value of an investment calculated as the sum of its initial cost and the *present value* of expected future cash-flows.

A positive NPV indicates that the project should be profitable, assuming that the estimated cash-flows are reasonably accurate. A negative NPV indicates that the project will probably be unprofitable and therefore should be adjusted, if not abandoned altogether.

NPV enables a management to consider the time-value of money it will invest. This concept holds that the value of money increases with time because it can always earn interest in a savings account. When the time-value-of-money concept is incorporated in the calculation of NPV, the value of a project's future net cash receipts in 'today's money' can be determined. This enables proper comparisons between different projects.

EXAMPLE If Global Manufacturing Ltd is considering the acquisition of a new machine, its management will consider all the factors: initial purchase and installation costs; additional revenues generated by sales of the new machine's products, plus the taxes on these new revenues. Having accounted for these factors in its calculations, the cash-flows that Global Manufacturing projects will generate from the new machine are:

Year 1:	−100,000 (initial cost of investment)
Year 2:	30,000
Year 3:	40,000
Year 4:	40,000
Year 5:	35,000
Net Total:	145,000

At first glance, it appears that cash flows total 45% more than the £100,000 initial cost, a sound investment indeed. But the time-value of money shrinks the return on the project considerably, since future pounds are worth less than present pounds in hand. NPV accounts for these differences with the help of present-value tables, which list the ratios that express the present value of expected cash-flow pounds, based on the applicable interest rate and the number of years in question.

In the example, Global Manufacturing's cost of capital is 9%. Using this figure to find the corresponding ratios on the present value table, the £100,000 investment cost and expected annual revenues during the five years in question, the NPV calculation looks like this:

Year	Cash-flow	Table factor (at 9%)	Present value
1	(£100,000) ×	1.000000 =	(£100,000)
2	£30,000 ×	0.917431 =	£27,522.93
3	£40,000 ×	0.841680 =	£33,667.20
4	£40,000 ×	0.772183 =	£30,887.32
5	£35,000 ×	0.708425 =	£24,794.88

NPV = £16,873.33

NPV is still positive. So, on this basis at least, the investment should proceed.

2. the difference between the sum of the projected discounted cash inflows and outflows attributable to a capital investment or other long-term project. *Abbr* **NPV**

net price the price paid for goods or services after all relevant discounts have been deducted

net proceeds the amount realised from a transaction minus the cost of making it

net profit an organisation's income as shown in a *profit and loss account* after all relevant expenses have been deducted

net profit margin *see profit margin*

net profit ratio the ratio of an organisation's net profit to its total net sales. Comparing the net profit ratios of companies in the same sector shows which are the most efficient.

net realisable value the value of an asset if sold, allowing for costs

net relevant earnings earnings which qualify for calculating pension contributions and against which relief against tax can be claimed. Such earnings can be income from employment which is not pensionable, such as the profits of a self-employed sole trader.

net residual value the anticipated proceeds of an asset at the end of its useful life, less the costs of selling it, for example, transport and commission. It is used when calculating the annual charge for the straight-line method of depreciation. *Abbr* **NRV**

net return the amount realised on an investment, taking taxes and transaction costs into account

net salvage value the amount expected to result from terminating a project, taking tax consequences into consideration

net worth the difference between the assets and liabilities of a person or company

net yield the rate of return on an investment after considering all costs and taxes

new economy a term used in the late 1990s and 2000s to describe the e-commerce sector and the *digital economy*, in which firms mostly trade online rather than in the bricks and mortar of physical premises in the high street

new issue 1. a new security, for example, a bond, debenture, or share, being offered to the public for the first time. *See also float (sense 1), initial public offering* **2.** a rights issue, or any further issue of an existing security

new issue market a market where companies can raise finance by issuing new shares or by a flotation

new issues market the part of the market in which securities are first offered to investors by the issuers. *See also float (sense 1), initial public offering, primary market*

newly industrialised economy a country whose industrialisation has reached a level beyond that of a developing country. Mexico and Malaysia are examples of newly industrialised economies.

new money finance provided by a new issue of shares or by the transfer of money from one account to another

new time the next account on a stock exchange where sales in the last few days of the previous account are credited to the following account

New York Mercantile Exchange the world's largest physical commodity exchange and North America's most important trading exchange for energy and precious metals. It deals in crude oil, petrol, heating oil, natural gas, propane, gold, silver, platinum, palladium, and copper. *Abbr* **NYMEX**

New York Stock Exchange *see NYSE*

New Zealand Stock Exchange the principal market in New Zealand for trading in securities. It was established in 1981, replacing the Stock Exchange Association of New Zealand and a number of regional trading floors. *Abbr* **NZSE**

New Zealand Trade Development Board a government body responsible for promoting New Zealand exports and facilitating foreign investment in New Zealand. *Also known as* **TRADENZ**

next futures contract an option for the month after the current month

NI *abbr* National Insurance

NIC *abbr* National Insurance contribution

niche company a company specialising in a particular type of produce or service, which occupies a market niche

niche player 1. an investment banker specialising in a particular field, for example, management buyouts **2.** a broking house that deals in securities of only one industry. *Also known as boutique investment house*

nickel (*US*) five basis points (*slang*)

Nifty Fifty (*US*) on Wall Street, the 50 most popular stocks among institutional investors (*slang*)

Nikkei 225 *or* **Nikkei Index** the Japanese share price index

Nikkei Index *see Nikkei 225*

nil paid with no money yet paid. This term is used in reference to the purchase of newly issued shares, or to the shares themselves, when the shareholder entitled to buy new shares has not yet made a commitment to do so and may sell the rights instead.

NMS *abbr* National Market System

NNP *abbr* net national product

no-brainer a transaction so favourable that no intelligence is required when deciding whether to enter into it (*slang*)

noise irrelevant or insignificant data which overload a feedback process. The presence of noise can confuse or divert attention from relevant information; efficiency in a system is enhanced as the ratio of information to noise increases.

noise traders uninformed market participants (*slang*)

no-load fund a unit trust that does not charge a fee for the purchase or sale of shares. *See also* **load fund**

nominal account a record of revenues and expenditures, liabilities and assets classified by their nature, for example, sales, rent, rates, electricity, wages, or share capital

nominal annual rate *see APR*

nominal capital the total value of all of a company's stock

nominal cash-flow cash-flow in terms of currency, without adjustment for inflation

nominal exchange rate the exchange rate as specified, without adjustment for transaction costs or differences in purchasing power

nominal interest rate the interest rate as specified, without adjustment for compounding or inflation

nominal ledger a ledger listing revenue, operating expenses, assets, and capital

nominal price the price of an item being sold when consideration does not reflect the value

nominal share capital *see authorised share capital*

nominal value the value of a newly issued share. *Also known as par value*

nominee account an account held not in the name of the real owner of the account, but instead in the name of another person, organisation, or *financial institution*. Shares can be bought and held in nominee accounts so that the owner's identity is not disclosed.

nominee holding a shareholding in a company registered in the name of a nominee, instead of that of the owner

nominee name a financial institution, or an individual employed by such an institution, that holds a security on behalf of the actual owner. While this may be to hide the owner's identity, for example, in the case of a celebrity, it is also to allow an institution managing any individual's portfolio to carry out transactions without the need for the owner to sign the required paperwork.

non-acceptance on the presentation of a bill of exchange, the refusal by the person on whom it is drawn to accept it

non-business days those days when banks are not open for business, for example, in the West, Saturdays, Sundays, and public holidays

non-cash item an item in an income statement that is not *cash*, such as *depreciation* expenses, and gains or losses from investments

non-conforming loan a loan that does not conform to the lender's standards, especially those of a US government agency

non-contributory pension scheme a pension scheme to which the employee makes no contribution

non-contributory pension plan (*US*) = *non-contributory pension scheme*

non-current asset *see fixed asset*

non-deductible not allowed to be deducted, especially as an allowance against income taxes

non-financial asset an asset that is neither money nor a financial instrument, for example, real or personal property

non-financial incentive scheme *see incentive scheme*

non-integrated accounts *see interlocking accounts*

non-interest-bearing bond a bond that is sold at a discount instead of with a promise to pay interest

non-judicial foreclosure a foreclosure on property without recourse to a court

non-linear programming a process in which the equations expressing the interactions of variables are not all linear but may, for example, be in proportion to the square of a variable

non-negotiable instrument a financial instrument that cannot be signed over to anyone else

non-operational balances accounts that banks maintain at the Bank of England without the power of withdrawal

non-optional not subject to approval by shareholders

non-participating preference share the most common type of preference share that pays a fixed dividend regardless of the profitability of the company. *See also participating preference share*

non-performing asset an asset that is not producing income

non-profit organisation an organisation that does not have financial profit as a main strategic objective. Non-profit organisations include charities, professional associations, trade unions, and religious, arts, community, research, and campaigning bodies. These organisations are not situated in either the *public* or *private sectors*, but in what has been called the **third sector**. Many have paid staff and working capital but, according to Peter Drucker, their fundamental purpose is not to provide a product or service, but to change people. They are led by values rather than financial commitments to shareholders.

non-recourse debt a debt for which the borrower has no personal responsibility, typically a debt of a limited partnership

non-recoverable relating to a debt that will never be paid, for example, because of the borrower's bankruptcy

non-recurring charge a charge that is made only once

non-recurring items special items in a set of accounts which appear only once

non-refundable relating to bonds that are not able to be retired through the issue of succeeding bonds

non-resident used to describe an individual who has left his or her native country to work overseas for a period. Non-residency has tax implications, for example, while a UK national is working overseas only their income and realised capital gains generated within the United Kingdom are subject to UK income tax. During a period of non-residency, many expatriates choose to bank offshore.

Non-Resident Withholding Tax a duty imposed by the New Zealand government on interest and dividends earned by a non-resident from investments. *Abbr* **NRWT**

non-tariff barrier *see NTB*

non-taxable not subject to tax

non-voting shares ordinary shares that are paid a dividend from the company's profits, but that do not entitle the shareholder to vote at the Annual General Meeting or any other meeting of shareholders. Such shares are unpopular with institutional investors. *Also called* **A shares**

normal capacity a measure of the long-run average level of capacity that may be expected. This is often used in setting the budgeted fixed overhead absorption rate which gives it stability over time, although budgeted fixed overhead volume variances are generally produced as a consequence.

normal loss an expected loss, allowed for in the budget, and normally calculated as a percentage of the good output from a process during a period of time. Normal losses are generally either valued at zero, or at their disposal values.

normal profit the minimum level of profit that will attract an entrepreneur to begin a business or remain trading

normal yield curve a yield curve with higher interest rates for long-term bonds than for short-term bonds. *See also* **yield curve**

normative economics economics based on value judgments, for example, that a country should shift employment from heavy industry to the services sector of its economy

nostro account an account which a bank has with a correspondent bank in another country

note issuance facility a bank's credit-providing service to customers unable to market their medium-term notes

note of hand a document where someone promises to pay money at a stated time without conditions

notes to the accounts an explanation of particular items in a set of accounts

notes to the financial statements an explanation of particular items in a set of financial statements

notice of coding a notice which informs a third party of the code number given to indicate the amount of tax allowances a person has

notice of default (*US*) = *default notice*

notional cost a cost used in product evaluation, decision-making, and performance measurement to represent the cost of using resources which have no conventional 'actual cost'. Notional interest, for example, may be charged for the use of internally generated funds.

notional income invisible benefit which is not money or goods and services

notional principal amount the value used to represent a loan in calculating *interest rate swaps*

notional rent an amount of money noted in accounts as rent where the company owns the building it is occupying and so does not pay an actual rent

not negotiable wording appearing on a cheque or bill of exchange that it is deprived of its inherent quality of negotiability. When such a document is transferred from one person to another, the recipient obtains no better title to it than the signatory. *See also **negotiable instrument***

novation an agreement to change a contract by substituting a third party for one of the two original parties

NPV *abbr* net present value

NRV *abbr* net residual value

NRWT *abbr* Non-Resident Withholding Tax

NSA *abbr* National Society of Accountants

NSB *abbr* National Savings Bank

NSC *abbr* National Savings Certificate

NTB *abbr* non-tariff barrier: a country's economic regulation on something such as safety standards that impedes imports, often from developing countries

numbered account a bank account identified by a number to allow the holder to remain anonymous

nuncupative will a will that is made orally in the presence of a witness, rather than in writing

NYMEX *abbr* New York Mercantile Exchange

NYSE *abbr* New York Stock Exchange: the leading stock exchange in New York which is self-regulatory but has to comply with the regulations of the US Securities and Exchange Commission

NZSE *abbr* New Zealand Stock Exchange

NZSE10 *abbr* NZSE10 Index

NZSE10 Index a measure of changes in share prices on the New Zealand Stock Exchange, based on the change in value of the stocks of the ten largest companies. *Abbr* **NZSE10**

NZSE30 Selection Index a measure of changes in share prices on the New Zealand Stock Exchange, based on the change in value of the stocks of the 30 largest companies. *Abbr* **NZSE30**

NZSE40 the principal measure of changes in share prices on the New Zealand Stock Exchange, based on the change in value of the stocks of the 40 largest companies. The composition of the index is reviewed every three months.

O

OBI *abbr* open buying on the Internet

OBSF *abbr* off-balance-sheet financing

obsolescence the loss of value of a fixed asset due to advances in technology or changes in market conditions for its product

OCF *abbr* operating cash-flow

OCR *abbr* official cash rate

O/D *abbr* overdraft

OECD *abbr* Organisation for Economic Co-operation and Development: a group of 30 member countries, with a shared commitment to democratic government and the market economy, that has active relationships with some 70 other countries via non-governmental organisations. Formed in 1961, its work covers economic and social issues from macroeconomics to trade, education, development, and scientific innovation. Its goals are to promote economic growth and employment in member countries in a climate of stability; to assist the sustainable economic expansion of both member and non-member countries; and to support a balanced and even-handed expansion of world trade.

OEIC *abbr* open-ended investment company

off-balance-sheet financing financing obtained by means other than debt and equity instruments, for example, partnerships, joint ventures, and leases. *Abbr* **OBSF**

offer the price at which a market maker will sell a security, or a unit trust manager in the United Kingdom will sell units. It is also the net asset value of a mutual fund plus any sales charges in the United States. It is the price investors pay when they buy a security. *Also known as* **ask**, **offering price**, **offer price**

offer by prospectus in the United Kingdom, one of the ways available to a lead manager of offering securities to the public. *See also* **float**, **initial public offering**, **new issue**, **offer for sale**

offer document a description of the loan a lender is offering to provide

offer for sale an invitation by a party other than the company itself to apply for shares in a company based on information contained in a prospectus

offering circular a document which gives information about a company whose shares are being sold to the public for the first time

offering memorandum a description of an offer to sell securities privately

offering price *see* **offer price**

offeror somebody who makes a bid

offer price the price at which somebody offers a share of a stock for sale. *Also known as* **offering price**

official bank a bank that has a charter from a government

official books of account the official financial records of an institution

official cash rate the current interest rate as set by a central bank. *Abbr* **OCR**

official development assistance money that the Organisation for Economic Co-operation and Development's Development Assistance Committee gives or lends to a developing country

official intervention an attempt by a government to influence the exchange rate by buying or selling foreign currency

official list in the United Kingdom, the list maintained by the Financial Services Authority of all the securities traded on the London Stock Exchange

official receiver an officer of the court who is appointed to wind up the affairs of an organisation that goes bankrupt. In the United Kingdom, an official receiver is appointed by the Department of Trade and Industry and often acts as a *liquidator*. The job involves realising any assets that remain to repay debts, for example, by selling property. *Abbr* **OR**

offset a transaction that balances all or part of an earlier transaction in the same security

offset clause a provision in an insurance policy that permits the balancing of credits against debits so that, for example, a party can reduce or omit payments to another party that owes it money and is bankrupt

offshore account an account in a *tax haven*

offshore bank a bank that offers only limited wholesale banking services to non-residents

offshore company a company that is registered in a country other than the one in which it conducts most of its business, usually for tax purposes. For example, many captive insurance companies are registered in the Cayman Islands.

offshore finance subsidiary a company created in another country to handle financial transactions, giving the owning company certain tax and legal advantages in its home country. *US term* **offshore financial subsidiary**

offshore financial centre a country or other political unit that has banking laws intended to attract business from industrialised nations

offshore financial subsidiary (*US*) = *offshore finance subsidiary*

offshore holding company a company created in another country to own other companies, giving the owning company certain legal advantages in its home country

offshore trading company a company created in another country to handle commercial transactions, giving the owning company certain legal advantages in its home country

off-the-shelf company a company for which all the legal formalities, except the appointment of directors, have been completed so that a purchaser can transform it into a new company with relative ease and low cost

OI *abbr* operating income

Old Lady of Threadneedle Street the Bank of England, which is located in Threadneedle Street in the City of London (*slang*)

oligopoly a market in which there are only a few, very large, suppliers

omitted dividend a regularly scheduled dividend that a company does not pay

omnibus account an account of one broker with another that combines the transactions of multiple investors for the convenience of the brokers

on account paid in advance against all or part of money due in the future

on demand 1. used to describe an account from which withdrawals may be made without giving a period of notice **2.** used to describe a loan, usually an overdraft, that the lender can request the borrower to repay immediately **3.** used to describe a bill of exchange that is paid upon presentation

one-stop shopping the ability of a single financial institution to offer a full range of financial services

one-to-one merger *see merger*

one-way trade an economic situation in which one country sells to another, but does not buy anything in return

one-year money money placed on a money market for a fixed period of one year, with either a fixed or variable rate of interest. It can be removed during the fixed term only upon payment of a penalty.

on-target earnings the amount earned by a person working on *commission* who has achieved the targets set. *Abbr* **OTE**

OPEC *abbr* Organization of the Petroleum Exporting Countries: an international organisation of 11 developing countries, each one largely reliant on oil revenues as its main source of income, that tries to ensure there is a balance between supply and demand by adjusting the members' oil output. OPEC's headquarters are in Vienna. The current members, Algeria, Indonesia, Iran, Iraq, Kuwait, Libya, Nigeria, Qatar, Saudi Arabia, the United Arab Emirates, and Venezuela, meet at least twice a year to decide on output levels and discuss recent and anticipated oil market developments.

open buying on the Internet a standard built round a common set of business requirements for electronic communication between buyers and sellers that, when implemented, allows different e-commerce systems to talk to one another. *Abbr* **OBI**. *See also* **open trading protocol**

open cheque 1. a cheque that is not crossed and so may be cashed by the payee at the branch of the bank where it is drawn **2.** (*US*) a signed cheque where the amount payable has not been indicated

open economy an economy that places no restrictions on the movement of capital, labour, foreign trade, and payments into and out of the country

open-end credit (*US*) = *open-ended credit*

open-ended credit a form of credit that does not have an upper limit on the amount that can be borrowed or a time limit before repayment is due

open-ended fund a unit trust that has a variable number of shares. *US term* *open-end fund*

open-ended investment company a unit trust, as distinguished from an investment trust, or *closed-end fund*. *See also* **open-ended fund**. *US term* *open-end investment company*

open-ended management company a company that sells unit trusts. *US term* *open-end management company*

open-ended mortgage a mortgage in which prepayment is allowed. *US term* *open-end mortgage*

open-end fund (*US*) = *open-ended fund*

open-end investment company (*US*) = *open-ended investment company*

open-end management company (*US*) = *open-ended management company*

open-end mortgage (*US*) = *open-ended mortgage*

opening balance the value of a financial quantity at the beginning of a period of time, such as a day or a year

opening balance sheet an account showing an organisation's opening balances

opening bell the beginning of a day of trading on a market

opening price a price for a security at the beginning of a day of trading on a market

opening purchase a first purchase of a series to be made in options of a particular type for a particular commodity or security

opening stock on a balance sheet, the closing stock at the end of one accounting period that is transferred forward and becomes the opening stock in the one that follows. *US term* **beginning inventory**

open interest options that have not yet been closed

open loop system a control system which includes no provision for corrective action to be applied to the sequence of activities

open-market operation a transaction by a central bank in a public market

open-market value the price that an asset or security would realise if it were offered on a market open to all

open trading protocol a standard designed to support Internet-based retail transactions that allows different systems to communicate with each other for a variety of payment-related activities. The *open buying on the Internet* protocol is a competing standard. *Abbr* **OTP**. *See also* **open buying on the Internet**

operating budget a budget of the revenues and expenses expected in a forthcoming accounting period

operating cash-flow the amount used to represent the money moving through a company as a result of its operations, as distinct from its purely financial transactions. *Abbr* **OCF**

operating income revenue minus the cost of goods sold and normal operating expenses. *Also known as* **earnings before interest and taxes**. *Abbr* **OI**

operating leverage the ratio of a business's fixed costs to its total costs.

As the fixed costs have to be paid regardless of output, the higher the ratio, the higher the risk of losses in an economic downturn.

operating margin *see* **profit margin**

operating profit the difference between a company's revenues and any related costs and expenses, not including income or expenses from any sources other than its normal methods of providing a good or a service

operating risk the risk of a high operating leverage

operating statement a regular report for management of actual costs and revenues, as appropriate. An operating statement usually compares actual costs with budgeted costs and shows variances.

operational control the management of daily activities in accordance with strategic and tactical plans

operational gearing the relationship of the fixed cost to the total cost of an operating unit. The greater the proportion of total costs that are fixed (high operational gearing), the greater the advantage to the organisation of increasing sales volume. Conversely, should sales volumes drop, a highly geared organisation would find the high proportion of fixed costs to be a major problem, possibly causing a rapid swing from profitability into significant loss-making. *See also* **leverage**

opportunity cost an amount of money lost as a result of choosing one investment rather than another

optimal portfolio a theoretical set of investments that would be the most profitable for an investor

optimal redemption provision a provision that specifies when an issuer can call a bond

optimise to allocate such things as resources or capital as efficiently as possible

option 1. a contract for the right to buy or sell an asset, typically a commodity, under certain terms. *Also known as option contract* **2.** the right of an option holder to buy or sell a specific asset on predetermined terms on, or before, a future date

option account a brokerage account used for trading in options

optionaire a millionaire whose wealth consists of share options (*slang*)

option buyer an investor who buys an option

option class a set of options that are identical with respect to type and underlying asset

option contract *see option* (*sense 1.*)

option elasticity the relative change in the value of an option as a function of a change in the value of the underlying asset

option income fund a unit trust that invests in options

option premium the amount per share that a buyer pays for an option

option price the price of an option

option pricing model a model that is used to determine the fair value of options

options clearing corporation (*US*) an organisation responsible for the listing of options and clearing trades in them

option seller *see option writer*

option series a collection of options that are identical in terms of what they represent

options market the trading in options, or a place where options trading occurs

options on physicals options on securities with fixed interest rates

option writer a person or institution who sells an option. *Also known as option seller*

OR *abbr* official receiver

order an occasion when a broker is told to buy or sell something for an investor's own account

order point the quantity of an item that is on hand when more units of the item are to be ordered

orders pending orders that have not yet resulted in transactions

ordinary interest interest calculated on the basis of a year having only 360 days

ordinary shares shares that entitle the holder to a dividend from the company's profits after holders of preference shares have been paid

Organisation for Economic Co-operation and Development *see OECD*

Organization of the Petroleum Exporting Countries *see OPEC*

original face value the amount of the principal of a mortgage on the day it is created

original issue discount the discount offered on the day of sale of a debt instrument

original maturity a date on which a debt instrument is due to mature

origination fee a fee charged by a lender for providing a mortgage, usually expressed as a percentage of the principal

OTC market *abbr* over-the-counter market

other capital capital that is not listed in specific categories

other current assets assets that are not cash and are due to mature within a year

other long-term capital long-term capital that is not listed in specific categories

other long-term liabilities obligations with terms greater than one year on which there is no charge for interest in the next year

other prices prices that are not listed in a catalogue

other short-term capital short-term capital that is not listed in specific categories

OTP *abbr* open trading protocol

out-of-date cheque a cheque which has not been presented to the bank on which it is drawn for payment within a reasonable time of its date (six months in the United Kingdom) and which may therefore be dishonoured by the bank without any breach of the banker–customer contract

out-of-the-money option an option whose underlying transaction shows a profit. *See in-the-money option*

output anything produced by a company, usually physical products

output gap the difference between the amount of activity that is sustainable in an economy and the amount of activity actually taking place

output method an accounting system that classifies costs according to the *outputs* for which they are incurred, not the inputs they have bought

output tax (*ANZ*) the amount of Goods and Services Tax paid to the tax office after the deduction of *input tax credits*

outsourcing the use of external suppliers as a source of finished products, components, or services

outstanding cheque a cheque which has been written and therefore has been entered in the company's ledgers, but which has not been presented for payment and so has not been debited from the company's bank account

outstanding share a share that a company has issued and somebody has bought

outstanding share capital the value of all of the stock of a company minus the value of retained shares

outwork work carried out for a company away from its premises, for example, by subcontractors or employees working from home

outworker a subcontractor or employee carrying out work for a company away from its premises

overall capitalisation rate net operating income other than debt service, divided by value

overall market capacity the amount of a service or good that can be absorbed in a market without affecting the price

overall rate of return the yield of a bond held to maturity, expressed as a percentage

overall return the aggregate of all the dividends received over an investment's life together with its capital gain or loss at the date of its realisation, calculated either before or after tax. It is one of the ways an investor can look at the performance of an investment.

overbid 1. to bid more than necessary **2.** an amount that is bid that is unnecessarily high

overbought used to describe a market or security considered to have risen too rapidly as a result of excessive buying

overbought market a market where prices have risen beyond levels that can be supported by fundamental analysis.

The market for Internet companies in 2001 was overbought and subsequently collapsed when it became clear that their trading performance could not support such price levels.

overcapitalise to supply a company with more capital than it needs or should have with the result that it is liable for unnecessary interest charges or dividend payments

overcapitalised used to describe a business that has more capital than can profitably be employed. An overcapitalised company could buy back some of its own shares in the market; if it has significant debt capital it could repurchase its bonds in the market; or it could make a large one-off dividend to shareholders.

overdraft the amount by which the money withdrawn from a bank account exceeds the balance in the account. *Abbr* **O/D**

overdraft facility a credit arrangement with a bank, allowing a person or company with an account to use borrowed money up to an agreed limit when nothing is left in the account

overdraft line an amount in excess of the balance in an account that a bank agrees to pay in honouring cheques on the account

overdraft protection the bank service, amounting to a line of credit, that assures that the bank will honour overdrafts, up to a limit and for a fee

overdraw to withdraw more money from a bank account than it contains, thereby exceeding an agreed credit limit

overdrawn in debt to a bank because the amount withdrawn from an account exceeds its balance

overdue an amount still owed after the date due

over-geared used to describe a company with debt capital and preference shares that outweigh its ordinary share capital

overhanging a large amount of commodities or securities that has not been sold and therefore has a negative effect on prices, for example, the element of a new issue left in the hands of the underwriters

overhead absorption rate a means of attributing overhead to a product or service, based, for example, on direct labour hours, direct labour cost, or machine hours. The choice of overhead absorption base may be made with the objective of obtaining 'accurate' product costs, or of influencing managerial behaviour, for example, overhead applied to labour hours or part numbers appears to make the use of these resources more costly, thus discouraging their use.

overhead capacity variance the difference between the overhead absorbed, based on budgeted hours, and actual hours worked

overhead costs the indirect recurring costs of running a business that are not linked directly to the goods or services produced and sold. Overhead costs can include payments for the rent of premises, utility bills, and employees' salaries. *Also called* **overheads**

overhead expenditure variance the difference between the budgeted *overhead costs* and the actual expenditure

overheads *see* *overhead costs*

over-insuring insuring an asset for a sum in excess of its market or replacement value. However, it is unlikely that an insurance company will pay out more in a claim for loss than the asset is worth or the cost of replacing it.

over-invested used to describe a business that invests heavily during an economic boom only to find that when it starts to produce an income, the demand for the product or service has fallen

overlap profit *profit* which occurs in two overlapping accounting periods and on which overlap relief can be claimed

overnight position a trader's position in a security or option at the end of a trading day

overnight repo a repurchase agreement where banks sell securities for cash and repurchase them the next day at a higher price. This type of agreement is used by central banks as a means of regulating the money markets.

overrated used to describe something that is valued more highly than it should be

overseas company a branch or subsidiary of a business that is incorporated in another country

Overseas Investment Commission an independent body reporting to the New Zealand government that regulates foreign investment in New Zealand. It was set up in 1973 and is funded by the Reserve Bank of New Zealand.

overseas taxation *see double taxation, double taxation agreement*

oversold used to describe a market or security that is considered to have fallen too rapidly as a result of excessive selling. *See also bear market*

overstocked used to describe a business that has more stock than it needs

oversubscribe to buy more of an offering than is available for sale

over-the-counter market a market in which trading takes place directly between licensed dealers, rather than through an auction system as used in most organised exchanges. *Abbr* **OTC market**

overtrading the condition of a business which enters into commitments in excess of its available short-term resources. This can arise even if the company is trading profitably, and is typically caused by financing strains imposed by a lengthy operating cycle or production cycle.

owners' equity a business's total assets less its total liabilities. *See also capital, ordinary shares*

P

packaging the practice of combining securities in a single trade

Pac Man defence a strategy to avoid the purchase of a company by making an offer to buy the prospective buyer

paid cheque a cheque which has been honoured by the bank on which it was drawn, and bears evidence of payment on its face

paid-up policy 1. an endowment assurance policy that continues to provide life cover while the cost of the premiums is covered by the underlying fund after the policyholder has decided not to continue paying premiums. If the fund is sufficient to pay the premiums for the remainder of the term, the remaining funds will be paid to the policyholder at maturity. **2.** (*US*) an insurance policy on which all the premiums have been paid

paid-up share a share for which shareholders have paid the full contractual amount. *See also* ***call, called-up share capital, paid-up share capital, share capital***

paid-up share capital the amount which shareholders are deemed to have paid on the shares issued and called up

painting the tape an illegal practice in which traders break large orders into smaller units in order to give the illusion of heavy buying activity. This encourages investors to buy, and the traders then sell as the price of the stock goes up. (*slang*)

panda one of a series of Chinese gold and silver bullion/collector coins, each featuring a panda, that were first issued in 1982. Struck with a highly polished surface, the smallest gold coin weighs 0.05 ounces, the largest 12 ounces.

P & L *see* ***profit and loss account***

Panel on Takeovers and Mergers *see City Code on Takeovers and Mergers*

panic buying an abnormal level of buying caused by fear or rumours of product shortages or by severe price rises

panic dumping of sterling a rush to sell sterling at any price because of possible devaluation

paper 1. a certificate of deposits and other securities **2.** a rights issue or an issue of bonds launched by a company to raise additional capital (*slang*) **3.** all the debt issued by a company (*slang*)

paper company a company that only exists on paper and has no physical assets

paper millionaire an individual who owns shares that are worth in excess of a million in currency, but which may fall in value. In 2001, many of the founders of dot-com companies were paper millionaires. *See also* ***paper profit***

paper money 1. banknotes **2.** payments in paper form, for example, cheques

paper profit an increase in the value of an investment that the investor has no immediate intention of realising

par the nominal value of a bond, being the price denominated for the purpose of setting the interest rate (coupon) payable

PAR *abbr* prime assets ratio

parallel pricing the practice of varying prices in a similar way and at the same time as competitors, which may be done by agreement with them

parent company a company with one or more subsidiary undertakings

Pareto's Law a theory of income distribution. Developed by Vilfredo Pareto, Pareto's Law states that regardless of political or taxation conditions, income will be distributed in the same way across all countries.

pari passu ranking equally

Paris Club *see Group of Ten*

Paris Inter Bank Offered Rate the French equivalent of the London Inter Bank Offered Rate. *Abbr* **PIBOR**

parity a situation when the price of a commodity, foreign currency, or security is the same in different markets. *See also* **arbitrage**

parity value *see conversion value*

park to place owned shares with third parties to disguise their ownership, usually illegally

parking 1. the transfer of shares in a company to a nominee name or the name of an associate, often for non-legitimate or illegal reasons (*slang*) **2.** (*US*) putting money into safe investments while deciding where to invest the money

Parquet an informal name for the Paris Bourse (*slang*)

participating bond a bond that pays the stockholders dividends as well as interest

participating insurance a form of insurance in which policyholders receive a dividend from the insurer's profits

participating preference share a type of preference share that entitles the holder to a fixed dividend and, in addition, to the right to participate in any surplus profits after payment of agreed levels of dividends to ordinary shareholders has been made. *See also* *non-participating preference share*

participative budgeting a budgeting system in which all budget holders are given the opportunity to participate in setting their own budgets. *Also known as bottom-up budgeting*

partly-paid share a share for which shareholders have not paid the full contractual amount. *See also* **call**, **share capital**

partnership according to the Partnership Act 1890, the relationship which exists between persons carrying on business in common with a view to profit. The liability of the individual partners is unlimited unless provided for by the partnership agreement. The Limited Partnership Act 1907 allows a partnership to contain one or more partners with limited liability so long as there is at least one partner with unlimited liability. A partnership consists of not more than 20 persons.

partnership accounts the capital and current accounts of each partner in a partnership, or the accounts recording the partnership's business activities

partnership agreement the document that sets up a partnership, detailing the capital contributed by each partner; whether an individual partner's liability is limited; the apportionment of the profit; salaries; and possibly procedures to be followed, for example, in the event of a partner retiring or a new partner joining. In the United Kingdom, when a partnership agreement is silent on any matter, the provisions of the Partnership Act 1890 apply. *Also known as* **articles of partnership**

par value *see nominal value*

passbook a small booklet issued by banks, building societies, and other financial institutions to record deposits, withdrawals, interest paid, and the balance on savings and deposit accounts. In all but the smaller building societies, it has now largely been replaced by statements.

passing off a form of fraud in which a company tries to sell its own product by deceiving buyers into thinking it is another product

passive investment management the managing of a unit trust or other investment portfolio by relying on automatic adjustments such as indexation instead of making personal judgments. *See also* ***active fund management***

passive portfolio strategy the managing of an investment portfolio by relying on automatic adjustments or tracking an index

patent
   to patent an invention to register an invention with the Patent Office to prevent other people from copying it

pathfinder prospectus a preliminary prospectus used in initial public offerings to gauge the reaction of investors. *Also known as* ***red eye***

pawnbroker a person who lends money against the security of a wide range of chattels, from jewellery to cars. The borrower may recover the goods by repaying the loan and interest by a certain date. Otherwise, the items pawned are sold and any surplus after the deduction of expenses, the loan, and interest is returned to the borrower.

pay a sum of money given in return for work done or services provided. Pay, in the form of ***salary*** or ***wages***, is generally provided in weekly or monthly fixed amounts, and is usually expressed in terms of the total sum earned per year. It may also be allocated using a piece-rate system, where workers are paid for each unit of work they carry out.

payable to order the legend on a bill of exchange or cheque, used to indicate that it may be transferred

Pay As You Earn in the United Kingdom, a system for collecting direct taxes that requires employers to deduct taxes from employees' ***pay*** before payment is made. *Abbr* **PAYE**

pay-as-you-go (*Canada*) a means of financing a pension system whereby benefits of current retirees are financed by current workers

Pay-As-You-Go (*ANZ*) a system used in Australia for paying income tax instalments on business and investment income. PAYG is part of the new tax system introduced by the Australian government on 1 July 2000. *Abbr* **PAYG**

payback the time required for the cash inflows from a capital investment project to equal the cash outflows

payback period the length of time it will take to earn back the money invested in a project.
EXAMPLE The straight payback period method is the simplest way of determining the investment potential of a major project. Expressed in time, it tells a management how many months or years it will take to recover the original cash cost of the project. It is calculated using the formula:

Cost of project / annual cash revenues = payback period

Thus, if a project cost £100,000 and was expected to generate £28,000 annually, the payback period would be:

100,000 / 28,000 = 3.57 years

If the revenues generated by the project are expected to vary from year to year, add the revenues expected for each succeeding year until you arrive at the total cost of the project.
   For example, say the revenues expected to be generated by the £100,000 project are:

Revenue	Total	Cum. Total
Year 1	£19,000	£19,000
Year 2	£25,000	£44,000
Year 3	£30,000	£74,000
Year 4	£30,000	£104,000
Year 5	£30,000	£134,000

Thus, the project would be fully paid for in Year 4, since it is in that year the total revenue reaches the initial cost of £100,000. The precise payback period would be calculated as:

$$((100,000 - 74,000) / (104,000 - 74,000)) \times 365 = 316 \text{ days} + 3 \text{ years}$$

The picture becomes complex when the time-value-of-money principle is introduced into the calculations. Some experts insist this is essential to determine the most accurate payback period. Accordingly, the annual revenues have to be discounted by the applicable interest rate, 10% in this example. Doing so produces significantly different results:

Revenue	Present value	Total	Cum. Total
Year 1	£19,000	£17,271	£17,271
Year 2	£25,000	£20,650	£37,921
Year 3	£30,000	£22,530	£60,451
Year 4	£30,000	£20,490	£80,941
Year 5	£30,000	£18,630	£99,571

This method shows that payback would not occur even after five years.

Generally, a payback period of three years or less is desirable; if a project's payback period is less than a year, some contend it should be judged essential.

PAYE *abbr* Pay As You Earn

payee 1. the person or organisation to whom a cheque is payable. *See also* *drawee* **2.** the person to whom a payment has to be made

payer the person making a payment

PAYG *abbr* (*ANZ*) Pay-As-You-Go

paying agent the institution responsible for making interest payments on a security and repaying capital at redemption. *Also known as* *disbursing agent*

paying banker the bank on which a bill of exchange or cheque is drawn

paying-in book a book of detachable slips that accompany money or cheques being paid into a bank account

payload the amount of cargo that a vessel can carry

paymaster the person responsible for paying an organisation's employees

payment by results a system of *pay* that directly links an employee's salary to his or her work output. The system is based on the view put forward by Frederick Winslow Taylor that payment by results will increase workers' productivity by appealing to their materialism. The concept is closely related to performance-related pay which rewards employees for behaviour and skills rather than quantifiable productivity measures.

payment gateway a company or organisation that provides an interface between a merchant's point-of-sale system, *acquirer* payment systems, and *issuer* payment systems. *Abbr* **GW**

payment in advance a payment made for goods when they are ordered and before they are delivered. *See also* *prepayment*

payment in due course the payment of a bill of exchange on a fixed date in the future

payment-in-kind an alternative form of *pay* given to employees in place of monetary reward but considered to be of equivalent value. A payment in kind may take the form of use of a car, purchase of goods at cost price, or other non-financial exchange that benefits the employee. It forms part of the total pay package rather than being an extra benefit.

payment-in-lieu payment that is given in place of an entitlement

payment terms the stipulation by a business as to when it should be paid for goods or services supplied, for example, cash with order, payment on delivery, or within a particular number of days of the invoice date

payout ratio an expression of the total dividends paid to shareholders as a percentage of a company's net profit in a given period of time. This measures the likelihood of dividend payments being sustained, and is a useful indication of sustained profitability. The lower the ratio, the more secure the dividend, and the company's future. The payout ratio is calculated by dividing annual dividends paid on ordinary shares by earnings per share:

Annual dividend / earnings per share = payout ratio

EXAMPLE Take the company whose earnings per share is £8 and its dividend payout is 2.1. Its payout ratio would be:

2.1 / 8 = .263 or 26.3%

A high payout ratio clearly appeals to conservative investors seeking income. When coupled with weak or falling earnings, however, it could suggest an imminent dividend cut, or that the company is short-changing reinvestment to maintain its payout. A payout ratio above 75% is a warning. It suggests the company is failing to reinvest sufficient profits in its business, that the company's earnings are faltering, or that it is trying to attract investors who otherwise would not be interested. *See also **dividend cover***

Pay Pal a web-based service that enables Internet users to send and receive payments electronically. To open a Pay Pal account, users register and provide their credit card details. When they decide to make a transaction via Pay Pal, their card is charged for the transfer.

pay-per-click a website that charges a *micropayment* to see digital information, for example, an e-book or e-magazine

pay-per-play a website that charges a *micropayment* to play an interactive game over the Internet

pay per view 1. a website that charges a *micropayment* to see digital information, for example, an e-book or e-magazine **2.** a method of collecting revenue from television viewers. The viewer pays a fee for watching an individual programme, typically a sports or entertainment event.

payroll a record showing for each employee his or her gross pay, deductions, and net pay. The payroll may also include details of the employer's associated employment costs.

payroll analysis an analysis of a payroll for cost accounting purposes, giving, for example, gross pay by department or operation, gross pay by class of labour, gross pay by product, or constituent parts of gross pay, such as direct pay and lost time

payroll giving scheme a scheme by which an employee pays money to a charity directly out of his or her salary. The money is deducted by the employer and paid to the charity, and the employee gets tax relief on such donations.

payslip a document given to employees when they are paid, providing a statement of *pay* for that period. A payslip includes details of deductions such as *income tax*, national insurance contributions, pension contributions, and trade union dues.

P/C *abbr* petty cash

P/DR *abbr* price/dividend ratio

P/E *abbr* price/earnings ratio

peg 1. to fix the exchange rate of one currency against that of another or of a basket of other currencies **2.** to fix wages and salaries during a period of inflation to help prevent an inflationary spiral

P/E multiple *abbr* price/earnings multiple

penalty an arbitrary pre-arranged sum that becomes payable if one party breaks a term of a contract or an undertaking. The most common penalty is a high rate of interest on an unauthorised overdraft. *See also* **overdraft**

penetration pricing setting prices low, especially for new products, in order to maximise market penetration

penny shares very low-priced stock that is a speculative investment

pension money received regularly after retirement, from a personal pension scheme, occupational pension scheme, or state pension scheme. *Also known as* **retirement pension**

pensionable earnings in an occupational pension scheme with a defined benefit, the earnings on which the pension is based. Generally, overtime payments, benefits in kind, bonuses, and territorial allowances, for example, payments for working in a large city, are not pensionable earnings. *US term* *final average monthly salary*

pension entitlement the amount of pension which someone has the right to receive when he or she retires

PEP *abbr* personal equity plan

P/E ratio *abbr* price/earnings ratio

per capita income the average income of each of a particular group of people, for example, citizens of a country

perceived value pricing *see market based pricing*

per diem a rate paid per day, for example, for expenses when an employee is working away from the office

perfect capital market a capital market in which the decisions of buyers and sellers have no effect on market price

perfect competition the condition in which no buyer or seller can influence prices. In practice, perfect markets are characterised by few or no barriers to entry and by many buyers and sellers.

perfect forward secrecy the property an encryption system has if the compromise of a key affects only one message

perfect hedge a hedge that exactly balances the risk of another investment

performance bond a guarantee given by a bank to a third party stating that it will pay a sum of money if its customer, the account holder, fails to complete a specified contract

performance criteria the standards used to evaluate a product, service, or employee

performance fund an investment fund designed to produce a high return, reflected in the higher risk involved

performance measurement the process of assessing the proficiency with which a reporting entity succeeds, by the economic acquisition of resources and their efficient and effective deployment, in achieving its objectives. Performance measures may be based on non-financial as well as on financial information.

performance share a share which is likely to show capital growth rather than income, which is normally provided by shares with a higher risk

period bill a bill of exchange payable on a certain date rather than on demand. *Also known as* **term bill**

period cost a cost which relates to a time period rather than to the output of products or services

periodicity concept the requirement to produce financial statements at set time intervals. This requirement is embodied, in the case of UK corporations, in the Companies Acts.

permanent interest-bearing shares shares issued by a building society to raise capital because the law prohibits it from raising capital in more conventional ways. *Abbr* **PIBS**

perpetual bond a bond that has no date of maturity

perpetual debenture a debenture that pays interest in perpetuity, having no date of maturity

perpetual inventory the daily tracking of inventory

perpetuity a periodic payment continuing for a limitless period. *See also annuity*

personal account a record of amounts receivable from or payable to a person or an entity. A collection of these accounts is known as a sales/debtor ledger, or a purchases/creditors ledger. The terms sales and purchases ledger are preferred. In the United States, the terms 'receivables ledger' and 'payables ledger' are used.

personal allowances the amount of money that an individual can earn without having to pay income tax. The allowances vary according to age, marital status, and whether the person is a single parent.

Personal Equity Plan a scheme sponsored by the UK government to promote investment in company shares, unit trusts, and equity-based investment trusts by offering tax benefits to investors. The arrival of ISAs in 1999 meant that no new personal equity plans could be opened, but existing plans carry on as before. *Abbr* **PEP**

personal financial planning short- and long-term financial planning by an individual, either independently or with the assistance of a professional advisor. It will include the use of tax efficient schemes such as Individual Savings Accounts, ensuring adequate provisions are being made for retirement, and examining short- and long-term borrowing requirements such as overdrafts and mortgages.

Personal Identification Number *abbr* **PIN**

Personal Investment Authority a self-regulatory organisation responsible for supervising the activities of financial intermediaries selling financial products to individuals. *Abbr* **PIA**

personal pension plan a pension plan which applies to one worker only, usually a self-employed person or a person not in a company pension scheme, rather than a group of employees

PESTLE an acronym that describes the six influences to which a market is subject, namely, political, economic, social, technological, legal, and environmental

petty cash a small store of cash used for minor business expenses. *Abbr* **P/C**

petty cash account a record of relatively small cash receipts and payments, the balance representing the cash in the control of an individual, usually dealt with under an imprest system

petty cash voucher a document supporting payments under a petty cash system

PFI *abbr* Private Finance Initiative

phantom bid a reported but non-existent attempt to buy a company

phantom income income that is subject to tax even though the recipient never actually gets control of it, for example, income from a limited partnership

physical asset an asset that has a physical embodiment, as opposed to cash or securities

physical market a market in futures that involves physical delivery of the commodities involved, instead of simple cash transactions

physical price the price of a commodity for immediate delivery

physicals commodities that can be bought and used, as contrasted with commodities traded on a futures contract

PIA *abbr* Personal Investment Authority

PIBOR *abbr* Paris Inter Bank Offered Rate

PIBS *abbr* permanent interest-bearing shares

picture the price and trading quantity of a particular stock on Wall Street, used for example, in the question to a specialist dealer 'What's the picture on ABC?'. The response would give the bid and offer price and number of shares for which there would be a buyer and seller. (*slang*)

piggyback loan a loan that is raised against the same security as an existing loan

piggyback rights the permission to sell existing shares in conjunction with the sale of like shares in a new offering

PIN *abbr* personal identification number

pink dollar (*US*) = *pink pound*

pink form in the United Kingdom, a preferential application form at an initial public offering that is reserved for the employees of the company being floated

pink pound money spent by the homosexual community. *US term* **pink dollar**

Pink 'Un the *Financial Times* (*slang*)

pit the area of an exchange where trading takes place. It was traditionally an octagonal stepped area with terracing so as to give everyone a good view of the proceedings during open outcry.

pit broker a broker who transacts business in the pit of a futures or options exchange. *Also known as* **floor broker**

placement *see* *placing, private placing*

placement fee a fee that a stockbroker receives for a sale of shares

placing a method of raising share capital in which there is no public issue of shares, the shares being issued, rather, in a small number of large 'blocks', to persons or institutions who have previously agreed to purchase the shares at a predetermined price

plain vanilla a financial instrument in its simplest form (*slang*)

plan comptable in France, a uniformly structured and detailed bookkeeping system with which companies are required to comply

planning the establishment of objectives, and the formulation, evaluation, and selection of the policies, strategies, tactics, and action required to achieve them. Planning comprises long-term/strategic planning and short-term operation planning. The latter is usually for a period of up to one year.

planning horizon the furthest time ahead for which plans can be quantified. It need not be the planning period. *See also* **planning, futuristic planning**

planning period the period for which a plan is prepared and used. It differs according to product or process life cycle. For example, forestry requires a period of many years whereas fashion garments require only a few months.

plastic *or* **plastic money** a payment system using a plastic card (*slang*) *See also* **credit card, debit card, multifunctional card**

plc *or* **PLC** *abbr* public limited company

plentitude a hypothetical condition of an economy in which manufacturing technology has been perfected and scarcity is replaced by an abundance of products

plough back to reinvest a company's earnings in the business instead of paying them out as dividends

ploughed back profits retained profits

plug and play relating to a new member of staff who does not require training (*slang*)

plum a successful investment (*slang*)

PN *abbr* promissory note

PO *abbr* purchase order

point (*US*) a unit used for calculation of a value, such as a hundredth of a percentage point for interest rates

poison pill a measure taken by a company to avoid a hostile takeover, for example, the purchase of a business interest that will make the company unattractive to the potential buyer (*slang*) *Also known as **show stopper***

policy an undated, long-lasting, and often unquantified statement of guidance regarding the way in which an organisation will seek to behave in relation to its stakeholders

policyholder a person or business covered by an insurance policy

political economy a country's economic organisation

poop (*US*) a person who has *inside information* on a financial deal (*slang*)

pooping and scooping (*US*) an illegal financial practice in which a person or group of individuals attempts to drive down a share price by spreading false unfavourable information. The advent

of the Internet has allowed pooping and scooping to become more widespread. (*slang*)

portable pension a pension plan that moves with an employee when he or she changes employer. *See also **stakeholder pension***

portfolio the range of investments, such as stocks and shares, owned by an individual or an organisation

portfolio immunisation measures taken by traders to protect their share portfolios (*slang*)

portfolio insurance options that provide hedges against stock in a portfolio

portfolio investment a form of investment that aims for a mixture of income and capital growth

portfolio management the buying and selling of shares by a specialist on behalf of a client

portfolio manager a person or company that specialises in managing an investment portfolio on behalf of investors

position the number of shares of a security that are owned by an individual or company

position audit part of the planning process which examines the current state of an entity in respect of the following: resources of tangible and intangible assets and finance; products, brands, and markets; operating systems such as production and distribution; internal organisation; current results; and returns to stockholders

position limit the largest amount of a security that any group or individual may own

positive economics the study of economic propositions that can be verified by observing the real economy

possessor in bad faith somebody who occupies land even though they do not believe they have a legal right to do so

possessor in good faith somebody who occupies land believing they have a legal right to do so

possessory action a lawsuit over the right to own a piece of land

post a credit to enter a credit item in a ledger

postal account an account for which all dealings are done by post, thereby reducing overhead costs and allowing a higher level of *interest* to be paid

postal vote an election in which the voters send in their ballot papers by post

Post Big Bang *see also* **Big Bang**

post-completion audit an objective and independent appraisal of the measure of success of a capital expenditure project in progressing the business as planned. The appraisal should cover the implementation of the project from authorisation to commissioning and its technical and commercial performance after commissioning. The information provided is also used by management as feedback which helps the implementation and control of future projects.

postdate to put a later date on a document or cheque than the date when it is signed, with the effect that it is not valid until the later date

postdated *see* **postdate**

post-purchase costs costs incurred after a capital expenditure decision has been implemented and facilities acquired. These costs may include training, maintenance, and the cost of upgrades.

potential GDP a measure of the real value of the services and goods that can be produced when a country's factors of production are fully employed

potentially exempt transfer *see* *chargeable transfer*

pot trust a trust, typically created in a will, for a group of beneficiaries

pound cost averaging investing the same amount at regular intervals in a security regardless of its price. *US term* *dollar cost averaging*

poverty trap a situation whereby low income families are penalised by a progressive tax system: an increase in income is either counteracted by a loss of social benefit payments or by an increase in taxation

power of appointment the power of a trustee to dispose of interests in property to another person

power of attorney a legal document granting one person the right to act on behalf of another

pp derived from the Latin 'per pro', used beside a signature at the end of a letter meaning 'on behalf of'

PPP *abbr* purchasing power parity

pre-acquisition profits/losses the profits or losses of a subsidiary undertaking, attributable to a period prior to its acquisition by a parent company. Such profits are not available for distribution as dividends by the parent company unless the underlying value of the subsidiary undertaking is at least equal to its net carrying value in the books of the parent company.

pre-authorised electronic debit a scheme in which a payer agrees to let a bank make payments from an account to somebody else's account

prebilling the practice of submitting a bill for a product or service before it has actually been delivered

preceding year the year before the accounting year in question

precious metals gold, silver, platinum, and palladium

predatory pricing the practice of setting prices for products that are designed to win business from competitors or to damage competitors. This may involve *dumping*, which is selling a product in a foreign market at below cost or below the domestic market price (subject to adjustments for taxation differences, transportation costs, specification differences, etc.).

pre-emptive right the right of a stockholder to maintain proportional ownership in a corporation by purchasing newly issued stock

preference option an option for preferred stock

preference share a share which carries a fixed rate of dividend. The holders, subject to the conditions of issue, have a prior claim to any company profits available for distribution.

preferential creditor a creditor who is entitled to payment, especially from a bankrupt, before other creditors

preferential form *see pink form*

preferential issue an issue of stock available only to designated buyers

preferential payment a payment to a preferential creditor

preferred ordinary shares ordinary shares of *preferred stock*

preferred risk somebody considered by an insurance company to be less likely to collect on a policy than the average person, for example, a non-smoker

preferred stock *(US)* = *preference shares*

pre-financing the practice of arranging funding for a project before the project begins

preliminary prospectus a document issued prior to a share issue that gives details of the shares available

premarket used to describe transactions between market members carried out prior to the official opening of the market. *Also known as* **pretrading**

premium 1. the price a purchaser of an option pays to its writer **2.** the difference between the futures price and the cash price of an underlying asset **3.** the consideration for a contract of insurance or assurance

at a premium 1. of a fixed interest security, at an issue price above its par value **2.** of a new issue, at a trading price above the one offered to investors **3.** at a price that is considered expensive in relation to others

premium bond in the United States, a bond with a selling price above its face or redemption value

Premium Bond in the United Kingdom, a non-marketable security issued by National Savings at £1 each that pays no interest but is entered into a draw every month to win prizes from £50 to £1 million. There are many lower value prizes, but only one £1 million prize. The bonds are repayable upon demand.

premium income the income earned by a life company or insurance company from premiums

premium pay plan an enhanced pay scale for high performing employees. A premium pay plan can be offered as an incentive to motivate employees, rewarding such achievements as high productivity, long service, or completion of training with an increased pay package.

prepaid interest interest paid in advance of its due date

prepayment the payment of a debt before it is due to be paid

prepayment penalty (*US*) a charge that may be levied against somebody who makes a payment before its due date. The penalty compensates the lender or seller for potential lost interest.

prepayment privilege the right to make a prepayment, for example, on a loan or mortgage, without penalty

prepayment risk the risk that a debtor will avoid interest charges by making partial or total prepayments, especially when interest rates fall

prescribed payments system (*ANZ*) a system under which employers are obliged to deduct a certain amount of tax from cash payments made to casual workers. The system was introduced in Australia in 1983.

present value 1. the amount that a future interest in a financial asset is currently worth, discounted for inflation **2.** the value now of an amount of money that somebody expects to receive at a future date, calculated by subtracting any interest that will accrue in the interim

preservation of capital an approach to financial management that protects a person's or company's capital by arranging additional forms of finance

pre-syndicate bid a bid made before a group of buyers can offer blocks of shares in an offering to the public

pretax before tax is considered or paid

pretax profit the amount of profit a company makes before taxes are deducted

pretax profit margin the profit made by a company, calculated as a percentage of sales, before taxes are considered

pretrading *see premarket*

price an amount of money that a vendor charges a customer for a good or service

price-book ratio *see price-to-book ratio*

price ceiling the highest price that a buyer is willing to pay

price competition a form of competition based on price rather than factors such as quality or design

price control a government regulation that sets maximum prices for commodities or controls price levels by means of credit controls

price differentiation a pricing strategy in which a company sells the same product at different prices in different markets

price discovery the process by which price is determined by negotiation in a free market

price discrimination the practice of selling the same product to different buyers at different prices

price/dividend ratio the price of a stock divided by the annual dividend paid on a share. *Abbr* **P/DR**

price/earnings multiple *abbr* **P/E multiple**

price/earnings ratio a company's share price divided by earnings per share (EPS).

While EPS is an actual amount of money, usually expressed in pence per share, the P/E ratio has no units, it is just a number. Thus if a quoted company has a share price of £100 and EPS of £12 for the last published year, then it has a historical P/E of 8.3. If analysts are forecasting for the next year EPS of, say, £14 then the forecast P/E is 7.1.

The P/E ratio is predominantly useful in comparisons with other shares rather than in isolation.

EXAMPLE If the average P/E in the market is 20, there will be many shares with P/Es well above and well below this, for a variety of reasons. Similarly, in a particular sector, the P/Es will frequently vary from the sector average, even though the constituent companies may all be engaged in similar businesses. The reason is that even two businesses doing the same thing will not always be doing it as profitably as each other. One may be far more efficient, as demonstrated by a history of rising EPS compared with the flat EPS picture of the other over a series of years, and the market might recognise this by awarding the more profitable share a higher P/E ratio. *Abbr* **P/E ratio**

price effect the impact of price changes on a market or economy

price elasticity of demand the percentage change in demand divided by the percentage change in price of a good

price elasticity of supply the percentage change in supply divided by the percentage change in price of a good

price escalation clause a contract provision that permits the seller to raise prices in response to increased costs

price fixing an often illegal agreement between producers of a good or service in order to maintain prices at a particular level

price floor the lowest price at which a seller is prepared to do business

price index an index, such as the Consumer Price Index, that measures inflation

price indicator a price that is a measurable variable and can be used, for example, as an index of the cost of living

price-insensitive used to describe a good or service for which sales remain constant no matter what its price because it is essential to buyers

price instability a situation in which the prices of goods alter daily or even hourly

price ring a group of traders who make an agreement, often illegally, to maintain prices at a particular level

prices and incomes policy a policy limiting price or wage increases through government regulations

price-sensitive used to describe a good or service for which sales fluctuate depending on its price, often because it is a non-essential item

price-sensitive information as yet unpublished information that will affect a company's share price. For example, the implementation of a new manufacturing process that will substantially cut production costs would have a positive impact, whereas the discovery of harmful side effects from a recently launched drug would have a negative impact.

price stability a situation in which there is little change in the price of goods or services

price support government assistance in keeping market prices from falling below a minimum level

price taker an economic agent whose size relative to that of the market in which it operates is so small that it cannot influence prices in that market

price-to-book ratio the ratio of the value of all of a company's stock to its *book value*. *Also known as* **price-book ratio**

price-to-cash-flow ratio the ratio of the value of all of a company's stock to its cash-flow for the most recent complete fiscal year

price-to-sales ratio the ratio of the value of all of a company's stock to its sales for the previous twelve months, a way of measuring the relative value of a share when compared with others.

The P/S ratio is obtained by dividing the market capitalisation by the latest published annual sales figure. So, a company with a capitalisation of £1 billion and sales of £3 billion would have a P/S ratio of 0.33.

P/S ratios will vary with the type of industry. You would expect, for example, that many retailers and other large-scale distributors of goods would have very high sales in relation to their market capitalisations—in other words, a very low P/S ratio. Equally, manufacturers of high-value items would generally have much lower sales figures and thus higher P/S ratios.

A company with a lower P/S is cheaper than one with a higher ratio, particularly if they are in the same sector so that a direct comparison is more appropriate. It means that each share of the lower P/S company is buying more of its sales than those of the higher P/S company.

It is important to note that a share which is cheaper only on P/S grounds is not necessarily the more attractive share. There will frequently be reasons why it has a lower ratio than that of another similar company, most commonly because it is less profitable.

price-weighted index an index of production or market value that is adjusted for price changes

pricing the determination of a selling price for a product or service

pricing model a computerised system for calculating prices, based on a variety of factors including costs and anticipated margins

primary account number an identifier for a credit card used in secure electronic transactions

primary banking system all the banks in the United Kingdom that transfer money between parties

primary commodities farm produce grown in large quantities, such as corn, rice, or cotton

primary earnings per (common) share (US) see **earnings per share**

primary liability a responsibility to pay before anyone else, for example, for damages covered by insurance

primary market the part of the market on which securities are first offered to investors by the issuer. The money from this sale goes to the issuer, rather than to traders or investors as it does in the secondary market. See also **secondary market**

primary sector the firms and corporations of the productive sector of a country's economy

prime see **prime rate**

prime assets ratio the proportion of total liabilities which Australian banks are obliged by the Reserve Bank to hold in secure assets such as cash and government securities. Abbr **PAR**

prime cost the total cost of direct material, direct labour, and direct expenses

prime interest rate see **prime rate**

prime rate the lowest interest rate that commercial banks offer on loans. Also known as **prime**, **prime interest rate**

principal the original amount of a loan, not including any **interest**. See also **mortgage**

principal budget factor a factor which will limit the activities of an undertaking and which is often the starting-point in budget preparation

principal shareholders the shareholders who own the largest percentage of shares in an organisation

prior charge capital capital which has a right to the receipt of interest or of preference dividends in precedence to any claim on distributable earnings on the part of the ordinary shareholders. On winding up, the claims of holders of prior charge capital also rank before those of ordinary shareholders.

prior charge percentage *see priority percentage*

priority-based budgeting a method of budgeting in which budget requests are accompanied by a statement outlining the changes which would occur if the prior period budget were to be increased or decreased by a certain amount or percentage. These changes are prioritised.

priority percentage the proportion of a business's net profit that is paid in interest to preference shareholders and holders of debt capital. *Also known as prior charge percentage*

prior lien bond a bond whose holder has more claim on a debtor's assets than holders of other types of bonds

prior year adjustment an adjustment made to accounts for previous years, because of changes in accounting policies or because of errors

private bank 1. a bank that is owned by a single person or a limited number of private shareholders **2.** a bank that provides banking facilities to high net worth individuals. *See also private banking* **3.** a bank that is not state-owned in a country where most banks are owned by the government

private banking a service offered by certain financial institutions to high net worth individuals. In addition to standard banking services, it will typically include portfolio management and advisory services on taxation, including estate planning.

private company a company which has not been registered as a public company under the Companies Act. The major practical distinction between a private and public company is that the former may not offer its securities to the public.

private cost *(US)* the cost incurred by individuals when they use scarce resources such as petrol

private debt money owed by individuals and organisations other than governments

private enterprise business or industry that is controlled by companies or individuals rather than the government

Private Finance Initiative a policy which is designed to harness private sector management and expertise in the delivery of public services. Under PFI, the public sector does not buy assets, it buys the asset-based services it requires, on contract, from the private sector, the latter having the responsibility for deciding how to supply these services, the investment required to support the services, and how to achieve the required standards. *Abbr* **PFI**

private placement *(US)* = *private placing*

private placing the sale of securities directly to institutions for investment rather than resale. *US term* **private placement**

private sector the section of the economy that is financed and controlled by individuals or private institutions, such as companies, shareholders, or investment groups. *See also* **public sector**

private sector investment investment by the private enterprise sector of an economy

private treaty the sale of land without an auction

privatisation the transfer of a company from ownership by either a government or a few individuals to the public via the issuance of stock

probability the likelihood of an event or a state of nature occurring, being measured in a range from 0 (no possibility) to 1 (certainty)

problem child 1. (*US*) a subsidiary company that is not performing well or is damaging the *parent company* in some way **2.** a product with a low market share but high growth potential. Problem children often have good long-term prospects, but high levels of investment may be needed to realise the potential, thereby draining funds that may be needed elsewhere. *See also Boston Consulting Group matrix*

proceeds the income from a transaction

process costing a method of costing something which is manufactured from a series of continuous processes, where the total costs of those processes are divided by the number of units produced

procurement exchange a group of companies that act together to buy products or services they need at lower prices

producer price index a statistical measure, the weighted average of the prices of commodities that firms buy from other firms

product bundling a form of discounting in which a group of related products is sold at a price which is lower than that obtainable by the consumer were the products to be purchased separately

production cost prime cost plus absorbed production overhead

productivity a measurement of the efficiency of production, taking the form of a ratio of the output of goods and services to the input of factors of production. **Labour productivity** takes account of inputs of employee hours worked; **capital productivity** takes account of inputs of machines or land; and **marginal productivity** measures the

additional output gained from an additional unit of input. Techniques to improve productivity include greater use of new technology, altered working practices, and improved training of the workforce.

product life cycle the period which begins with the initial product specification and ends with the withdrawal from the market of both the product and its support. It is characterised by defined stages including research, development, introduction, maturity, decline, and abandonment.

product-sustaining activities activities undertaken in support of production, the costs of which are linked to the number of separate products produced rather than to the volume of output. Engineering change is a product-sustaining activity. *See also hierarchy of activities*

profile a description of a company, including its products and finances

profit the difference between the selling price and the purchase price of a security or financial instrument when the selling price is higher

profitability 1. the degree to which an individual, company, or single activity makes a *profit* **2.** the condition of making a *profit*

profitability index the present value of the money an investment will earn divided by the amount of the investment

profitability threshold the point at which a business begins to make profits

profitable used to refer to a product, service, or organisation which makes money

profit and loss the difference between a company's income and its costs

profit and loss account *or* **profit and loss statement** the summary record of a company's sales revenues and expenses over a period, providing a calculation of profits or losses during that time.

Companies typically issue P&L reports monthly. It is customary for the reports to include year-to-date figures, as well as corresponding year-earlier figures to allow for comparisons and analysis.

There are two P&L formats, multiple-step and single-step. Both follow a standard set of rules known as *Generally Accepted Accounting Principles* (GAAP). These rules generally adhere to requirements established by governments to track receipts, expenses, and profits for tax purposes. They also allow the financial reports of two different companies to be compared.

The multiple-step format is much more common, because it includes a larger number of details and is thus more useful. It deducts costs from revenues in a series of steps, allowing for closer analysis. Revenues appear first, then expenses, each in as much detail

as management desires. Sales may be broken down by product line or location, while expenses such as salaries may be broken down into base salaries and commissions.

Expenses are then subtracted from revenues to show profit (or loss). A basic multiple-step P&L looks like the table below:

P&Ls of public companies may also report income on the basis of earnings per share. For example, if the company issuing this statement had 12,000 shares outstanding, earnings per share would be £5.12, that is, £61,440 divided by 12,000 shares. *Abbr* **P & L**

profit before tax the amount that a company or investor has made, without taking taxes into account

profit centre a part of a business accountable for both costs and revenues

profit distribution the allocation of profits to different recipients such as

MULTIPLE-STEP PROFIT & LOSS ACCOUNT		(£)
NET SALES	750,000	
Less: cost of goods sold	450,000	
Gross profit		300,000
LESS: OPERATING EXPENSES		
Selling expenses		
Salaries & commissions	54,000	
Advertising	37,500	
Delivery/transportation	12,000	
Depreciation/store equipment	7,500	
Other selling expenses	5,000	
Total selling expenses		116,000
General & administrative expenses		
Administrative/office salaries	74,000	
Utilities	2,500	
Depreciation/structure	2,400	
Misc. other expenses	3,100	
Total general & admin expenses		82,000
Total operating expenses		198,000
OPERATING INCOME		102,000
LESS (ADD): NON-OPERATING ITEMS		
Interest expenses	11,000	
Interest income earned	(2,800)	8,200
Income before taxes		93,800
Income taxes		32,360
Net Income		**61,440**

shareholders and owners, or for different purposes such as research or investment

profiteer an individual or organisation that aims to make excessive profits, often with a detrimental effect on others

profit from ordinary activities profits earned in the normal course of business, as opposed to profits from extraordinary sources such as windfall payments

profit margin sales less cost of sales, expressed either as a value or as a percentage of sales value. The profit margin may be calculated at different stages, hence the terms **gross profit margin** and **net profit margin**. The level of profit reported is also influenced by the extent of the application of accounting conventions, and by the method of product costing used, for example, marginal or *absorption costing*.

profit motive the desire of a business or service provider to make profit

profit per employee an indication of the effectiveness of the employment of staff. When there are full- and part-time employees, full-time equivalents should be used. It is calculated as follows:

Profit for the year before interest and tax / Average number of employees.

See also *sales per employee*

profit-related pay a *profit sharing* scheme, approved by the Inland Revenue, in which employees received tax-free payments in addition to their basic salary. Profit-related pay was phased out during 2000.

profit retained for the year non-distributed profit retained as a distributable reserve

profit sharing the allocation of a proportion of company profit to employees by an issue of shares or other means

profit-sharing debenture a debenture held by an employee, the payouts from which depend on the employing company's financial success

profit squeeze the inability to maintain an individual or an organisation's profit in a venture in comparison to previous ventures

profits tax a tax on profits, for example, corporation tax (*slang*)

profit–volume/contribution graph a graph showing the effect on contribution and on overall profit of changes in sales volume or value

profit warning a statement by a company's executives that the company may realise less profit in a coming quarter than investors expect

pro-forma financial statement a projection showing a business's financial statements after the completion of a planned transaction

pro-forma invoice an invoice sent to the purchaser in advance of goods, for completion of business formalities (usually for payment before despatch of goods)

programme trading the trading of securities electronically, by sending messages from the investor's computer to a market

programming *see* *dynamic programming, linear programming, non-linear programming*

program trading the buying and selling of shares according to instructions given by a computer program. The computer is programmed to buy or sell when certain prices are reached or when a certain volume of sales on the market is reached.

progressive tax a tax with a rate that increases proportionately with taxable income. *See also* *proportional tax, regressive tax*

project costing *see* *costing, contract costing*

project finance money, usually non-recourse finance, raised for a specific self-contained venture, usually a construction or development project

projection an expected future trend pattern obtained by extrapolation. It is principally concerned with quantitative factors, whereas a forecast includes judgments.

project management the integration of all aspects of a project in order to ensure that the proper knowledge and resources are available when and where needed, and above all to ensure that the expected outcome is produced in a timely, cost-effective manner. The primary function of a project manager is to manage the trade-offs between performance, timeliness, and cost.

promissory carrying or in the nature of a promise, as of an agreement to pay money

promissory note a contract to pay money to a person or organisation for a good or service received. *Abbr* **PN**

property *assets*, such as land or goods, that an individual or organisation owns

property bond a bond, especially a bail bond, for which a property is collateral

property damage insurance insurance against the risk of damage to property

proportional tax a tax which is strictly proportional in amount to the value of the item being taxed, especially income. *See also progressive tax, regressive tax*

proprietors' interest an amount of money which the owners of a business have invested in the business

ProShare a group that acts in the interests of private investors in securities of the London Stock Exchange

prospectus a description of a company's operations, financial background, prospects, and the detailed terms and conditions relating to an offer for sale or placing of its shares by notice, circular, advertisement, or any form of invitation which offers securities to the public

protectionism a government economic policy of restricting the level of imports by using measures such as tariffs and *NTBs* in order to protect a country's domestic industries

protective put buying the purchase of *puts* for stocks already owned

protective tariff a tariff imposed to restrict imports into a country

protocol a set of rules that govern and regulate a process

provision a sum set aside in the accounts of an organisation in anticipation of a future expense, often for doubtful debts. *See also bad debt*

provisional tax tax paid in advance on the following year's income, the amount being based on the actual income from the preceding year

proxy fight the use of proxy votes to settle a contentious issue at a company meeting

proxy statement a notice that a company sends to stockholders allowing them to vote and giving them all the information they need to vote in an informed way

prudence concept the principle that revenue and profits are not anticipated but are included in the *profit and loss account* only when realised in the form either of *cash* or of other assets, the ultimate cash realisation of which can be assessed with reasonable certainty. Provision is made for all known liabilities (expenses and losses) whether the amount of these is known with certainty, or is a best estimate in the light of the information available.

prudential ratio the ratio of capital to assets which, according to European

Union regulations, a bank feels it is prudent to have

prudent man rule the rule that trustees who make financial decisions on behalf of other people should act carefully (as a normal prudent person would)

PSBR *abbr* Public Sector Borrowing Requirement

Pty *abbr* (*S Africa*) used in company names to indicate a private limited liability company

Public Accounts Committee a committee of the House of Commons which examines the spending of each department and ministry

public corporation a state-owned organisation established to provide a particular service, for example, the British Broadcasting Corporation. *See also* ***corporation***

public debt the money that a government or a set of governments owes

public deposits in the United Kingdom, the government's credit monies held at the Bank of England

public expenditure spending by the government of a country on things such as pension provision and infrastructure enhancement

public finance law legislation relating to the financial activities of government or public sector organisations

public issue a way of making a new issue of shares by offering it for sale to the public. An issue of this type is often advertised in the press. *See also* ***offer for sale***, ***offer by prospectus***

public-liability insurance insurance against the risk of being held financially liable for injury to somebody

public limited company a company in the United Kingdom that is required to have a minimum authorised capital of £50,000 and to offer its shares to the public. A public limited company has the letters 'plc' after its name. In the United Kingdom, only public limited companies can be listed on the London Stock Exchange. *US term* ***publicly held corporation***. *Abbr* **PLC**

publicly held corporation (*US*) = ***public limited company***

public monopoly a situation of limited competition in the public sector, usually relating to nationalised industries

public offering a method of raising money used by a company by which it invites the public to apply for shares

public placing placing shares in a public company. *See also* ***private placing***

public sector the organisations in the section of the economy that is financed and controlled by central government, local authorities, and publicly funded corporations. *See also* ***private sector***

public sector borrowing requirement *abbr* **PSBR**. *See* ***public sector cash requirement***

public sector cash requirement the difference between the income and the expenditure of the public sector. It was formerly called the **public sector borrowing requirement**.

public spending spending by the government of a country on publicly provided goods and services

published accounts a company's financial statements that must by law be published. *US term* ***earnings report***

puff to overstate the virtues of a product, especially a stock (*slang*)

pump priming the injection of further investment in order to revitalise a company in stagnation, or to help a start-up over a critical period. Pump priming has a similar effect to the provision of ***seed capital***.

purchase contract a form of agreement to buy specified products at an agreed price

purchase money mortgage (*US*) a mortgage whose proceeds the borrower uses to buy the property that is collateral for the loan

purchase order a written order for goods or services specifying quantities, prices, delivery dates, and contract terms

purchase price the price that somebody pays to buy a good or service

purchase requisition an internal instruction to a buying office to purchase goods or services, stating their quantity and description and generating a *purchase order*

purchasing manager an individual with responsibility for all activities concerned with purchasing. The responsibilities of a purchasing manager can include ordering, commercial negotiations, and delivery chasing. *Also known as buying manager*

purchasing power a measure of the ability of a person, organisation, or sector to buy goods and services

purchasing power parity a theory that the exchange rate between two currencies is in equilibrium when the purchasing power of a currency is the same in each country. If a basket of goods costs £100 in the United Kingdom and US $150 for an equivalent in the United States, for equilibrium to exist, the exchange rate would be expected to be £1 = US $1.50. If this is were not the case, *arbitrage* would be expected to take place until equilibrium was restored. *Abbr* **PPP**

purchasing routine the various stages involved in organising the purchase of a product or service

pure competition a situation in which there are many sellers in a market and there is free flow of information

pure economic rent a payment to a factor in an economy greater than the amount necessary to keep it in its existing employment

pure endowment a gift whose use is fully prescribed by the donor

purpose credit credit used for trade in securities

put *or* **put option** an option to sell stock within a specified time at a specified price

put option *see put*

PYB *abbr* preceding year basis

Q

qualification payment (*ANZ*) an additional payment sometimes made to employees of New Zealand companies, who have gained an academic qualification relevant to their job

qualified auditor's report *see adverse opinion*

qualified domestic trust a trust for the non-citizen spouse of a US citizen, affording tax advantages at the time of the citizen's death

qualified lead a sales prospect whose potential value has been carefully researched

qualified listed security a security that is eligible for purchase by a regulated entity such as a trust

qualified valuer a person conducting a valuation who holds a recognised and relevant professional qualification. The person must also have recent post-qualification experience and sufficient knowledge of the state of the market with reference to the location and category of the tangible fixed asset being valued.

qualifying distribution the payment to a shareholder of a dividend, on which *Advance Corporation Tax* is paid

qualifying ratio a calculation of how much mortgage a borrower can afford, by comparing his or her monthly incoming against monthly outgoings

qualitative analysis the subjective appraisal of a project or investment for which there is no quantifiable data. *See also chartist, fundamental analysis, quantitative analysis, technical analysis*

qualitative factors factors which are relevant to a decision, but which are not expressed numerically

qualitative lending guideline a rule for evaluating creditworthiness that is not objective

quality bond a bond issued by an organisation that has an excellent credit rating

quality equity an equity with a good track record of earnings and dividends. *See also blue chip*

quango an acronym derived from quasi-autonomous non-governmental organisation. Established by the government and answerable to a government minister, some, but not all, quangos are staffed by civil servants and some have statutory powers in a specified field.

quantitative analysis the appraisal of a project or investment using econometric, mathematical, and statistical techniques. *See also chartist, fundamental analysis, qualitative analysis, technical analysis*

quantitative factors factors which are relevant to a decision and which are expressed numerically

quantitative research the gathering and analysis of data that can be expressed in numerical form. Quantitative research involves data that is measurable and can include statistical results, financial data, or demographic data.

quantum meruit a Latin phrase meaning 'as much as has been earned'

quarterly report *see interim statement*

quasi-contract a decree by a UK court stipulating that one party has a legal obligation to another, even though there is no legally binding contract between the two parties

quasi-loan an arrangement whereby one party pays the debts of another, on the condition that the sum of the debts will be reimbursed by the indebted party at some later date

quasi-money *see near money*

quasi-public corporation (*US*) an organisation that is owned partly by private or public shareholders and partly by the government

quasi-rent the short-run excess earnings made by a firm, the difference between production cost (the cost of labour and materials) and selling cost

queuing time the time between the arrival of material at a workstation and the start of work on it

quick asset *see near money*

quick ratio 1. a measure of the amount of cash a potential borrower can acquire in a short time, used in evaluating creditworthiness **2.** the ratio of liquid assets to current debts

quid pro quo a Latin phrase meaning 'something for something'

quorum the minimum number of people required in a meeting for it to be able to make decisions that are binding on the organisation. For a company, this is stated in its *articles of associ-*

ation, for a partnership, in its partnership agreement.

quota 1. the maximum sum to be contributed by each party in a joint venture or joint business undertaking **2.** the maximum number of investments that may be purchased and sold in a given situation or market **3.** the maximum amount of a particular commodity, product, or service that can be imported into or exported out of a country

quote a statement of what a person is willing to accept when selling a product or service

quoted company a company whose shares are listed on a stock exchange

quoted price a documented amount that a person is willing to accept when selling something, for example, a security

quote driven used to describe a share dealing system where prices are initially generated by dealers' and market makers' quotes before market forces come into play and prices are determined by the interaction of supply and demand. The London Stock Exchange's dealing system, as well as those of many over-the-counter markets, have quote driven systems.

quoted securities securities or shares that are listed on a stock exchange

R

R150 Bond the benchmark South African government bond which has a fixed interest rate of 12% and matures in 2005

raid the illegal practice of selling shares short to drive the price down. *Also known as **bear raid***

raider a person or company that makes hostile takeover bids

rake it in to make a great deal of money (*slang*)

rake-off commission (*slang*)

rally a rise in share prices after a fall

ramp to buy shares with the objective of raising their price. *See also **rigged market***

rand the South African unit of currency, equal to 100 cents

Randlord originally a Johannesburg-based mining magnate or tycoon of the late 19th or early 20th centuries, now used informally for any wealthy or powerful Johannesburg businessman

range pricing the pricing of individual products so that their prices fit logically within a range of connected products offered by one supplier, and differentiated by a factor such as weight of pack or number of product attributes offered

ratchet effect the result when households adjust more easily to rising incomes than to falling incomes, as, for example, when their consumption drops by less than their income in a recession

rateable value the value of something as calculated with reference to a rule, such as the value of a commercial property as a basis for calculating local taxes

rate cap *see cap*

rate of exchange *see exchange rate*

rate of interest a percentage charged on a loan or paid on an investment for the use of the money

rate of return an accounting ratio of the income from an investment to the amount of the investment, used to measure financial performance.

There is a basic formula that will serve most needs, at least initially:

[(Current value of amount invested – Original value of amount invested) / Original value of amount invested] × 100% = rate of return

EXAMPLE If £1,000 in capital is invested in stock, and one year later the investment yields £1,100, the rate of return of the investment is calculated like this:

[(1100 – 1000) / 1000] × 100% = 100 / 1000 × 100% = 10% rate of return

Now, assume £1,000 is invested again. One year later, the investment grows to £2,000 in value, but after another year the value of the investment falls to £1,200. The rate of return after the first year is:

[(2000 – 1000) / 1000] × 100% = 100%

The rate of return after the second year is:

[(1200 – 2000) / 2000] × 100% = –40%

The average annual return for the two years (also known as average annual arithmetic return) can be calculated using this formula:

(Rate of return for Year 1 + Rate of return for Year 2) / 2 = average annual return

Accordingly:

(100% + –40%) / 2 = 30%

The average annual rate of return is a percentage, but one that is accurate over only a short period, so this method should be used accordingly.

The geometric or compound rate of return is a better yardstick for measuring investments over the long term, and takes into account the effects of compounding. This formula is more complex and technical.

The real rate of return is the annual return realised on an investment, adjusted for changes in the price due to inflation. If 10% is earned on an investment but inflation is 2%, then the real rate of return is actually 8%. *Also known as return*

rating agency an organisation which gives a rating to companies or other organisations issuing bonds

ratio analysis the use of ratios to measure financial performance

ratio pyramid the analysis of a primary ratio into mathematically linked secondary ratios

raw material goods purchased for incorporation into products for sale

RBA *abbr* Reserve Bank of Australia

RBNZ *abbr* Reserve Bank of New Zealand

RD *abbr* refer to drawer

RDP *abbr* Reconstruction and Development Program: a policy framework by means of which the South African government intends to correct the socio-economic imbalances caused by apartheid

RDPR *abbr* refer to drawer please represent

Reaganomics the economic policy of former US President Reagan in the 1980s, who reduced taxes and social security support and increased the national budget deficit to an unprecedented level

real after the effects of inflation are taken into consideration

real asset a non-movable asset such as land or a building

real balance effect the effect on income and employment when prices fall and consumption increases

real capital assets that can be assigned a monetary value

real exchange rate an exchange rate that has been adjusted for inflation

real GDP *GDP* adjusted for changes in prices

real growth the growth of a country or a household adjusted for changes in prices

real interest rate an interest rate approximately calculated by subtracting the rate of inflation from the nominal interest rate

real investment the purchase of assets such as land, property, and plant and machinery as opposed to the acquisition of securities

realisation concept the principle that increases in value should only be recognised on realisation of assets by arm's-length sale to an independent purchaser

realise to change an *asset* into cash by selling it

real option an option based on the right to buy/sell a tangible, rather than a financial, asset

real purchasing power the purchasing power of a country or a household adjusted for changes in prices

real time credit card processing the online authorisation of a credit card indicating that the credit card has been approved or rejected during the transaction

real time transaction an Internet payment transaction that is approved or rejected immediately when the customer completes the online order form

rebadge to buy a product or service from another company and sell it as part of your own product range

rebate 1. money returned because a payment exceeded the amount required, for example, a tax rebate **2.** a discount **3.** of a broker, to reduce part of the commission charged to the client as a promotional offer

recapitalise 1. to increase the *capital* owned by an individual, company, or industry **2.** to change the organisation of a company's *capital*, usually in response to a major financial problem, such as *bankruptcy*

recd *abbr* received

receipt a document acknowledging that something, for example, a payment, has been received

receipts and payments account a report of cash transactions during a period. It is used in place of an income and expenditure account when it is not considered appropriate to distinguish between capital and revenue transactions or to include accruals.

receiver a person appointed to sell the assets of a company that is insolvent. The proceeds of the sale are used to discharge debts to creditors, with any surplus distributed to *shareholders*.

Receiver of Revenue 1. a local office of the South African Revenue Service **2.** an informal term for the South African Revenue Service as a whole

receivership 1. a state of *insolvency* prior to *liquidation*, and *bankruptcy*. During receivership, receivers may attempt to undertake turnaround management or decide that the company must go into liquidation. **2.** the control of a receiver, who is appointed by secured creditors or by the court to take control of company property. The most usual reason for the appointment of a receiver is the failure of a company to pay principal sums or interest due to debenture holders whose debt is secured by fixed or floating charges over the assets of the company.

recession a stage of the *business cycle* in which economic activity is in slow decline. Recession usually follows a boom, and precedes a *depression*. It is characterised by rising unemployment and falling levels of output and investment.

recessionary gap a shortfall in the amount of *aggregate demand* in an economy needed to create full employment

reciprocal cost allocation a method of secondary cost allocation generally used to re-allocate service department costs over user departments. Service department costs are re-charged over user departments (including other service departments) in a number of iterations until all of the service department costs have been re-charged to users.

recognised investment exchange a stock exchange, futures exchange, or commodity exchange recognised by the *Financial Services Authority*

reconciliation the adjustment of an account, such as an individual's own record of a bank account, to match more authoritative information

Reconstruction and Development Program *see RDP*

recourse a source of redress should a debt be dishonoured at maturity

recourse agreement an agreement in a hire purchase contract whereby the retailer repossesses the goods being purchased in the event of the hirer failing to make regular payments

recoverable ACT *Advance Corporation Tax* which can be set against corporation tax payable for the period

recoverable amount the value of an asset, either the price it would fetch if sold, or its value to the company when used, whichever is the larger figure

recovery the return of a country to economic health after a crash or a depression

recovery fund a fund that invests in *recovery stock*

recovery stock a share that has fallen in price because of poor business performance but is now expected to climb due to an improvement in the company's prospects

rectification note an authorisation for more work to be done to improve a product which did not originally meet the required standard

recurring billing transaction an electronic payment facility based on the automatic charging of a customer's credit card in each payment period

recurring payments 1. an electronic payment facility that permits a merchant to process multiple authorisations by the same customer either as multiple payments for a fixed amount or recurring billings for varying amounts **2.** payments, such as mortgage interest or payments on a hire purchase agreement, which are made each month

red the colour of debit or overdrawn balances in some bank statements
  in the red in debt, or making a loss (*slang*)

Red Book a copy of the Chancellor of the Exchequer's speech published on the day of the Budget. It can be regarded as the country's financial statement and report.

Red chips good risk-free Chinese companies

red day (*US*) an unprofitable day (*slang*) *See also* **green day**

redeemable bond *see bond*

redeemable gilt *see gilt-edged security*

redeemable government stock stock which can be redeemed for cash at some time in the future

redeemable preference share a *preference share* which must be bought back by the company at a certain date and for a certain price. The company will set aside money in a special fund for the purpose of redeeming these shares at due date.

redeemable security a security which can be redeemed at its face value at a certain date in the future

redeemable shares shares which are issued on terms which may require them to be bought back by the issuer at some future date, at the discretion either of the issuer or of the holder. Redemption must comply with the conditions of the Companies Act 1985.

redemption repayment, this term being most frequently used in connection with preference shares and debentures

redemption date the date on which a redeemable security is due to be repaid

redemption yield the rate of interest at which the total of the discounted values of any future payments of interest and capital is equal to the current price of a security

red eye (*US*) *see pathfinder prospectus* (*slang*)

red herring a statement or action intended to mislead

redistributive effect the tendency towards equalisation of people's wealth that results from a progressive tax or benefit

red screen market in the United Kingdom, a market where the prices are down and are being shown as red on the dealing screens

red tape excessive bureaucracy

reducing balance depreciation *see depreciation*

redundancy package a package of benefits that an employer gives to somebody who is made redundant. *US term* ***severance package***

reference *see banker's reference*

reference rate a benchmark rate, for example, a bank's own base rate or LIBOR. Lending rates are often expressed as a margin over a reference rate.

referred share a share that is *ex dividend*

refer to drawer to refuse to pay a cheque because the account from which it is drawn has too little money in it. *Abbr* **RD**

refer to drawer please represent in the United Kingdom, written on a cheque by the paying banker to indicate that there are currently insufficient funds to meet the payment, but that the bank believes sufficient funds will be available shortly. *See also* ***refer to drawer****. Abbr* **RDPR**

refinance to replace one loan with another, especially at a lower rate of interest

refinancing 1. the process of taking out a loan to pay off other loans **2.** a loan taken out for the purpose of repaying another loan or loans

reflation a method of reducing unemployment by increasing an economy's ***aggregate demand****. See also* ***recession***

refugee capital people and resources that come into a country because they have been forced to leave their own country for economic or political reasons

regional fund a unit trust that invests in the markets of a geographical region

registered bond a bond the ownership of which is recorded on the books of the issuer

registered broker a broker registered on a particular exchange

registered capital *see authorised capital*

registered company in the United Kingdom, a company that has lodged official documents with the ***Registrar of Companies*** at Companies House. A registered company is obliged to conduct itself in accordance with company law. All organisations must register in order to become companies.

registered name in the United Kingdom, the name of a company as it is registered at Companies House. It must appear, along with the company's registered number and office, on all its letterheads and orders. *See also* ***company***, ***corporation***

registered number in the United Kingdom, a unique number assigned to a company registered at Companies House. It must appear, along with the company's registered name and office, on all its letterheads and orders. *See also* ***company, corporation***

registered security a security where the holder's name is recorded in the books of the issuer. *See also* ***nominee name***

registered share a share the ownership of which is recorded on the books of the issuer

registered share capital *see authorised share capital*

register of companies in the United Kingdom, the list of companies maintained at Companies House. *See also* ***company, corporation***

register of directors and secretaries a record that every ***registered company*** in the United Kingdom must maintain of the names and residential addresses of directors and the company secretary together with their nationality, occupation, and details of other directorships held. Public companies must also record the date of birth of their directors. The record must be kept at the company's registered office and be available for inspection by shareholders without charge and by members of the public for a nominal fee.

register of directors' interests a record that every *registered company* in the United Kingdom must maintain of the *shares* and other *securities* that have been issued by the company and are held by its directors. It has to be made available for inspection during the company's *annual general meeting*.

registrar an organisation that registers a company's shares

Registrar of Companies the official charged with the duty of holding and registering the official start-up and constitutional documents of all *registered companies* in the United Kingdom

registration statement in the United States, a document that corporations planning to issue securities to the public have to submit to the Securities and Exchange Commission. It features details of the issuer's management, financial status, and activities, and the purpose of the issue. *See also* **shelf registration**

regressive tax a tax with a rate that decreases proportionally as the value of the item being taxed, especially income, rises. US social security taxes are regressive. *See also* **progressive tax**, **proportional tax**

regulated price a selling price set within guidelines laid down by a regulatory authority, normally governmental

regulated superannuation fund (*ANZ*) an Australian superannuation fund that is regulated by legislation and therefore qualifies for tax concessions.

To attain this status, a fund must either show that its main function is the provision of pensions, or adopt a corporate trustee structure.

regulation the use of laws or rules stipulated by a government or regulatory body, such as the Financial Services Authority, to provide orderly procedures and to protect consumers and investors

regulatory body an independent organisation, usually set up by government, that regulates the activities of companies in an industry

regulatory framework the set of legal and professional requirements with which the financial statements of a company must comply. Company reporting is influenced by the requirements of law, of the accountancy profession, and of the stock exchange (for listed companies).

regulatory pricing risk the risk an insurance company faces that a government will regulate the prices it can charge

reinsurance a method of reducing risk by transferring all or part of an insurance policy to another insurer

reinvestment rate the interest rate at which an investor is able to reinvest income received from another investment

reinvestment risk the risk that it will not be possible to invest the proceeds of an investment at as high a rate as they earned

reinvestment unit trust a unit trust that uses dividends to buy more shares in the company issuing them

rejects units of output which fail a set quality standard and are subsequently rectified, sold as sub-standard, or disposed of as scrap

relative income hypothesis the theory that consumers are concerned less with their absolute living standards than with consumption relative to other consumers

relevancy concept the principle that management accounting must ensure that flexibility is maintained in assembling and interpreting information. This facilitates the exploration and presentation, in a clear, understandable, and timely manner, of as many alternatives as are necessary for impartial and confident decisions to be taken. The process is essentially forward-looking and dynamic. Therefore, the information must satisfy the criteria of being applicable and appropriate.

relevant costs/revenues costs and revenues appropriate to a specific management decision. These are represented by future cash-flows whose magnitude will vary depending upon the outcome of the management decision made. If stock is sold by a retailer, the relevant cost, used in the determination of the profitability of the transaction, would be the cost of replacing the stock, not its original purchase price, which is a sunk cost. Abandonment analysis, based on relevant cost and revenues, is the process of determining whether or not it is more profitable to discontinue a product or service than to continue it.

relevant interest (*ANZ*) the legal status held by share investors who can legally dispose of, or influence the disposal of, shares

relevant range the activity levels within which assumptions about cost behaviour in breakeven analysis remain valid

reliability concept the principle that management accounting information must be of such quality that confidence can be placed in it. Its reliability to the user is dependent on its source, integrity, and comprehensiveness.

relocation package payments made by an employer to an employee when the employee is asked to move to a new area in order to work. Some of these payments may be exempt from tax if they are below the minimum level.

remitting bank *see collecting bank*

remuneration *see earnings*

renounceable document written proof of ownership for a limited period, for example, a letter of allotment. *See also letter of renunciation*

renting back *see sale and leaseback*

renunciation *see letter of renunciation*

reorder level a level of stock at which a replenishment order should be placed. Traditional 'optimising' systems use a variation on the computation of maximum usage multiplied by maximum lead, which builds in a measure of safety stock and minimises the likelihood of a stock running out.

reorganisation bond in the United States, a bond issued to creditors of a business that is undergoing a Chapter 11 form of reorganisation. Interest is normally only paid when the company can make the payments from its earnings.

repayment mortgage a long-term loan, usually for the purchase of a property, in which the borrower makes monthly payments, part of which cover the interest on the loan and part of which cover the repayment of the principal. In the early years, the greater proportion of the payment is used to cover the interest charged but, as the principal is gradually repaid, the interest portion diminishes and the repayment portion increases. *See also mortgage*

replacement cost the cost of replacing an asset or service with its current equivalent

replacement cost accounting a method of valuing company assets based on their replacement cost

replacement price the price at which identical goods or capital equipment could be purchased at the date of valuation

replacement ratio the ratio of the total resources received when unemployed to those received when in employment

repo 1. a repurchase agreement (*slang*) **2.** (*US*) an open market operation undertaken by the Federal Reserve to purchase securities and agree to sell them back at a stated price on a future date **3.** a Bank of England repurchase agreement with market makers in gilt-edged securities. It is used to provide securities for short positions.

report a written or verbal statement analysing a particular issue, incident, or state of affairs, usually with some form of recommendations for future action

reporting entity any organisation, such as a limited company, which reports its accounts to its shareholders

repossession the return of goods bought on hire purchase when the purchaser fails to make the required regular payments. *See also* **recourse agreement**

representative office an office of a foreign company not incorporated or registered in Singapore. *Abbr* **RO**

repudiation a refusal to pay or acknowledge a debt

repurchase of a fund manager, to buy the units in a unit trust when an investor sells

repurchase agreement in the bond and money markets, a spot sale of a security combined with its repurchase at a later date and pre-agreed price. In effect, the buyer is lending money to the seller for the duration of the transaction and using the security as collateral. Dealers finance their positions by using repurchase agreements. *Also known as* **repo**

required rate of return the minimum return for a proposed project investment to be acceptable. *See also* **discounted cash-flow**

required reserves (*US*) the minimum reserves that member banks of the Federal Reserve System have to maintain

requisition an official order form used by companies when purchasing a product or service

research the examination of statistics and other information regarding past, present, and future trends or performance that enables analysts to recommend to investors which shares to buy or sell in order to maximise their return and minimise their risk. It may be used either in the top-down approach (where the investor evaluates a market, then an industry, and finally a specific company) or the bottom-up approach (where the investor selects a company and confirms his or her findings by evaluating the company's sector and then its market). Careful research is likely to help investors find the best deals, in particular *value shares* or *growth equities*. *See also* **fundamental analysis, technical analysis**

reserve bank (*US*) a bank such as a US Federal Reserve bank that holds the reserves of other banks

Reserve Bank the South African Reserve Bank, South Africa's central bank

Reserve Bank of Australia Australia's central bank, which is responsible for managing the Commonwealth's monetary policy, ensuring financial stability, and printing and distributing currency. *Abbr* **RBA**

Reserve Bank of New Zealand New Zealand's central bank, which is responsible for managing the government's monetary policy, ensuring financial stability, and printing and distributing currency. *Abbr* **RBNZ**

reserve currency foreign currency that a central bank holds for use in international trade

reserve for fluctuations money set aside to allow for changes in the values of currencies

reserve price a price for a particular lot, set by the vendor, below which an auctioneer may not sell

reserve ratio the proportion of a bank's deposits that must be kept in reserve.

In the United Kingdom and in certain European countries, there is no compulsory ratio, although banks will have their own internal measures and targets to be able to repay customer deposits as they forecast they will be required. In the United States, specified percentages of deposits—established by the Federal Reserve Board—must be kept by banks in a non-interest-bearing account at one of the twelve Federal Reserve banks located throughout the country.

In Europe, the reserve requirement of an institution is calculated by multiplying the reserve ratio for each category of items in the reserve base, set by the European Central Bank, with the amount of those items in the institution's balance sheets. These figures vary according to the institution.

The required reserve ratio in the United States is set by federal law, and depends on the amount of checkable deposits a bank holds. The first $44.3 million of deposits are subject to a 3% reserve requirement. Deposits in excess of $44.3 million are subject to a 10%

reserve requirement. These breakpoints are reviewed annually in accordance with money supply growth. No reserves are required against certificates of deposit or savings accounts.

The reserve ratio requirement limits a bank's lending to a certain fraction of its demand deposits. The current rule allows a bank to issue loans in an amount equal to 90% of such deposits, holding 10% in reserve. The reserves can be held in any combination of till money and deposit at a Federal Reserve bank.

reserve requirements the requirements an agency levies on a nation's banks to hold reserves

reserves 1. the money that a bank holds to ensure that it can satisfy its depositors' demands for withdrawals **2.** profits made by a company in previous accounting periods that have not yet been made available to shareholders **3.** a sum of money held by an individual or company to finance unexpected business opportunities. *See also* ***war chest***

residual income pretax profits less an imputed interest charge for invested capital. It is used to assess divisional performance.

residual value the value of an asset after it has been depreciated in the company's accounts

residuary legatee the person to whom a testator's estate is left after specific bequests have been made

resistance level a price or index level, at which investors feel that the price of a share is too high or too low

resolution a proposal put to a meeting, for example, an Annual General Meeting of shareholders, on which those present and eligible can vote. *See also* ***extraordinary resolution***, ***special resolution***

resource drivers measurement units which are used to assign resource costs to activity cost pools based on some measure of usage. Thus area may be used to assign office occupancy costs to purchasing, accounting services, etc.

responsibility accounting the keeping of financial records with an emphasis on who is responsible for each item

responsibility centre a department or organisational function whose performance is the direct responsibility of a specific manager

restated balance sheet a balance sheet reframed to serve a particular purpose, such as highlighting depreciation of assets

restricted tender an offer to buy shares only under specified conditions

restrictive covenant an agreement by a borrower not to sell an asset which he or she has used as collateral for a loan

retail banking services provided by commercial banks to individuals as opposed to business customers, that include current accounts, deposit and savings accounts, as well as credit cards, mortgages, and investments. In the United Kingdom, although this service was traditionally provided by high street banks, separate organisations, albeit offshoots of established financial institutions, are now providing Internet and telephone banking services.

retail investor an investor who buys and sells shares in retail organisations

Retail Price Index a listing of the average levels of prices charged by retailers for goods or services. The retail price index is calculated on a set range of items, and usually excludes luxury goods. It is updated monthly, and provides a running indicator of changing costs. *Abbr* **RPI**

retained earnings (*US*) the share of a company's profits remaining after the distribution of dividends that is kept as capital. = *earnings retained*

retained profits the amount of profit remaining after tax and distribution to shareholders that is retained in a business and used as a reserve or as a means of financing expansion or investment. *Also known as* ***earnings retained***

retention money or payments withheld an agreed proportion of a contract price withheld for a specified period after contract completion as security for fulfilment of obligations

retirement annuity an annuity paid to a person at a certain age, normally 60 for a woman or 65 for a man, from funds paid into a retirement annuity contract

retirement benefits benefits which are payable by a pension scheme to a person on retirement

retirement pension *see pension*

Retirement Savings Account a type of bank account offered by Australian financial institutions as an alternative to conventional superannuation funds. RSAs attract similar concessional tax rates to superannuation funds but offer the security of a bank account and lower management charges. *Abbr* **RSA**

retrenchment the reduction of costs in order to improve profitability

return 1. the income derived from an activity **2.** *see* ***rate of return*** **3.** *see* ***tax return***

return on assets a measure of profitability calculated by expressing a company's net income as a percentage of total assets.
Because the ROA formula reflects total revenue, total cost, and assets

deployed, the ratio itself reflects a management's ability to generate income during the course of a given period, usually a year.

EXAMPLE To calculate ROA, net income is divided by total assets, then multiplied by 100 to express the figure as a percentage:

Net income / total assets × 100 = ROA

If net income is £30, and total assets are £420, the ROA is:

30 / 420 = 0.0714 × 100 = 7.14%

A variation of this formula can be used to calculate return on net assets (RONA):

**Net income / fixed assets +
working capital = RONA**

And, on occasion, the formula will separate after-tax interest expense from net income:

**Net income + interest expense /
total assets = ROA**

It is therefore important to understand what each component of the formula actually represents.

Some experts recommend using the net income value at the end of the given period, and the assets value from the beginning of the period or an average value taken over the complete period, rather than an end-of-the-period value; otherwise, the calculation will include assets that have accumulated during the year, which can be misleading. *Abbr* **ROA**

return on capital a ratio of the profit made in a financial year as a percentage of the *capital employed*

return on capital employed 1. the profitability of a corporation expressed as a percentage of its capital **2.** an indication of the productivity of *capital employed*.

The denominator is normally calculated as the average of the capital employed at the beginning and end of year. Problems of seasonality, new capital introduced, or other factors may necessitate taking the average of a

number of periods within the year. The ROCE is known as the primary ratio in a ratio pyramid. *Abbr* **ROCE**. *See also* *capital employed*

return on equity the ratio of a company's net income as a percentage of shareholders' funds.

Return on equity is easy to calculate and is applicable to a majority of industries. It is probably the most widely used measure of how well a company is performing for its shareholders.

EXAMPLE It is calculated by dividing the net income shown on the income statement (usually of the past year) by shareholders' equity, which appears on the balance sheet:

**Net income / owners' equity × 100% =
return on equity**

For example, if net income is £450 and equity is £2,500, then:

**450 / 2,500 = 0.18 × 100% =
18% return on equity**

Return on equity for most companies should be in double figures; investors often look for 15% or higher, while a return of 20% or more is considered excellent. Seasoned investors also review five-year average ROE, to gauge consistency. *Abbr* **ROE**

return on investment a ratio of the profit made in a financial year as a percentage of an investment

EXAMPLE The most basic expression of ROI can be found by dividing a company's net profit (also called net earnings) by the total investment (total debt plus total equity), then multiplying by 100 to arrive at a percentage:

Net profit / Total investment × 100 = ROI

If, say, net profit is £30 and total investment is £250, the ROI is:

30 / 250 = 0.12 × 100 = 12%

A more complex variation of ROI is an equation known as the Du Pont formula:

**(Net profit after taxes / Total assets) =
(Net profit after taxes / Sales) ×
Sales / Total assets**

If, for example, net profit after taxes is £30, total assets are £250, and sales are £500, then:

$$30 / 250 = 30 / 500 \times 500 / 250 = 12\% =$$
$$6\% \times 2 = 12\%$$

Champions of this formula, which was developed by the Du Pont Company in the 1920s, say that it helps reveal how a company has both deployed its assets and controlled its costs, and how it can achieve the same percentage return in different ways.

For shareholders, the variation of the basic ROI formula used by investors is:

Net income + (current value − original value) / original value × 100 = ROI

If, for example, somebody invests £5,000 in a company and a year later has earned £100 in dividends, while the value of the shares is £5,200, the return on investment would be:

$$100 + (5,200 - 5,000) / 5,000 \times 100 =$$
$$(100 + 200) / 5,000 \times 100 = 300 / 5,000 =$$
$$.06 \times 100 = 6\% \text{ ROI}$$

It is vital to understand exactly what a return on investment measures, for example, assets, equity, or sales. Without this understanding, comparisons may be misleading. It is also important to establish whether the net profit figure used is before or after provision for taxes. *Abbr* **ROI**

return on net assets a ratio of the profit made in a financial year as a percentage of the assets of a company

return on sales a company's operating profit or loss as a percentage of total sales for a given period, typically a year. EXAMPLE Return on sales shows how efficiently management uses the sales income, thus reflecting its ability to manage costs and overheads and operate efficiently. It also indicates a firm's ability to withstand adverse conditions such as falling prices, rising costs, or declining sales. The higher the figure, the better a company is able to endure price wars and falling prices. It is calculated using the basic formula:

Operating profit / total sales × 100 = Percentage return on sales

So, if a company earns £30 on sales of £400, its return on sales is:

$$30 / 400 = 0.075 \times 100 = 7.5\%$$

Some calculations use operating profit before subtracting interest and taxes; others use after-tax income. Either figure is acceptable as long as ROS comparisons are consistent. Using income before interest and taxes will produce a higher ratio.

Return on sales has its limits, since it sheds no light on the overall cost of sales or the four factors that contribute to it: materials, labour, production overheads, and administrative and selling overheads.

See also ***profit margin***. *Abbr* **ROS**

returns to scale the proportionate increase in a country's or firm's output as a result of increases in all its inputs

revaluation a rise in the value of a country's currency in relation to other currencies

revaluation method a method of calculating the depreciation of assets by which the asset is depreciated by the difference in its value at the end of the year from its value at the beginning of the year

revaluation of assets the revaluation of a company's ***assets*** to take account of inflation or changes in value since the assets were acquired

revaluation of currency an increase in the value of a currency in relation to others. In situations where there is a floating exchange rate, a currency will normally find its own level automatically but this will not happen if there is a fixed exchange rate. Should a government have persistent balance of payment surpluses, it may exceptionally decide to revalue its currency, making imports cheaper but its exports more expensive.

revaluation reserve money set aside to account for the fact that the value of assets may vary as a result of accounting in different currencies

revaluation reserve account *see* *revaluation of assets*

revenue the income generated by a product or service over a period of time

revenue account an accounting system which records the revenue and expenditure incurred by a company during its normal business

revenue anticipation note a government-issued debt instrument for which expected income from taxation is collateral

revenue bond a bond that a government issues, to be repaid from the money made from the project financed with it

revenue centre a centre devoted to raising revenue with no responsibility for costs, for example, a sales centre

revenue expenditure expenditure on purchasing stock (but not on capital items) which is then sold during the current accounting period

revenue ledger a record of all the income received by an organisation

revenue reserves retained earnings which are shown in the company's balance sheet as part of the shareholders' funds

revenue sharing 1. distribution to states by the US federal government of money that it collects in taxes **2.** the distribution of income within limited partnerships

revenue stamp a stamp that a government issues to certify that somebody has paid a tax

revenue tariff a tax levied on imports or exports to raise revenue for a national government

reversal stop a price at which a trader stops buying and starts selling a security, or vice versa

reverse engineering the decomposition and analysis of competitors' products in order to determine how they are made, costs of production, and the way in which future development may proceed

reverse leverage 1. the negative flow of cash **2.** the borrowing of money at a rate of interest higher than the expected rate of return on investing the money borrowed

reverse mortgage a financial arrangement in which a lender such as a bank takes over a mortgage then pays an annuity to the homeowner

reverse split the issuing to shareholders of a fraction of one share for every share that they own. *See also* **split**

reverse yield gap the amount by which bond yield exceeds equity yield, or interest rates on loans exceed rental values as a percentage of the costs of properties

reversionary annuity an annuity paid to someone on the death of another person

revolving bank facility *see* *revolving loan*

revolving charge account a charge account with a company for use in buying that company's goods with *revolving credit*

revolving credit a credit facility which allows the borrower, within an overall credit limit and for a set period, to borrow or repay debt as required

revolving fund a fund the resources of which are replenished from the revenue of the projects that it finances

revolving loan a loan facility whereby the borrower can choose the number and timing of withdrawals against their bank loan and any money repaid may be reborrowed at a future date. Such loans are available both to businesses and personal customers.

rigged market a market where two or more parties are buying and selling securities among themselves to give the impression of active trading with the intention of attracting investors to purchase the shares. This practice is illegal in most jurisdictions. *See also* **ramp**

rights issue the raising of new capital by giving existing **shareholders** the right to subscribe to new shares or **debentures** in proportion to their current holdings. These **shares** are normally issued at a discount to market price. A shareholder not wishing to take up a rights issue may sell the rights. *Also known as* **rights offer**

rights letter *see letter of allotment*

rights offer *see rights issue*

rights offering an offering for sale of a *rights issue*

ring 1. a trading pit **2.** a trading session on the London Metal Exchange

ring-fence 1. to set aside a sum of money for a specific project **2.** to allow one company within a group to go into liquidation without affecting the viability of the group as a whole or any other company within it

ring member a member of the London Metal Exchange

ring trading business conducted in a trading pit

rising bottoms a pattern on a graph of the price of a security or commodity against time that shows an upward price movement following a period of low prices (*slang*) *See also* **chartist**

risk a condition in which there exists a quantifiable dispersion in the possible outcomes from any activity

risk-adjusted return on capital return on capital calculated in a way that takes into account the risks associated with income.

Being able to compare a high-risk, potentially high-return investment with a low-risk, lower-return investment helps to answer a key question that confronts every investor: is it worth the risk?

There are several ways to calculate risk-adjusted return. Each has its strengths and shortcomings. All require particular data, such as an investment's rate of return, the risk-free return rate for a given period, and a market's performance and its standard deviation.

The choice of calculation depends on an investor's focus: whether it is on upside gains or downside losses.

Perhaps the most widely used is the Sharpe ratio. This measures the potential impact of return volatility on expected return and the amount of return earned per unit of risk. The higher a fund's Sharpe ratio, the better its historical risk-adjusted performance, and the higher the number the greater the return per unit of risk. The formula is:

(Portfolio return – Risk-free return) / Std deviation of portfolio return = Sharpe ratio

EXAMPLE Take, for example, two investments, one returning 54%, the other 26%. At first glance, the higher figure clearly looks like the better choice, but because of its high volatility it has a Sharpe ratio of .279, while the investment with a lower return has a ratio of .910. On a risk-adjusted basis the latter would be the wiser choice.

The Treynor ratio also measures the excess of return per unit of risk. Its formula is:

(Portfolio return – Risk-free return) / Portfolio's beta = Treynor ratio

In this formula (and others that follow), **beta** is a separately calculated figure that describes the tendency of an investment to respond to marketplace swings. The higher beta the greater the volatility, and vice versa.

A third formula, Jensen's measure, is often used to rate a money manager's performance against a market index, and whether or not an investment's risk was worth its reward. The formula is:

(Portfolio return – Risk-free return) – Portfolio's beta × (Benchmark return – Risk-free return) = Jensen's measure

risk arbitrage *arbitrage* without certainty of profit

risk-based capital assessment an internationally approved system of calculating a bank's capital value by assessing the risk attached to its assets. Cash deposits and gold, for example, have no risk, while loans to less-developed countries have a high risk.

risk-bearing economy of scale conducting business on such a large scale that the risk of loss is reduced because it is spread over so many independent events, as in the issuance of insurance policies

risk capital *see venture capital*

risk-free return the profit made from an investment that involves no risk

risk management the process of understanding and managing the risks that an organisation is inevitably subject to in attempting to achieve its corporate objectives. For management purposes, risks are usually divided into categories such as operational, financial, legal compliance, information, and personnel.

ROA *abbr* return on assets

ROCE *abbr* return on capital employed

rocket scientist an employee of a financial institution who creates innovative securities that usually include derivatives (*slang*)

rodo kinko in Japan, a financial institution specialising in providing credit for small businesses

ROE *abbr* return on equity

rogue trader a dealer in stocks and shares who uses illegal methods to make profits

ROI *abbr* return on investment

rolling budget a budget continuously updated by adding a further accounting period (month or quarter) when the earliest accounting period has expired. Its use is particularly beneficial where future costs and/or activities cannot be forecast accurately. *Also known as **continuous budget***

rolling forecast a continuously updated forecast whereby each time actual results are reported, a further forecast period is added and intermediate period forecasts are updated

rollover relief tax relief that applies when the profit on the sale of an asset is used to acquire another asset. The profit on the eventual sale of this second asset will be taxed unless the proceeds of the second sale are also invested in new assets.

roll up the addition of interest amounts to principal in loan repayments

ROS *abbr* return on sales

round figures figures that have been adjusted up or down to the nearest 10, 100, 1,000, and so on

routing number (*US*) = *sort code*

royalties a proportion of the income from the sale of a product paid to its creator, for example, an inventor, author, or composer

RPI *abbr* Retail Price Index

RPIX an index based on the Retail Price Index that excludes mortgage interest payments and is commonly referred to as the underlying rate of inflation

RPIY an index based on the Retail Price Index that excludes mortgage interest payments and indirect taxation

RSA *see Retirement Savings Account*

rule of 78 a method used to calculate the rebate on a loan with front-loaded interest that has been repaid early. It takes into account the fact that as the loan is repaid, the share of each monthly payment related to interest decreases, while the share related to repayment increases.

rumortrage (*US*) speculation in securities issued by companies that are rumoured to be the target of an imminent takeover attempt (*slang*)

run 1. an incidence of bank customers en masse and simultaneously withdrawing their entire funds because of a lack of confidence in the institution **2.** an incidence of owners of holdings in a particular currency selling en masse and simultaneously usually because of a lack of confidence in the currency

running account credit an overdraft facility, credit card, or similar system that allows customers to borrow up to a specific limit and reborrow sums previously repaid by either writing a cheque or using their card

running total a total carried from one column of figures to the next

running yield *see yield*

S

SA *abbr* Société Anonyme *or* Sociedad Anónima *or* Sociedade Anónima

SADC *abbr* Southern African Development Community: an organisation that aims to harmonise economic development in Southern Africa. The member countries are Angola, Botswana, Democratic Republic of Congo, Lesotho, Malawi, Mauritius, Mozambique, Namibia, South Africa, Seychelles, Swaziland, Tanzania, Zambia, and Zimbabwe.

safe custody *see safe keeping*

safe hands 1. investors who buy securities and are unlikely to sell in the short- to medium-term **2.** securities held by friendly investors

safe keeping the holding of share certificates, deeds, wills, or a locked deed box on behalf of customers by a financial institution. Securities are often held under the customer's name in a locked cabinet in the vault so that if the customer wishes to sell, the bank can forward the relevant certificate to the broker. A will is also normally held in this way so that it may be handed to the executor on the customer's death. Deed boxes are always described as 'contents unknown to the bank'. Most institutions charge a fee for this service. *Also known as* **safe custody**

safety stock the quantity of stocks of raw materials, work in progress, and finished goods which are carried in excess of the expected usage during the lead time of an activity. The safety stock reduces the probability of operations having to be suspended due to running out of stocks.

St. Ex. *abbr* stock exchange

salaried partner a partner, often a junior one, who receives a regular salary, detailed in the partnership agreement

salary a form of *pay* given to employees at regular intervals in exchange for the work they have done. Traditionally, a salary is a form of remuneration given to professional employees on a monthly basis. In modern usage, the word refers to any form of pay that employees receive on a regular basis, and it is often used interchangeably with the term *wages*. A salary is normally paid straight into an employee's account.

salary ceiling the highest level on a pay scale that a particular employee can achieve under their contract

salary review a reassessment of an individual employee's rate of *pay*, usually carried out on an annual basis

sale and leaseback the sale of an asset, usually buildings, to a third party that then leases it back to the owner. It is used by a company as a way of raising finance. *Also known as* **renting back**

sale by instalments *see hire purchase*

sale by tender the sale of an asset to interested parties who have been invited to make an offer. The asset is sold to the party that makes the highest offer.

sale or return a system where the retailer sends goods back if they are not sold and pays the supplier only for goods sold

sales order an acknowledgment by a supplier of a purchase order. It may contain terms which override those of the purchaser.

sales per employee an indicator of labour productivity. *See also* **profit per employee**

samurai bond a bond issue denominated in yen and issued in Japan by a foreign institution

sandbag in a hostile *takeover* situation, to enter into talks with the bidder and attempt to prolong them as long as possible, in the hope that a *white knight* will appear and rescue the target company (*slang*)

S&L *abbr* savings and loan association

S&P 500 *abbr* Standard & Poor's Composite 500 Stock Index

S&P Index *abbr* Standard & Poor's Composite 500 Index

Santa Claus rally (*US*) a rise in stock prices in the last week of the year

SARL *abbr* société à responsabilité limitée

SARS *abbr* South African Revenue Service

SAS *abbr* Statement of Auditing Standards

save as you earn a system for saving on a regular basis that is encouraged by the government through tax concessions. *Abbr* **SAYE**

savings money set aside by consumers for a particular purpose, to meet contingencies, or to provide an income during retirement. Savings, money in deposit and savings accounts, differ from investments, for example, on the stock market, in that they are not subject to price fluctuations and are thus considered safer.

savings account an account with a financial institution that pays interest. *See also* **gross interest**, **net interest**

savings and loan association a chartered bank that offers savings accounts, pays dividends, and invests in new mortgages. *See also* **thrift institution**. *Abbr* **S&L**

savings bank a bank that specialises in managing small investments. *See also* **thrift institution**

savings bond a US bond that an individual buys from the federal government

savings certificate *see* **National Savings Certificate**

savings function an expression of the extent to which people save money instead of spending it

savings ratio the proportion of the income of a country or household that is saved in a particular period

SAYE *abbr* save as you earn

SC *abbr* Securities Commission

Schedule C a schedule to the Finance Acts under which tax was charged on income from public sources, such as government stock

scheme of arrangement a scheme drawn up by an individual or company to offer ways of paying debts, so as to avoid bankruptcy proceedings

scorched earth policy destructive actions taken by an organisation in defence against a hostile *takeover*. Extreme actions under a scorched earth policy may include voluntary liquidation or selling off critical assets. A scorched earth policy may come into play if the value of the company to be acquired exceeds the value of the company making a hostile bid. (*slang*)

scrap discarded material that has some value

scrip dividend a dividend paid by the issue of additional company shares, rather than by cash

scrip issue a proportional issue of free shares to existing shareholders. *US term* **stock split**. *Also known as* **bonus shares**, **share split**

scripophily the collecting of valueless share or bond certificates

Sdn *abbr* Sendirian

SDR *see* **special drawing rights**

SEAQ *abbr* Stock Exchange Automated Quotations system: the London Stock Exchange's system for UK securities. It is a continuously updated computer database containing quotations that also records prices at which transactions have been struck.

SEAQ International *abbr* Stock Exchange Automated Quotations system International: the London Stock Exchange's system for overseas securities. It is a continuously updated computer database containing quotations that also records prices at which transactions have been struck.

seasonal adjustment an adjustment made to accounts to allow for any short-term seasonal factors, such as Christmas sales, that may distort the figures

seasonal business trade that is affected by seasonal factors, for example, trade in goods such as suntan products or Christmas trees

seasoned equity shares that have traded long enough to have a well-established value

seasoned issue an issue for which there is a pre-existing market. *See also* **unseasoned issue**

SEATS *abbr* Stock Exchange Automatic Trading System: the electronic screen-trading system operated by the Australian Stock Exchange. It was introduced in 1987.

SEC *abbr* Securities and Exchange Commission

secondary issue an offer of listed shares that have not previously been publicly traded

secondary market a market that trades in existing shares rather than new share issues, for example, a stock exchange. The money earned from these sales goes to the dealer or investor, not to the issuer.

secondary offering an offering of securities of a kind that is already on the market

Secondary Tax on Companies (*S Africa*) *see* **STC**

second mortgage a loan that uses the equity on a mortgaged property as security and is taken out with a different lender from the first mortgage. As the first mortgagee holds the deeds, the second mortgagee has to register its interest with the Land Registry and cannot foreclose without the first mortgagee's permission.

second-tier market a market in stocks and shares where the listing requirements are less onerous than for the main market, as in, for example, London's Alternative Investment Market

secret reserves *see* **hidden reserves**

Section 21 Company (*S Africa*) a company established as a **non-profit organisation**

sector index an index of companies in particular parts of a market whose shares are listed on a general or specialist stock exchange

secured 1. used to describe borrowing when the lender has a charge over an asset or assets of the borrower, for example, a mortgage or floating charge **2.** used to describe a creditor who has a charge over an asset or assets of the borrower, for example, a mortgage or floating charge. *See also* **collateral**, **security**

secured bond a collateralised bond

secured creditors creditors whose claims are wholly or partly secured on the assets of a business

secure server a combination of hardware and software that secures e-commerce credit card transactions so that there is no risk of unauthorised people gaining access to credit card details online

securities account an account that shows the value of financial assets held by a person or organisation

securities analyst a professional person who studies the performance of securities and the companies that issue them

Securities and Exchange Commission the US government agency responsible for establishing standards of financial reporting and accounting for public companies. *Abbr* **SEC**

Securities and Futures Authority a self-regulatory organisation responsible for supervising the activities of institutions advising on corporate finance activity, or dealing or facilitating deals in securities or derivatives. *Abbr* **SFA**

Securities and Investment Board *abbr* **SIB**. *See* *Financial Services Authority*

Securities Commission a statutory body responsible for monitoring standards in the New Zealand securities markets and for promoting investment in New Zealand. *Abbr* **SC**

securities deposit account a brokerage account into which securities are deposited electronically

Securities Institute of Australia a national professional body that represents people involved in the Australian securities and financial services industry. *Abbr* **SIA**

Securities Investor Protection Corporation in the United States, a corporation created by Congress in 1970 that is a mutual insurance fund established to protect clients of securities firms. In the event of a firm being closed because of bankruptcy or financial difficulties, the SIPC will step in to recover clients' cash and securities held by the firm. The corporation's reserves are available to satisfy cash and securities that cannot be recovered up to a maximum of $500,000, including a maximum of $100,000 on cash claims. *Abbr* **SIPC**

securities lending the loan of securities to those who have *sold short*

securitisation the conversion of financial or physical assets into financial instruments which can be traded

securitised mortgage *see securitisation*

securitised paper the *bond* or *promissory note* resulting from *securitisation*

security 1. a tradable financial asset, for example, a bond, stock, a share, or a warrant **2.** the collateral for a loan or other borrowing

security deposit an amount of money paid before a transaction occurs to compensate the seller in the event that the transaction is not concluded and this is the buyer's fault

security investment company a financial institution that specialises in the analysis and trading of securities

security of tenure the right to keep a job or rented accommodation, provided that certain conditions are met

security printer a printer who prints paper money, share prospectuses, and confidential government documents

seed capital a usually modest amount of money used to convert an idea into a viable business. Seed capital is a form of *venture capital*. *US term seed money*

self-assessment in the United Kingdom, a system that enables taxpayers to assess their own income tax and capital gains tax payments for the fiscal year

self-insurance the practice of saving money to pay for a possible loss rather than taking out an insurance policy against it

self-liquidating providing enough income to pay off the amount borrowed for financing

self-regulatory organisations (SRO)s professional bodies licensed by the *SIB* and responsible for policing the range of investment activities undertaken by their members; for ensuring that compensation is available in cases of negligence or fraud; and for ensuring that there is sufficient professional indemnity

self-tender in the United States, the repurchase by a corporation of its stock by way of a tender

seller's market a market in which sellers can dictate prices, typically because demand is high or there is a product shortage

selling cost the cost incurred in securing orders, usually including salaries, commissions, and travelling expenses

selling season a period in which market conditions are favourable to sellers

sell short to sell commodities, currencies, or securities that one does not own in the expectation that prices will fall before delivery to the seller's profit

semi-variable cost a cost that contains both fixed and variable components and is thus partly affected by a change in the level of activity

Sendirian Malay term for 'limited'. Companies can use 'Sendirian Berhad' or 'Sdn Bhd' in their name instead of 'plc'. *Abbr* **Sdn**

senior capital capital in the form of secured loans to a company which, in the event of liquidation, is repaid before junior capital, such as shareholders' equity

senior debt a debt whose holder has more claim on the debtor's assets than the holder of another debt. *See also **junior debt***

senior mortgage a mortgage whose holder has more claim on the debtor's assets than the holder of another mortgage. *See also **junior mortgage***

sensitivity analysis a modelling and risk assessment procedure in which changes are made to significant variables in order to determine the effect of these changes on the planned outcome. Particular attention is thereafter paid to variables identified as being of special significance.

SERPS *abbr* State Earnings-Related Pension Scheme: in the United Kingdom, a state scheme designed to pay retired employees an additional pension to the standard state pension. Contributions, collected through National Insurance payments, and benefits are related to earnings. Individuals may opt out of SERPS and have their contributions directed to an occupational or personal pension.

service charge a fee for any service provided, or additional fee for any enhancements to an existing service. For example, banks may charge a fee for obtaining foreign currency for customers. Residents in blocks of flats may pay an annual maintenance fee that is also referred to as a service charge.

service cost centre a cost centre providing services to other cost centres. When the output of an organisation is a service, rather than goods, an alternative name is normally used, for example, support cost centre or utility cost centre.

service/function costing cost accounting for services or functions, for example, canteens, maintenance, or personnel

service industry an industry which does not make products, but instead offers a service such as banking, insurance, or transport

service level agreement a contract between service provider and customer which specifies in detail the level of service to be provided over the contract period (quality, frequency, flexibility, charges, etc.) as well as the procedures to implement in the case of default

servicing borrowing paying the interest due on a loan

set-aside *see reserves*

set-off an agreement between two parties to balance one debt against another or a loss against a gain

settlement the payment of a debt or charge

settlement date the date on which an outstanding debt or charge is due to be paid

seven-day money funds that have been placed on the money market for a term of seven days

severance package (*US*) = *redundancy package*

SFA *abbr* Securities and Futures Authority

SFAS *abbr* Statement of Financial Accounting Standards

SFE *abbr* Sydney Futures Exchange

shadow ACT a system which commenced on 6 April 1999 to allow relief for surplus Advance Corporation Tax which has accumulated at 5 April 1999

shadow market *see black market*

shadow price 1. the *opportunity cost* to an individual or economy of engaging in an economic activity **2.** an increase in value which would be created by having available one additional unit of a limiting resource at its original cost. This represents the opportunity cost of not having the use of the one extra unit. This information is routinely produced when mathematical programming (especially linear programming) is used to model activity.

shakeout the elimination of weak or cautious investors during a crisis in the financial market (*slang*)

share a fixed identifiable unit of capital which has a fixed nominal or face value, which may be quite different from the market price of the share

share account 1. an account at a building society where the account holder is a member of the society. Building societies usually offer another type of account, a deposit account, where the account holder is not a member. A share account is generally paid a better rate of interest, but in the event of the society going into liquidation, deposit account holders are given preference. **2.** (*US*) an account with a credit union that pays dividends rather than interest

share buyback an arrangement whereby a company buys its own shares on the stock market

share capital the amount of capital that a company raises by issuing shares

share certificate a document that certifies ownership of a share in a company. *US term* **stock certificate**

shared services a business strategy which involves centralising certain business activities, such as accounting and other transaction-oriented activities in order to reduce costs and provide better customer service

share exchange a service provided by certain collective investment schemes whereby they exchange investors' existing individual shareholdings for units or shares in their funds. This saves the investor the expense of selling holdings, which can be uneconomical when dealing with small shareholdings.

share-for-share offer a *takeover* bid where the bidder offers its own shares, or a combination of cash and shares, for the target company

shareholder a person or organisation that owns shares in a limited company or partnership. A shareholder has a stake in the company and becomes a member of it, with rights to attend the *annual general meeting*. Since shareholders have invested money in a company, they have a vested interest in its performance and can be a powerful influence on company policy; they should consequently be considered *stakeholders* as well as shareholders. Some pressure groups have sought to exploit this by becoming shareholders in order to get a particular viewpoint or message across. At the same time, managers must, in order to maintain or increase the company's market value, consider their responsibility to shareholders when formulating strategy. It has been argued that on some occasions the desire to make profits to raise returns for shareholders has damaged companies because it has limited the amount of money spent in other areas, such as the development of facilities, or health and safety.

shareholders' equity a company's share capital and reserves

shareholders' perks benefits offered to shareholders in addition to dividends, often in the form of discounts on the company's products and services

shareholder value the total return to the shareholders in terms of both dividends and share price growth, calculated as the present value of future free cash-flows of the business discounted at the weighted average cost of the capital of the business less the market value of its debt

shareholder value analysis a calculation of the value of a company made by looking at the returns it gives to its shareholders. Shareholder value analysis, like the *economic theory of the firm* and *economic value added*, assumes that the objective of a company director is to maximise the wealth of the company's shareholders. It is based on the premise that discounted cash-flow principles can be applied to the business as a whole. Shareholder value analysis can be applied to assess the contribution of a business unit or to evaluate individual projects. It is a concept also used for managing long-term financial decisions so that the value of the business is increased. It takes the view that standard accounting methods for calculating the value of a business are outmoded: they either dwell on a backward-looking historical perspective, or are simply too short-term. Business decisions that are based on techniques such as price/earnings ratios or growth in profits are inadequate, because it is possible to make decisions which improve these measures in the short-term (such as reducing training or research expenditure), but which reduce the long-term value of the business. The concept of shareholder value works from the premise that a business only adds value for its shareholders when equity returns exceed equity costs. SVA is therefore focused on long-term profit flows. Applying shareholder value analysis requires a long-term perspective, possibly involving significant change in what the organisation does and how it does it. *Abbr* **SVA**

shareholding the shares in a limited company owned by a shareholder. *US term* **stockholding**

share incentive scheme a type of financial *incentive scheme* in which employees can acquire shares in the company in which they work and so have an interest in its financial performance. A share incentive scheme is a type of *employee share scheme*, in which employees may be given shares by their employer, or shares may be offered for purchase at an advantageous price, as a reward for personal or group performance. A *share option* is a type of share incentive scheme.

share index *see index*

share issue the offering for sale of shares in a business. The *capital* derived from share issues can be used for investment in the core business or for expansion into new commercial ventures.

share option a type of *share incentive scheme* in which an employee is given the option to buy a specified number of shares at a future date, at an agreed price. Share options provide a financial benefit to the recipient only if the share price rises over the period the option is available. If the share price falls over the period, the employee is under no obligation to buy the shares. There may be a tax advantage to the employees who participate in such a scheme. Share options may be available to all employees or operated on a discretionary basis.

shareowner somebody who owns a share of stock

share premium the amount payable for a share above its nominal value. Most shares are issued at a premium to their nominal value. Share premiums are credited to the company's *share premium account*.

share premium account the special reserve in a company's balance sheet to which *share premiums* are credited. Expenses associated with the issue of shares may be written off to this account.

share register a list of the shareholders in a particular company

share shop the name given by some financial institutions to the office open to the public where shares may be bought and sold

shares of negligible value shares which are considered in income tax terms as having no value because the company has ceased to exist. The shares of companies in receivership are not deemed to be of negligible value, although they may eventually end up as such.

share split *see scrip issue*

Share Transactions Totally Electronic (*S Africa*) *see STRATE*

share transfer form *see transfer deed*

shark watcher in the United States, a firm specialising in monitoring the stock market for potential takeover activity (*slang*)

Sharpe ratio *see risk-adjusted return on capital*

shelf registration a registration statement, lodged with the Securities and Exchange Commission two years before a corporation issues securities to the public. The statement, which has to be updated periodically, allows the corporation to act quickly when it considers that the market conditions are right, without having to start the registration procedure from scratch.

shell company a company that has ceased to trade but is still registered, especially one sold to enable the buyer to begin trading without having to set up a new company

shibosai the Japanese term for a private placing

shibosai bond a *samurai bond* sold direct to investors by the issuing company as opposed to a financial institution

shinyo kinku in Japan, a financial institution that provides financing for small businesses

shinyo kumiai in Japan, a credit union that provides financing for small businesses

shipping confirmation an e-mail message informing the purchaser that an order has been shipped

shogun bond a bond denominated in a currency other than the yen that is sold on the Japanese market by a non-Japanese financial institution. *Also known as geisha bond. See also samurai bond*

short 1. a short-dated gilt (*slang*) **2.** an asset in which a dealer has a short position

short account a brokerage account on which short sales are made

short covering the purchase of foreign exchange, commodities, or securities by a firm or individual that has been *selling short*. Such purchases are undertaken when the market has begun to move upwards, or when it is thought to be about to do so.

short-dated gilt *see gilt-edged security*

short-dated gilts government stocks which mature in less than five years from the date of purchase

shorting the act of *selling short*

short interest the number of shares on an exchange that have been sold short and not covered with purchases

short selling *see sell short*

short-term bond a bond on the corporate bond market that has an initial maturity of less than two years

short-term capital funds raised for a period of less than 12 months. *See also working capital*

short-term debt debt with a term of 12 months or less

short-term economic policy an economic policy with objectives that can be met within a period of months or a few years

show stopper *see poison pill*

shrinkage 1. a reduction in the amount of a company's inventories, often caused by production processes **2.** a term used to describe goods that leave a retail outlet but are not logged as sales. Shrinkage can include goods that are stolen by shoplifters, damaged, or broken in some capacity.

SI *abbr* Statutory Instrument

SIA *abbr* Securities Institute of Australia

SIB *abbr* Securities and Investment Board

sickness and accident insurance a form of permanent health insurance that may be sold with some form of credit, for example, a credit card or personal loan. In the event of the borrower being unable to work because of accident or illness, the policy covers the regular payments to the credit card company or lender.

sight bill a bill of exchange that is payable on sight

sight deposit a bank deposit against which the depositor can immediately draw

sight draft a bill of exchange that is payable on delivery. *See also time draft*

signature guarantee a stamp or seal, usually from a bank or a broker, that vouches for the authenticity of a signature

signature loan *see unsecured loan*

silent partner (*US*) = *sleeping partner*

simple interest interest charged simply as a constant percentage of principal and not compounded. *See also* **compound interest**

simultaneous engineering *see concurrent engineering*

Singapore dollar Singapore's unit of currency, whose exchange rate is quoted as S$ per US$

Singapore Exchange a merger of the Stock Exchange of Singapore and the Singapore International Monetary Exchange, established in 1999. It provides securities and derivatives trading, securities clearing and depository, and derivatives clearing services. *Abbr* **SGX**

single currency denominated entirely in one currency

single customs document a standard universally used form for the passage of goods through customs

single-entry a type of bookkeeping where only one entry, reflecting both a credit to one account and a debit to another, is made for each transaction

single market *see EU*

single-payment bond a bond redeemed with a single payment combining principal and interest at maturity

single premium assurance life cover where the premium is paid in one lump sum when the policy is taken out, rather than in monthly instalments

single premium deferred annuity an annuity that is paid for with a single payment at inception and pays returns regularly after a set date. It gives a tax advantage.

single tax a tax that supplies all revenue, especially on land

sinking fund 1. an account in which money is accumulated for use in the retirement of debt **2.** money put aside periodically to settle a liability or replace an *asset*. The money is invested

to produce a required sum at an appropriate time.

SIPC *abbr* Securities Investor Protection Corporation

SITE (*S Africa*) a tax deducted from an employee's income as part of the Pay-As-You-Earn system, for remuneration below an amount set by the South African Revenue Service. Income above this amount necessitates the additional submission of an annual tax return.

six-month money funds invested on the money market for a period of six months

skimming the unethical and usually illegal practice of taking small amounts of money from accounts that belong to other individuals or organisations

slack variables the amount of each resource which will be unused if a specific linear programming solution is implemented

sleeping partner a person or organisation that invests money in a company but takes no active part in the management of the business. Although sleeping partners are inactive in the operation of the business, they have legal obligations and benefits of ownership and are therefore fully liable for any debts. *US term* **silent partner**

slowdown a fall in demand that causes a lowering of economic activity, less severe than a *recession* or *slump*

slump a severe downturn phase in the business cycle

slumpflation a collapse in all economic activity accompanied by wage and price inflation. This happened, for example, in the United States and Europe in 1929. (*slang*)

slush fund a fund used by a company for illegal purposes, such as bribing officials to obtain preferential treatment for planned work or expansion

small change a quantity of coins that a person might carry with them

Small Order Execution System on the NASDAQ, an automated execution system for bypassing brokers when processing small order agency executions of NASDAQ securities of up to 1,000 shares

smart card a small plastic card containing a microprocessor that can store and process transactions and maintain a bank balance, thus providing a secure, portable medium for electronic money. Financial details and personal data stored on the card can be updated each time the card is used.

smart market a market in which all transactions are carried out electronically using network communications

social cost tangible and intangible costs and losses sustained by third parties or the general public as a result of economic activity, for example, pollution by industrial effluent

socially-conscious investing see *ethical investment*

social marginal cost the additional cost to a society of a change in an economic variable, for example, the price of petrol or bread

social responsibility accounting the identification, measurement, and reporting of the social costs and benefits resulting from economic activities

Sociedad Anónima the Spanish equivalent of a private limited company. *Abbr* **SA**

Sociedade Anónima the Portuguese equivalent of a private limited company. *Abbr* **SA**

Società a responsabilità limitata an Italian limited liability company that is unlisted. *Abbr* **Srl**

Società per Azioni an Italian public limited company. *Abbr* **SpA**

Société Anonyme the French equivalent of a private limited company. *Abbr* **SA**

société à responsabilité limitée a French limited liability company that is unlisted. *Abbr* **SARL**

société d'investissement à capital variable the French term for collective investment. *Abbr* **SICAV**

Society for Worldwide Interbank Financial Telecommunication see *SWIFT*

socio-economic involving both social and economic factors. Structural unemployment, for example, has socio-economic causes.

Sod's Law the principle that if something can go wrong, it will. *US term* *Murphy's Law*

soft capital rationing see *capital rationing*

soft commissions brokerage commissions that are rebated to an institutional customer in the form of, or to pay for, research or other services

soft commodities commodities, such as foodstuffs, that are neither metals nor other solid raw materials. *Also known as* **softs**. *See also* **future**, **hard commodities**

soft currency a currency that is weak, usually because there is an excess of supply and a belief that its value will fall in relation to others. *See also* **hard currency**

soft landing the situation when a country's economic activity has slowed down but demand has not fallen far enough or rapidly enough to cause a recession

soft loan a loan on exceptionally favourable terms, for example, for a project that a government considers worthy

soft market a market in which prices are falling

softs *see soft commodities*

sold short *see sell short*

sole distributor a retailer who is the only one in an area who is allowed by the manufacturer to sell a certain product or service

sole trader a person carrying on business with total legal responsibility for his or her actions, neither in partnership nor as a company

solicit to ask another person or company for money

solvency margin 1. a business's liquid assets that exceed the amount required to meet its liabilities **2.** the extent to which an insurance company's assets exceed its liabilities

solvency ratio 1. a ratio of assets to liabilities, used to measure a company's ability to meet its debts **2.** in the United Kingdom, the ratio of an insurance company's net assets to its non-life premium income

solvent used to refer to a situation in which the *assets* of an individual or organisation are worth more than their *liabilities*

sort code a combination of numbers that identifies a bank branch on official documentation, such as bank statements and cheques. *US term* ***routing number***

sou marqué a French coin that circulates in Canada

source and application of funds statement *see cash-flow statement*

source document a document upon which details of transactions or accounting events are recorded and from which information is extracted to be subsequently entered into the internal accounting system of an organisation, for example, a sales invoice or credit note

sources and uses of funds statement *see cash-flow statement*

Southern African Development Community *see SADC*

sovereign loan a loan by a financial institution to an overseas government, usually of a developing country. *See also sovereign risk*

sovereign risk the risk that an overseas government may refuse to repay or may default on a *sovereign loan*

SpA *abbr* Società per Azioni

special clearing *see special presentation*

Special Commissioner an official appointed by the Treasury to hear cases where a taxpayer is appealing against an income tax assessment

special damages damages awarded by a court to compensate for a loss which can be calculated, such as the expense of repairing something

special deposit 1. an amount of money set aside for the rehabilitation of a mortgaged house **2.** a large sum of money which a commercial bank has to deposit with the Bank of England

special drawing rights a measure of a country's reserves, as internationally recognised. *Abbr* **SDR**. *Also known as paper gold*

specialist (*US*) *see market maker*

special notice notice of a proposal to be put before a meeting of the shareholders of a company which is issued less than 28 days before the meeting

special presentation the sending of a cheque directly to the paying banker rather than through the clearing system. *Also known as special clearing. See also advice of fate*

special purpose bond a bond for one particular project, financed by levies on the people who benefit from the project

special resolution *see extraordinary resolution*

specie coins, as opposed to banknotes, that are legal tender

specific charge a fixed charge as opposed to a floating charge

specific order costing the basic cost accounting method applicable where work consists of separately identifiable contracts, jobs, or batches

speculation a purchase made solely to make a profit when the price or value increases

split 1. an issuance to shareholders of more than one share for every share owned. *See also* **reverse split 2.** an award of some number of, usually additional, shares for each share a person owns

split-capital investment trust an investment trust set up for a specific timescale where the shares are divided at launch into two different classes: income shares and capital shares. Income shareholders receive all or most of the income generated by the trust and a predetermined sum at liquidation, while capital shareholders receive no interest but the remainder of the capital at liquidation. *Also known as* **split-level trust**, **split trust**

split commission *commission* that is divided between two or more parties in a transaction

split coupon bond *see zero coupon bond*

split-level trust *see split-capital investment trust*

split trust *see split-capital investment trust*

spot currency market *see spot market*

spot exchange rate the exchange rate used for immediate currency transactions

spot goods a commodity traded on the spot market

spot interest rate an interest rate that is determined when a loan is made

spot market a market that deals in commodities or foreign exchange for immediate rather than future delivery

spot month *see nearby month*

spot price the price for immediate delivery of a commodity or foreign exchange

spot rate the rate of interest to maturity currently offered on a particular type of security

spot transaction a transaction in commodities or foreign exchange for immediate delivery

spread 1. the difference between the buying and selling price of a share on a stock exchange **2.** the range of investments in a portfolio

spreadsheet a computer program that provides a series of ruled columns in which data can be entered and analysed

sprinkling trust a trust with multiple beneficiaries whose distributions occur at the trustees' discretion

squeeze a government policy of restriction, commonly affecting the availability of credit in an economy

Srl *abbr* Società a responsabilità limitata

SSAP *abbr* Statement of Standard Accounting Practice

stabilisation fund a fund created by a government as an emergency savings account for international financial support

staff costs the costs of employment which include gross pay, paid holidays, and employer's contributions to national insurance, pension schemes, sickness benefit schemes, and other benefits, for example, protective clothing and canteen subsidies

stagflation the result when both inflation and unemployment exist at the same time in an economy. There was stagflation in the United Kingdom and the United States in the 1970s, for example.

stakeholder a person or organisation with a vested interest in the successful operation of a company or organisation. A stakeholder may be an employee, customer, supplier, partner, or even the local community within which an organisation operates.

stakeholder pension a pension, bought from a private company, in which the retirement income depends on the level of contributions made during a person's working life. Stakeholder pensions are designed for people without access to an occupational pension scheme, and are intended to provide a low-cost supplement to the State Earnings-Related Pension Scheme. A stakeholder pension scheme can either be trust-based, like an occupational pension scheme, or contract-based, similar to a personal pension. Subject to certain exceptions, employers must provide access to a stakeholder pension scheme for employees, although they are not required to establish a stakeholder pension scheme themselves. Membership of a stakeholder pension scheme is voluntary. *See also **Keough Plan***

stakeholders groups or individuals having a legitimate interest in the activities of an organisation, generally comprising customers, employees, the community, shareholders, suppliers, and lenders

stakeholder theory the theory that an organisation can enhance the interests of its shareholders without damaging the interests of its wider **stakeholders**. Stakeholder theory grew in response to the **economic theory of the firm**, and contrasts with Theory E. One of the difficulties of stakeholder theory is allocating importance to the values of different groups of stakeholders, and a solution to this is proposed by **stakeholder value analysis**.

stakeholder value analysis a method of determining the values of all **stakeholders** within an organisation for the purposes of making strategic and operational decisions. Stakeholder value analysis is one method of justifying an approach based on **stakeholder theory** rather than the **economic theory of the firm**. It involves identifying groups of stakeholders and eliciting their views on particular issues in order that these views may be taken into account when making decisions.

stale bull an investor who bought shares hoping that they would rise, and now finds that they have not risen and wants to sell them

stamp duty in the United Kingdom, a duty that is payable on some legal documents and is shown to have been paid by a stamp being fixed to the document

Standard & Poor's 500 a US index of 500 general share prices selected by the Standard & Poor agency. *Abbr* **S&P Index**

Standard & Poor's rating a share rating service provided by the US agency Standard & Poor

standard cost the planned unit cost of the products, components, or services produced in a period. The main uses of standard costs are in performance measurement, control, stock valuation, and in the establishment of selling prices.

standard cost card a document or other record detailing, for each individual product, the standard inputs required for production as well as the standard selling price. Inputs are normally divided into material, labour, and overhead categories, and both price and quantity information is shown for each.

standard costing a control technique which compares standard costs and revenues with actual results to obtain variances which are used to stimulate improved performance

standard direct labour cost the planned average cost of direct labour

standard for deferred payments the money with which a hire-purchase agreement, for example, is paid

standard hour the amount of work achievable, at standard efficiency levels, in an hour

standard of living a measure of economic well-being based on the ability of people to buy the goods and services they desire

standard performance–labour the level of efficiency which appropriately trained, motivated, and resourced employees can achieve in the long run

standard rate 1. the rate of income tax paid by the majority of workers in the United Kingdom. The **Inland Revenue** is responsible for the administration of income tax and publishes information on rates and allowances on its website. **2.** the rate of *VAT* normally payable on goods or services

standard time the total time in which a task should be completed by employees working at standard levels of efficiency

standby credit credit drawing rights given to a developing country by an international financial institution to fund industrialisation or other growth policies

standby loan a loan given to a developing country by an international financial institution, to fund technology hardware purchase or other growth policies

standing instructions instructions, that may be revoked at any time, for a particular procedure to be carried out in the event of a certain occurrence, for example, for the monies from a fixed-term account that has just matured to be placed on deposit for a further fixed period

standing order an instruction given by an account holder to a bank to make regular payments on given dates to the same payee. *US term **automatic debit***

staple commodity any basic food or a raw material which is important in a country's economy

star an investment that is performing extremely well (*slang*)

start-up costs the initial sum required to establish a business or to get a project underway. The costs will include the capital expenditure and related expenses before the business or project generates revenue.

state bank a bank chartered by a state of the United States

state capitalism a way of organising society in which the state controls most of a country's means of production and capital

State Earnings-Related Pension Scheme *see SERPS*

statement a summary of all transactions, such as deposits or withdrawals, that have occurred in an account over a given period of time

statement of account a summary of recent transactions between two parties. It can include a list of sums due, usually relating to unpaid invoices, items paid on account but not offset against particular invoices, credit notes, debit notes, and discounts

statement of affairs a statement, usually prepared by a receiver, in a prescribed form, showing the estimated financial position of a debtor or of a company which may be unable to meet its debts. It contains a summary of the debtor's assets and liabilities. The assets are shown at their estimated realisable values. The various classes of creditors, such as preferential, secured, partly secured, and unsecured, are shown separately.

Statement of Auditing Standards an auditing standard, issued by the Auditing Practices Board (APB), containing prescriptions as to the basic principles and practices which members of the UK accountancy bodies are expected to follow in the course of an audit. *Abbr* **SAS**

statement of cash-flows a statement that documents actual receipts and expenditures of cash

statement-of-cash-flows method a method of accounting that is based on flows of cash rather than balances on accounts

statement of changes in financial position a financial report of a company's incomes and outflows during a period, usually a year or a quarter

Statement of Financial Accounting Standards in the United States, a statement detailing the standards to be adopted for the preparation of financial statements. *Abbr* **SFAS**

statement of source and application of funds *see* **cash-flow statement**

Statement of Standard Accounting Practice an accounting standard issued by the Accounting Standards Committee (ASC). *Abbr* **SSAP**

statement of total recognised gains and losses a financial statement showing changes in shareholders' equity during an accounting period

statistic a piece of information in numerical form

statistical significance the level of importance at which an event influences a set of *statistics*

statistics information in numerical form and its collection, analysis, and presentation

statute-barred debt a debt that cannot be pursued as the time limit laid down by law has expired

statutory auditor a professional person qualified to carry out an audit required by the Companies Act

statutory body an entity formed by Act of Parliament

STC *abbr* (*S Africa*) Secondary Tax on Companies: a secondary tax levied on corporate dividends

stealth wealth advantage that the owners of a company do not realise it has (*slang*)

stipend a regular remuneration or allowance paid to an individual holding a particular office

stock 1. a form of security that offers fixed interest **2.** the *capital* made available to an organisation after a *share issue*

stockbroker somebody who arranges the sale and purchase of stocks

stock capital an amount of fully paid-up capital, any part of which can be transferred, for example, a block of £1,000 of stock out of a total holding of £15,000

stock certificate (*US*) = *share certificate*

stockcount profit gained from ownership of a stock or share

stock exchange a registered market in securities

Stock Exchange Automated Quotations system *see SEAQ*

Stock Exchange Automated Quotations system International *see SEAQ International*

Stock Exchange Automatic Trading System *see SEATS*

stockholding (*US*) = *shareholding*

stockjobber (*India*) *see market maker*

stock market the trading of stocks, or a place where this occurs

stock market manipulation an attempt or series of attempts to influence the price of shares by buying or selling in order to give the impression that the shares are widely traded

stock market rating the price of a share on the stock market, which shows how investors and financial advisors generally consider the value of the company

stock option *see option*

stock split (*US*) = *scrip issue*

stock symbol a shortened version of a company's name, usually made up of two to four letters, used in screen-based trading systems

stock turnover the total value of stock sold in a year divided by the average value of goods held in stock. This checks that cash is not tied up in stock for too long, losing its value over time.

stock turns *or* **stock turnover** *see inventory turnover*

stokvel (*S Africa*) an informal, widely used co-operative savings scheme that provides small-scale loans

stop-go the alternate tightening and loosening of fiscal and monetary policies. This characterised the UK economy in the 1960s and 1970s.

stop limit order in the United States, an order to trade only if and when a security reaches a specified price

stop loss (*US*) an order to trade only if and when a security falls to a specified price

stop order (*US*) an order to trade only if and when a security rises above or falls below its current price

stores requisition *see materials requisition*

story stock a stock that is the subject of a press or financial community story that may affect its price

straight-line depreciation a form of depreciation in which the cost of a fixed asset is spread equally over each year of its anticipated lifetime

Straits Times Industrial Index an index of 30 Singapore stocks, the most commonly quoted indicator of stock market activity in Singapore

STRATE *abbr* (*S Africa*) Share Transactions Totally Electronic: the electronic share transactions system of the Johannesburg Stock Exchange

strategic business unit a section within a larger organisation, responsible for planning, developing, producing, and marketing its own products or services

strategic financial management the identification of the possible strategies capable of maximising an organisation's net present value, the allocation of scarce capital resources among the competing opportunities, and the implementation and monitoring of the chosen strategy so as to achieve stated objectives

strategic investment appraisal a method of investment appraisal which allows the inclusion of both financial and non-financial factors. Project benefits are appraised in terms of their contribution to the strategies of the organisation, either by their financial contribution or, for non-financial benefits, by the use of index numbers or other means.

strategic management accounting a form of management accounting in which emphasis is placed on information which relates to factors external to the firm, as well as non-financial information and internally generated information

strategic plan a statement of long-term goals along with a definition of the strategies and policies which will ensure achievement of these goals

strategy a course of action, including the specification of resources required, to achieve specific objectives

street name (*US*) a broker who holds a customer's security in the broking house's name to facilitate transactions

strike pay *or* **strike benefit** a benefit or allowance paid by a trade union to its members during the course of official strike action to help offset loss of earnings. *Also known as* **dispute benefit**

strike price the price for a security or commodity that underlies an option

stripped bond a bond that can be divided into separate zero-coupon bonds to represent its principal repayment and its interest

stripped stock stock whose rights to dividends have been separated and sold

strips the parts of a bond that entitle the owner only to *interest* payments or only to the repayment of *principal*

structural adjustment the reallocation of resources in response to a change in the output composition of an economy. *Also known as* **structural change**

structural change *see* **structural adjustment**

structural fund a unit trust that invests in projects that contribute to the economic development of poorer nations in the European Union

structural inflation inflation that naturally occurs in an economy, without any particular triggering event

structural unemployment unemployment resulting from a change in demand, or technology changes, so that there is a surplus of labour in a particular location or skills area

stub equity the money raised through the sale of high-risk bonds in large amounts or quantities, as in a leveraged takeover or a leveraged buy-out

subject to collection dependent upon the ability to collect the amount owed

subordinated debt *see junior debt*

subordinated loan a loan that ranks below all other borrowings with regard to both the payment of interest and repayment of the principal. *See also pari passu*

subscribed share capital *see issued share capital*

subscriber 1. a buyer, especially one who buys shares in a new company or new issues **2.** a person who signs a company's Memorandum of Association

subscription an agreement to buy, for example, shares in an offering

subscription right a right to buy, for example, shares in an offering

subscription share a share purchased by a subscriber when a new company is formed

subsidiary account an account for one of the individual people or organisations that jointly hold another account

subsistence allowance *expenses* paid by an employer, usually within pre-set limits, to cover the cost of accommodation, meals, and incidental expenses incurred by employees when away on business

subtreasury a place where some of a nation's money is held

sum 1. an amount of money **2.** the total amount of any given item, such as stocks or securities **3.** the total arising from the addition of two or more numbers

sum at risk an amount of any given item, such as money, stocks, or securities, that an investor may lose

sum insured the maximum amount that an insurance company will pay out in the event of a claim

sum-of-digits method a method of depreciating a fixed asset where the cost of the asset (less its residual value) is multiplied by a fraction based on the number of years of its expected useful life. The fraction changes each year and charges the highest costs to the earliest years.

sum-of-the-year's-digits depreciation accelerated depreciation, conferring tax advantage by assuming more rapid depreciation when an asset is new

sumptuary expense an amount, regulated for moral purposes, that is spent for a purpose related to personal behaviour

sunk cost a cost which has been irreversibly incurred or committed prior to a decision point and which cannot therefore be considered relevant to subsequent decisions

sunshine law a law that requires public disclosure of a government act

superannuation plan a pension plan in Australia

superannuation scheme a pension plan in New Zealand

supplier an organisation that delivers materials, components, goods, or services to another organisation

supply and demand the quantity of goods available for sale at a given price, and the level of consumer need for those goods. The balance of supply and demand fluctuates as external economic factors such as the cost of materials and the level of competition in the marketplace influence the level of demand from consumers and the desire and ability of producers to supply the goods. Supply and demand is recognised as an economic force, and is often referred to as the **law of supply and demand**.

supply shock a sudden rise in productivity which gives higher output and profits without *inflation*

supply-side economics the study of the way economic agents behave when supply is affected by changes in price

support price the price of a product that is fixed or stabilised by a government so that it cannot fall below a certain level

surety 1. a guarantor **2.** the collateral given as security when borrowing

surplus *see budget surplus*

surrender value the sum of money offered by an insurance company to somebody who cancels a policy before it has completed its full term

surtax a tax paid in addition to another tax, typically levied on a corporation with very high income

survivalist enterprise (*S Africa*) a business that has no paid employees, generates income below the poverty line, and is considered the lowest level of micro-enterprise

sushi bond a bond that is not denominated in yen and is issued in any market by a Japanese financial institution. This type of bond is often bought by Japanese institutional investors. (*slang*)

suspense account an account in which debits or credits are held temporarily until sufficient information is available for them to be posted to the correct accounts

SVA *abbr* shareholder value analysis

swap 1. an exchange of *credits* or *liabilities*. *See also asset swap, bond swap, interest rate swap* **2.** an arrangement whereby two organisations contractually agree to exchange payments on different terms, for example, in different currencies, or one at a fixed rate and the other at a floating rate

swap book a broker's list of stocks or securities that clients wish to swap

swaption an option to enter into a *swap* contract (*slang*)

sweep facility the automatic transfer of sums from a current account to a deposit account, or from any low interest account to a higher one. For example, a personal customer may have the balance transferred just before receipt of their monthly salary, or a business may stipulate that when a balance exceeds a certain sum, the excess is to be transferred.

sweetener 1. a feature added to a security to make it more attractive to investors **2.** a security with a high yield that has been added to a portfolio to improve its overall return. *See also kicker*

SWIFT *abbr* Society for Worldwide Interbank Financial Telecommunication: a non-profit co-operative organisation with the mission of creating a shared worldwide data processing and communications link and a common language for international financial transactions. Established in Brussels in 1973 with the support of 239 banks in 15 countries, it now has over 7,000 live users in 192 countries, exchanging millions of messages valued in trillions of dollars every business day.

swing trading the trading of stock by individuals that takes advantage of sudden price movements that occur especially when large numbers of traders have to cover short sales

switch 1. to exchange a specific security with another within a portfolio, usually because the investor's objectives have changed **2.** a swap exchange rate. *See also swap* **3.** to move a commodity from one location to another

Switch a debit card widely used in the United Kingdom

switching the simultaneous sale and purchase of contracts in futures with different expiry dates, as, for example, when a business decides that it would like to take delivery of a commodity earlier or later than originally contracted

switching discount the discount available to holders of collective investments who move from one fund to another offered by the same fund manager. The discount is usually a lower initial charge compared to the one made to new investors or when existing investors make a further investment.

Sydney Futures Exchange the principal market in Australia for trading financial and commodity futures. It was set up in 1962 as a wool futures market, the Sydney Greasy Wool Futures Exchange, but adopted its current name in 1972 to reflect its widening role. *Abbr* **SFE**

T

T+ an expression of the number of days allowed for settlement of a transaction

tactical plan a short-term plan for achieving an entity's objectives

tailgating the practice by a broker of buying or selling a security immediately after a client's transaction, in order to take advantage of the impact of the client's deal

take a flyer to speculate (*slang*)

take a hit to make a loss on an investment (*slang*)

take a view to form an opinion on the likely direction a market will take, and to take a position to benefit if the opinion proves correct

take-home pay the amount of *pay* an employee receives after all deductions, such as income tax, national insurance, or pension contributions. *Also known as net pay*

takeout financing loans used to replace bridge financing

takeover the acquisition by a company of a controlling interest in the voting share capital of another company, usually achieved by the purchase of a majority of the voting shares

takeover approach the price at which a suitor offers to buy a corporation's shares. *US term* **tender offer**

takeover battle the result of a hostile takeover bid. The bidder may raise the offer price and write to the shareholders extolling the benefits of the takeover. The board may contact other companies in the same line of business hoping that a *white knight* may appear. It could also take action to make the company less desirable to the bidder. *See also* **poison pill**

takeover ratio the book value of a company divided by its market capitalisation. If the resulting figure is greater than one, then the company is a candidate for a takeover. *See also* **appreciation**, **asset-stripping**

taker 1. the buyer of an option **2.** a borrower

takings a retailer's net receipts

talon a form attached to a bearer bond that the holder of the bond uses to order new coupons when those attached to the bond have been depleted

tangible assets assets that are physical, such as buildings, cash, and stock. Leases and securities, although not physical in themselves, are classed as tangible assets because the underlying assets are physical.

tangible book value the book value of a company after intangible assets, patents, trademarks, and the value of research and development have been subtracted

tangible fixed asset statement a summary of the opening and closing balances for tangible fixed assets and acquisitions, disposals, and depreciation in the period

tank to fall precipitously. This term is used especially with reference to stock prices. (*slang*)

tap CD the issue of certificates of deposit, normally in large denominations, when required by a specific investor

tape
   don't fight the tape don't go against the direction of the market (*slang*)

target cash balance the amount of cash that a company would like to have in hand

target company a company that is the object of a takeover bid

target cost a product cost estimate derived by subtracting a desired profit margin from a competitive market price. This may be less than the planned initial product cost, but will be expected to be achieved by the time the product reaches the mature production stage.

targeted repurchase a company's purchase of its own shares from somebody attempting to buy the company

target savings motive the motive that people have not to save when their families are growing up but to save when they are in middle age and trying to build up a pension

tariff 1. a government duty imposed on imports or exports to stimulate or dampen economic activity **2.** a list of prices at which goods or services are supplied

Tariff Concession Scheme a system operated by the Australian government in which imported goods that have no locally produced equivalent attract reduced duties. *Abbr* **TCS**

tariff office an insurance company whose premiums are determined according to a scale set collectively by several companies

tax a charge levied by a government on individuals and companies to pay for public services. The amount of money required from a person or organisation depends on their income and assets.

taxability the extent to which a good or individual is subject to a *tax*

taxable base the amount subject to taxation

taxable income income that is subject to taxes

taxable matters goods or services that can be taxed

tax and price index an index number showing the percentage change in gross income that taxpayers need if they are to maintain their real disposable income

taxation *see* **tax**

tax auditor a government employee who investigates taxpayers' declarations

tax avoidance the organisation of a taxpayer's affairs so that the minimum tax liability is incurred. Tax avoidance involves making the maximum use of all legal means of minimising liability to taxation.

tax bracket a range of income levels subject to marginal tax at the same rate

tax break an investment that is tax efficient or a legal arrangement that reduces the liability to tax. *See also* **tax avoidance, tax shelter**

tax consultant a professional who advises on all aspects of taxation from tax avoidance to estate planning

tax-deductible that which is able to be subtracted from taxable income before tax is paid

tax-deductible public debt any debt instrument that is exempt from US federal income tax

tax-deferred not to be taxed until a later time

tax disc a prominent sticker displayed inside the window of a motor vehicle to prove that the owner has paid road tax on it. *US term* **registration sticker**

tax dodge an illegal method of paying less tax than an individual or company is legally obliged to pay

tax domicile a place that a government levying a tax considers to be a person's home

tax-efficient financially advantageous by leading to a reduction of taxes to be paid

tax-efficient investment an investment that is tax-efficient

tax evasion the illegal practice of paying less money in taxes than is due. *See also **tax avoidance***

tax evasion amnesty a governmental measure that affords those who have evaded a tax in some specified way freedom from punishment for their violation of the tax law

tax-exempt not subject to tax

tax exemption the status of not being subject to tax

Tax Exempt Special Savings Account a UK savings account in which investors could save up to £9,000 over a period of five years and not pay any tax provided they made no withdrawals over that time. The advent of the ISA in 1999 meant that no new accounts of this type could be opened, but those opened prior to 1999 will continue under their original terms until their expiry date. *Abbr* **TESSA**

tax exile a person or business that leaves a country to avoid paying taxes, or the condition of having done this

tax-favoured asset an asset that receives more favourable tax treatment than some other asset

tax file number 1. an identification number assigned to each taxpayer in Australia. *Abbr* **TFN 2.** a numeric code assigned to all members of the Australian workforce for the purpose of paying income tax

tax-free not subject to tax

tax harmonisation the enactment of taxation laws in different jurisdictions, such as neighbouring countries, prov-

inces, or states of the United States, that are consistent with one another

tax haven 1. a country that has very low taxes **2.** a country that has generous tax laws, especially one that encourages non-citizens to base operations in the country to avoid higher taxes in their home countries

tax holiday an exemption from tax granted for a specified period of time. *See also **tax subsidy***

taxi industry the privately owned minibus taxi services in South Africa, which constitute the largest sector of public transport in that country

tax incentive a tax reduction afforded to people for particular purposes, for example, sending their children to college

tax inspector a government employee who investigates taxpayers' declarations

tax invoice (*ANZ*) a document issued by a supplier which stipulates the amount charged for goods or services as well as the amount of **GST** payable

tax law the body of laws on taxation, or one such law

tax lien a lien that a government places on a property because taxes on it are unpaid

tax loophole an ambiguity in a tax law that enables some individuals or companies to avoid or reduce taxes

tax loss a loss of money that can serve to reduce tax liabilities

tax loss carry-back the reduction of taxes in a previous year by subtraction from income for that year of losses suffered in the current year

tax loss carry-forward the reduction of taxes in a future year by subtraction from income for that year of losses suffered in the current year

taxman a government organisation or person that collects a tax

tax obligation the amount of tax a person or company owes

tax on capital income a tax on the income from sales of capital assets

tax payable the amount of tax a person or company has to pay

taxpayer an individual or corporation who pays a tax

tax pressure the financial difficulty that a company may face because of the taxes it must pay

tax rate the rate at which a tax is payable, usually expressed as a percentage

tax refund an amount that a government gives back to a taxpayer who has paid more taxes than were due

tax relief 1. the reduction in the amount of taxes payable, as, for example, on capital goods a company has purchased **2.** (*US*) money given to a certain group of people by a government in the form of a reduction of taxes

tax return an official form on which a company or individual enters details of income and expenses, used to assess tax liability. *Also known as* **return**

tax revenue money that a government receives in taxes

tax sale (*US*) a sale of an item by a government to recover overdue taxes on a taxable item

tax shelter a financial arrangement designed to reduce tax liability. *See also* **abusive tax shelter**

tax subsidy a tax reduction that a government gives a business for a particular purpose, usually to create jobs. *See also* **tax holiday**

tax system a scheme for imposing and collecting taxes

tax treaty an international agreement that deals with taxes, especially taxes by several countries on the same individuals

tax year a period covered by a statement about taxes

T-bill *abbr* Treasury bill

TCS *abbr* Tariff Concession Scheme

TDB *abbr* Trade Development Board

teaser rate a temporary concessionary interest rate offered on mortgages, credit cards, or savings accounts in order to attract new customers

technical analysis the analysis of past movements in the prices of financial instruments, currencies, commodities, etc., with a view to predicting future price movements by applying analytical techniques. *See also* **fundamental analysis**

technical correction a situation where a share price or a currency moves up or down because it was previously too low or too high, because of technical factors

technical rally a temporary rise in security or commodity prices while the market is in a general decline. This may be because investors are seeking bargains, or because analysts have noted a support level.

technical reserves the assets that an insurance company maintains to meet future claims

technological risk the risk that a newly designed plant will not operate to specification

Technology and Human Resources for Industry Programme (*S Africa*) *see* **THRIP**

technology stock stock issued by a company that is involved in new technology

teeming and lading 1. an attempt to hide missing funds by delaying the recording of cash receipts in a business's books. *US term **lapping*** **2.** a fraud based on a continuous cycle of stealing and later replacing assets (generally cash), each theft being used in part, or in full, to repay a previous theft in order to avoid detection

telebanking electronic banking carried out by using a telephone line to communicate with a bank

telegraphic transfer a method of transferring funds from a bank to a financial institution overseas using telegraphs. *Abbr* **TT**

telephone banking a system in which customers can access their accounts and a range of banking services up to 24 hours a day by telephone. Apart from convenience, customers usually benefit from higher interest rates on savings accounts and lower interest when borrowing, as providers of telephone banking have lower overheads than traditional high street banks.

teleshopping the use of telecommunications and computers to shop for and purchase goods and services

teller a bank cashier

tender to bid for securities at auction. The securities are allocated according to the method adopted by the issuer. In the standard auction style, the investor receives the security at the price they tendered. In a Dutch style auction, the issuer announces a strike price after all the tenders have been examined. This is set at a level at which all the issue is sold. Investors who submitted a tender above the strike price only pay the strike price. The Dutch style of auction is increasingly being adopted in the United Kingdom. US Treasury Bills are also sold using the Dutch system. *See also **offer for sale**, **sale by tender***

tender offer *(US)* = *takeover approach*

10-K the filing of a US company's annual accounts with the New York Stock Exchange

tenor the period of time that has to elapse before a bill of exchange becomes payable

10-Q the filing of a US company's quarterly accounts with the New York Stock Exchange

term the period of time that has to elapse from the date of the initial investment before a security or other investment, such as a term deposit or endowment assurance, becomes redeemable or reaches its maturity date

term account an account where money is invested for a fixed period at a rate of interest higher than that available in current accounts

term assurance 1. a life policy that will pay out upon the death of the life assured or in the event of the death of the first life assured with a joint life assurance **2.** insurance, especially life assurance, that is in effect for a specified period of time

term bill *see **period bill***

term deposit a deposit account held for a fixed period. Withdrawals are either not allowed during this period, or they involve a fee payable by the depositor.

terminal date the day on which a futures contract expires

terminal market an exchange on which futures contracts or spot deals for commodities are traded

term insurance insurance, especially life assurance, that is in effect for a specified period of time

term loan a loan for a fixed period, usually called a personal loan when it is for non-business purposes. While a personal loan is normally at a fixed rate of interest, a term loan to a business may be at either a fixed or variable rate. Term loans may be either secured or unsecured. An early repayment fee is usually payable when such a loan is repaid before the end of the term. *See also balloon loan, bullet loan*

term shares a share account in a building society that is for a fixed period of time. Withdrawals are usually not allowed during this period. However, if they are, then a fee is normally payable by the account holder.

terotechnology *see life-cycle costing*

tertiary sector the part of the economy made up of non-profit organisations, such as consumer associations and self-help groups

TESSA *abbr* Tax Exempt Special Savings Account

testacy the legal position of a person who has died leaving a valid will

testate used to refer to a person who has died leaving a valid will

testator a man who has made a valid will

testatrix a woman who has made a valid will

TFN *abbr* tax file number

TFN Withholding Tax *abbr* (*ANZ*) Tax File Number Withholding Tax: a levy imposed on financial transactions involving an individual who has not disclosed his or her tax file number

theory of constraints an approach to production management which aims to maximise sales revenue less material and variable overheads cost. It focuses on factors such as bottlenecks which act as constraints to this maximisation. *Abbr* **TOC**

thin market a market where the trading volume is low. A characteristic of such a market is a wide spread of bid and offer prices.

third market a market other than the main stock exchange in which stocks are traded

three generic strategies strategies of differentiation, focus, and overall cost leadership outlined by Porter as offering possible means of outperforming competitors within an industry, and of coping with the five competitive forces

3i a finance group owned by the big UK high street banks which provides finance to other companies, especially small ones

three steps and a stumble a rule of thumb used on the US stock market that if the Federal Reserve increases interest rates three times consecutively, stock market prices will go down (*slang*)

thrift institution *or* **thrift** a bank that offers savings accounts. *See also savings and loan association, savings bank*

THRIP *abbr* (*S Africa*) Technology and Human Resources for Industry Programme: a collaborative programme involving industry, government, and educational and research institutions, that supports research and development in technology, science, and engineering

throughput accounting a management accounting system which focuses on ways by which the maximum return per unit of bottleneck activity can be achieved

TIBOR *abbr* Tokyo Inter Bank Offered Rate

tick the least amount by which a value such as the price of a stock or a rate of interest can rise or fall. This could be, for example, a hundredth of a percentage point.

tied loan a loan made by one national government to another on the condition that the funds are used to purchase goods from the lending nation

tiger any of the key markets in the Pacific Basin region, except Japan: Hong Kong, South Korea, Singapore, and Taiwan

tight money a situation where it is expensive to borrow because of restrictive government policy or high demand

TILA *abbr* Truth in Lending Act

time and material pricing a form of cost plus pricing in which price is determined by reference to the cost of the labour and material inputs to the product/service

time bargain a stock market transaction in which the securities are deliverable at a future date beyond the exchange's normal settlement day

time deposit a US savings account or a certificate of deposit, issued by a financial institution. While the savings account is for a fixed term, deposits are accepted with the understanding that withdrawals may be made subject to a period of notice. Banks are authorised to require at least 30 days' notice. While a certificate of deposit is equivalent to a term account, passbook accounts are generally regarded as funds readily available to the account holder.

time draft a bill of exchange drawn on and accepted by a US bank. It is either an after date or after sight bill.

time sheet a record of how a person's time has been spent. It is used to calculate pay, assess the efficient use of time, or charge for work done.

time spread the purchase and sale of options in the same commodity or security with the same price and different maturities

time value the premium at which an option is trading relative to its *intrinsic value*

timing difference a difference between the balances held on related accounts which is caused by differences in the timing of the input of common transactions. For example, a direct debit will appear on the bank statement before it is entered into the bank account. Knowledge of the timing difference allows the balances on the two accounts to be reconciled.

tip a piece of useful expert information. Used in the sense of a 'share tip', it is a share recommendation published in the financial press, usually based on research published by a financial institution.

tip-off a warning based on confidential information. *See also* **insider trading, money laundering**

title a legal term meaning ownership. Deeds to land are sometimes referred to as title deeds. If a person has good title to a property, their proof of ownership is beyond doubt.

toasted used to refer to someone or something that has lost money (*slang*)

TOC *abbr* theory of constraints

toehold (*US*) a stake in a corporation built up by a potential bidder which is less than 5% of the corporation's stock. It is only when a 5% stake is reached that the holder has to make a declaration to the Securities and Exchange Commission.

Tokyo Inter Bank Offered Rate on the Japanese money markets, the rate at which banks will offer to make deposits in yen with each other, often used as a reference rate. The deposits are for terms from overnight up to five years. *Abbr* **TIBOR**

tombstone a notice in the financial press giving details of a large lending facility to a business. It may relate to a management buyout or to a package that may include an interest rate cap and *interest rate collars* to finance a specific package. More than one bank may be involved. Although it may appear to be an advertisement, technically in most jurisdictions it is regarded as a statement of fact and therefore falls outside the advertisement regulations. The borrower generally pays for the advertisement, though it is the financial institutions that derive the most benefit.

top-down budget *see imposed budget*

top slicing 1. selling part of a shareholding that will realise a sum that is equal to the original cost of the investment. What remains therefore represents potential pure profit. **2.** in the United Kingdom, a complex method used by the Inland Revenue for assessing what tax, if any, is paid when certain investment bonds or endowment policies mature or are cashed in early

total absorption costing a method used by a cost accountant to price goods and services, allocating both direct and indirect costs. Although this method is designed so that all of an organisation's costs are covered, it may result in opportunities being missed because of high prices. Consequently sales may be lost that could contribute to overheads. *See also* **marginal costing**

total assets the total *net book value* of all assets

total asset turnover ratio a measure of the use a business makes of all its assets. It is calculated by dividing sales by total assets.

total-debt-to-total-assets the premium at which an option is trading relative to its *intrinsic value*

total overhead cost variance the difference between the overhead costs absorbed and the actual overhead costs incurred (both fixed and variable)

total quality management an integrated and comprehensive system of planning and controlling all business functions so that products or services are produced which meet or exceed customer expectations. TQM is a philosophy of business behaviour, embracing principles such as employee involvement, continuous improvement at all levels, and customer focus, as well as being a collection of related techniques aimed at improving quality such as full documentation of activities, clear goal-setting, and performance measurement from the customer perspective. *Abbr* **TQM**

total return the total percentage change in the value of an investment over a specified time period, including capital gains, dividends, and the investment's appreciation or depreciation.

The total return formula reflects all the ways in which an investment can earn or lose money, resulting in an increase or decrease in the investment's net asset value (NAV):

(Dividends + Capital gains distributions +/- Change in NAV) / Beginning NAV = Total return × 100%

EXAMPLE If, for instance, you buy a stock with an initial NAV of £40, and after one year it pays an income dividend of £2 per share and a capital gains distribution of £1, and its NAV has increased to £42, then the stock's total return would be:

(2 + 1 + 2) / 40 = 5 / 40 = 0.125 × 100% = 12.5%

The total return time frame is usually one year, and it assumes that dividends have been reinvested. It does not take into account any sales charges that an investor paid to invest in a fund, or taxes they might owe on the income dividends and capital gains distributions received.

touch the difference between the best bid and the best offer price quoted by all market makers for a particular security

touch price the best bid and offer price available

tracker fund *see index fund*

tracking error the deviation by which an index fund fails to replicate the index it is aiming to mirror

tracking stock a stock whose dividends are tied to the performance of a subsidiary of the corporation that owns it

trade agreement an international agreement between countries over general terms of trade

trade balance *see balance of trade*

trade barrier a condition imposed by a government to limit free exchange of goods internationally. *NTBs*, safety standards, and tariffs are typical trade barriers.

trade bill a bill of exchange between two businesses that trade with each other. *See also* **acceptance credit**

trade credit credit offered by one business when trading with another. Typically this is for one month from the date of the invoice, but it could be for a shorter or longer period.

trade creditors money owed to suppliers for goods and services. Other money owed, including employers' National Insurance and taxation, is to be shown under the heading 'other creditors'.

trade date the date on which an enterprise becomes committed to buy a financial asset

trade debt a debt that originates during the normal course of trade

trade debtors debtors who owe money to a company in the normal course of that company's trading

Trade Development Board a government agency that was established in 1983 to promote trade and explore new markets for Singapore products, and offers various schemes of assistance to companies. *Abbr* **TDB**

traded option 1. an option that is bought and sold on an exchange **2.** an option that is traded on an exchange that is different from the one on which the asset underlying the option is traded

trade gap a balance of payments deficit

trade investment the action or process of one business making a loan to another, or buying shares in another. The latter may be the first stages of a friendly takeover.

trade mission a visit by business-people from one country to another for the purpose of discussing trade between their respective nations

TRADENZ *abbr* New Zealand Trade Development Board

trade point a stock exchange that is less formal than the major exchanges

trade war a competition between two or more countries for a share of international or domestic trade

trade-weighted index an index that measures the value of a country's currency in relation to the currencies of its trading partners

trading account *see profit and loss account*

trading asset or liability a security that an enterprise intends to buy or sell

trading financial assets financial assets acquired or held in order to produce profit from short-term changes in price

trading floor *see floor*

trading halt a stoppage of trading in a stock on an exchange, usually in response to information about a company, or concern about rapid movement of the share price

trading loss a situation in which the amount of money an organisation takes in sales is less than its expenditure

trading pit *see pit*

trading profit *see gross profit*

trading, profit and loss account an account which shows the gross profit or loss generated by an entity for a period (**trading account**), and after adding other income and deducting various expenses shows the profit or loss of the business (the profit and loss account). Some small entities combine the two accounts.

tranche a portion of an investment or loan, usually a large amount of money or a block of shares

tranche CD one of a series of certificates of deposit that are sold by the issuing bank over time. Each tranche CD has a common maturity date.

transaction 1. any item or collection of sequential items of business that are enclosed in encrypted form in an electronic envelope and transmitted between trading partners **2.** a trade of a security

transaction costs incremental costs that are directly attributable to the buying or selling of an asset. Transaction costs include commissions, fees, and direct taxes.

transaction date 1. the date on which control of an asset passes from the seller to the buyer **2.** the date on which an offer for sale is accepted

transaction e-commerce the electronic sale of goods and services, either business-to-business or business-to-customer

transaction exposure the susceptibility of an organisation to the effect of foreign exchange rate changes during the transaction cycle associated with the export or import of goods or services. Transaction exposure is present from the time a price is agreed until the payment has been made or received in the domestic currency.

transaction history a record of all of an investor's transactions with a broker

transactions motive the motive that consumers have to hold money for their likely purchases in the immediate future

transfer 1. the movement of money from one account to another at the same branch of the same bank **2.** the movement of money through the domestic or international banking system. *See also* **BACS**, **Fedwire**, **SWIFT 3.** the change of ownership of an asset

transfer deed a document that must be signed by the seller of shares in order to enable the sale. *Also called share transfer form*

transferee the person to whom an asset is transferred

transfer of value *see chargeable transfer*

transferor a person who transfers an asset to another person

transfer-out fee a fee for closing an account with a broker

transfer stamp the mark embossed onto transfer deeds to signify that stamp duty has been paid

transfer value the value of an individual's rights in a pension when they are lost in preference to rights in a new pension. *See also vested rights*

transit time the period between the completion of an operation and the availability of the material at the succeeding workstation

translation *see foreign currency translation*

translation exposure the susceptibility of a balance sheet and income statement to the effect of foreign exchange rate changes

transparency the condition in which nothing is hidden. This is an essential condition for a free market in securities. Prices, the volume of trading, and factual information must be available to all.

travel accident insurance a form of insurance cover offered by some credit card companies when the whole or part of a travel arrangement is paid for with the card. In the event of death resulting from an accident in the course of travel, or the loss of eyesight or a limb, the credit card company will pay the cardholder or his or her estate a pre-stipulated sum. *See also* ***travel insurance***

travel insurance a form of insurance cover that provides medical cover while abroad as well as covering the policyholder's possessions and money while travelling. Many travel insurance policies also reimburse the policyholder if a holiday has to be cancelled and pay compensation for delayed journeys. *See also* ***travel accident insurance***

treasurer somebody who is responsible for an organisation's funds

Treasurer (*ANZ*) the minister responsible for financial and economic matters in a national, state, or territory government

treasuries the generic name for negotiable debt instruments issued by the US government

treasury the department of a company or corporation that deals with all financial matters

Treasury in some countries, the government department responsible for the nation's financial policies as well as the management of the economy

Treasury bill a short-term security issued by the government. *Abbr* **T-bill**

Treasury bill rate the rate of interest obtainable by holding a Treasury bill. Although Treasury bills are non-interest bearing, by purchasing them at a discount and holding them to redemption, the discount is effectively the interest earned by holding these instruments. The Treasury bill rate is the discount expressed as a percentage of the issue price. It is annualised to give a rate per year.

treasury bond a long-term bond issued by the US government that bears interest

treasury management the corporate handling of all financial matters, the generation of external and internal funds for business, the management of currencies and cash-flows, and the complex strategies, policies, and procedures of corporate finance

treasury note 1. a note issued by the US government **2.** a short-term debt instrument issued by the Australian federal government. Treasury notes are issued on a tender basis for periods of 13 and 26 weeks.

treasury product any financial item produced by a government for sale, such as bonds

treasury shares (*US*) *see* ***treasury stock***

treasury stock (*US*) a company's shares that have been bought back by the company and not cancelled. In the United States, these rules are shown as deductions from ***equity***, in the United Kingdom, they are shown as ***assets*** in the ***balance sheet***. *Also called* ***treasury shares***

treaty 1. a written agreement between nations, such as the Treaty of Rome (1957) that was the foundation of the European Union **2.** a contract between an insurer and the reinsurer whereby the latter is to accept risks from the insurer **3.** *see* ***private treaty***

trend analysis the use of trends in averages and other statistics to examine a company's performance over a period in order to predict future performance

Treynor ratio *see risk-adjusted return on capital*

trial balance a list of account balances in a double-entry accounting system. If the records have been correctly maintained, the sum of the debit balances will equal the sum of the credit balances, although certain errors such as the omission of a transaction or erroneous entries will not be disclosed by a trial balance.

trickle-down theory the theory that if markets are open and programmes exist to improve basic health and education, growth will extend from successful parts of a developing country's economy to the rest

triple tax exempt (*US*) exempt from federal, state, and local income taxes

troubleshooter an independent person, often a consultant, who is called in by a company in difficulties to help formulate a strategy for recovery

troy ounce the traditional unit used when weighing precious metals such as gold or silver. It is equal to approximately 1.097 ounces avoirdupois or 31.22 grams.

true and fair view a phrase used in the United Kingdom and the European Union to refer to the legal requirement that financial statements present information that is factual and not misleading

Trueblood Report a report, 'Objectives of Financial Statements', published by the American Institute of Certified Public Accountants in 1971, that recommended a conceptual framework for financial accounting and led to the Statements of Financial Accounting Concepts issued by the Financial Accounting Standards Board in the United States

true interest cost the effective rate of interest paid by the issuer on a debt security that is sold at a discount

truncation the removal of some of the final digits of a number, rather than rounding them up or down

trust 1. a collection of assets held by somebody for another person's benefit **2.** a company that has a *monopoly*

trust account a bank account that is held in trust for somebody else

trust bank a Japanese bank that acts commercially in the sense of accepting deposits and making loans and also in the capacity of a trustee

trust company a company whose business is administering trusts

trust corporation a US state-chartered institution that may undertake banking activities. A trust corporation is sometimes known as a non-bank bank.

trust deed 1. a note that is a loan for which property that becomes the trust of the lender is collateral **2.** a legal document that creates and sets out the arrangements of a trust

trustee somebody who holds assets in trust

trustee in bankruptcy somebody appointed by a court to manage the finances of a bankrupt person or company

trustee investment an investment that is made by a trustee and is subject to legal restrictions

trusteeship the holding of a trust, or the term of such a holding

trust fund assets held in trust by a trustee for the trust's beneficiaries

trust officer somebody who manages the assets of a trust, especially for a bank that is acting as a trustee

Truth in Lending Act in the United States, a law requiring lenders to disclose the terms of their credit offers accurately so that consumers are not misled and are able to compare the various credit terms available. The Truth in Lending Act requires lenders to disclose the terms and costs of all loan plans, including the following: annual percentage rate, points, and fees; the total of the principal amount being financed; payment due date and terms, including any balloon payment where applicable and late payment fees; features of variable-rate loans, including the highest rate the lender would charge, how it is calculated and the resulting monthly payment; total finance charges; whether the loan is assumable; application fee; annual or one-time service fees; pre-payment penalties; and, where applicable, confirm the address of the property securing the loan. *Abbr* **TILA**

TT *abbr* telegraphic transfer

turbulence unpredictable and swift changes in an organisation's external or internal environments which affect its performance. The late 20th century was considered a turbulent environment for business because of the rapid growth in technology and globalisation, and the frequency of restructuring and merger activity.

turkey a poorly performing investment or business (*slang*)

turn the difference between a market maker's bid and offer prices

turnover 1. the total sales *revenue* of an organisation for an accounting period. This is shown net of *VAT*, trade discounts, and any other taxes based on the revenue in a *profit and loss*

account. **2.** the rate at which staff leave and are replaced in an organisation

turnover of shares the total value of shares bought and sold on the Stock Exchange during the year. This covers both sales and purchases, so each transaction is counted twice.

turnover ratio a measure of the number of times in a year that a business's stock or inventory is turned over. It is calculated as the cost of sales divided by the average book value of inventory/stock.

20-F a document compiled by non-US companies listed on the New York Stock Exchange for the US SEC that gives detailed corporate information

twenty-four hour trading the ability to trade in currencies or securities at any time of day or night by means of trading floors being continually open at different locations in different time zones. A financial institution with offices in the Far East, Europe, and the United States can offer its clients 24-hour trading either by the client contacting their offices in each area, or by the customer's local office passing the orders on to another centre.

two-tier tender offer in the United States, a takeover bid in which the acquirer offers to pay more for shares bought in order to gain control than for those acquired at a later date. The ploy is to encourage shareholders to accept the offer. This form of bidding is outlawed in some jurisdictions, including the United Kingdom.

tyre kicker a prospective customer who asks for a lot of information and requires a lot of attention but does not actually buy anything (*slang*)

U

UBR *abbr* uniform business rate

UCITS *abbr* undertakings for collective investments in transferable securities

UEC the Union Européenne des Experts Comptables Economiques et Financiers, a representative body of European accountants, which was absorbed into the Fédération des Experts Comptables Européens in 1986

UIF *abbr* (*S Africa*) Unemployment Insurance Fund: a system, administered through payroll deductions, that insures employees against loss of earnings through being made unemployed by such causes as retrenchment, illness, or maternity

ultimate holding company the top company in a group consisting of several layers of parent companies and subsidiaries

ultra vires the Latin for 'beyond the powers', used to refer to an activity that normally falls beyond the scope of the instrument from which an organisation's authority is derived, and thus may be challenged by the courts. A company's powers are limited by the objectives in its *memorandum of association*. Most company's objectives are wide-ranging, but should it act outside of these objectives, any resulting agreement may be unenforceable.

ultra vires activity an act that is not permitted by applicable rules, such as a corporate charter. Such acts may lead to contracts being void.

umbrella fund a collective investment based offshore that invests in other offshore collective investments

umbrella liability insurance insurance against risks, such as jury awards, that are not covered by conventional liability insurance

unadjusted trial balance a *trial balance* that has not yet been adjusted at a period end for items such as closing stock

unallotted shares shares that have been issued but not yet allocated to particular shareholders

unappropriated profits profits that have neither been distributed to a company's shareholders as dividends nor set aside as specific reserves

unbalanced growth the situation when not all sectors of an economy can grow at the same rate

unbundling the division of a company into separate constituent companies, often to sell all or some of them after a takeover

uncalled share capital the amount of the nominal value of a share which is unpaid and has not been called up by the company

uncertainty the inability to predict the outcome from an activity due to a lack of information about the required input/output relationships or about the environment within which the activity takes place

uncollected funds money deriving from the deposit of an instrument that a bank has not been able to negotiate

uncollected trade bill an account with an outstanding balance for purchases made from the company that holds it

unconditional bid in a takeover battle, a situation in which a bidder will pay the offered price irrespective of how many shares are acquired

unconsolidated not grouped together, as of shares or holdings

unconsolidated subsidiary a subsidiary that is not included in the consolidated financial statements of the group to which it belongs. An unconsolidated subsidiary would appear on a consolidated balance sheet as an investment.

uncontested bid an offering of a contract by a government or other organisation to one bidder only, without competition

uncontrollable costs costs appearing on a management accounting statement that are regarded as not within the control of that particular level of management

uncovered bear a person who sells stock which he or she does not hold, hoping to be able to buy stock later at a lower price when he needs to settle

UNCTAD *abbr* United Nations Conference on Trade and Development: the focal point within the UN system for the integrated treatment of development and interrelated issues in trade, finance, technology, and investment

undated stock securities that have no redemption date

underabsorbed overhead in absorption costing, the amount of an organisation's overhead for a period that has not been charged to production. *US term* *underapplied overhead*

underapplied overhead *(US)* = *underabsorbed overhead*

underbanked without enough brokers to sell a new issue

undercapitalisation a situation in which a company has insufficient funds for its scale of operations. Undercapitalisation usually occurs when a company expands too rapidly.

underlying asset an asset that is the subject of an option

underlying inflation the rate of inflation that does not take mortgage costs into account

underlying security a security that is the subject of an option

undermargined account an account that does not have enough money to cover its margin requirements, resulting in a margin call

understandability when referring to financial information, the quality of being sufficiently clearly expressed as to be understood by anybody with a reasonable knowledge of business

undertaking in the United Kingdom, a legal term for a business such as a company, partnership, or unincorporated association, that is run with the aim of making a profit

undertakings for collective investments in transferable securities securities such as unit trusts which can be sold in any EU country. *Abbr* **UCITS**

undervalued used to describe an asset that is available for purchase at a price lower than its worth

undervalued currency a currency that costs less to buy with another currency than its worth in goods

underwrite to assume risk, especially for a new issue or an insurance policy

underwriter a person or organisation that buys an issue from a corporation and sells it to investors

underwriters' syndicate a group of organisations that buys an issue from a corporation and sells it to investors

underwriting the buying of an issue from a corporation for the purpose of selling it to investors

underwriting expenses the costs incurred when a company engages a financial institution to act as underwriter for a new issue of shares

underwriting income the money that an insurance company makes because the premiums it collects exceed the claims it pays out

underwriting spread an amount that is the difference between what an organisation pays for an issue and what it receives when it sells the issue to investors

underwriting syndicate a group of organisations that together underwrite a new securities issue

undistributable profit profit that is not legally available for distribution to shareholders as dividends

undistributable reserves in the United Kingdom, reserves that are not legally available for distribution to shareholders as dividends according to the Companies Act (1985)

undistributed profit profit that has not been paid out to shareholders as dividends

undistributed reserves profits for the current and previous period that have not been paid out to shareholders as dividends

UNDP *abbr* United Nations Development Programme: the world's largest source of grants for sustainable human development. Its aims include the elimination of poverty, environmental regeneration, job creation, and advancement of women.

unearned finance income the difference between the minimum lease payments, plus any unguaranteed residual value, of a finance lease; and that total discounted at the interest rate implicit in the lease

unearned income income received from sources other than employment

unearned increment an increase in the value of a property that arises

from causes other than the owner's improvements or expenditure

unearned premium the amount repaid by an insurance company when a policy is terminated

uneconomic not profitable for a country, firm, or investor in the short or long term

unemployment the situation when some members of a country's labour force are willing to work but cannot find employment

Unemployment Insurance Fund (*S Africa*) *see* **UIF**

unexpired cost the net book value, or depreciated historical cost of an asset, not yet charged to the profit and loss account

unfavourable variance an adverse difference between actual performance and forecast, or standard, performance

unfranked investment income amounts received by a company net of basic rate tax, for example, patent royalties

unfunded debt short-term debt requiring repayment within a year from issuance

unguaranteed residual value the amount of the residual value of a leased asset whose realisation is not assured

uniform accounting a system by which different organisations in the same industry adopt common concepts, principles, and assumptions in order to facilitate interfirm comparison, or a system of classifying financial accounts in a similar manner within defined business sectors of a national economy, to ensure comparability

uniform accounting policies the use of the same accounting policies for all the companies in a group, for the preparation of consolidated financial statements

uniform business rate the rate of tax set by the central government that is to be collected from businesses by the local authority. *Abbr* **UBR**

uniform costing the use by several undertakings of the same costing methods, principles, and techniques

uniformity the principle of using common measurements, accounting standards, and methods of presentation across different organisations, to ensure comparability

unincorporated association an association of people that is not a corporation

uninsurable considered unsuitable for insurance, especially because of being a poor risk

uninsured not covered by an insurance policy

unissued share capital stock that is authorised but has not been issued. *US term* **unissued stock**

unissued stock (*US*) = *unissued share capital*

unit a collection of securities traded together as one item

unitary taxation a method of taxing a corporation based on its worldwide income rather than on its income in the country of the tax authority

unit cost the cost to a company of producing one item that it markets

United Nations Conference on Trade and Development *see* *UNCTAD*

United Nations Development Programme *see* *UNDP*

unitholder a person who has an investment in a unit trust

uniting of interests the international accounting standards term for merger accounting

unit of account a unit of a country's currency that can be used in payment for goods or in a firm's accounting

unit of trade the smallest amount that can be bought or sold of a share of stock, or a contract included in an option

unit price the price at which a company sells one item that it markets

units of production method of depreciation a method of calculating depreciation that determines the cost of an asset over its useful economic life according to the number of units it is expected to produce over that period

unit trust an investment company that sells shares to investors and invests for their benefit. *US term* **mutual fund**

unlimited company a registered company whose shareholders have unlimited liability for the company's debts. In the United Kingdom, unlimited companies do not have to publish financial statements.

unlimited liability full responsibility for the obligations of a general partnership

unlimited risk a risk whose potential loss is unlimited, such as futures trading

unlisted used to refer to security that is not traded on an exchange

unlisted company a company that has none of its securities listed on a stock exchange. *Also called* **unquoted company**

unlisted securities market a market for stocks that are not listed on an exchange. *See also* **AIM**. *Abbr* **USM**

unpaid cheque a cheque that has been returned to the payee by the payee's bank because the amount cannot be transferred. If the cheque is unpaid because of insufficient funds it is returned marked 'refer to drawer'.

unpresented cheque a cheque that is in the possession of the payee but has not yet been deposited in a bank

unquoted having no publicly stated price, usually referring to an unlisted security

unquoted company *see unlisted company*

unquoted investments investments which are difficult to value, such as shares which have no stock exchange listing or land of which the *asset* value is difficult to estimate

unrealisable gains apparent increases in the value of assets that could not be turned into realised profit

unrealised capital gain *or* **unrealised gain** a profit from the holding of an asset worth more than its purchase price, but not yet sold

unrealised profit/loss a profit or loss that need not be reported as income, for example, deriving from the holding of an asset worth more/less than its purchase price, but not yet sold

unregistered company in the United States, a company that is not registered with the Securities and Exchange Commission

unremittable gain a capital gain that cannot be imported into the taxpayer's country, especially because of currency restrictions

unrestricted income funds a charity's funds that are available to its trustees to use for the purposes set out in the charity's governing document

unseasoned issue an issue of shares or bonds for which there is no existing market. *See also* **seasoned issue**

unsecured without collateral

unsecured debt money borrowed without supplying collateral

unsecured loan a loan made with no collateral. *Also known as* **signature loan**

unsecured loan stock debt securities for which no specific assets have been set aside to be sold if the borrower cannot repay the loan

unstable equilibrium a market situation in which if there is a movement (of price or quantity) away from the equilibrium, existing forces will push the price even further away

upside potential the possibility of gain, for example, the possibility for a share to increase in value

upstairs market the place where traders for major brokerages and institutions do business at an exchange

upstream transactions transactions from an investee to an investor, for example, sales from an associate to its investor or to other parts of the investor's group.

Urgent Issues Task Force in the United Kingdom, an organisation whose aim is to assist the ASB in areas where unsatisfactory or conflicting interpretations of an accounting standard have developed, or seem likely to develop. *Abbr* **UITF**

used credit the portion of a line of *credit* that is no longer available for use

useful economic life *or* **useful life** the period of time during which a depreciable asset can be expected to be used. This is sometimes expressed as the number of units that can be expected to be produced by the asset.

USM *abbr* unlisted securities market

utopian socialism a form of socialism in which the use and production of all services and goods are held collectively by the group or community, rather than by a central government

V

value the total amount of money for which something can be exchanged in a *market*

value-added reseller a merchant who buys products at retail and packages them with additional items for sale to customers. *Abbr* **VAR**

value-added statement a simplified financial statement that shows how much wealth has been created by a company. A value-added statement calculates total output by adding sales, changes in stock, and other incomes, then subtracting depreciation, interest, taxation, dividends, and the amounts paid to suppliers and employees.

value-added tax *see VAT*

value-based management a management team preoccupation with searching for and implementing the activities which will contribute most to increases in shareholder value

value chain the sequence of business activities by which, in the perspective of the end user, value is added to products or services produced by an organisation

value driver an activity or organisational focus which enhances the perceived value of a product or service in the perception of the consumer and which therefore creates value for the producer. Advanced technology, reliability, or reputation for customer care can all be value drivers.

value engineering an activity which helps to design products which meet customer needs at the lowest cost while assuring the required standards of quality and reliability

value for customs purposes only the stated value of an import into the United States

value for money audit an investigation into whether proper arrangements have been made for securing economy, efficiency, and effectiveness in the use of resources. *Abbr* **VFM**. *Also known as comprehensive auditing*

value in use the present value of the estimated future net cash-flows from an object, including the amount expected from its disposal at the end of its useful life. Value in use replaces book value when an asset suffers impairment.

value proposition a proposed scheme for making a profit (*slang*)

value share a share that is considered to be currently underpriced by the market and therefore an attractive investment prospect

value to the business *see deprival value*

value to the owner *see deprival value*

VAR *abbr* value-added reseller

variable annuity *see annuity*

variable cost *see cost behaviour*

variable costing *see marginal costing*

variable cost of sales the sum of direct materials, direct wages, variable production overheads, and variable selling and distribution overheads

variable cost ratio an organisation's variable costs over a given period, divided by sales

variable interest rate an interest rate that changes, usually in relation to a standard index, during the period of a loan

variable overheads indirect costs that vary with the volume of operations. Variable overheads include production costs as well as commission paid to salespeople.

variable production overheads indirect production costs, including indirect costs of materials and labour, that vary with the volume of operations

variable rate note a note the interest rate of which is tied to an index, such as the prime rate in the United States or the London InterBank Offering Rate (LIBOR) in the United Kingdom. *Abbr* **VRN**

variance the difference between a planned, budgeted, or standard cost and the actual cost incurred. The same comparisons may be made for revenues.

variance accounting a method of accounting by means of which planned activities (quantified through budgets and standard costs and revenues) are compared with actual results. It provides information for *variance analysis*.

variance analysis the evaluation of performance by means of variances, whose timely reporting should maximise the opportunity for managerial action

VAT *abbr* value-added tax: a tax added at each stage in the manufacture of a product. It acts as a replacement for a sales tax in almost every industrialised country outside North America. It is levied on selected goods and services, paid by organisations on items they buy and then charged to customers.

VAT declaration a statement declaring VAT income to the VAT office

VAT group in the United Kingdom, a group of related companies that is treated as one taxpayer for VAT purposes

VAT inspector a government official who examines VAT returns and checks that VAT is being paid

VAT paid with the VAT already paid

VAT receivable with the VAT for an item not yet collected by a taxing authority

VAT registration the process of listing with a European government as a company eligible for return of VAT in certain cases

VCM *abbr* Venture Capital Market

velocity of circulation of money the rate at which money circulates in an economy

velocity of money the speed with which a sum of money circulates in an economy

vendor placing the practice of issuing shares to acquire a business, where an agreement has been made to allow the vendor of the business to place the shares with investors for cash

venture capital 1. money used to finance new companies or projects, especially those with high earning potential and high risk. *Also known as risk capital* **2.** the money invested in a new company or business venture

venture capital fund a fund which invests in finance houses providing *venture capital*

Venture Capital Market a sector on the *JSE* Securities Exchange for listing smaller developing companies. Criteria for listing in the VCM sector are less stringent than for the DCM (*Development Capital Market*) sector. *See also Development Capital Market*. *Abbr* **VCM**

venture funding the round of funding for a new company that follows seed funding, provided by venture capitalists

venturer one of the parties involved in a *joint venture*

verification in an audit, a substantive test of the existence, ownership, and valuation of a company's assets and liabilities

vertical equity the principle that people with different incomes should pay different rates of tax

vertical form the presentation of a financial statement in which the debits and credits are shown in one column of figures

vertical merger *see merger*

vested employee benefits employee benefits that are not conditional on future employment

vested rights the value of somebody's rights in a pension in the United States if he or she leaves a job

VFM *abbr* value for money audit

v-form a graphic representation that something had been falling in value and is now rising

virement the authority to apply saving under one expenditure heading to meet excesses on others

visible trade trade in physical goods and merchandise

voetstoots (*S Africa*) purchased at the buyer's risk or without warranty

volume of retail sales the amount of trade in goods carried out in the retail sector of an economy in a particular period

volume of trade the number of shares sold on the Stock Exchange during a day's trading

volume variances differences in costs or revenues compared with budgeted amounts, caused by differences between the actual and budgeted levels of activity

voluntary arrangement an agreement the terms of which are not legally binding on the parties

voluntary liquidation liquidation of a solvent company that is supported by the shareholders

voluntary registration in the United Kingdom, registration for *VAT* by a trader whose turnover is below the registration threshold. This is usually done in order to reclaim tax on inputs.

vostro account an account held by a local bank on behalf of a foreign bank

votes on account in the United Kingdom, money granted by Parliament in order to continue spending in a fiscal year before final authorisation of the totals for the year

voting shares shares whose owners have voting rights. *US term voting stock*

voting trust a group of individuals who have collectively received voting rights from shareholders

voucher documentary evidence supporting an accounting entry

vouching an auditing process in which documentary evidence is matched with the details recorded in an accounting record in order to check for validity and accuracy

Vredeling Directive a proposal, presented to the European Council of Ministers in 1980, for obligatory information, consultation, and participation of workers at headquarters level in multinational enterprises

VRN *abbr* variable rate note

Vulcan nerve pinch the uncomfortable hand position required to reach all the keys for certain computer commands (*slang*)

vulture capitalist a venture capitalist who structures deals on behalf of an entrepreneur in such a way that the investors benefit rather than the entrepreneur (*slang*)

W

wage drift the difference between wages and money actually earned, the difference being made up by bonus or overtime payments

wage earner a person in paid employment

wage freeze government policy of preventing *pay* rises in order to combat inflation

wage incentive a monetary benefit offered as a reward to those employees who perform well in a specified area

wage-price spiral a situation where price rises encourage higher wage demands, which in turn make prices rise

wages a form of *pay* given to employees in exchange for the work they have done. Traditionally, the term applied to the weekly pay of manual, or non-professional workers. In modern usage, the term is often used interchangeably with *salary*.

wages costs the costs of paying employees' salaries. Along with other costs, such as pension contributions and salaries, these costs typically form the largest single cost item for a business.

wages payable account an account showing the gross wages and employer's *National Insurance contributions* paid during a certain period

waiting time the period for which an operator is available for production but is prevented from working by shortage of material or tooling, or by machine breakdown

waiver of premium a provision of an insurance policy that suspends payment of premiums, for example, if the insured suffers a disabling injury

wallet technology a software package providing *digital wallets* or purses on the computers of merchants and customers to facilitate payment by digital cash

wallflower an investment that does not attract a lot of interest from potential investors because it has not been profitable enough

wallpaper a disparaging term used to describe a situation where a company issues and sells many new shares in order to finance a series of takeovers

Wall Street 1. a collective name for the US financial industry **2.** the area of New York City where the financial industry is based and does much of its business

war chest a large amount of money held by a person or a company in *reserves* that can be used to finance the *takeover* of other companies (*slang*)

war loan a government bond that pays a fixed rate of *interest* and has no *redemption date*. War loans were originally issued to finance military expenditure.

warrant a contract that gives the right to buy a predetermined number of shares in the future

warrants risk warning notice a statement that a broker gives to clients to alert them to the risks inherent in trading in options

waste discarded material having no value

wasting asset a fixed asset which is consumed or exhausted in the process of earning income, such as a mine or a quarry

watchdog an independent organisation whose remit it is to police a particular industry, ensuring that member companies do not act illegally

watered stock shares in a company that are worth less than the total *capital* invested

watermark a design inserted into documents to prove their authenticity. For example, banknotes all carry watermarks to prevent forgery.

WDA *abbr* writing down allowances

WDV *abbr* written down value

weak currency a currency which is trading at a low level against other currencies

weak market a share market in which prices tend to fall because there are no buyers

wealth physical assets such as a house or financial assets such as stocks and shares that can yield an income for their holder

wealth tax a tax on somebody's accumulated wealth, as opposed to their income

wear and tear the deterioration of a tangible fixed asset as a result of normal use. This is recognised for accounting purposes by *depreciation*.

WEF *abbr* World Economic Forum

weighted average cost a method of unit cost determination often applied to stocks. When a new purchase quantity is received, an average unit cost is calculated by dividing the sum of the cost of the opening stock plus the cost of the acquisitions by the total number of units in stock.

weighted average cost of capital the average cost of a company's finance (equity, debentures, bank loans) weighted according to the proportion each element bears to the total pool of capital. Weighting is usually based on market valuations, current yields, and costs after tax.

The weighted average cost of capital is often used as the measure to be used as the hurdle rate for investment decisions, and as the measure to be minimised in order to find the optimal capital structure for the company.

weighted average cost price a value for the cost of each item of a specific type in an inventory, taking into account what quantities were bought at what prices

weighted average number of ordinary shares the number of ordinary shares at the beginning of a period, adjusted for shares cancelled, bought back, or issued during the period, multiplied by a time-weighting factor. This number is used in the calculation of *earnings per share*.

welfare economics the analysis of consumers' behaviour in a society to achieve desirable outcomes, for example, free healthcare, for the society as a whole

Wheat Report a report produced by a committee in 1972 that set out to examine the principles and methods of accounting in the United States. Its publication led to the establishment of the *FASB*.

whisper estimates *see whisper number*

whisper number an estimate of a company's earnings that is based on rumours

whisper stock a stock about which there is talk of a likely change in value, usually upwards, and often related to a takeover

white coat rule a US Federal Trade Commission rule prohibiting the use of actors dressed as doctors to promote a product in TV commercials (*slang*)

white elephant a product or service that has not sold well, despite large amounts of money being pumped into its development

white knight a person or company liked by a company's management, who buys the company when a hostile company is trying to buy it. *See also knight*

whizz kid a young, exceptionally successful person, especially one who makes a lot of money in large financial transactions, including takeovers

wholesale price a price charged to customers who buy large quantities of an item for resale in smaller quantities to others

wholesale price index a government-calculated index of wholesale prices, indicative of inflation in an economy

wholesale trade trade at wholesale prices

wholly-owned subsidiary a company that is completely owned by another company. A wholly-owned subsidiary is a *registered company* with board members who all represent one *holding company* or corporation. Board members may be directly from the holding company or acting as its nominees, or they may be from other wholly-owned subsidiaries of the holding company.

widow-and-orphan stock (*US*) a stock considered extremely safe as an investment

windfall gains and losses unexpected gains and losses

windfall profit a sudden large profit, subject to extra tax

windfall tax the tax a government levies on a company that makes extraordinarily large profits in times of unusual circumstances, for example, during a war

winding-up the legal process of closing down a company

winding-up petition a formal request to a court for the compulsory liquidation of a company

window dressing a *creative accounting* practice in which changes in short-term funding have the effect of disguising or improving the reported liquidity position of the reporting organisation

WIP *abbr* work in progress

witching hour (*US*) the time when a type of derivative financial instrument such as a *put*, a *call*, or a contract for advance sale becomes due (*slang*)

withdrawal the regular disbursements of dividend or capital gain income from an open-end unit trust

withholding tax 1. in the United States, the money that an employer pays directly to the government as a payment of the income tax on the employee **2.** the money deducted from a dividend or interest payment that a financial institution pays directly to the government as a payment of the income tax on the recipient

work cell a group of employees or machines dedicated to performing a specific manufacturing task or a group of related tasks

working capital the funds that are readily available to operate a business.
Working capital comprises the total net current assets of a business minus its liabilities and is calculated as follows:

Current assets – current liabilities

Current assets are cash and assets that can be converted to cash within one year or a normal operating cycle; current liabilities are monies owed that are due within one year.
EXAMPLE If a company's current assets total £300,000 and its current liabilities total £160,000, its working capital is:

£300,000 – £160,000 = £140,000

working capital cycle the period of time which elapses between the point at which cash begins to be expended on the production of a product, and the collection of cash from the purchaser

working capital ratio *see current ratio*

working hours directive government regulations that aim to protect employees' health and safety at work by making sure that they do not work for too long, have too little rest, or have disrupted patterns of work. According to the directive, employees must not work more than an average of 48 hours per week, although they may opt out and work longer if they so choose. They must not be forced to work for more than eight hours a night on average. Employees are also legally entitled to one day off each week; 11 hours rest a day; an in-work rest break if they work for more than six hours per day; and four weeks' paid leave annually.

Working Time Directive a European Union directive concerning the maximum number of hours an employee can work. The directive currently limits weekly working hours to a maximum of 48, but employees can choose to opt out and work more hours than this.

work in process *(US)* = *work in progress*

work in progress any product that is in the process of being made. Such items are included in stocks and usually valued according to their production costs. *US term* **work in process**

World Bank one of the largest sources of funding for less developed countries in the world. It is made up of five organisations: the International Bank for Reconstruction and Development, the International Development Association, the International Finance Corporation, the Multilateral Investment Guarantee Agency, and the International Centre for Settlement of Investment Disputes. The World Bank was founded at the 1944 Bretton Woods Conference in the United States and has over 180 member countries. Its head office is based in Washington DC, but the Bank has field offices in over 100 countries. Its focus has shifted dramatically since the 1980s, when over one-fifth of its lending was made up of investment in the power industry. Its current priorities are education, health, and nutrition in the most economically challenged countries of the world.

world class manufacturing a position of international manufacturing excellence, achieved by developing a culture based on factors such as continuous improvement, problem prevention, zero defect tolerance, customer-driven just-in-time production, and *total quality management*

World Economic Forum an independent economic organisation whose stated mission is to 'improve the state of the world'. Based in Switzerland, the WEF was formed in the 1970s by Professor Klaus Schwab, who set out to bring together the CEOs of leading European companies in order to discuss strategies that would enable Europe to compete in the global marketplace. Since then, over 1,000 companies around the world have become members of the WEF and its interests have diversified to cover health, corporate citizenship, and peace-building activities. However, it has attracted criticism from some quarters, and anti-globalisation protesters gather regularly at its meetings. *Abbr* **WEF**

world economy the global marketplace that has grown up since the 1970s in which goods can be produced wherever the production costs are cheapest

World Trade Organization the international organisation charged with regulating global rules of trade. Based in Geneva, and established in 1995, the World Trade Organization performs a variety of roles within its overall remit, including administering trade agreements, settling trade disputes, and reviewing national trade policies. *Abbr* **WTO**

wrap fund *(S Africa)* a registered fund, not itself a unit trust but with similar status to that of a stockbroker's portfolio, which invests in a range of underlying unit trusts, each of which is treated as a discrete holding

write-down a reduction in the recorded value of an asset to comply with the concept of prudence. The valuation of stock at the lower cost or net realisable value may require the values of some stock to be written down.

write-off a reduction in the recorded value of an asset, usually to zero

writing-down allowance a form of capital allowance giving tax relief to companies acquiring fixed assets which are then depreciated. *Abbr* **WDA**

written-down value *see net book value*. *Abbr* **WDV**

wrongful trading the continuation of trading when a company's directors know that it cannot avoid insolvent liquidation

WTO *abbr World Trade Organization*

X

XBRL *abbr* Extensible Business Reporting Language: a computer language for financial reporting. It allows companies to publish, extract, and exchange financial information through the Internet and other electronic means.

Y

Yankee bond a bond issued in the US domestic market by a non-US company

year-end relating to the end of a financial or fiscal (tax) year

year-end closing the financial statements issued at the end of a company's fiscal (tax) year

year to date the period from the start of a specified financial year to the current time. A variety of financial information, such as a company's profits, losses, or sales, may be displayed in this way. *Abbr* **YTD**

Yellow Book a book, *Admission of Securities to Listing*, which sets out the regulations for admission to, and continuing membership of, the official list of quoted companies on the London Stock Exchange (*slang*)

yield a percentage of the amount invested that is the annual income from an investment.

Yield is calculated by dividing the annual cash return by the current share price and expressing that as a percentage.

Yields can be compared against the market average or against a sector average, which in turn gives an idea of the relative value of the share against its peers. Other things being equal, a higher yield share is preferable to that of an identical company with a lower yield.

An additional feature of the yield (unlike many of the other share analysis ratios) is that it enables comparison with cash. Cash placed in an interest-bearing source, such as a bank account or a government stock, produces a yield—the annual interest payable. This is usually a safe investment. The yield from this cash investment can be compared with the yield on shares, which are far riskier. This produces a valuable basis for share evaluation.

Share yield is less reliable than bank interest or government stock interest yield, because, unlike banks paying interest, companies are under no obligation at all to pay dividends. Frequently, if they go through a bad patch, even the largest companies will cut dividends or abandon paying them altogether.

yield curve a visual representation of relative interest rates of short- and long-term bonds. It can be normal, flat, or inverted.

yield gap an amount representing the difference between the yield on a very safe investment and the yield on a riskier one

yield to call the yield on a bond at a date when the bond can be called

yield to maturity (*US*) = *gross yield to redemption*

YK *abbr* yugen kaisha

YTD *abbr* year to date

yugen kaisha in Japan, a private limited liability corporation. Usually, the number of shareholders must be less than 50. The minimum capital of a limited liability corporation is 3 million yen. The par value of each share must be 50,000 yen or more. *Abbr* **YK**

Z

ZBB *abbr* zero-based budgeting

Z bond a bond whose holder receives no accrued interest until all of the holders of other bonds in the same series have received theirs

zero-balance account a bank account that does not hold funds continuously, but has money automatically transferred into it from another account when claims arise against it

zero-based budgeting a method of budgeting which requires each cost element to be specifically justified, as though the activities to which the budget relates were being undertaken for the first time. Without approval, the budget allowance is zero. *Abbr* **ZBB**

zero-coupon returning principal and a premium over the purchase price at maturity, but no interest

zero-coupon bond a bond that pays no interest and is sold at a large discount. *Also known as* **accrual bond**

zero fund to assign no money to a

business project without actually cancelling it (*slang*)

zero growth a fall in output for two successive quarters

zero-rated supplies *or* **zero-rated goods and services** taxable items or services on which **VAT** is charged at zero rate, such as food, books, public transport, and children's clothes

zillionaire a very wealthy person (*slang*)

zombie (*US*) a business that continues to trade even though it is officially insolvent (*slang*)

Z score a single figure, produced by a financial model, which combines a number of variables (generally financial statements ratios), whose magnitude is intended to aid the prediction of failure. A Z score model may predict that a company with a score of 1.8 or less is likely to fail within 12 months. Individual companies are scored against this benchmark.

FACTS AND
FIGURES

NATIONAL AND INTERNATIONAL ACCOUNTING ORGANISATIONS

American Accounting Association (AAA)
5717 Bessie Drive
Sarasota, FL 34233-2399
USA
T: 00 1 (941) 921-7747
F: 00 1 (941) 923-4093
www.accounting.rutgers.edu/raw/aaa/

American Institute of Certified Public Accountants
1211 Avenue of the Americas
New York, NY 10036-8775
USA
T: 00 1 212 596 6200
F: 00 1 212 596 6213
www.aicpa.org

Association of Chartered Accountants in the United States (ACAUS)
341 Lafayette Street
Suite 4246
New York, NY 10012-2417
USA
T: 00 1 (212) 334-2078
www.acaus.org/

Association of Chartered Certified Accountants (ACCA)
64 Finnieston Square
Glasgow
G3 8DT
T: 00 44 (0)141 582 2000
F: 00 44 (0)141 582 2222
www.acca.co.uk

Australian Accounting Standards Board (AASB)
PO Box 204
Collins St West
VIC 8007
Australia
T: 00 61 (3) 9617 7600
T: 00 61 (3) 9617 7608
www.aasb.com.au/

British Accounting Association (BAA)
c/o Sheffield University Management School
9 Mappin Street
Sheffield
S1 4DT
T: 00 44 (0)114 222 3462
F: 00 44 (0)114 222 3348
www.shef.ac.uk/~baa/

Chartered Institute of Management Accountants (CIMA)
26 Chapter Street
London
SW1P 4NP
T: 00 44 (0)20 7663 5441
F: 00 44 (0)20 7663 5442
www.cimaglobal.com

Chartered Institute of Public Finance and Accountancy (CIPFA)
3 Robert Street
London
WC2N 6RL
T: 00 44 (0)20 7543 5600
F: 00 44 (0)20 7543 5700
www.cipfa.org

CMA Canada
Mississauga Executive Centre
One Robert Speck Parkway, Suite 1400
Mississauga, ON L4Z 3M3
Canada
T: 00 1 905 949 4200
www.cma-canada.org

Institute of Chartered Accountants in England and Wales (ICAEW)
Chartered Accountants' Hall
PO Box 433
London
EC2P 2BJ
T: 00 44 (0)20 7920 8100
F: 00 44 (0)20 7920 0547
www.icaew.co.uk

Institute of Chartered Accountants in Ireland (ICAI)
CA House
87-89 Pembroke Road
Dublin 4
 Tel: 00 353 1 637 7200
Fax: 00 353 1 668 0842

11 Donegall Road South
Belfast
BT1 5JE
Tel: 028 9032 1600
Fax: 028 9023 0071
www.icai.ie

Institute of Chartered Accountants of New Zealand (ICANZ)

Level 2, Cigna House
40 Mercer Street
PO Box 11 342
Wellington 6034
New Zealand
T: 00 64 4 474 7840
F: 00 64 4 473 6303
www.icanz.co.nz

Institute of Chartered Accountants of Scotland

CA House
21 Haymarket Yards
Edinburgh
EH12 5BH
T: 00 44 (0)131 347 0100
F: 00 44 (0)131 347 0105
www.icas.org.uk

Institute of Financial Accountants

Burford house
44 London Road
Sevenoaks
Kent
TN13 1AS
T: 00 44 (0)1732 458080
F: 00 44 (0)1732 455848
www.accountingweb.co.uk/ifa/

National Society of Accountants (NSA)

1010 North Fairfax Street
Alexandria, VA 22314
USA
T: 00 1 703 549 6400
F: 00 1 703 549 2984
www.nsacct.org

INTERNET

Accountants World

www.accountantsworld.com
This is an extensive US-based portal with links to a wide range of websites of interest to accountants. It relates mainly to US accounting practice.

Accounting Web

www.accountingweb.co.uk
This site is an extensive UK-based online resource. It contains material from a number of providers intended for accountancy and finance professionals. It has received an award as the New Media Business Website of the Year.

The Dyer Partnership

http://netaccountants.com
The site provides a wide range of information on UK tax and accounting matters and other business issues of interest to owners and managers of UK businesses.

Financial Accounting Standards Board

www.fasb.org
This is the website for the Financial Accounting Standards Board, the independent private-sector entity that establishes generally accepted accounting principles (GAAP). The Board issues formal accounting guidance on the treatment and reporting of financial transactions and performance.

INFLATION
LOWEST INFLATION 1990–99

	INFLATION (% P.A.) 1990–2000		INFLATION (% P.A.) 1990–2000		INFLATION (% P.A.) 1990–2000
Bahrain	-0.1	Puerto Rico	3.7	Indonesia	15.5
Japan	0.1	Italy	3.8	Costa Rica	17.2
Brunei*	1.1	Macao	3.8	Lebanon	17.4
Cuba	1.1	Malaysia	3.9	Algeria	18.1
French Polynesia	1.2	Spain	3.9	Mexico	18.9
Singapore	1.3	Bangladesh	4.0	Hungary	19.3
Switzerland	1.3	Palau	4.0	Slovenia	20.4
Canada	1.4	Hong Kong	4.1	Colombia	21.1
Australia	1.5	Thailand	4.2	Tanzania	21.5
France	1.5	Tunisia	4.5	Poland	23.4
New Zealand	1.5	South Korea	5.0	Jamaica	24.1
New Caledonia	1.7	Cameroon	5.1	Zimbabwe	25.5
Belgium	1.9	Argentina	5.2	Iran	26.2
Finland	1.9	Portugal	5.3	Ghana	26.7
Netherlands	1.9	Trinidad & Tobago	5.5	Peru	26.8
Panama	1.9	Mauritius	5.9	Nigeria	28.9
Austria	2.0	Gabon	6.2	Uruguay	31.1
Germany	2.0	Syria	6.7	Mozambique	32.6
Sweden	2.1	Ethiopia	7.0	Ecuador	37.1
United States	2.1	China	7.1	Venezuela	45.5
Denmark	2.2	Chile	7.3	Latvia	49.2
Luxembourg	2.2	El Salvador	7.4	Zambia	51.4
Saudi Arabia	2.2	Côte d'Ivoire	7.5	Estonia	53.1
United Arab Emirates	2.3	Papua New Guinea	7.9	Sudan	60.8
Antigua & Barbuda*	2.5	India	8.0	Lithuania	75.2
Grenada	2.5	Egypt	8.2	Turkey	76.3
Bahamas	2.7	Philippines	8.4	Croatia	86.2
Belize	2.7	Bolivia	8.5	Romania	98.0
Malta	2.8	Sri Lanka	9.1	Bulgaria	102.8
Morocco	2.8	Greece	9.2	Russia	162.0
Norway	2.8	Dominican Republic	9.4	Kazakhstan	204.7
St Lucia	2.9	Namibia	9.5	Brazil	207.7
United Kingdom	2.9	South Africa	9.6	Uzbekistan	246.6
Dominica	3.0	Botswana	9.7	Ukraine	271.3
Kuwait	3.0	Israel	10.0	Belarus	355.1
St Kitts & Nevis	3.0	Pakistan	10.2	Georgia	387.5
Barbados	3.1	Guatemala	10.3	Angola	740.6
Iceland	3.2	Slovakia	10.6		
Jordan	3.2	Czech Republic	11.5	* 1999 data	
Seychelles	3.3	Uganda	12.4		
Bermuda	3.5	Paraguay	12.5		
Cyprus	3.5	Kenya	13.9		
Ireland	3.5	Vietnam	15.4		

HIGHEST INFLATION 1990–99

	INFLATION (% P.A.) 1990–2000		INFLATION (% P.A.) 1990–2000		INFLATION (% P.A.) 1990–2000
Angola	740.6	Guatemala	10.3	Barbados	3.1
Georgia	387.5	Pakistan	10.2	Dominica	3.0
Belarus	355.1	Israel	10.0	Kuwait	3.0
Ukraine	271.3	Botswana	9.7	St Kitts & Nevis	3.0
Uzbekistan	246.6	South Africa	9.6	St Lucia	2.9
Brazil	207.7	Namibia	9.5	United Kingdom	2.9
Kazakhstan	204.7	Dominican Republic	9.4	Malta	2.8
Russia	162.0	Greece	9.2	Morocco	2.8
Bulgaria	102.8	Sri Lanka	9.1	Norway	2.8
Romania	98.0	Bolivia	8.5	Bahamas	2.7
Croatia	86.2	Philippines	8.4	Belize	2.7
Turkey	76.3	Egypt	8.2	Antigua & Barbuda*	2.5
Lithuania	75.2	India	8.0	Grenada	2.5
Sudan	60.8	Papua New Guinea	7.9	United Arab Emirates	2.3
Estonia	53.1	Côte d'Ivoire	7.5	Denmark	2.2
Zambia	51.4	El Salvador	7.4	Luxembourg	2.2
Latvia	49.2	Chile	7.3	Saudi Arabia	2.2
Venezuela	45.5	China	7.1	Sweden	2.1
Ecuador	37.1	Ethiopia	7.0	United States	2.1
Mozambique	32.6	Syria	6.7	Austria	2.0
Uruguay	31.1	Gabon	6.2	Germany	2.0
Nigeria	28.9	Mauritius	5.9	Belgium	1.9
Peru	26.8	Trinidad & Tobago	5.5	Finland	1.9
Ghana	26.7	Portugal	5.3	Netherlands	1.9
Iran	26.2	Argentina	5.2	Panama	1.9
Zimbabwe	25.5	Cameroon	5.1	New Caledonia	1.7
Jamaica	24.1	South Korea	5.0	Australia	1.5
Poland	23.4	Tunisia	4.5	France	1.5
Tanzania	21.5	Thailand	4.2	New Zealand	1.5
Colombia	21.1	Hong Kong	4.1	Canada	1.4
Slovenia	20.4	Bangladesh	4.0	Singapore	1.3
Hungary	19.3	Palau	4.0	Switzerland	1.3
Mexico	18.9	Malaysia	3.9	French Polynesia	1.2
Algeria	18.1	Spain	3.9	Brunei*	1.1
Lebanon	17.4	Italy	3.8	Cuba	1.1
Costa Rica	17.2	Macao	3.8	Japan	0.1
Indonesia	15.5	Puerto Rico	3.7	Bahrain	–0.1
Vietnam	15.4	Bermuda	3.5		
Kenya	13.9	Cyprus	3.5	* 1999 data	
Paraguay	12.5	Ireland	3.5		
Uganda	12.4	Seychelles	3.3		
Czech Republic	11.5	Iceland	3.2		
Slovakia	10.6	Jordan	3.2		

ECA INTERNATIONAL COST OF LIVING RANKING, DECEMBER 2001

RANK 2001	MOST EXPENSIVE COUNTRIES FOR EXPATRIATES	RANK 2001	MOST EXPENSIVE COUNTRIES FOR EXPATRIATES	RANK 2001	MOST EXPENSIVE COUNTRIES FOR EXPATRIATES
2	Japan	53	Mexico	114	Lithuania
4	Bermuda	56	Trinidad & Tobago	115	Ghana
5	Uzbekistan	57	Jordan	119	Malta
6	Cayman Islands	58	Oman	120	Spain
7	Angola	59	United Kingdom	121	Kenya
9	Russia	60	Austria	123	Cyprus
10	French Polynesia	62	Kuwait	124	Tunisia
11	Norway	63	Belize	125	Uganda
12	Guam	66	Singapore	127	Estonia
13	Zimbabwe	67	United Arab Emirates	128	Portugal
14	Iceland	68	Uruguay	129	Ethiopia
15	French Guiana	69	Sweden	131	Australia
16	New Caledonia	70	Luxembourg	132	Poland
17	Seychelles	71	El Salvador	134	Slovenia
18	Barbados	72	Guatemala	135	Egypt
19	Bahamas	77	France	136	Malaysia
20	Switzerland	78	Germany	138	Bolivia
21	Hong Kong	80	Costa Rica	139	Papua New Guinea
22	South Korea	81	Bahrain	140	Mauritius
23	Israel	82	Qatar	141	Vietnam
24	Martinique	84	Belgium	142	New Zealand
25	Sudan	85	Panama	146	Zambia
26	British Virgin Islands	86	Ireland	148	Serbia
27	Antigua & Barbuda	87	Syria	149	Czech Republic
28	Cuba	88	Indonesia	150	Paraguay
30	Lebanon	89	Gibraltar	151	Thailand
31	Denmark	90	Italy	152	Bulgaria
32	Taiwan	92	Netherlands	153	Chile
33	St Lucia	94	Brunei	155	Philippines
34	Libya	95	Tanzania	156	Turkey
36	Netherlands Antilles	96	Peru	157	Hungary
37	Argentina	98	Georgia	158	Brazil
38	Côte d'Ivoire	99	Colombia	159	Bangladesh
39	Finland	100	Canada	161	Mozambique
40	China	101	Morocco	162	Slovakia
41	Dominican Republic	102	Greece	163	Romania
42	Palau	104	Croatia	165	Sri Lanka
46	Puerto Rico	105	Ecuador	166	India
48	Venezuela	108	Iran	167	Botswana
49	Ukraine	109	Latvia	168	Namibia
51	Nigeria	111	Cameroon	169	Pakistan
52	Monaco	112	Saudi Arabia	172	South Africa

ECA INTERNATIONAL COST OF LIVING RANKING, DECEMBER 2001

RANK 2001	LEAST EXPENSIVE COUNTRIES FOR EXPATRIATES	RANK 2001	LEAST EXPENSIVE COUNTRIES FOR EXPATRIATES	RANK 2001	LEAST EXPENSIVE COUNTRIES FOR EXPATRIATES
172	South Africa	111	Cameroon	49	Ukraine
169	Pakistan	109	Latvia	48	Venezuela
168	Namibia	108	Iran	46	Puerto Rico
167	Botswana	105	Ecuador	42	Palau
166	India	104	Croatia	41	Dominican Republic
165	Sri Lanka	102	Greece	40	China
163	Romania	101	Morocco	39	Finland
162	Slovakia	100	Canada	38	Côte d'Ivoire
161	Mozambique	99	Colombia	37	Argentina
159	Bangladesh	98	Georgia	36	Netherlands Antilles
158	Brazil	96	Peru	34	Libya
157	Hungary	95	Tanzania	33	St Lucia
156	Turkey	94	Brunei	32	Taiwan
155	Philippines	92	Netherlands	31	Denmark
153	Chile	90	Italy	30	Lebanon
152	Bulgaria	89	Gibraltar	28	Cuba
151	Thailand	88	Indonesia	27	Antigua & Barbuda
150	Paraguay	87	Syria	26	British Virgin Islands
149	Czech Republic	86	Ireland	25	Sudan
148	Serbia	85	Panama	24	Martinique
146	Zambia	84	Belgium	23	Israel
142	New Zealand	82	Qatar	22	South Korea
141	Vietnam	81	Bahrain	21	Hong Kong
140	Mauritius	80	Costa Rica	20	Switzerland
139	Papua New Guinea	78	Germany	19	Bahamas
138	Bolivia	77	France	18	Barbados
136	Malaysia	72	Guatemala	17	Seychelles
135	Egypt	71	El Salvador	16	New Caledonia
134	Slovenia	70	Luxembourg	15	French Guiana
132	Poland	69	Sweden	14	Iceland
131	Australia	68	Uruguay	13	Zimbabwe
129	Ethiopia	67	United Arab Emirates	12	Guam
128	Portugal	66	Singapore	11	Norway
127	Estonia	63	Belize	10	French Polynesia
125	Uganda	62	Kuwait	9	Russia
124	Tunisia	60	Austria	7	Angola
123	Cyprus	59	United Kingdom	6	Cayman Islands
121	Kenya	58	Oman	5	Uzbekistan
120	Spain	57	Jordan	4	Bermuda
119	Malta	56	Trinidad & Tobago	2	Japan
115	Ghana	53	Mexico		
114	Lithuania	52	Monaco		
112	Saudi Arabia	51	Nigeria		

ECA INTERNATIONAL EXPATRIATE ACCOMMODATION COST RANKING

HIGHEST MONTHLY RENT

	CITY	COUNTRY	MONTHLY RENT ($) 2001
1	Hong Kong	China	7,627
2	Tokyo	Japan	7,601
3	New York	United States	5,653
4	Seoul	South Korea	4,756
5	Moscow	Russia	4,346
6	London	United Kingdom	4,296
7	Beijing	China	4,081
8	Shanghai	China	3,993
9	Singapore	Singapore	3,522
10	Mumbai	India	3,323

Note: Accommodation costs are one of the largest expenditures a company may face when sending an expatriate abroad. When costing an assignment, accommodation accounts for as much as 26% of expenditure and in some cases, the cost of accommodation may exceed the expatriate's salary.

LOWEST MONTHLY RENT

	CITY	COUNTRY	MONTHLY RENT ($) 2001
1	Karachi	Pakistan	487
2	Nairobi	Kenya	843
3	Doha	Qatar	911
4	Muscat	Oman	940
5	Johannesburg	South Africa	951
6	Montreal	Canada	1,036
7	Melbourne	Australia	1,175
8	Frankfurt	Germany	1,225
9	Helsinki	Finland	1,225
10	Hamburg	Germany	1,254

Note: Accommodation costs are one of the largest expenditures a company may face when sending an expatriate abroad. When costing an assignment, accommodation accounts for as much as 26% of expenditure and in some cases, the cost of accommodation may exceed the expatriate's salary.

INVESTMENT

TOTAL INWARD FLOWS OF FOREIGN DIRECT INVESTMENT (FDI) 1997–2000

	TOTAL INWARD FLOWS OF FDI ($ MILLION) 1997–2000	TOTAL GDP ($ MILLION) 1997–2000	INWARD FLOWS OF FDI (% GDP) 1997–2000		TOTAL INWARD FLOWS OF FDI ($ MILLION) 1997–2000	TOTAL GDP ($ MILLION) 1997–2000	INWARD FLOWS OF FDI (% GDP) 1997–2000
Algeria	29	195,597	0.0	Lebanon	898	65,908	1.4
Angola	4,879	32,507	15.0	Lithuania	2,147	42,269	5.1
Argentina	48,389	1,191,269	4.1	Malaysia	13,319	339,660	3.9
Australia	32,493	1,549,387	2.1	Mauritius	380	17,222	2.2
Austria	20,400	815,292	2.5	Mexico	47,787	1,854,720	2.6
Bangladesh	902	177,188	0.5	Morocco	1,535	137,403	1.1
Belarus	664	101,949	0.7	Mozambique	771	14,357	5.4
Bolivia	3,222	33,167	9.7	Namibia	187	13,351	1.4
Botswana	262	21,227	1.2	Netherlands	130,363	1,500,555	8.7
Brazil	117,003	2,945,553	4.0	New Zealand	4,887	221,971	2.2
Bulgaria	2,707	46,741	5.8	Nigeria	4,677	157,339	3.0
Cameroon	166	35,882	0.5	Norway	16,621	613,967	2.7
Canada	111,533	2,511,147	4.4	Oman	279	56,988	0.5
Chile	22,951	293,834	7.8	Pakistan	2,051	244,828	0.8
China	165,139	3,930,424	4.2	Panama	2,861	36,834	7.8
Colombia	12,505	366,529	3.4	Papua New Guinea	737	15,789	4.7
Costa Rica	1,694	50,999	3.3	Paraguay	660	34,050	1.9
Côte d'Ivoire	1,218	41,832	2.9	Peru	6,609	231,993	2.8
Croatia	3,595	80,290	4.5	Philippines	5,537	298,556	1.9
Czech Republic	13,516	212,302	6.4	Poland	27,885	607,138	4.6
Denmark	51,839	681,530	7.6	Portugal	10,835	427,600	2.5
Dominican Republic	3,387	67,959	5.0	Romania	5,312	143,747	3.7
Ecuador	2,808	70,726	4.0	Russia	15,028	1,376,141	1.1
Egypt	4,267	346,188	1.2	Singapore	29,223	357,895	8.2
El Salvador	439	48,812	0.9	Slovakia	3,133	78,656	4.0
Estonia	1,539	20,086	7.7	Slovenia	843	75,865	1.1
Ethiopia	149	25,755	0.6	South Africa	4,612	519,569	0.9
Finland	28,036	494,463	5.7	South Korea	26,875	1,627,450	1.7
France	133,044	5,546,037	2.4	Spain	62,292	2,239,749	2.8
Gabon	200	19,955	1.0	Sri Lanka	973	63,063	1.5
Georgia	313	16,139	1.9	Sudan	1,134	41,824	2.7
Germany	259,778	8,211,457	3.2	Sweden	110,791	920,132	12.0
Ghana	313	27,349	1.1	Switzerland	33,334	1,017,209	3.3
Greece	3,051	481,404	0.6	Syria	362	71,675	0.5
Guatemala	1,148	73,917	1.6	Tanzania	706	32,723	2.2
Hungary	7,657	187,601	4.1	Thailand	20,265	511,771	4.0
India	10,470	1,715,872	0.6	Trinidad & Tobago	2,353	26,455	8.9
Indonesia	-2,974	604,917	-0.5	Tunisia	2,068	79,299	2.6
Iran	198	418,814	0.0	Turkey	3,510	774,350	0.5
Ireland	47,516	344,254	13.8	Uganda	822	25,938	3.2
Israel	11,311	409,832	2.8	Ukraine	2,457	163,736	1.5
Italy	26,293	4,562,356	0.6	United Kingdom	324,348	5,500,029	5.9
Jamaica	1,486	24,845	6.0	United States	850,036	35,053,937	2.4
Japan	27,003	17,161,703	0.2	Uruguay	851	81,069	1.0
Jordan	1,048	30,821	3.4	Uzbekistan	698	70,802	1.0
Kazakhstan	5,316	78,216	6.8	Venezuela	17,173	405,209	4.2
Kenya	156	42,814	0.4	Vietnam	5,907	112,058	5.3
Kuwait	163	122,899	0.1	Zambia	505	13,278	3.8
Latvia	1,633	25,333	6.4	Zimbabwe	284	28,244	1.0

LARGEST INWARD FLOWS OF FDI 1997–99

	TOTAL INWARD FLOWS OF FDI ($ MILLION) 1997–2000		TOTAL INWARD FLOWS OF FDI ($ MILLION) 1997–2000
United States	850,036	Slovakia	3,133
United Kingdom	324,348	Greece	3,051
Germany	259,778	Panama	2,861
China	165,139	Ecuador	2,808
France	133,044	Bulgaria	2,707
Netherlands	130,363	Ukraine	2,457
Brazil	117,003	Trinidad & Tobago	2,353
Canada	111,533	Lithuania	2,147
Sweden	110,791	Tunisia	2,068
Spain	62,292	Pakistan	2,051
Belgium-Luxembourg	56,294	Costa Rica	1,694
Denmark	51,839	Latvia	1,633
Argentina	48,389	Estonia	1,539
Mexico	47,787	Morocco	1,535
Ireland	47,516	Jamaica	1,486
Switzerland	33,334	Côte d'Ivoire	1,218
Australia	32,493	Guatemala	1,148
Singapore	29,223	Sudan	1,134
Finland	28,036	Jordan	1,048
Poland	27,885	Sri Lanka	973
Japan	27,003	Bangladesh	902
South Korea	26,875	Lebanon	898
Italy	26,293	Uruguay	851
Chile	22,951	Slovenia	843
Austria	20,400	Uganda	822
Thailand	20,265	Mozambique	771
Venezuela	17,173	Papua New Guinea	737
Norway	16,621	Tanzania	706
Russia	15,028	Uzbekistan	698
Czech Republic	13,516	Belarus	664
Malaysia	13;319	Paraguay	660
Colombia	12,505	Zambia	505
Israel	11,311	El Salvador	439
Portugal	10,835	Mauritius	380
India	10,470	Syria	362
Hungary	7,657	Georgia	313
Peru	6,609	Ghana	313
Vietnam	5,907	Zimbabwe	284
Philippines	5,537	Oman	279
Kazakhstan	5,316	Botswana	262
Romania	5,312	Gabon	200
New Zealand	4,887	Iran	198
Angola	4,879	Namibia	187
Nigeria	4,677	Cameroon	166
South Africa	4,612	Kuwait	163
Egypt	4,267	Kenya	156
Croatia	3,595	Ethiopia	149
Turkey	3,510	Algeria	29
Dominican Republic	3,387	Indonesia	−2,974
Bolivia	3,222		

LARGEST INWARD FLOWS OF FDI 1997–99 AS A SHARE OF GDP

	INWARD FLOWS OF FDI (% GDP) 1997–2000		INWARD FLOWS OF FDI (% GDP) 1997–2000
Angola	15.0	Norway	2.7
Ireland	13.8	Tunisia	2.6
Sweden	12.0	Mexico	2.6
Bolivia	9.7	Portugal	2.5
Trinidad & Tobago	8.9	Austria	2.5
Netherlands	8.7	United States	2.4
Singapore	8.2	France	2.4
Chile	7.8	Mauritius	2.2
Panama	7.8	New Zealand	2.2
Estonia	7.7	Tanzania	2.2
Denmark	7.6	Australia	2.1
Kazakhstan	6.8	Georgia	1.9
Latvia	6.4	Paraguay	1.9
Czech Republic	6.4	Philippines	1.9
Jamaica	6.0	South Korea	1.7
United Kingdom	5.9	Guatemala	1.6
Belgium-Luxembourg	5.8	Sri Lanka	1.5
Bulgaria	5.8	Ukraine	1.5
Finland	5.7	Namibia	1.4
Mozambique	5.4	Lebanon	1.4
Vietnam	5.3	Botswana	1.2
Lithuania	5.1	Egypt	1.2
Dominican Republic	5.0	Ghana	1.1
Papua New Guinea	4.7	Morocco	1.1
Poland	4.6	Slovenia	1.1
Croatia	4.5	Russia	1.1
Canada	4.4	Uruguay	1.0
Venezuela	4.2	Zimbabwe	1.0
China	4.2	Gabon	1.0
Hungary	4.1	Uzbekistan	1.0
Argentina	4.1	El Salvador	0.9
Slovakia	4.0	South Africa	0.9
Brazil	4.0	Pakistan	0.8
Ecuador	4.0	Belarus	0.7
Thailand	4.0	Greece	0.6
Malaysia	3.9	India	0.6
Zambia	3.8	Ethiopia	0.6
Romania	3.7	Italy	0.6
Colombia	3.4	Bangladesh	0.5
Jordan	3.4	Syria	0.5
Costa Rica	3.3	Oman	0.5
Switzerland	3.3	Cameroon	0.5
Uganda	3.2	Turkey	0.5
Germany	3.2	Kenya	0.4
Nigeria	3.0	Japan	0.2
Côte d'Ivoire	2.9	Kuwait	0.1
Peru	2.8	Iran	0.0
Spain	2.8	Algeria	0.0
Israel	2.8	Indonesia	−0.5
Sudan	2.7		

MARKET CAPITALISATION OF STOCK MARKETS 1990 AND 2001

	MARKET CAPITALISATION ($ MILLION) 2001	MARKET CAPITALISATION ($ MILLION) 2001	GROWTH IN MARKET CAPITALISATION (%) 1990–2001	MARKET	MARKET CAPITALISATION ($ MILLION) 2001	GROWTH IN CAPITALISATION ($ MILLION) 2001	MARKET CAPITALISATION (%) 1990–200
Argentina	192,499	192,499	0	Malaysia	120,007	120,007	0
Australia	372,794	372,794	0	Mauritius	1,063	1,063	0
Austria	29,935	29,935	0	Mexico	121,403	121,403	0
Bangladesh	1,145	1,145	0	Morocco	9,087	9,087	0
Belgium	182,481	182,481	0	Namibia	151	151	0
Bolivia	116	116	0	Netherlands	640,456	640,456	0
Botswana	1,269	1,269	0	New Zealand	18,613	18,613	0
Brazil	186,238	186,238	0	Nigeria	5,404	5,404	0
Bulgaria	505	505	0	Norway	65,034	65,034	0
Canada	841,385	841,385	0	Oman	2,606	2,606	0
Chile	56,310	56,310	0	Pakistan	4,944	4,944	0
China	523,952	523,952	0	Panama	3,584	3,584	0
Colombia	13,217	13,217	0	Paraguay	423	423	0
Costa Rica	2,303	2,303	0	Peru	11,134	11,134	0
Côte d'Ivoire	1,165	1,165	0	Philippines	41,523	41,523	0
Croatia	3,319	3,319	0	Poland	26,017	26,017	0
Czech Republic	9,331	9,331	0	Portugal	60,681	60,681	0
Denmark	107,666	107,666	0	Romania	2,124	2,124	0
Dominican Republic	141	141	0	Russia	76,198	76,198	0
Ecuador	1,417	1,417	0	Saudi Arabia	73,199	73,199	0
Egypt	24,335	24,335	0	Singapore	152,827	152,827	0
El Salvador	2,672	2,672	0	Slovakia	665	665	0
Estonia	1,483	1,483	0	Slovenia	2,839	2,839	0
Finland	293,635	293,635	0	South Africa	139,750	139,750	0
France	1,446,634	1,446,634	0	South Korea	220,046	220,046	0
Germany	1,270,243	1,270,243	0	Spain	504,219	504,219	0
Ghana	528	528	0	Sri Lanka	1,332	1,332	0
Greece	86,538	86,538	0	Sweden	328,339	328,339	0
Guatemala	215	215	0	Switzerland	792,316	792,316	0
Hong Kong	623,398	623,398	0	Tanzania	181	181	0
Hungary	10,367	10,367	0	Thailand	36,340	36,340	0
India	110,396	110,396	0	Trinidad & Tobago	5,035	5,035	0
Indonesia	23,006	23,006	0	Tunisia	2,303	2,303	0
Iran	21,830	21,830	0	Turkey	47,150	47,150	0
Ireland	81,882	81,882	0	Ukraine	1,365	1,365	0
Israel	55,964	55,964	0	United Arab Emirates	23,262	23,262	0
Italy	768,364	768,364	0	United Kingdom	2,576,992	2,576,992	0
Jamaica	4,703	4,703	0	United States	15,104,037	15,104,037	0
Japan	3,157,222	3,157,222	0	Uruguay	168	168	0
Jordan	6,316	6,316	0	Uzbekistan	119	119	0
Kazakhstan	2,260	2,260	0	Venezuela	6,216	6,216	0
Kenya	1,050	1,050	0	Yugoslavia	10,817	10,817	0
Kuwait	20,772	20,772	0	Zambia	291	291	0
Latvia	697	697	0	Zimbabwe	2,972	2,972	0
Lebanon	1,243	1,243	0				
Lithuania	1,199	1,199	0				

Source: Standard & Poor's

LARGEST MARKET CAPITALISATION IN 2000

	MARKET CAPITALISATION ($ MILLION) 2001		MARKET CAPITALISATION ($ MILLION) 200		MARKET CAPITALISATION ($ MILLION) 200
United States	15,104,037	Portugal	60,681	Oman	2,606
Japan	3,157,222	Chile	56,310	Costa Rica	2,303
United Kingdom	2,576,992	Israel	55,964	Tunisia	2,303
France	1,446,634	Turkey	47,150	Kazakhstan	2,260
Germany	1,270,243	Philippines	41,523	Romania	2,124
Canada	841,385	Thailand	36,340	Estonia	1,483
Switzerland	792,316	Austria	29,935	Ecuador	1,417
Italy	768,364	Poland	26,017	Ukraine	1,365
Netherlands	640,456	Egypt	24,335	Sri Lanka	1,332
Hong Kong	623,398	United Arab Emirates	23,262	Botswana	1,269
China	523,952	Indonesia	23,006	Lebanon	1,243
Spain	504,219	Iran	21,830	Lithuania	1,199
Australia	372,794	Kuwait	20,772	Côte d'Ivoire	1,165
Sweden	328,339	New Zealand	18,613	Bangladesh	1,145
Finland	293,635	Colombia	13,217	Mauritius	1,063
South Korea	220,046	Peru	11,134	Kenya	1,050
Argentina	192,499	Yugoslavia	10,817	Latvia	697
Brazil	186,238	Hungary	10,367	Slovakia	665
Belgium	182,481	Czech Republic	9,331	Ghana	528
Singapore	152,827	Morocco	9,087	Bulgaria	505
South Africa	139,750	Jordan	6,316	Paraguay	423
Mexico	121,403	Venezuela	6,216	Zambia	291
Malaysia	120,007	Nigeria	5,404	Guatemala	215
India	110,396	Trinidad & Tobago	5,035	Tanzania	181
Denmark	107,666	Pakistan	4,944	Uruguay	168
Greece	86,538	Jamaica	4,703	Namibia	151
Ireland	81,882	Panama	3,584	Dominican Republic	141
Russia	76,198	Croatia	3,319	Uzbekistan	119
Saudi Arabia	73,199	Zimbabwe	2,972	Bolivia	116
Norway	65,034	Slovenia	2,839		
Portugal	60,681	El Salvador	2,672		

NATIONAL PROSPERITY
NATIONAL INCOME AND GROWTH

	GNI ($ MILLION) 2000	GNI PER CAPITA 2000	GDP GROWTH (% P.A.) 1990–2000		GNI ($ MILLION) 2000	GNI PER CAPITA 2000	GDP GROWTH (% P.A.) 1990–2000
United States	9,601,505	34,100	3.5	Chile	69,850	4,590	6.8
Japan	4,519,067	35,620	1.3	Pakistan	61,022	440	3.7
Germany	2,063,734	25,120	1.5	Czech Republic	53,925	5,250	0.9
United Kingdom	1,459,500	24,430	2.5	Peru	53,392	2,080	4.7
France	1,438,293	24,090	1.7	New Zealand	49,750	12,990	3.0
Italy	1,163,211	20,160	1.6	Algeria	47,897	1,580	1.9
China	1,062,919	840	10.3	Bangladesh	47,864	370	4.8
Canada	649,829	21,130	2.9	Hungary	47,249	4,710	1.5
Brazil	610,058	3,580	2.9	Romania	37,380	1,670	−0.7
Spain	595,255	15,080	2.5	Kuwait	35,771	18,030	3.2
Mexico	497,025	5,070	3.1	Ukraine	34,565	700	−9.3
India	454,800	450	6.0	Morocco	33,940	1,180	2.3
South Korea	421,069	8,910	5.7	Nigeria	32,705	260	2.4
Netherlands	397,544	24,970	2.8	Vietnam	30,439	390	7.9
Australia	388,252	20,240	4.1	Belarus	28,735	2,870	−1.6
Taiwan	313,900	14,188	—	Croatia	20,240	4,620	0.6
Argentina	276,228	7,460	4.3	Tunisia	20,057	2,100	4.7
Switzerland	273,829	38,140	0.8	Uruguay	20,010	6,000	3.4
Belgium	251,583	24,540	2.0	Slovenia	19,979	10,050	2.7
Russia	241,027	1,660	−4.8	Slovakia	19,969	3,700	2.1
Sweden	240,707	27,140	1.9	Guatemala	19,164	1,680	4.1
Austria	204,525	25,220	2.1	Kazakhstan	18,773	1,260	−4.1
Turkey	202,131	3,100	3.7	Luxembourg	18,439	42,060	—
Hong Kong	176,157	25,920	4.0	Dominican Republic	17,847	2,130	6.0
Denmark	172,238	32,280	2.5	Lebanon	17,355	4,010	6.0
Poland	161,832	4,190	4.6	Sri Lanka	16,408	850	5.3
Norway	155,064	34,530	3.6	Ecuador	15,256	1,210	1.8
Saudi Arabia	149,932	7,230	1.5	Syria	15,146	940	5.8
Finland	130,106	25,130	2.8	Costa Rica	14,510	3,810	5.3
South Africa	129,171	3,020	2.0	El Salvador	12,569	2,000	4.7
Greece	126,269	11,960	2.1	Bulgaria	12,391	1,520	−2.1
Thailand	121,602	2,000	4.2	Lithuania	10,809	2,930	−3.1
Indonesia	119,871	570	4.2	Kenya	10,610	350	2.1
Portugal	111,291	11,120	2.7	Yugoslavia	10,028	940	0.6
Iran	106,707	1,680	3.5	Sudan	9,599	310	8.1
Israel	104,128	16,710	5.1	Côte d'Ivoire	9,591	600	3.5
Venezuela	104,065	4,310	1.6	Cyprus	9,361	12,370	—
Singapore	99,404	24,740	7.8	Panama	9,308	3,260	4.1
Egypt	95,380	1,490	4.6	Tanzania	9,013	270	2.9
Ireland	85,979	22,660	7.3	Uzbekistan	8,843	360	−0.5
Colombia	85,279	2,020	3.0	Cameroon	8,644	580	1.7
Philippines	78,778	1,040	3.3	Iceland	8,540	30,390	—
Malaysia	78,727	3,380	7.0	Jordan	8,360	1,710	5.0

NATIONAL INCOME AND GROWTH (CONT.)

	GNI ($ MILLION) 2000	GNI PER CAPITA 2000	GDP GROWTH (% P.A.) 1990–2000		GNI ($ MILLION) 2000	GNI PER CAPITA 2000	GDP GROWTH (% P.A.) 1990–2000
Bolivia	8,206	990	4.0	Angola	3,847	290	1.3
Paraguay	7,933	1,440	2.2	Mozambique	3,746	210	6.4
Latvia	6,925	2,920	−3.4	Papua New Guinea	3,607	700	4.0
Jamaica	6,883	2,610	0.5	Namibia	3,569	2,030	4.1
Ethiopia	6,737	100	4.7	Malta	3,559	9,120	—
Uganda	6,699	300	7.0	New Caledonia	3,203	15,060	—
Ghana	6,594	340	4.3	Georgia	3,183	630	−13.0
Trinidad & Tobago	6,415	4,930	3.0	Zambia	3,026	300	0.5
Macao	6,385	14,580	—	Barbados	2,469	9,250	—
Zimbabwe	5,851	460	2.5	Belize	746	3,110	—
Botswana	5,280	3,300	4.7	Antigua & Barbuda	642	9,440	—
Estonia	4,894	3,580	−0.5	St Lucia	642	4,120	—
Bahamas	4,533	14,960	—	Seychelles	573	7,050	—
Mauritius	4,449	3,750	5.3	Grenada	370	3,770	—
French Polynesia	4,064	17,290	—	St Kitts & Nevis	269	6,570	—
Gabon	3,928	3,190	2.8	Dominica	234	3,250	—

HIGHEST GNI PER CAPITA

		GNI PER CAPITA ($) 2000			GNI PER CAPITA ($) 2000			GNI PER CAPITA ($) 2000
1	Luxembourg	42,060	44	Czech Republic	5,250	87	Paraguay	1,440
2	Switzerland	38,140	45	Mexico	5,070	88	Kazakhstan	1,260
3	Japan	35,620	46	Trinidad & Tobago	4,930	89	Ecuador	1,210
4	Norway	34,530	47	Hungary	4,710	90	Morocco	1,180
5	United States	34,100	48	Croatia	4,620	91	Philippines	1,040
6	Denmark	32,280	49	Chile	4,590	92	Bolivia	990
7	Iceland	30,390	50	Venezuela	4,310	93	Syria	940
8	Sweden	27,140	51	Poland	4,190	94	Yugoslavia	940
9	Hong Kong	25,920	52	St Lucia	4,120	95	Sri Lanka	850
10	Austria	25,220	53	Lebanon	4,010	96	China	840
11	Finland	25,130	54	Costa Rica	3,810	97	Papua New Guinea	700
12	Germany	25,120	55	Grenada	3,770	98	Ukraine	700
13	Netherlands	24,970	56	Mauritius	3,750	99	Georgia	630
14	Singapore	24,740	57	Slovakia	3,700	100	Côte d'Ivoire	600
15	Belgium	24,540	58	Brazil	3,580	101	Cameroon	580
16	United Kingdom	24,430	59	Estonia	3,580	102	Indonesia	570
17	France	24,090	60	Malaysia	3,380	103	Zimbabwe	460
18	Ireland	22,660	61	Botswana	3,300	104	India	450
19	Canada	21,130	62	Panama	3,260	105	Pakistan	440
20	Australia	20,240	63	Dominica	3,250	106	Vietnam	390
21	Italy	20,160	64	Gabon	3,190	107	Bangladesh	370
22	Kuwait	18,030	65	Belize	3,110	108	Uzbekistan	360
23	French Polynesia	17,290	66	Turkey	3,100	109	Kenya	350
24	Israel	16,710	67	South Africa	3,020	110	Ghana	340
25	Spain	15,080	68	Lithuania	2,930	111	Sudan	310
26	New Caledonia	15,060	69	Latvia	2,920	112	Uganda	300
27	Bahamas	14,960	70	Belarus	2,870	113	Zambia	300
28	Macao	14,580	71	Jamaica	2,610	114	Angola	290
29	Taiwan	14,188	72	Dominican Republic	2,130	115	Tanzania	270
30	New Zealand	12,990	73	Tunisia	2,100	116	Nigeria	260
31	Cyprus	12,370	74	Peru	2,080	117	Mozambique	210
32	Greece	11,960	75	Namibia	2,030	118	Ethiopia	100
33	Portugal	11,120	76	Colombia	2,020			
34	Slovenia	10,050	77	El Salvador	2,000			
35	Antigua & Barbuda	9,440	78	Thailand	2,000			
36	Barbados	9,250	79	Jordan	1,710			
37	Malta	9,120	80	Guatemala	1,680			
38	South Korea	8,910	81	Iran	1,680			
39	Argentina	7,460	82	Romania	1,670			
40	Saudi Arabia	7,230	83	Russia	1,660			
41	Seychelles	7,050	84	Algeria	1,580			
42	St Kitts & Nevis	6,570	85	Bulgaria	1,520			
43	Uruguay	6,000	86	Egypt	1,490			

LOWEST GNI PER CAPITA

		GNI PER CAPITA ($) 2000			GNI PER CAPITA ($) 2000			GNI PER CAPITA ($) 2000
1	Ethiopia	100	45	Peru	2,080	89	New Zealand	12,990
2	Mozambique	210	46	Tunisia	2,100	90	Taiwan	14,188
3	Nigeria	260	47	Dominican Republic	2,130	91	Macao	14,580
4	Tanzania	270	48	Jamaica	2,610	92	Bahamas	14,960
5	Angola	290	49	Belarus	2,870	93	New Caledonia	15,060
6	Uganda	300	50	Latvia	2,920	94	Spain	15,080
7	Zambia	300	51	Lithuania	2,930	95	Israel	16,710
8	Sudan	310	52	South Africa	3,020	96	French Polynesia	17,290
9	Ghana	340	53	Turkey	3,100	97	Kuwait	18,030
10	Kenya	350	54	Belize	3,110	98	Italy	20,160
11	Uzbekistan	360	55	Gabon	3,190	99	Australia	20,240
12	Bangladesh	370	56	Dominica	3,250	100	Canada	21,130
13	Vietnam	390	57	Panama	3,260	101	Ireland	22,660
14	Pakistan	440	58	Botswana	3,300	102	France	24,090
15	India	450	59	Malaysia	3,380	103	United Kingdom	24,430
16	Zimbabwe	460	60	Brazil	3,580	104	Belgium	24,540
17	Indonesia	570	61	Estonia	3,580	105	Singapore	24,740
18	Cameroon	580	62	Slovakia	3,700	106	Netherlands	24,970
19	Côte d'Ivoire	600	63	Mauritius	3,750	107	Germany	25,120
20	Georgia	630	64	Grenada	3,770	108	Finland	25,130
21	Papua New Guinea	700	65	Costa Rica	3,810	109	Austria	25,220
22	Ukraine	700	66	Lebanon	4,010	110	Hong Kong	25,920
23	China	840	67	St Lucia	4,120	111	Sweden	27,140
24	Sri Lanka	850	68	Poland	4,190	112	Iceland	30,390
25	Syria	940	69	Venezuela	4,310	113	Denmark	32,280
26	Yugoslavia	940	70	Chile	4,590	114	United States	34,100
27	Bolivia	990	71	Croatia	4,620	115	Norway	34,530
28	Philippines	1,040	72	Hungary	4,710	116	Japan	35,620
29	Morocco	1,180	73	Trinidad & Tobago	4,930	117	Switzerland	38,140
30	Ecuador	1,210	74	Mexico	5,070	118	Luxembourg	42,060
31	Kazakhstan	1,260	75	Czech Republic	5,250			
32	Paraguay	1,440	76	Uruguay	6,000			
33	Egypt	1,490	77	St Kitts & Nevis	6,570			
34	Bulgaria	1,520	78	Seychelles	7,050			
35	Algeria	1,580	79	Saudi Arabia	7,230			
36	Russia	1,660	80	Argentina	7,460			
37	Romania	1,670	81	South Korea	8,910			
38	Guatemala	1,680	82	Malta	9,120			
39	Iran	1,680	83	Barbados	9,250			
40	Jordan	1,710	84	Antigua & Barbuda	9,440			
41	El Salvador	2,000	85	Slovenia	10,050			
42	Thailand	2,000	86	Portugal	11,120			
43	Colombia	2,020	87	Greece	11,960			
44	Namibia	2,030	88	Cyprus	12,370			

HIGHEST GDP GROWTH 1990–99

		GDP GROWTH (% P.A.) 1990–2000
1	China	10.3
2	Sudan	8.1
3	Vietnam	7.9
4	Singapore	7.8
5	Ireland	7.3
6	Malaysia	7.0
7	Uganda	7.0
8	Chile	6.8
9	Mozambique	6.4
10	Dominican Republic	6.0
11	India	6.0
12	Lebanon	6.0
13	Oman	5.9
14	Syria	5.8
15	South Korea	5.7
16	Costa Rica	5.3
17	Mauritius	5.3
18	Sri Lanka	5.3
19	Israel	5.1
20	Jordan	5.0
21	Bangladesh	4.8
22	Botswana	4.7
23	El Salvador	4.7
24	Ethiopia	4.7
25	Peru	4.7
26	Tunisia	4.7
27	Egypt	4.6
28	Poland	4.6
29	Argentina	4.3
30	Ghana	4.3
31	Cuba	4.2
32	Indonesia	4.2
33	Thailand	4.2
34	Australia	4.1
35	Guatemala	4.1
36	Namibia	4.1
37	Panama	4.1
38	Bolivia	4.0
39	Hong Kong	4.0
40	Papua New Guinea	4.0
41	Pakistan	3.7
42	Turkey	3.7
43	Norway	3.6
44	Côte d'Ivoire	3.5

		GDP GROWTH (% P.A.) 1990–2000
45	Iran	3.5
46	United States	3.5
47	Uruguay	3.4
48	Philippines	3.3
49	Kuwait	3.2
50	Mexico	3.1
51	Puerto Rico	3.1
52	Colombia	3.0
53	New Zealand	3.0
54	Trinidad & Tobago	3.0
55	Brazil	2.9
56	Canada	2.9
57	Tanzania	2.9
58	United Arab Emirates	2.9
59	Finland	2.8
60	Gabon	2.8
61	Netherlands	2.8
62	Portugal	2.7
63	Slovenia	2.7
64	Denmark	2.5
65	Spain	2.5
66	United Kingdom	2.5
67	Zimbabwe	2.5
68	Nigeria	2.4
69	Morocco	2.3
70	Paraguay	2.2
71	Austria	2.1
72	Greece	2.1
73	Kenya	2.1
74	Slovakia	2.1
75	Belgium	2.0
76	South Africa	2.0
77	Algeria	1.9
78	Sweden	1.9
79	Ecuador	1.8
80	Cameroon	1.7
81	France	1.7
82	Italy	1.6
83	Venezuela	1.6
84	Germany	1.5
85	Hungary	1.5
86	Saudi Arabia	1.5
87	Angola	1.3
88	Japan	1.3

		GDP GROWTH (% P.A.) 1990–2000
89	Czech Republic	0.9
90	Switzerland	0.8
91	Croatia	0.6
92	Yugoslavia	0.6
93	Jamaica	0.5
94	Zambia	0.5
95	Estonia	−0.5
96	Uzbekistan	−0.5
97	Romania	−0.7
98	Belarus	−1.6
99	Bulgaria	−2.1
100	Lithuania	−3.1
101	Latvia	−3.4
102	Kazakhstan	−4.1
103	Russia	−4.8
104	Ukraine	−9.3
105	Georgia	−13.0

LOWEST GDP GROWTH 1990–99

		GDP GROWTH (% P.A.) 1990–2000
1	Georgia	-13.0
2	Ukraine	-9.3
3	Russia	-4.8
4	Kazakhstan	-4.1
5	Latvia	-3.4
6	Lithuania	-3.1
7	Bulgaria	-2.1
8	Belarus	-1.6
9	Romania	-0.7
10	Estonia	-0.5
11	Uzbekistan	-0.5
12	Jamaica	0.5
13	Zambia	0.5
14	Croatia	0.6
15	Yugoslavia	0.6
16	Switzerland	0.8
17	Czech Republic	0.9
18	Angola	1.3
19	Japan	1.3
20	Germany	1.5
21	Hungary	1.5
22	Saudi Arabia	1.5
23	Italy	1.6
24	Venezuela	1.6
25	Cameroon	1.7
26	France	1.7
27	Ecuador	1.8
28	Algeria	1.9
29	Sweden	1.9
30	Belgium	2.0
31	South Africa	2.0
32	Austria	2.1
33	Greece	2.1
34	Kenya	2.1
35	Slovakia	2.1
36	Paraguay	2.2
37	Morocco	2.3
38	Nigeria	2.4
39	Denmark	2.5
40	Spain	2.5
41	United Kingdom	2.5
42	Zimbabwe	2.5
43	Portugal	2.7

		GDP GROWTH (% P.A.) 1990–2000
44	Slovenia	2.7
45	Finland	2.8
46	Gabon	2.8
47	Netherlands	2.8
48	Brazil	2.9
49	Canada	2.9
50	Tanzania	2.9
51	United Arab Emirates	2.9
52	Colombia	3.0
53	New Zealand	3.0
54	Trinidad & Tobago	3.0
55	Mexico	3.1
56	Puerto Rico	3.1
57	Kuwait	3.2
58	Philippines	3.3
59	Uruguay	3.4
60	Côte d'Ivoire	3.5
61	Iran	3.5
62	United States	3.5
63	Norway	3.6
64	Pakistan	3.7
65	Turkey	3.7
66	Bolivia	4.0
67	Hong Kong	4.0
68	Papua New Guinea	4.0
69	Australia	4.1
70	Guatemala	4.1
71	Namibia	4.1
72	Panama	4.1
73	Cuba	4.2
74	Indonesia	4.2
75	Thailand	4.2
76	Argentina	4.3
77	Ghana	4.3
78	Egypt	4.6
79	Poland	4.6
80	Botswana	4.7
81	El Salvador	4.7
82	Ethiopia	4.7
83	Peru	4.7
84	Tunisia	4.7
85	Bangladesh	4.8
86	Jordan	5.0

		GDP GROWTH (% P.A.) 1990–2000
87	Israel	5.1
88	Costa Rica	5.3
89	Mauritius	5.3
90	Sri Lanka	5.3
91	South Korea	5.7
92	Syria	5.8
93	Oman	5.9
94	Dominican Republic	6.0
95	India	6.0
96	Lebanon	6.0
97	Mozambique	6.4
98	Chile	6.8
99	Malaysia	7.0
100	Uganda	7.0
101	Ireland	7.3
102	Singapore	7.8
103	Vietnam	7.9
104	Sudan	8.1
105	China	10.3